Design in Legal Education

This visually rich, experience-led collection explores what design can do for legal education. In recent decades design has increasingly come to be understood as a resource to improve other fields of public, private and civil society practice; and legal design—that is, the application of design-based methods to legal practice—is increasingly embedded in lawyering across the world. This collection brings together experts from multiple disciplines, professions and jurisdictions to reflect upon how designerly mindsets, processes and strategies can enhance teaching and learning across higher education, public legal information and legal practice; and will be of interest and use to those teaching and learning in any and all of those fields.

Emily Allbon is an Associate Professor at the City Law School (City, University of London). She is known for her work in developing the award-winning Lawbore resource—a website to support and engage those studying law, as well as for her activities in the field of legal design. She was proud to launch TL;DR—the less textual legal gallery in late 2019—which showcases ways of making law more accessible to all. She has worked with charities, law firms and independent organisations too; helping them find better solutions for communicating the law to their clients.

Her work has been recognised via awards both from her previous profession (librarianship and information science) and the academic law community; she was awarded the Routledge/ALT Teaching Law with Technology Prize 2013. In 2013 the Higher Education Academy named her one of 55 National Teaching Fellows—the UK's most prestigious awards for excellence in higher education teaching and support for learning. She is also a Senior Fellow of the HEA. Her interests lie in legal education, legal research and legal information literacy, student engagement, legal design and visualisation and the use of technology in teaching and learning.

Amanda Perry-Kessaris SFHEA is Professor of Law at Kent Law School where she convenes a unique design-driven postgraduate research methods course, Research Methods in Law. She is author of *Doing Sociolegal Research in Design Mode* funded by the Leverhulme Trust and the Socio-Legal Studies Association and published by Routledge in 2021. She has worked with a wide range of collaborators to use designerly ways to enhance legal thinking and practice in academic and beyond, and is currently working on a project entitled Approaching the Economic Lives of Law in Design Mode to be published in monograph form by Routledge. She blogs at https://amandaperrykessaris.org/approaching-law/ and tweets @amandaperrykessaris

For additional multimedia content, including a visual conversation between the editors, downloadable artefacts, background interviews and author biographies see DesigninLegalEducation.net

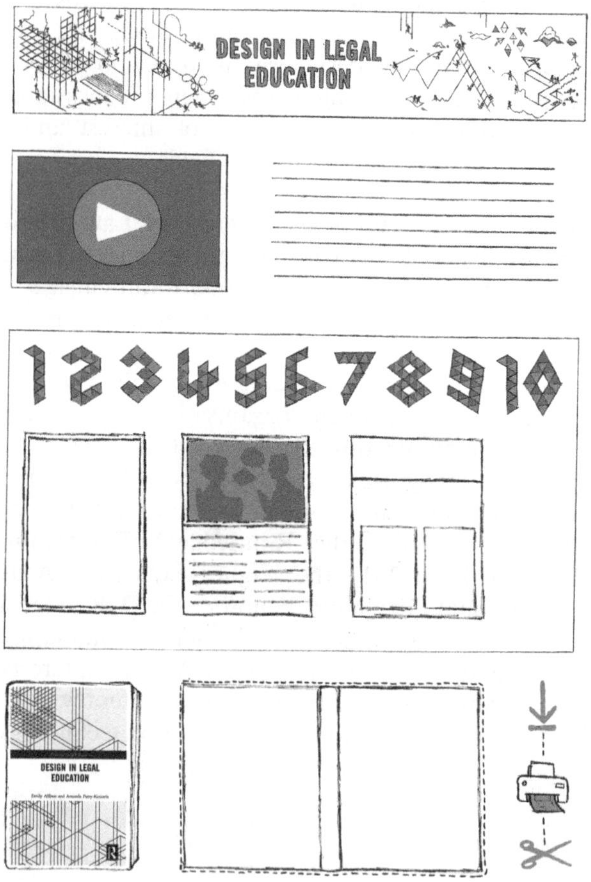

Emerging Legal Education

Series Editors:
Paul Maharg, *Osgoode Hall Law School, York University, ON, Canada*,
Elizabeth Mertz, *University of Wisconsin-Madison/American Bar Foundation, USA* and
Meera Deo, *Thomas Jefferson School of Law, San Diego, CA, USA*

Emerging Legal Education is a forum for analysing the discourse of legal education and creating innovative ways of learning the law. The series focuses on research, theory and practice within legal education, drawing attention to historical, interdisciplinary and international characteristics, and is based upon imaginative and sophisticated educational thinking. The series takes a broad view of theory and practice. Series books are written for an international audience and are sensitive to the diversity of contexts in which law is taught, learned and practised.

Other titles in this series:

Affect and Legal Education
Emotion in Learning and Teaching the Law
Edited by Paul Maharg and Caroline Maughan

Imperatives for Legal Education Research
Then, Now and Tomorrow
Edited by Ben Golder, Marina Nehme, Alex Steel and Prue Vines

Better Law for a Better World
New Approaches to Law Practice and Education
Liz Curran

Public Legal Education
The Role of Law Schools in Building a More Legally Literate Society
Richard Grimes

Clinical Legal Education
Philosophical and Theoretical Perspectives
Omar Madhloom and Hugh McFaul

https://www.routledge.com/Emerging-Legal-Education/book-series/ELE

Design in Legal Education

Edited by
Emily Allbon and Amanda Perry-Kessaris

Routledge
Taylor & Francis Group
NEW YORK AND LONDON

First published 2023
by Routledge
605 Third Avenue, New York, NY 10158

and by Routledge
4 Park Square, Milton Park, Abingdon, Oxon OX14 4RN

Routledge is an imprint of the Taylor & Francis Group, an informa business

British Library Cataloguing-in-Publication Data
A catalogue record for this book is available from the British Library

Library of Congress Cataloging-in-Publication Data
A catalog record has been requested for this book

ISBN: 978-0-367-07579-8 (hbk)
ISBN: 978-1-032-27156-9 (pbk)
ISBN: 978-0-429-02141-1 (ebk)

DOI: 10.4324/9780429021411

Typeset in Times New Roman
by Taylor & Francis Books

For young people everywhere, hoping that all they have given during the pandemic will be repaid.

Contents

List of figures xii
List of tables xv
List of boxes xvi
Acknowledgements xvii

1 What can design do for legal education? 1
EMILY ALLBON AND AMANDA PERRY-KESSARIS

PART I
Higher Education 15

2 Socio-legal methods labs as pedagogical spaces: Experimentation, knowledge building, community development 17
SIDDHARTH PETER DE SOUZA AND LISA HAHN

3 Using personas, vignettes and diagrams in legal education 29
CLARE WILLIAMS

4 Objects and visual devices in teaching for peace in Colombia: Narrowing the gaps between social sciences and law 43
XIMENA SIERRA-CAMARGO

5 Psychologically-Informed Design in Legal Education 58
SARAH STEIN LUBRANO

6 Service design comes to Blackstone's tower: Applying design thinking to curriculum development in legal education 67
MICHAEL DOHERTY AND TINA MCKEE

7 Teaching innovation in the age of technology: Educating lawyers for digital disruption using visually-oriented legal design principles 81
LISA TOOHEY, MONIQUE MOORE AND SARA RAYMENT

8 Teaching IT Law through the lens of legal design 97
ROSSANA DUCATO AND ALAIN STROWEL

9 Making a racism reporting tool: A legal design case study 110
ANDY UNGER AND LUCIA OTOYO

10 Teaching comic book contracting 121
CAMILLA BAASCH ANDERSEN

PART II
Public Legal Education 133

11 Using human-centred design to break down barriers to legal participation 135
GRÁINNE MCKEEVER AND LUCY ROYAL-DAWSON

12 Judging by appearances 151
ISOBEL WILLIAMS

13 Designing to dismantle 165
HALLIE JAY POPE

14 Taking a co-design workshop online 178
EMILY ALLBON AND RACHEL WARNER

15 Designing access to the law: An ethical perspective 192
EMILY MACLOUD

PART III
Legal Practice 201

16 Visualisation in contract education and practice: The first 25 years 203
HELENA HAAPIO

17 How Legal Design is shaping satisfaction, standards and substance in legal practice 218
ERIKA CONCETTA PAGANO

18 Design in legal publishing 229
EMILY ALLBON AND AMANDA PERRY-KESSARIS

19 Lawyers are still lawyers. Except when they're not. 238
RAE MORGAN

Index 243

Figures

1.1 Screenshot from TL;DR including interactive subsite Coltsfoot Vale. Images © Emily Allbon. 6

1.2 Judith Onwubiko presenting (top left), and recreating in clay (top right), a collection of manillas (metal shaped in the form of a bracelet, commonly used as currency in C15th–C20th West Africa, including as part the Transatlantic slave trade) at the British Museum; and postgraduate research students making models of their projects at Kent Law School (bottom). Images © Amanda Perry-Kessaris. 10

2.1 A brainstorm outcome on dichotomies in research. 20

2.2 A mind map of discussions from the Socio-Legal Lab 2019 in Göttingen. 21

3.1 Mainstream or orthodox approaches to law, economy and society as silos of research and practice. 31

3.2 ESL through a looking glass. Ann asks her students to imagine holding a sociological magnifying glass over the spheres of law, economy and society, such that the three spheres shift closer together. 32

3.3 Ann might develop a persona to introduce her students to ESL. She introduces them to 'Policy Polly' (top) who is based on the real-life characteristics of someone she knows. She asks her students to summarise the information about Polly (middle); and then develops Policy Polly into a vignette (bottom), including Polly's intentions, attitudes and general dissatisfaction with current approaches. 33

4.1 Visualisation of 'The marginal road in the jungle' by Zulma González and Nohora Blanco. Image by creators 2020. Reproduced with permission. 47

4.2 Visual representation of 'Embroidering a future of peace, from coca to banana'. Image by creators 2020. Reproduced with permission. 49

4.3 Visualisation of 'Let's make love to fear' by Diana Jimena Ordóñez and Juan Roberto Rengifo. Image by creators 2020. Reproduced with permission. 51
6.1 Stages of UCLan design process presented in terms of the Stanford model (original diagram © Stanford University). 70
6.2 User personas developed for the UCLan law curriculum project. 74
8.1 Data protection canvas—mind map. The students annotate their answers (in the form of keywords) on Post-it® notes which are then applied on the different squares. 99
8.2 Papers and groups allocation in the jigsaw seminar. From top to bottom, representation of the seed groups and the post-seed groups, where the number indicates the paper. 101
8.3 EITLab's Legal Design cycle. 103
9.1 Clarifying the report racism feature (left) and discussing the first version of the page layout (right). 114
9.2 Early design of the 'report racism' feature. 115
9.3 'Frontend' desktop view of the racism reporting tool homepage. 117
10.1 Images by Louis Silvestro used by the author in BLIP lectures on contract innovation and to illustrate (a) the impact of legal jargon (left) and (b) and the question 'Does anyone actually read them?' (right). Copyright Camilla Baasch Andersen. 125
10.2 'Of course comic contracts are binding'. Image by Stuart Medley and Bruce Mutard used by the author in BLIP lectures on contract innovation. Reproduced with permission. 127
11.1 Example of persona template used in the Human Centred Design process. Image: authors. 138
11.2 Persona litigation journey mapping example. Image: authors. 141
11.3 Example of a design concept fleshed out into a prototype. Image: authors. 142
12.1 During the first lockdown, the all-party law reform and human rights organisation Justice experimented with mock Crown Court trials online, to assess their workability and fairness. In one crucial innovation, people in the virtual public gallery could see non-confidential court documents displayed on the screen: transparency campaigners would like this to continue in court. 151
12.2 Some of the negative space in *The Supreme Court: A Guide for Bears*—in this book I point out that there is no jury in the court. 161
12.3 Lynn Shellfish Limited and others v Loose and another, UK Supreme Court, 9 February 2016. 161
12.4 The Naked Rambler and his brief, Matthew Scott. The lower part of the dock is not transparent, being made of wood, but I have met and drawn Stephen Gough before, in a private house, so I cheat for the sake of the drawing. 163

13.1 Detail from the pamphlet 'Bail Bonds', a collaboration between Iowa Legal Aid and the Graphic Advocacy Project (2019). 168

13.2 Detail from a visual evictions guide created by the Community Justice Project and the Graphic Advocacy Project (2020). 172

13.3 Detail from a comic about multi-stakeholder cooperatives created by Co-op Dayton and the Graphic Advocacy Project (2017). 173

13.4 The original (left) and final (right) versions of an image for 'Bail Bonds', a pamphlet created by Iowa Legal Aid and the Graphic Advocacy Project (2019). 175

14.1 A diagram of our design process loosely based on the discover, define, develop and deliver aspects of the Double Diamond model. This chapter focusses on the 'kick-off workshop' and 'insights evaluation' activities within the project. 179

14.2 Extract from a Persona seeking immigration information and advice. The boxes at the top indicate the headings underneath which are responses from the workshop participants. 184

14.3 Extract of journey map for someone seeking immigration information and advice. Participants add key touch points along the *Timeline*. 185

16.1 A brief chronology of my contract visualisation journey. Image: Author. Reproduced with permission. 208

16.2 Sample pages of a 1997 contract workshop visualisation. Images: Annika Varjonen. Reproduced with permission. 208

16.3 Two timelines that make different understandings visible. Image: Author and Stefania Passera. Reproduced with permission. 209

18.1 Detail of vLex Precedent Map showing the relationships between cases relevant to the case of *Tinsley v Milligan*. The small circles in the centre represent cases mentioned within *Tinsley* and the larger circles outside represent those cases which have cited *Tinsley*. Note that the arrowed lines are in colour which indicates if positive or negative treatment given. The larger the circle, the more the case has in common with the main case. Image: vLex. Reproduced with permission. 230

Tables

9.1 Minimum viable product user stories 114
9.2 Examples of feedback from Black Lives Matters protestors extracted from the Design Report 116
10.1 Data from the Comic Contracting Project, UWA Law School, funded by Aurecon 123
11.1 Design group members 139
11.2 Workshop activities mapped onto the human-centred design stages 140
14.1 Selected contributions to the empathy map 183
16.1 Moving to Next Generation Contracts 210

Box

1 Lockdown experiences 152

Acknowledgements

Thanks to all the students, academics, lawyers and non-governmental organisations who have experimented with us over the years; to all those who contributed their time, energy and braincells to this collection; and to Daniel Rozenberg for liaising with authors.

Emily Allbon and Amanda Perry-Kessaris

1 What can design do for legal education?

Emily Allbon[1] and Amanda Perry-Kessaris[2]

This collection explores what design can do for legal education. It defines design broadly to include a wide range of practices that are devoted to the planning and making by humans of tangibles and intangibles including, for example, product design, graphic design, system design and interaction design; and it addresses a wide range of legal education contexts including higher education, public legal information and legal practice.

In this chapter we introduce some key characteristics of design, and suggest how they might support core objectives in legal education. In the process we demonstrate that designerly ways can influence any and all levels of legal pedagogy—from the top—the relatively abstract, overarching 'approach', including conceptual frames and underpinning normative 'aspirations'; to the bottom—the relatively concrete, specific and action-oriented 'tasks' that learners and teachers perform independently or together.[3] And we take care to attend not only to the potential rewards of drawing on designerly ways, but also to some of the risks.

What are designerly ways?

In recent decades design has increasingly come to be understood as a resource to improve other fields of public, private and civil society practice.[4] Since the early 2000s our attention has been drawn to what design can do for law by, for example, Colette Brunschwig, who was the first to highlight the potential of visual communication in the legal sphere[5]; Helena Haapio (see Chapter 16) and Stefania Passera, who were the first to focus on contract visualisation especially through the process of a design sprint;[6] Caitlin Moon, who has opened the door to radical change by introducing legal practitioners to human-centred design;[7] and Margaret Hagan, who has pioneered the use of design labs to explore how legal services might be made more accessible and engaging.[8] Today legal design—that is, the application of design-based methods to legal practice—is not only a recognised speciality, but also increasingly embedded across the world in leading law firms and in-house legal departments.[9] Which is why we see Rae Morgan—formerly Product Development Lead at LexisNexis, now principal consultant at design agency Wilson Fletcher—calling

DOI: 10.4324/9780429021411-1

in Chapter 19 of this volume for future-focused students and their teachers to pro-actively engage with designerly ways so that they might distinguish themselves in their future legal practice.

Opinions differ as to the core characteristics of design, as to which terminologies best capture them and as to how they might contribute to other fields of practice. We focus on designerly mindsets, processes, strategies. Designerly mindsets are simultaneously practical—that is, seeking and able to make things happen; critical—that is, seeking and able to identify what is wrong and why; and imaginative—that is, seeking and able to conjure what is not yet/still present. We all need and have these abilities—indeed, as we shall see, they are central to lawyering. And these abilities can be enhanced by designerly processes and strategies.[10] How?

Designerly strategies emphasise making ideas visible and tangible. Most forms of design, are explicitly and primarily about producing visible and/or tangible artefacts for end-users—whether a poster, an app, a pair of shoes or indeed a visual contract. Furthermore, in part because they tend to be devoted to making visible and tangible things, designers tend to communicate visibly and tangibly along the way—to themselves and to others. For example, they make prototypes of their ideas—anything from a carboard table-top model to a full-scale set complete with props—to help them to see, to think and to collaborate.[11]

Designerly processes tend to emphasise experimentation, both in the sense of generating and following new possibilities; and in the sense of testing hypotheses. Design is about making, and making is an experimental process of generating and testing. Designers do this by prompting and facilitating iterative, divergent and convergent thinking. In so doing they produce a sense of 'structured freedom' in which we can more effectively work with ideas.[12]

In combination these mindsets, processes and strategies can generate 'enabling ecosystems' in which our objectives become more possible and probable.[13] In order to consider how design might contribute to legal education we must establish what are and ought to be the objectives of legal education.

What is legal education for?

Answers to this question will, of course, vary. We propose that legal education is and ought to be aimed at prompting and facilitating people—including students, publics and clients—to work effectively with law. Furthermore, we propose that, like designers, those who wish to work effectively with law must be practical, critical and imaginative. They must be practical, in the sense of knowing how the law is likely to be interpreted, and how to make things happen smoothly and predictably. Those who wish to work effectively with law must also be critical—not only in the sense of identifying multiple sides of every argument, but also in the sense of keeping an eye on what is wrong with law. And those who wish to work with law must be imaginative—not only in the sense of being able to work conceptually, but also in the sense of being able to envisage how whatever is wrong with law might be made right.[14]

But how do we judge what is wrong or right in the context of legal education? Here we can draw on Roger Cotterrell's call to nurture and promote the 'well-being of law as a practical idea' and as a 'communal', as opposed to solely private, 'resource'. For law to function as a practical, communal resource it must be inclusive of the perceptions, expectations and experiences of all those within its actual and potential jurisdiction. Likewise legal educational spaces.[15]

An inclusive education ecosystem is one 'in which pedagogy, curricula and assessment are designed and delivered to engage students in learning that is meaningful, relevant and accessible to all'; and it entails not only 'taking account of', but proactively 'valuing', difference. The call for inclusive approaches to education originated in disabilities studies literature, which in turn drew on design literature to argue that both retrospective adaptation and proactive specialisation are expensive and exclusionary. Better, they argued, to adopt a 'universal design' approach which anticipates diversity, and which builds in the flexibility necessary to value and include it in all its forms.[16] Despite often being used interchangeably, there are distinctions to be drawn between universal design and inclusive design. As Kat Holmes notes, the former has primarily focused on the accessibility of physical space (primarily architecture), and the latter from digital technologies—for example, 'captioning for people who are deaf and audio record books for blind communities'.[17] Most importantly, she notes that inclusive design is committed to the principle of co-design—that is, to the idea that designers must work *with* excluded communities rather than creating *for* them. Examples of co-design in action can be found across several contributions in this volume.

So how might designerly ways support the development of legal education ecosystems that promote practical-critical-imaginative thinking, as well as being inclusive? The following section begins to answer this question by highlighting two designerly 'ways'—visual and material communication strategies, and experimental processes. It draws on our own experiences, as well as the experiences reported in the contributions to this volume and by others working at the intersection of design and law.

Visual and material communication strategies, experimental processes

Text remains empress of the legal world. But by supplementing the textual with visual and material formats, and by encouraging experimentation, we can make legal communications more inclusive—that is, more meaningful, relevant and accessible. The following subsections focus on how designerly ways can prompt and facilitate us not only to see legal ideas, but also to actively explore them: to move among them, and in so doing to better understand, even to change, them.[18]

Seeing

Information design is the sub-field of design most commonly applied to help us see law. It is devoted to making dense and/or complex information accessible. Information designers aim to transform pieces of data into information, which the user can then convert into knowledge. Richard Saul Wurman famously proposed that, while 'information may be infinite', there are only five methods by which to 'structure' it so that it can begin to be transformed into knowledge: category, time, location, alphabet or continuum. The trick is to choose the method that is most suitable, depending on what knowledge you wish to convey, to whom and in what context.[19] So information designers draw on insights from disciplines ranging from interface design to cognitive psychology, information science to journalism and marketing to socio-linguistics; and they use design processes to ensure that those insights are applied 'to all aspects of information, including its content and language', as well as its visual form.[20] Successful information design ensures that information is 'attractive' and relevant to 'the situation in which it appears'; and it 'reduces fatigue and errors in information processing', and thereby 'speeds up tasks'.[21] For example, as Sarah Stein Lubrano explains in Chapter 5, strategies such as visual mapping can, among other things, activate affective context and help to manage cognitive load.

Two examples designed by Emily Allbon illustrate the point. First, Lawbore is an award-winning community site that is designed to offer law students an engaging pathway to free online legal resources. It integrates, and thereby leavens, text with images chosen carefully to intrigue, to deepen communication and to make users smile. It is the product of nearly two decades of experimentation, having been continuously redesigned in response to the changing needs and experiences of users, including the addition of new sub-sites every few years such as Future Lawyer and Learnmore.[22] Second, TL;DR[23] (social media shorthand for 'too long, didn't read'), goes further by prompting and facilitating law students and academics without design expertise to experiment with designing legal information and share the results via the site. Perhaps most significantly, the site carves out a space in which students and academics can engage with each other *through* a wide range of designed materials including visual explainers, whiteboard animations, graphic novels, factsheets, animations, interactive games, videos. Each source includes a description of how and why it was created, which helps to give confidence to others to take up the baton and discover how they might give it a try.

Additional examples are to be found in the contributions to this volume. Clare Williams argues that devices such as personas and graphics can help us to, among other things, make complex ideas accessible by telling compelling stories, and 'empirically grounding the conceptual' (Chapter 3). Turning to the sphere of public legal education, Hallie Jay Pope, founder of Graphic Advocacy (Chapter 13) and artist Isobel Williams (Chapter 12) illustrate how their creative work can hit home where words cannot. Pope introduces an important note of caution by emphasising the associated responsibility, in particular the need to depict 'real stories told by the people who experienced them'. In Chapter 18, we report on our interviews with four experts on design in legal publishing: Robin Chesterman, Global Head of Product and Matthew Terrell, Head of Marketing, both at vLexJustis; and Karen Waldron, Director of Product and Matt Wardle, UX Director both at LexisNexis. They speak with palpable passion about how design can radically enhance the density of legal communications, whilst at the same time enhancing their accessibility: 'You can genuinely be transformative', especially when these techniques are deployed as part of a wider design-driven process.

Exploring

Formal education tends to promote 'technical rationality, analysis and logic over other kinds of knowing'. But Allison James and Stephen Brookfield argue that we ought to make more 'space' for—to develop and value—our 'personal antennae', 'intuition' and 'gut feelings'. In particular, we need to make space for imagination. 'The capacity to imagine is part of what makes us human', and it is essential to any effort to 'conceive of, and realize' something new. In an educational context, imagination is about activating and enhancing the abilities of students, publics and clients to experiment or 'play' with existing ideas and new possibilities. A 'playful student or teacher … embarks on a process in a spirit of optimistic trust.' They are 'not afraid to suspend [their] disbelief when faced with the unexpected', and 'will travel willingly and curiously to see what it might reveal'.[24] A designerly way to activate and enhance imagination, whilst still keeping ourselves practical and critical, is to experiment with making ideas visible and tangible.[25]

Making ideas visible can give students and teachers the confidence to draw on intuition to develop a personal sense of a subject. For example, Coltsfoot Vale is a site created by Allbon which supports the teaching and learning of Land Law through interactive storytelling (see Figure 1.1).[26] Students click on locations within a fictitious English village to reveal a 'story' or 'scenario' about the people living in it, and associated commentary and questions help students get a handle on land law concepts and principles. Coltsfoot Vale places land law in an accessible context; engaging students in the story and allowing them to develop empathy—to put themselves into the shoes of another.[27] It is hoped that other academics and practitioners may also in future be inspired to experiment by 'adopting a property' and developing a scenario for it.

If we also make ideas tangible, we can maximise inclusion. Sarah Frug has observed that those engaging in legal design have too often assumed that visual communication is universally inclusive. One manifestation of this tendency is that '[p]rominent visual law projects have published images, with non-descriptive, incomplete, or misleading alternative text.' The result is 'a

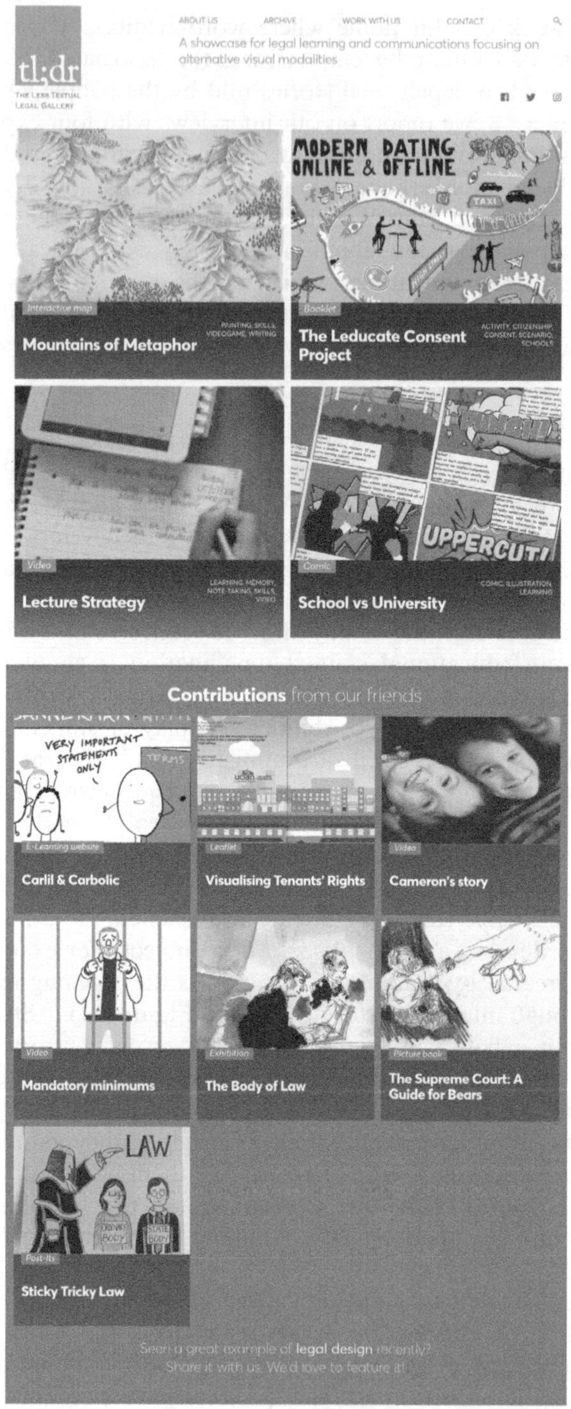

Figure 1.1 Screenshot from TL;DR including interactive subsite Coltsfoot Vale. Images © Emily Allbon.

data-impoverished environment' in which those with visual impairments, as well as others who draw indirectly on machine-generated summaries of legal sources, 'are effectively barred from access to meaningful content'.[28] By making things not only visible but also tangible, and by encouraging each other to narrate those visible and tangible representations of our ideas, we can ensure that we make use all available senses to activate and enhance our imaginations. For example, in the first session of a module that Perry-Kessaris teaches on International Economic Law she invites students to use LEGO® to collaboratively prototype what they expect the module will cover, and what they feel that it ought to cover; and to record themselves as they narrate their model. The aim is to prompt and facilitate them to take some individual and communal ownership of the module from the outset, and reflect back on those early imaginings at the end of the module. Here the 'ensuing discussion'—for example, around 'how different models connect with each other and how they can be adjusted' is as important as the 'building'.[29] A further example is provided in this volume by Ximena Sierra Camargo, who in her MA Peacebuilding programme in Colombia prompts and facilitates the building of bridges across a diverse student body, split across 'divides of discipline and of lived experience', by inviting them to communicate through objects and visual devices (Chapter 4).

We can also use existing artefacts in the visual and material world as new sources for communicating about law. As Audre Lorde famously observed, '[t]he master's tools will never dismantle the master's house. They may allow us to temporarily beat him at his own game, but they will never enable us to bring about genuine change'.[30] So, for example, the manifesto of DecoloniseUKC—a student-led campaign at the University of Kent argued that we must 'promote academic risk-taking', combat the 'fear' of using sources 'beyond the "white canon"'.[31] And such calls are echoed among specialists in gender, sexuality and disability. Drawing on the established practice of object-based learning,[32] Perry-Kessaris worked with colleagues Lisa Dickson and Sophie Vigneron to prompt and facilitate LLM students at Kent Law School to use museum artefacts as alternative sources.[33] The KLS LLM Legal Treasure Tours were held annually 2014–2016 at the British Museum. Students identified a legal object in the collection, presented a commentary in front of it, and then re-created the object on-site as a clay model.[34] Reporting for the group in 2015, student Sophie Bannister said the Tour offered 'a break from what [they] see as typical law elements and gave [them] the opportunity to look at historical objects and artefacts and find law within them, around them and amongst them'.[35]

Enabling ecosystems

Especially when used in combination, these designerly ways can generate practical-critical-imaginative, structured-yet-free, potentially enabling ecosystems. Within such ecosystems the ability of those who work with law to understand and meet the challenges of nurturing and sustaining law as a practical, communal resource is enhanced.[36] Different ecosystems will be required depending on the timeframe and objectives.

When time is short, and our objectives are relatively precise and discrete, we can use an ad-hoc fast and furious design 'sprint' format. Here ideas are made visible and tangible in iterative rounds of hands-on, sketching, prototyping and testing.[37] Participants are prompted and facilitated to think carefully about who their user might be—what are their perceptions, expectations and experiences? They are supported to be imaginative in their problem-solving, experiment with different ideas, to prototype solutions and test without worrying about being 'wrong'. This is important in a legal context, given that lawyers tend to find it especially difficult to 'embrace' the possibility that 'failure can have a positive connotation'.[38] And because sprints emphasise collaboration, they can help to highlight and challenge entrenched institutional silos, exclusionary homogeneity and hierarchy.

The sprint format can be applied across a wider range of legal education contexts. For example, Allbon has run sprints with Nepali lawyers in order to better explore the challenges in communicating reproductive rights to citizens; and as part of formal legal education.[39] Contributions in this volume demonstrate a variety of other applications. In Chapter 6, Michael Doherty and Tina McKee detail how they used a sprint to redesign the delivery of a higher education programme, emphasising that service design process and strategies can be productive no matter what your level of experience. From Camilla Baasch Andersen (Chapter10) we learn of a module on contracting innovation which emerged out of the Comic Contracting Project at the University of Western Australia; and from Lisa Toohey, Monique Moore and Sara Rayment (Chapter 7), we have the first dedicated module in Australia on legal design thinking, which was introduced at Newcastle Law School. In Chapter 8, Rossana Ducato and Alain Strowel talk us through their 'European IT Law by Design' module at UCLouvain in Belgium, including provocative micro level details of activities carried out in class to build skills. In Chapter 9 we see a cross-disciplinary collaboration between Andy Unger (Law) and Lucia Otoyo (Computer Science), who have joined forces to teach 'Law and Technology' to both law and computer science students at London's South Bank University; and discover how this has resulted in important positive impact beyond academia: namely, a spin-off project to create a racism reporting tool for a local community group. Turning to a public legal education context, Gráinne McKeever and Lucy Royal-Dawson detail their ongoing adventures in using human-centred design as part of their Litigants in Person in Northern Ireland project (Chapter 11); and Emily Allbon and Rachel Warner explain how, working with civil liberties organisation Liberty, they adapted a co-design workshop to be delivered online in response to the pandemic (Chapter 14). Each contribution includes practical insights into strategies, processes, challenges and findings, giving a clear sense of how and why to do it.

When we are working to a longer timeframe, and our objectives are more diffuse, we can take a slower, more open approach. For example, Perry-Kessaris has redesigned Research Methods in Law—a compulsory year-long module for postgraduate research students at Kent Law School—around a series of design briefs, each of which invites students to collaboratively experiment with a different aspect of the research process through their own project, often in visible and tangible ways.[40] The aim is to make students 'good hunters' by training them in 'the art of inquiry', by 'sharpen[ing] their powers of observation' and by 'encourag[ing] them to think *through* observation rather than *after* it'.[41] We tend to think of 'reflection as a cognitive process', but in fact we 'perceive' and, therefore, 'reflect with' all 'senses in an embodied, mobile existence'.[42] So it is productive to ground learning in practical activities: 'the quality of discussions' whilst completing such practical activities tends to be 'quite unlike anything experienced in an ordinary seminar'.[43] Students on Research Methods in Law have reflected that such tasks made them more willing to '"give things a go", rather than obsessively overthinking'; more 'aware' that 'answer[s] may lie … anywhere … not just … in textbooks and journal articles'; more 'free to experiment with different ideas and a bit more open'; and they see the module as a kind of 'intention-setting for the sort of open and collegiate academic life we should hope for in future'.[44] Further examples of the creation of longer term ecosystems can be found among the contributions to this volume. In Chapter 2, Siddharth De Souza and Lisa Hahn explain how they sought to develop a sense of community among postgraduate researchers, and make collaboration more possible and probable, through their creation of a 'Socio-Legal Lab' which emphasises experimentation with different research methods, and sharing experiences of 'how it feels to use them'. Likewise, Erika Pagano, Head of Legal Innovation and Design at Simmons Wavelength, offers valuable insights into how design can break down silos and hierarchies in law firms, as well as how to make it happen (Chapter 17).

Conclusion

Across the world, law firms and in-house legal departments alike are increasingly investing in legal design expertise.[45] And in the UK, there are signs that regulators of the legal professions are considering, or are being encouraged to consider, more human-centred approaches that align closely with the aims and strengths of designerly mindsets, strategies and processes. For example, the Legal Services Board, which is the statutory body responsible for regulating the regulators of the legal profession including the Law Society and the Bar Council, proposed in its State of Legal Services Report 2020 the development of 'simple legal products' to promote accessibility in legal communications. It also argued that regulatory bodies must 'put the interests of the public and consumers at the heart of everything they do'. And it noted that this requires not only directly encouraging or forcing the professions to

Figure 1.2 Judith Onwubiko presenting (top left), and recreating in clay (top right), a collection of manillas (metal shaped in the form of a bracelet, commonly used as currency in C15th–C20th West Africa, including as part the Transatlantic slave trade) at the British Museum; and postgraduate research students making models of their projects at Kent Law School (bottom). Images © Amanda Perry-Kessaris.

improve services, but also ensuring that consumers have 'the information and tools they need' to choose the legal services and providers that best suit their needs, thereby promoting 'competition' so that current and potential providers are pushed to 'redesign legal services that respond to [those] needs'.[46] These objectives were echoed in the 10 year strategy for 'reshaping legal services', launched by the LSB in 2021, which includes 'fairer outcomes, stronger confidence and better services' as key themes.[47] Steve Brooker, Head of Policy Development and Research at the LSB, is convinced that design can directly enhance our ability to meet those objectives, and thereby 'have a transformational impact on improving access to justice'. Specifically, he argues that designerly ways can help by 'increasing public understanding of the citizen's legal rights and duties, making it easier for people to navigate the market and building trust in technologies'. And he is passionate about the relevance and value of inclusive design principles to regulators, drawing directly, for example, on the work of entrepreneurial, design-driven organisations such as Fair By Design.[48] Meanwhile, also in 2020, the Bar Council co-hosted a legal design sprint run by Allbon for university students in celebration of Justice Week. Joanne Kane, a barrister who acted as judge, considered the legacy of the event, stating it 'must be a shared determination between legal practitioners and designers to make online legal resources accessible to all, for the benefit of society as a whole'.[49]

All of this suggests that law students ought to be introduced to and, ideally, trained in designerly mindsets, strategies and processes before they enter the professions. However, that introduction must be critical, for like law, design is not inherently 'good'. Designers are as prone as any other professional to being exclusive; and they sometimes ignore, misread or fail to anticipate users—especially users who are not like them.[50] So the design-based interventions proposed above are not a panacea—not least because they will be experienced differently by different users. If they are to enhance the experience of those who work with law now and in the future, they must be part of a proactively inclusive ecosystem. And educators have a foundational, dynamic and reflective role to play in developing such ecosystems. For instance, as Emily MacLoud explains in Chapter 15, understanding our own ethical lens in relation to accessibility and engagement is pivotal to the successful deployment of designerly ways in legal education.

We hope that this volume prompts and facilitates you to reflect on how you already do, and how you might in future, use designerly ways in legal education; and to place those efforts in a wider legal, design and educational context.

Notes

1 Associate Professor of Law, City Law School, City, University of London.
2 Professor of Law, Kent Law School, University of Kent.
3 Melanie Nind and Sarah Lewthwaite, 'A Conceptual-Empirical Typology of Social Science Research Methods Pedagogy' (2020) 35.4 Research Papers in Education 467–487. For example, influenced by her experiences as a part-time student of visual communication and then graphic design, Amanda Perry-Kessaris began by introducing occasional design-based tasks into her teaching of Research Methods in Law but eventually came to take a design-based approach to the module as a whole.
4 K Dorst, L Kaldor, L Klippan, and R Watson, *Designing for the Common Good* (BIS 2016) 3. See also L Kimbell, 'Rethinking Design Thinking: Part I' (2011) 3 Design and Culture 285.
5 CR Brunschwig, *Visualisierung von Rechtsnormen: Legal Design* [Visualization of Legal Norms: Legal Design] (Schulthess 2001).
6 See for example, H Haapio and S Passera, 'Visual Law: What Lawyers Need to Learn from Information Designers' VoxPopuLII, 15 May 2013 https://blog.law.cornell.

edu/voxpop/2013/05/15/visual-law-what-lawyers-need-to-learn-from-information-designers/; and Legal Design Jam, http://legaldesignjam.com/.

7 'Making Law Better with Caitlin Moon', Legal Design Podcast, Episode 10, 2 May 2021, http://legaldesignpodcast.com/10-making-law-better-with-cat-moon/.

8 See the Legal Design Lab, https://www.legaltechdesign.com and M Hagan, *Law by Design* (undated). Available at: http://www.lawbydesign.co/en/home/.

9 For regular contemporary insights in legal design thinking and practice see The Legal Design Podcast at http://legaldesignpodcast.com/.

10 Here we are drawing on the framework developed by Amanda Perry-Kessaris, which builds in particular on the findings and terminology of social designer Ezio Manzini. See A Perry-Kessaris, *Doing Sociolegal Research in Design Mode* (Routledge 2021); E Manzini, *Design, When Everybody Designs* (MIT Press 2015).

11 Perry-Kessaris 2021, Chapter 2.

12 Perry-Kessaris 2021, Chapter 1.

13 See Perry-Kessaris 2021, Chapter 2.

14 A Perry-Kessaris, 'Legal Design for Practice, Activism, Policy and Research' (2019) 46.2 Journal of Law and Society 185–210.

15 Perry-Kessaris 2019. See R Cotterrell, *Law, Culture and Society: Legal Ideas in the Mirror of Social Theory* (Ashgate 2006); R Cotterrell, *Sociological Jurisprudence: Juristic Thought and Social Inquiry* (Routledge 2018).

16 C Hockings, 'Inclusive Learning and Teaching in Higher Education: A Synthesis of Research'. Advance HE (2010), https://www.advance-he.ac.uk/knowledge-hub/inclusive-learning-and-teaching-higher-education-synthesis-research, pp. 1 and 4. See also L Thomas and H May, *Inclusive Learning and Teaching in Higher Education*, Advance HE (2010), https://www.advance-he.ac.uk/knowledge-hub/inclusive-learning-and-teaching-higher-education; Advance HE (2019) *Equality + Higher Education Staff Statistical Report 2019*, https://www.advance-he.ac.uk/knowledge-hub/equality-higher-education-statistical-report-2019; S Ahmed, *On Being Included: Racism and Diversity in Institutional Life* (Duke University Press 2012); and P Goodrich and L Mills, 'The Law of White Spaces: Race, Culture, and Legal Education' (2001) 51.1 Journal of Legal Education 15–38.

17 K Holmes, *Mismatch: How Inclusion Shapes Design* (MIT Press 2018) 55–56.

18 E Allbon, 'Changing Mindsets: Encouraging Law Teachers to See Beyond Text' (2019) 7.1 *Journal of Open Access Law* Special issue on "Visual Law" Available at https://ojs.law.cornell.edu/index.php/joal/article/view/96.

19 RS Wurman, *Information Anxiety* (Doubleday 1989) 59.

20 R Waller ([1995] 2011) 'Information Design: How the Disciplines Work Together'. Simplification Centre Technical Paper no 14. https://www.reading.ac.uk/web/files/simplification/SC14DisciplinesTogether-7.pdf.

21 J Frascara, *Information Design as Principled Action: Making Information Accessible, Relevant, Understandable, and Usable* (Common Ground Publishing 2015) 8.

22 http://lawbore.net/.

23 http://tldr.legal/home.html.

24 A James and SD Brookfield, *Engaging Imagination: Helping Students Become Creative and Reflective Thinkers* (Jossey-Bass 2014) 116.

25 A Perry-Kessaris, *Doing Sociolegal Research in Design Mode* (Routledge 2021).

26 E Allbon, 'A Day in Coltsfoot Vale'. TL:DR (undated), https://tldr.legal/resource/a-day-in-coltsfoot-vale.html.

27 Allbon 2019. Research conducted at UCL in 2010–2012 found that most students across a range of disciplines found object-based learning more effective than a lecture: H Chatterjee and R Duhs, 'OBL in Higher Education', CETLD Learning at the Interface Conference Proceedings (2010), http://arts.brighton.ac.uk/__data/assets/pdf_file/0010/18649/01-Object-based-learning-in-higher-education.pdf.

28 Sara Frug, 'Toward Inclusive Design for Visual Law' (2019) 7.1 Journal of Open Access to Law 1–11, https://ojs.law.cornell.edu/index.php/joal/issue/view/8.

29 A James and SD Brookfield, *Engaging Imagination: Helping Students Become Creative and Reflective Thinkers* (Jossey-Bass 2014) 116.

30 A Lorde, *Sister Outsider: Essays and Speeches* (Crossing Press 1984).

31 See RA Memon and S Jivraj , 'Trust, Courage and Silence: Carving Out Decolonial Spaces in Higher Education Through Student–Staff Partnerships' (2020) 54.4 *The Law Teacher* 475–488. Note that the term 'decolonizing the curriculum' is used very broadly to capture the dominance of law as a discipline and profession: RA MacDonald and TB McMorrow, 'Decolonizing Law School' (2014) 51.4 Alberta Law Review 717. But some, especially indigenous, scholars argue that decolonization is very specifically about 'the repatriation of Indigenous land and life' in settler colonies and, ought not to be appropriated by or deployed as 'a metaphor for other things we want to do to improve our societies': E Tuck and KW Wang, 'Decolonization is Not a Metaphor' (2012) 1.1 Decolonization: Indigeneity, Education and Society 1–40, 1.

32 See generally Helen Chatterjee and Leonie Hannan, *Engaging the Senses: Object-Based Learning in Higher Education* (Routledge 2015). See also L Morgan, 'Understanding Dworkin Through Art: Object-Based Learning and Law' (2017) 52.1 The Law Teacher 53–67.

33 https://amandaperrykessaris.org/legaltreasure/.

34 See further A Perry-Kessaris, 'The Pop-Up Museum of Legal Objects Project: An Experiment in Sociolegal Design' (2017) 68:2 Northern Ireland Legal Quarterly Special Issue on the Pop Up Museum of Legal Objects 225–44.

35 S Bannister, 'Legal Treasure Hunt'. Mastering Law, blog post, 19 June 2015, https://blogs.kent.ac.uk/klsllm/2015/06/19/legal-treasure-hunt/.

36 See further Perry-Kessaris 2021, Chapter 2.

37 See J Knapp, J Zeratsky and B Kowitz, *Sprint: How to Solve Big Problems and Test New Ideas in Just Five Days* (Bantam Press 2016).

38 https://www.ft.com/content/e66d15b2-8f39-11e7-9084-d0c17942ba93.

39 An example is a sprint hosted by the Bar Council as part of Justice Week 2020: Emily Allbon, 'The Legal Design Sprint—the Perfect End to Justice Week 2020'. Law Bore, blog post, 1 March 2020, https://blog.lawbore.net/2020/03/the-legal-design-sprint-the-perfect-end-to-justice-week-2020/.

40 A Perry-Kessaris (2016) Sociolegal model making 1: Decision. Film. Available at https://vimeo.com/174647035.

41 Ingold 2013, p. 11.

42 James and Brookfield 2014, p. 13. See also N Brown and J Collins, 'Using LEGO to Understand Emotion Work in Doctoral Education' (2018) 5.4 International Journal of Management and Applied Research 193–209.

43 Ingold 2013, p. 9.

44 See A Perry-Kessaris, 'Making Sociolegal Research More Social by Design: Anglo-German Roots, Rewards and Risks' (2020) 21.6 German Law Journal 1427–1445.

45 See 'Episode 13: Legal Designing Financial Services with Fiona Philipps' (Legal Design Podcast, 23 May 2021), http://legaldesignpodcast.com/13-episode-legal-designing-financial-services-with-fiona-phillips/, accessed 19 July 2021.

46 Legal Services Board, *State of Legal Services 2020 Report*, https://legalservicesboard.org.uk/state-of-legal-services-report-2020, accessed 19 July 2021.

47 Legal Services Board, *Reshaping Legal Services*, March 2021, https://legalservicesboard.org.uk/our-work/reshaping-legal-services-a-sector-wide-strategy.

48 Email from Steve Brooker to the authors (12 August 2021). See also Fair By Design website: https://fairbydesign.com/.

49 Joanna Kane, 'Elevating Publicly Available Legal Resources: The Legal Design Sprint'. Young Bar Blog (undated), https://www.barcouncil.org.uk/resource/

young-bar-blog-elevating-publicly-available-legal-resources-the-legal-design-sprint.html, accessed 19 July 2021. See also Emily Allbon, 'The Legal Design Sprint—The Perfect End to Justice Week 2020'. Law Bore, blog post, 1 March 2020, https://blog.lawbore.net/2020/03/the-legal-design-sprint-the-perfect-end-to-justice-week-2020/.

50 See for example C Criado Perez, *Invisible Women: Exposing Data Bias in a World Designed For Men* (Vintage 2020).

Part I

Higher Education

2 Socio-legal methods labs as pedagogical spaces

Experimentation, knowledge building, community development

Siddharth Peter de Souza[1] *and Lisa Hahn*[2]

Introduction

Many of the exciting questions that drive early career scholars for their first research project are difficult to answer with just one disciplinary approach. The realities of law are not revealed simply by interpreting a legal norm or analysing a legal text; reversely, understanding the societal relevance of law—as a system of norms, a regulating force or an economic factor—benefits from an understanding of law's internal logic, the process of law-making and of legal application. With this need to think of law from different standpoints, there is a great interest among doctoral students in both law and social sciences to expand the toolbox of methods they have learned during their mostly mono-disciplinary university education. Despite students' thirst for methods, learning spaces for interdisciplinary legal research are rare and often ad hoc. And when students auto-didactically try to improve their methodological skill set, they quickly realise that interdisciplinary work means more than reading method books about, for example, the art of interviewing or methods of legal interpretation. Field research skills are learned in the field and legal methods are understood when law is applied to real cases.[3]

The Socio-Legal Lab aims to create just such an open learning space, where methodological skills are acquired and applied collaboratively.[4] It began as a student initiative to create a platform of exchange about methods of interdisciplinary legal research and as an opportunity for graduate students working on socio-legal studies in Germany to connect and collaborate. This sparked the idea of a sustainable project that facilitated a critical, reflective but yet practical use of socio-legal methods in the development of research projects. It involved exploring assumptions that exist in terms of how (legal) knowledge is constructed, questioning the politics of why methods are used and circulated,[5] and then finding ways to build allies and communities in order to develop agendas for action.[6]

In this chapter, we explore how socio-legal methods can be brought alive and enhanced through the deployment of a lab as a space for interactive learning. We discuss how it is possible to build a more experiential way of learning socio-legal methods with a mixture of literature, visualisations and

DOI: 10.4324/9780429021411-3

games to make socio-legal methods more approachable as well as closely connected to law in action. The first section of the chapter introduces the idea of learning through a lab and how this format seeks to enable students to practice and work through strands of socio-legal theory, methods and science communication in an application-oriented, participatory and didactically creative way. In the second section, we explore some of the design aspects of a lab and the challenges that can emerge in its implementation. The chapter responds to the needs of emerging researchers, who face multiple challenges when designing and actually conducting an empirical research project at the intersection of law and other disciplines.

Learning through a lab

Our intervention of learning socio-legal methods through a lab connects to two larger trends in education and practice: the laboratory turn and the design turn in law. The laboratory turn in education describes didactical ambitions to introduce clinics or labs as experiential learning spaces.[7] Through creating an atmosphere where problems can be 'labbed', the idea is to encourage a more learning by doing mindset which is hands on and connected with real life problems.[8] The design turn as a second trend seeks to develop new mediums for law beyond text through design. Legal design has become a buzzword that is associated with the hope of making law more accessible and 'more human'.[9] According to Hagan, legal design focusses both on the front- and back-end of the legal system.[10] On the front-end, it aims to make legal processes easier to navigate for its users with better design; on the back-end, legal design means building more intuitive procedures and laws. Perry-Kessaris argues that work at the intersection of law and design entails 'the deployment of designerly ways to address lawyerly concerns'.[11] Legal design builds on the assumption that such designerly ways—experimentation, communication, visualisations—have the potential to improve lawyerly communication and create 'new structured-yet-free spaces in which lawyers can be at once practical, critical, and imaginative'.[12]

These objectives very much echo what we aim for didactically when we suggest learning through a lab: making socio-legal studies more accessible and participatory, encouraging critical thinking about law and society. Accordingly, when developing curriculums and workshops, we started from a user-perspective with an analysis of the audience's needs: Why do students struggle to engage in socio-legal studies, despite their seemingly great interest? How can we actually tackle their anxieties? And in doing so, which mediums can we use to make it work for different cognitive types and to build supportive communities?

Labs as a remedy for methodological anxieties

Our search for a format through which we could discuss research methods was prompted primarily by a realisation that deciding on one's methodological approach was a source of anxiety and confusion for many of our fellow graduate students. Conversations revealed that many felt that, although there was very good material available on how to build a research project or understand the framework of a method, there was a general hesitancy about how to apply and use the method in practice. The reasons for this hesitancy varied with disciplinary background: Lawyers expressed a great uncertainty and discomfort when engaging with any method beyond doctrinal legal research; while social scientists—all well trained in non-doctrinal research—described emotional barriers when engaging with law, a magical black-box to all those without legal training. These reports pointed us to a clear student need: a space in which they can learn not only about different methods, but also about how it feels to use them, including the serendipity and uncertainty of a research process.[13] These needs echo the demands identified by Lewthwaite and Nind in their survey of experts across the social sciences for more experiential forms of learning with an offer that brings people together to share, reflect and study in a collaborative and open environment.[14]

We decided to develop the 'Socio-Legal Lab' as a pedagogical space in which to incubate new ideas, as well as to find and generate a community, in which problems can be demystified through hands on practice, and which would become an integral aspect of a research process.[15] We began by organizing workshops to find out about the methods that participants use, reflecting on the suitability of these methods to their projects and examining the research protocols that they require. In doing so, we sought to give participants a space to test hypotheses as well as offer them opportunities to be able to also fail in a safe community. This would also allow for experimentation through using different theories and practices where participants could receive feedback on the project and build conversations and collaborations with others.[16] In this sense, the lab goes beyond just being a physical or virtual space to also being project and programme with a purpose and desired impact.[17] It uses designerly ways to make socio-legal methods both 'visible and tangible' and to create community.[18]

In sum, we suggest that the lab approach has the potential to address anxieties about socio-legal methods because it aims to create an atmosphere and mindset in which students move back and forth between law in books and law in action, deal with different dichotomies in socio-legal research from micro to macro problems, descriptive to analytical questions and critical to applied research and in the process experience the messy realities of law in action.[19]

Three steps of experiential learning: Information-gathering, framing, testing

Through the Socio-Legal Lab, we endeavoured to provide graduate students with a toolkit and a set of practical strategies for interdisciplinary legal research. In terms of content, this requires a comprehensive overview of current theoretical and methodological debates and options. Our socio-legal

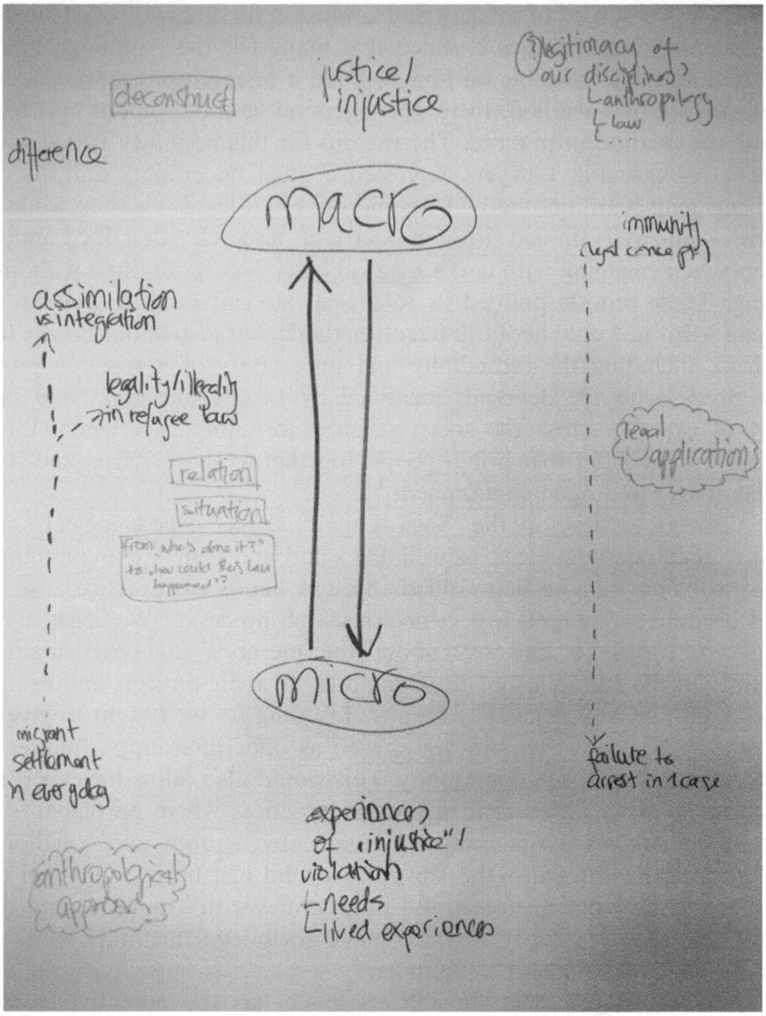

Figure 2.1 A brainstorm outcome on dichotomies in research.

methods workshops thus covered the role that interdisciplinarity plays in the study of law and society, interrogating the positionality of the researcher[20] and evaluating the assumptions that determine how knowledge is produced. We introduced qualitative and quantitative methods through which data can be collected and analysed and offered ways to enhance the outreach and impact of research through communication strategies.[21]

Our pedagogical aim was to build the Socio-Legal Lab as a space for experimentation, knowledge building and community development. Throughout our workshops, we used design aids such as visualisations and games. In order to work through each of the thematic blocks, we employed a three-step approach:

information-gathering, framing and testing. These steps have proven helpful in order to structure a session and to build an experiential learning environment when introducing a new topic. Individual researchers can use the three-step approach likewise when approaching a new theory or method.

The first step is to *gather information* on a certain topic through reading seminal texts. This stage is about looking at why the text is important to read, what the assumptions are and the representations it makes and finally what the agenda for action is. Secondly, the text can be used as a basis to *frame overarching questions* about the state of research and the kinds of issues it raises. In doing so, mind maps are a particular suitable tool to visually organize the information gathered according to particular networks and relationships. We employed mind maps for instance to document framing questions for the Lab such as exploring the interrelations between law and society, and how these questions animate the work of the participants.

After developing a series of framing questions, the third step is to *test the conclusions* of the method through a series of activities. In this last stage of application and testing, games are particularly useful. Generally, games are a popular educational tool: Mock trials are used in law schools to prepare students for legal practice; and digital simulations are supposed to enable lay people to better understand the law and navigate its institutions, e.g. represent themselves in court.[22] In the socio-legal methods labs, we have transferred this

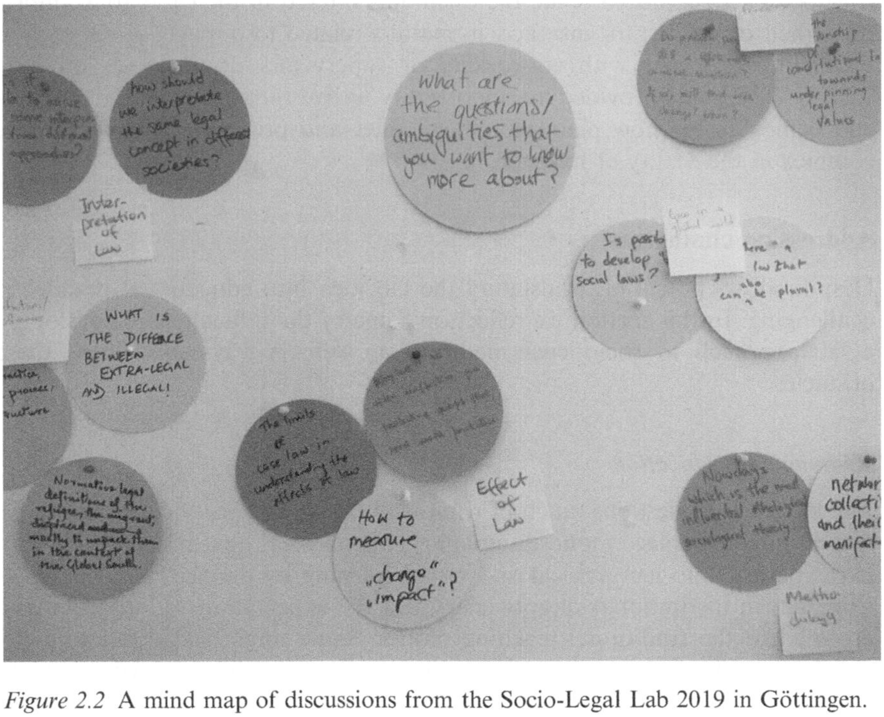

Figure 2.2 A mind map of discussions from the Socio-Legal Lab 2019 in Göttingen.

idea to simulating the research process. Here, gamification can serve as a medium to solve problems through creating artificial scenarios, providing obstacles and constraints, and asking participants to work with speculative situations.[23] For instance, when studying courtroom ethnography, after reading about how researchers approach the documentation and analysis of courtroom arguments, we simulated a courtroom setting by providing participants with recordings of a real trial. Despite participants being given similar readings and framing questions, we found they approached the ethnography of the courtroom differently depending on whether they were trained in law or social science. While the lawyers concentrated on the procedural aspects of the case, the sociologists focussed on the material aspects of the room, and the atmosphere under which the hearing took place. Each group was surprised at what the other group found, particularly as both thought their findings were the most obvious. The benefit of these two different approaches in the same room allowed participants to examine what kind of information was otherwise overlooked or ignored by them in their analysis. This offered the group an opportunity to benefit from how researchers apply similar methods differently in practice.

One further example for testing through gamification was a session on research ethics in which we used the Dilemma Game developed by the Erasmus University Rotterdam to play out practical challenges to integrity and professionalism in scientific research.[24] The feedback on this exercise was that it helped participants to relate the dilemmas offered in the cases to examples from their own lives; for instance, in matters related to impacts of research in the field, challenges with co-workers or supervisors or protocols on data sharing. The game provided an opportunity to live through potential conflicts and demonstrated how plausible ethical rules and principles are much more complex in the reality of research.

Addressing challenges

Despite all its potential, translating the lab idea into educational practice is challenging. In this section we reflect on some of the difficulties in developing a lab approach to socio-legal methods, as well as ways to address these obstacles.

Re-imagining education

The lab format questions much of what traditional university education looks like: it aims to replace mono-disciplinary, hierarchical, text-based inputs with participatory, anti-hierarchical and visual learning by doing. Thus, one challenge lies in institutional receptiveness and the expectations of students who are used to the traditional teaching model. Some might judge reflexive elements as academic self-help and consider games as inadequate for university education in terms of rigor or depth. However, it is precisely those moments of irritation which learning through a lab seeks to provoke. Moments of irritation are also part of any research process, just in a different way. For example, there can be instances where the turnout of your first survey is too small, an interview partner is not talkative, or a new court ruling contradicts the argument you develop in your project.

The lab aims to enable participants to quickly respond to such changing conditions creatively. Using experiential learning devices is less about trivializing science and more about preparing participants for the unpredictable reality of conducting research. Jackson has described a similar experience in his work on law and design with the Northeastern University School of Law Lab (NuLawLab). He advances that it is about reimagining 'the law as a creative pursuit by exploring structured methods like empathy via observation, prototyping, and the embrace of failure, with learning outcomes that hold the potential to transform how lawyers approach their role'.[25]

Merging multiple ways of thinking

Disciplinary socialisation influences the way we understand and apply socio-legal research methods; it shapes the questions we ask and the aspects of reality we consider relevant for our research. Legal thinking is conditioned to rational-analytical problem solving,[26] whereas other disciplines encourage ways of thinking in which specifying, measuring and describing problems extensively has an intrinsic value. Design thinking even breaks with that and experiments openly by moving from goals to solutions through iteration.[27] Merging these unique ways of thinking is challenging.

When design thinking and techniques are used to create an alternative learning space like a lab, it is unsurprising that experimentation is what students struggle with most. One activity during the Socio-Legal Labs in which this was particularly evident was the use of LEGO®. Inspired by the work of Perry-Kessaris,[28] we also asked participants to visualise aspects of their research by building physical models with LEGO®, and to use these models as tools to articulate concepts, challenges or research questions in a non-textual manner. These visualisations of research are meant to enable the participant to make their ideas and concepts more tangible and explore whether in the process of communicating the law differently they are able to identify any gaps in their research outcomes.[29] However, it always took a while before participants touched the first LEGO® pieces, and the concluding evaluation was very mixed: from pure joy and eureka-moments to rejection. Jackson describes comparable challenges in the NuLawLab: lawyers who are trained to narrow down things as soon as possible and get it right the first time feel uncomfortable when confronted with imperfection and being asked to test prototypes.[30] He offers a pragmatic strategy to deal with this in class: playfully interrupt the process of thinking, e.g. with a physical exercise such as jumping jacks.[31]

Becoming visually literate

When it comes to visuals as a medium of communication, one scepticism about legal design also applies to the lab: it requires visual literacy—both for creators and recipients. Communicating socio-legal methods through a lab does not mean simply reshaping text into a smart-art. It is—like legal design more generally[32]—about merging different styles of thinking. When it comes to design thinking, lawyers and social scientists are usually not familiar with it and tend to ignore principals of good design.[33] Pragmatically, this can be solved by working together with designers in co-creating and developing course curriculums and learning materials.

However, the question remains whether all content is suitable for visualisation. While all sorts of processes flow naturally in charts, one can think of content that is more challenging to be visualised. From a legal point of view, sceptics might argue that law as a knowledge system only works with texts. Visuals can hardly be interpreted using the traditional methods of legal interpretation—do we thus need new dogmatics for visuals in law?[34] What problems does the proliferation of visuals more generally pose to legal theory? [35] And how can we develop a 'new visual legal realism' that reflects the fact that legal decision-making processes are increasingly based on a mixture of fictional and non-fictional sources?[36] Furthermore, attempts to visualise can raise sensitive social and ethical considerations—for example, what is the impact of videos of police brutality? It is important not to reproduce stereotypes when using icons to represent human beings, social structures and interactions. For instance, Andersen provides the example of how in a project on disability rights, in creating an avatar, one of the mistakes she made was to first only show disability with a cane but, ultimately, changed this to move beyond showing just physical disability.[37] Similarly in one of their illustrations they showed a nurse with a nurse's cap, but reworked this as the industry had moved away from this image.[38]

In addition to these very fundamental theoretical questions, one might ask from a learning-psychology-perspective: How far do we read pictures differently than words?[39] Sceptics might say, there are limits to visualisations as didactical tools: they alienate coherent texts and, if done poorly, cause misunderstandings; topics that don't lend themselves well to visualisation tend to be ignored; visuals simplify and trivialise complex contents and images, videos and graphics are only suitable for visual learners.[40] The latter can also be said about texts as medium: the complexity of—above all legal—texts is a barrier to many people when engaging with law.[41] However, sceptics of visualisation argue that the educational outcome is minimised because students do not have to work through the content themselves but are being presented with a ready-made summary.[42]

All these doubts are to be taken seriously, but they do not necessarily mean refraining from visualisations. On the contrary: they call for investing more effort into creating meaningful visuals. Visuals that show processes and connections; that are clear and precise; that make it easier to get started with a topic without claiming to cover it comprehensively; that do not only summarise content but stimulate further thinking.[43] One strategy to address concerns about visuals is to incorporate findings from learning psychology. For example, visuals should be used together with words, as research on cognitive-oriented legal visualisation research recommends.[44] Overall, it is likely that digitalisation will continue to change the way we think and communicate about law and society. Instead of demonizing this trend, we should aim to improve visual literacy: by becoming aware of the cognitive and emotional effects of multimedia, by developing a 'critical visual intelligence' and by creating manuals for using multidisciplinary toolkits.[45]

Building trust, empowerment and community through games

Sceptics might argue that using games trivialises sciences and that gaming elements distract from learning goals.[46] In the Socio-Legal Lab, we have experienced quite the opposite: games have a particular value when used in addition to other mediums as they enable students to apply the learned content.

Trust is another reason why we have used games to build a community between participants. In the past three years of running the lab, we have found that a comforting atmosphere is essential for the lab to function. Trust is a prerequisite for sharing vulnerabilities of research as well as receiving constructive and collaborative feedback. To create an empowering environment in a short period of time, we used ice-breaker games where participants get to know each other by doing something that interrupts the monotony of serious academic debate. For instance, we played a game called Two Truths and a Lie which encourages participants to tell others about themselves through choosing mundane or amusing personal details, one of which must be a lie. This exercise through its silliness sets the tone of the lab, as an informal yet secure space to be able to understand and discuss methodological matters. We also encouraged participants to experiment with elevator pitches and role-plays as more creative means to convey the purpose and intentions of research as well as to share more details about themselves and their work.[47] A confidential environment is also important to allow for a joint reflection of the possible impacts of one's research. Tools like the Research Impact Canvas by Fecher and Kobsda can facilitate such an exchange. It is one way of thinking about one's audiences, different stakeholders, users and then finding ways to do meaningful work.[48]

The community-building function of games became even more obvious when the Socio-Legal Lab 2020 had to take place online during the Covid-19-pandemic. Sessions with games turned out to work best as gamification broke the digital fatigue that many participants felt from having to work and learn remotely. Overall, we discovered that communities did develop in much the same way online as offline. This was in part due to the ability to change formats around.

Conclusion

This chapter has introduced the idea of a lab as an experimental space to explore socio-legal studies. We have argued that learning through a lab has the potential to make socio-legal methods more approachable and user-oriented. In our experiences of running the Socio-Legal Lab, we have found that different aspects determine its success: Besides an open and safe atmosphere, the interdisciplinary composition of the participants is essential. This is not only because of the possibilities for diverse conversations but also for peer-to-peer learning, whether in terms of domain expertise or even practical strategies to develop new communities of learning. Creating this social aspect of the lab as a space for interaction is particularly difficult in an online format, the new normal during the Covid-19-pandemic. Being virtual leaves less opportunity for spontaneity and makes it more exhausting to share the same material for both instructors and participants. Despite all challenges both offline and online, we can echo Jackson's conclusion for labs as learning spaces: 'The good news is that the use of design pedagogies within legal education, while not always easy, is *fun*'.[49]

Notes

1 Postdoctoral Researcher, Tilburg University.
2 Ph.D. Candidate, Humboldt University, Berlin.
3 See generally for a discussion on understanding the mechanics of research through engaging in its practice: Daniel Kilburn, Melanie Nind and Rose Wiles, 'Learning as Researchers and Teachers: The Development of a Pedagogical Culture for Social Science Research Methods?' (2014) 62 British Journal of Educational Studies 191.
4 Lisa Hahn and Siddharth de Souza, 'The Socio-Legal Lab: Beyond Methods' (*Rechtswirklichkeit*), https://barblog.hypotheses.org/2047, accessed 13 January 2021.
5 For research on the how legal knowledge is circulated and presented see Daniel Bonilla, 'The Political Economy of Legal Knowledge' in Daniel Bonilla and Colin Crawford (eds), *Constitutionalism in the Americas* (Edward Elgar 2018).
6 Sarah Masefield, 'Use Peer Support to Improve Well-Being and Research Outcomes' (2019) 572 Nature 407.
7 Urszula Pawlicka-Deger, 'The Laboratory Turn: Exploring Discourses, Landscapes, and Models of Humanities Labs' (2020) 14 Digital Humanities Quarterly.
8 N Alexander Aguado, 'Teaching Research Methods: Learning by Doing' (2009) 15 Journal of Public Affairs Education 251.
9 'The Legal Design Manifesto v. 2' (*Legal Design Alliance*), https://www.legaldesignalliance.org/, accessed 9 January 2021.
10 Margaret Hagan, 'Legal Design', *Law by Design*, https://www.lawbydesign.co/legal-design/, accessed 13 January 2021.
11 Amanda Perry-Kessaris, 'Legal Design for Practice, Activism, Policy, and Research' (2019) 46 Journal of Law and Society 185, 193.
12 ibid 192.
13 The work of Schmidt and Halliday was pivotal in allowing us to lean on and understand how seminal socio-legal projects that similarly often had chance and unplanned moments in their research process: Patrick Schmidt and Simon Halliday (eds), 'Introduction: Beyond Methods—Law and Society in Action', in

Conducting Law and Society Research: Reflections on Methods and Practices (Cambridge University Press 2009).

14 Sarah Lewthwaite and Melanie Nind, 'Teaching Research Methods in the Social Sciences: Expert Perspectives on Pedagogy and Practice' (2016) 64 British Journal of Educational Studies 413.

15 For more on the didactic approach of the lab see Lisa Hahn and Siddharth de Souza, 'Introduction to the Blog Symposium: The Socio-Legal Lab as a Didactic Format' (*Rechtswirklichkeit*), https://barblog.hypotheses.org/3437, accessed 11 January 2021.

16 ibid.

17 See also Pawlicka-Deger (n 7).

18 Amanda Perry-Kessaris, 'Making Socio-Legal Research More Social by Design: Anglo-German Roots, Rewards, and Risks' (2020) 21 German Law Journal 1427, 1442.

19 Lisa Hahn and Siddharth de Souza, 'Self-reflecting, Constructing and Positioning: Intersecting Debates in Socio-Legal Studies' (*Rechtswirklichkeit*), https://barblog.hypotheses.org/2988, accessed 7 December 2020.

20 See for the importance of a reflexive mode in interdisciplinary research Larissa Vetters, Judith Eggers and Lisa Hahn, 'Migration and the Transformation of German Administrative Law. An Interdisciplinary Research Agenda' (Max Planck Institute for Social Anthropology 2017) Working Paper Series (188) 36, http://www.eth.mpg.de/cms/de/publications/working_papers/wp0188, accessed 17 May 2018.

21 Hahn and de Souza, 'Introduction to the Blog Symposium' (n 15); Hahn and de Souza, 'Self-Reflecting, Constructing and Positioning' (n 19).

22 Dan Jackson and Martha F Davis, 'Gaming a System: Using Digital Games to Guide Self-Represented Litigants' (Northeastern University School of Law 2016), Northeastern University School of Law Research Paper No 252, https://papers.ssrn.com/abstract=2719926, accessed 6 January 2021.

23 Daniel M Ferguson, 'The Gamification of Legal Education: Why Games Transcend the Langdellian Model and How They Can Revolutionize Law School' (2016) 19 Chapman Law Review 629.

24 'Dilemma Game' (*Erasmus University Rotterdam*), https://www.eur.nl/en/about-eur/policy-and-regulations/integrity/research-integrity/dilemma-game, accessed 13 January 2021.

25 Dan Jackson, 'Human-Centered Legal Tech: Integrating Design in Legal Education' (2016) 50 Law Teacher 82, 82.

26 Gerlinde Berger-Walliser, Thomas D Barton and Helena Haapio, 'From Visualization to Legal Design: A Collaborative and Creative Process' (2017) 54 American Business Law Journal 347, 360.

27 ibid 360.

28 Amanda Perry-Kessaris, 'Sociolegal Model Making 1: Decision' (*Amanda Perry-Kessaris*, 15 July 2016), https://amandaperrykessaris.org/2016/07/15/model-making-for-sociolegal-research-part-1/, accessed 9 January 2021; Perry-Kessaris (n 18) 1440.

29 Emily Allbon, 'Changing Mindsets: Encouraging Law Teachers to Think beyond Text' (2019) 7 Journal of Open Access to Law; Siddharth Peter de Souza, 'Communicating the Law: Thinking through Design, Visuals and Presentation of Legal Content' in Siddharth Peter de Souza and Maximilian Spohr (eds), *Technology, Innovation and Access to Justice: Dialogues on the Future of Law* (Edinburgh University Press 2021).

30 Jackson (n 25) 95.

31 ibid.

32 Berger-Walliser, Barton and Haapio (n 26) 350; Emily Allbon, 'Beyond Text: Exploiting the Visual in Law' (2018) 26 Australian Law Librarian 54.

33 Tania Leiman, 'Where Are the Graphics? Communicating Legal Ideas Effectively Using Images and Symbols' (2016) 26 Legal Education Review 47, 56.
34 ibid 55.
35 Neal Feigenson, 'The Visual in Law: Some Problems for Legal Theory' (2014) 10 Law, Culture and the Humanities 13.
36 Richard K Sherwin, 'A Manifesto for Visual Legal Realism Symposium: Access to Justice: Law and Popular Culture' (2007) 40 Loyola of Los Angeles Law Review 719.
37 Camilla Baasch Andersen, 'Musings on the Comic Book Contract Project and Legal Design Thinking' (2020) 11 Journal of Graphic Novels and Comics 1.
38 ibid.
39 Christina Spiesel, 'Reflections on Reading: Words and Pictures and Law' (2006) 2 International Journal of Law in Context 305.
40 Bernhard Bergmans, *Visualisierungen in Rechtslehre und Rechtswissenschaft—Ein Beitrag zur Rechtsvisualisierung* (Logos 2009) 25; Leiman (n 33) 55.
41 Siddharth de Souza, 'Vernacularizing the Law: Can It Be Made More Accessible?', https://winklerinstitute.ca/vernacularizing-the-law-can-it-be-made-more-accessible/, previously accessed 4 January 2021.
42 Bergmans (n 40) 25.
43 de Souza, 'Vernacularizing the Law: Can It Be Made More Accessible?' (n 41); Siddharth de Souza, 'Proactive Contracting for Platform Work: Making the Design of Terms and Conditions More Participatory' (*FemLab.Co*, 23 October 2020), https://femlab.co/2020/10/23/proactive-contracting-for-platform-work-making-the-design-of-terms-and-conditions-more-participatory/, accessed 14 January 2021; Siddharth de Souza, 'Making the Law Speak: Empowering Workers through Legal Engagement' (*FemLab.Co*, 3 July 2020), https://femlab.co/2020/07/03/making-the-law-speak-empowering-workers-through-legal-engagement/, accessed 6 July 2020.
44 Berger-Walliser, Barton and Haapio (n 26) 349.
45 Richard K Sherwin, Neal Feigenson and Christina Spiesel, 'Law in the Digital Age: How Visual Communication Technologies Are Transforming the Practice, Theory, and Teaching of Law' (2006) 12 Boston University Journal of Science & Technology Law 227, 260.
46 On the purpose and heuristics of learning games Fengfeng Ke, 'Designing and Integrating Purposeful Learning in Game Play: A Systematic Review' (2016) 64 Educational Technology Research and Development 219.
47 Mary Tran, 'Deconstructing the Elevator Speech' (*WI+RE – Quick and practical research and writing tutorials, collaboratively designed by students at UCLA.*, 12 April 2017), https://uclalibrary.github.io/research-tips/deconstructing-the-elevator-speech/, accessed 13 January 2021.
48 Benedikt Fecher and Christian Kobsda, 'Meet the Research Impact Canvas: A Structured Guide for Planning Your Science Communication Activities', https://elephantinthelab.org/meet-the-research-impact-canvas-a-structured-guide-for-planning-your-science-communication-activities/, accessed 13 January 2021.
49 Jackson (n 25) 91.

3 Using personas, vignettes and diagrams in legal education

Clare Williams[1]

Introduction

Personas, vignettes and visual technologies of communication offer us ways of telling memorable and engaging stories about the law, making them a useful tool in legal education.[2] In addition to diagrams and other visual forms, fictional renders of characters in the form of personas, and their intentions and motivations in the form of vignettes, can complement text-based materials by illustrating and interrogating core concepts. They illustrate by empirically grounding the conceptual, offering a tangible embodiment that brings three principal benefits to both student and teacher: the simplification of complexity, the reduction of text fatigue and the provision of spaces for knowledge co-production. Used in combination with visualisations, two further interrogatory benefits can be noted for both students and teachers. Firstly, these approaches offer short cuts to sites at which meaning is created and shared, allowing students to engage critically with the law as a social institution and site of shared expectations.[3] Secondly, visual approaches allow us to sidestep some of the limitations of linguistic framing. This chapter will address each of these through the experiences of Academic Ann—one of three fictional personas I am developing in my own research into the relationships between law, economy and society—as she uses visual methods to teach legal concepts.

The discussion operates at three layers of analysis. Zooming out, the first suggests a general proposition regarding the use of personas, vignettes and visualisations as tools for teaching legal theory. This responds to imperatives of both legal aesthetics and Economic Sociology of Law (ESL) in engaging students with legal theory as a contextualised yet varied social institution. Zooming in, the second layer focuses on the fictional persona of 'Academic Ann' in her role as teacher and researcher. Zooming in yet further, the third layer explores the teaching resources that Ann develops for her students. These include the creation of the persona and vignette of 'Policy Polly' along with some diagrams introducing ESL. To begin, I start at the second layer of analysis by introducing Ann.

DOI: 10.4324/9780429021411-4

Introducing Ann

Academic Ann teaches law at a university, although her own research sits at the interface between law and economy. She is now reconsidering her methodology before carrying out empirical research into the experiences of foreign investors with the law. But she is frustrated with mainstream or orthodox ways of doing, talking, and thinking about the law and economy. She has noticed that there are important voices and interests that are side-lined by mainstream frames and she wants a way of reframing law and economy that can accommodate other, non-economic interests. Ann finds that a range of interdisciplinary approaches that is sometimes referred to collectively as an Economic Sociology of Law (ESL) offers a flexible alternative that can balance competing voices, and she applies ESL to her own research. She also wants to introduce her students to ESL and its merits, but realises that this is a tricky and complex area. She needs to draw up a map of the field to guide her students across the basic topography but wonders how best to engage them. In addition to the reading lists and slides she has prepared, she creates a persona, a vignette and diagrams to both illustrate and interrogate some of the relationships between legal, economic, and social phenomena and explore what an ESL frame can offer. As the following discussion shows, this not only engages her students but prompts Ann with different questions and perspectives, deepening her own understanding in the process.

Communicating relationships between law, economy and society (Ann's teaching dilemma)

The complexity of ESL in reshaping how we do, talk, and think about law, economy, and society is the first of Ann's dilemmas. The second relates to the way that the mainstream vocabularies and grammars we use to talk about law and economy shape the mental models that we work with. These tend to be, respectively, doctrinal and neoclassical, the political manifestation of which is neoliberalism.[4] These approaches in turn reveal and conceal problems and solutions, and enable or disable our ability to imagine alternatives. Thus, the vocabulary of neoliberalism shapes our (neoliberal) mental models, making it difficult to conceive of alternative (non-neoliberal) solutions to financial crashes, social crises and environmental catastrophes.

Introducing an Economic Sociology of Law (ESL)

As an ESL is more a 'frame of mind' than a fixed methodology, several ESL-inspired lenses can be noted here, including actor-network theory,[5] relational work[6] and a community lens.[7] Ann likes the way that ESL re-sites law and economy socially, presenting the legal and economic as aspects of interactions. She also likes how it accommodates the differently-rational while denying claims of neutral objectivity that characterise mainstream approaches, challenging the metaphorical fictions of the separate silos of 'law' and 'economy'.[8] Ann wants her students to appreciate the historical and cultural contingency of the separation of law, economy, and society, and designs diagrams that will highlight the entrenched mental models that ESL responds to. Zooming in to the third layer of analysis, we can explore Ann's visual teaching materials.

Visualising ESL

Visuals can be simple without being superficial. Ann's diagrams are designed to be eye-catching and memorable as well as to spark a deeper curiosity and discussion. Her starting point is to draw what an ESL might look like, and, combining symbols with text, she begins with the mainstream approaches, illustrating the silos of law, economy and society.

She then asks the students to imagine holding a 'sociological magnifying glass' and moving it over the diagram, such that the circles shift closer together, eventually merging. She asks her students to notice that ESL sits at the interface of the three spheres, and that a sociological understanding of law and economy can give us different points of access, perspective and reference. She notes that the relationship between the three initial spheres has shifted, too, and asks her students what this might mean for how we think and talk about the relationships between law, economy and society.

Nevertheless, Ann realises that in avoiding linguistic metaphors, she is introducing visual metaphors with their own accompanying benefits and limitations and some of these are discussed in the final section.[9]

Personas and vignettes

Having introduced her students to ESL, Ann wants them to explore the difference it might make in practice. She creates the fictional persona of 'Policy

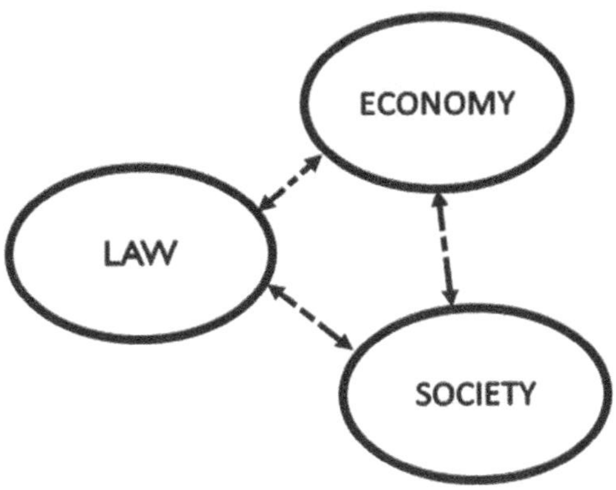

Figure 3.1 Mainstream or orthodox approaches to law, economy and society as silos of research and practice.

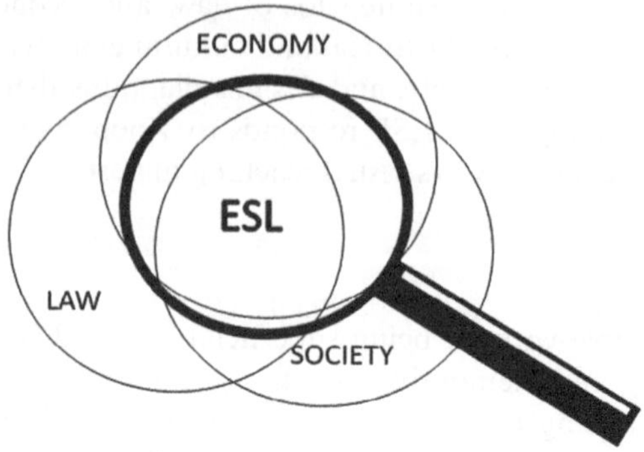

Figure 3.2 ESL through a looking glass. Ann asks her students to imagine holding a sociological magnifying glass over the spheres of law, economy and society, such that the three spheres shift closer together.

Polly', a researcher at the World Bank, who is based on a friend of hers that she had met on a previous fieldwork trip to Sri Lanka. In creating the persona of Polly, Ann sets out the characteristics that are relevant to her students (Figure 3.3). Ann might begin by asking her students to summarise the information we know.

Based on real-life discussions, Ann might include a project or area of research that Polly is engaged in, asking her students to imagine what tools and concepts Polly might use in her work at the World Bank as she researches the interface between law and economy, specifically which frameworks, methodologies and data sets.

Reflecting the Latin origins of the term, a *persona* is a fictional rendition of a character. This technique is used frequently in design where personas based on data or observation are created to embody key characteristics of the anticipated users of a designed output. Thus, the process is user-focused, and Ann keeps in mind that the end users (her students) must both identify with and invest in Polly. Personas also contextualise the discussion and there are two immediate observations here. Firstly, the persona of Polly not only provides an empirical application of the embodiment of theory but contextualises interpretation and understanding. In creating the persona of Policy Polly, Ann's students are asked to take account of Polly's surroundings, background, intentions and self-perception. In keeping with the distinction drawn in the theory of symbolic interactionism, developed by George Herbert Mead and Herbert Blumer, between the 'I' (the spontaneous self) and the 'me' (the other self in which social constraints are played out), personas enable a reflexive separation that appreciates not only the character as the product of her surroundings, but her own self-perception in that context.[10] Secondly, in contextualising an empirical embodiment of theory, the persona of Polly reminds her students to appreciate the social context of law as a site of shared expectations.[11] This is developed further in the vignette of Polly (Figure 3.3).

Figure 3.3 Ann might develop a persona to introduce her students to ESL. She introduces them to 'Policy Polly' (top) who is based on the real-life characteristics of someone she knows. She asks her students to summarise the information about Polly (middle); and then develops Policy Polly into a vignette (bottom), including Polly's intentions, attitudes and general dissatisfaction with current approaches.

The shift to Polly's beliefs, intentions and actions develops the initial persona into a vignette, although keen-eyed readers will have noticed that mentions of Polly's preferences in the first persona shifted towards a vignette. Originating mainly in psychology, a *vignette* comprises a short description or snapshot of a situation or context that references important points in the study of 'perceptions, beliefs, and attitudes'.[12] This can offer a powerful way of crafting and delivering narrative that both captures and contextualises core research methods and findings. These 'short stories about a hypothetical person',[13] simulations, real-life stories, anecdotes or simply a narrative form of presentation can be constructed through text or images, and can be both a method of conducting research and a way of interpreting and communicating results.[14] It is difficult to draw a clear dividing line between personas and vignettes when used in the social sciences, however vignettes can be a useful tool in addressing the reporting gap in qualitative research between what actors do, and what they say they do, and they can offer a situated context in which to explore real world values in a selective setting. They can, therefore, allow us to interrogate core arguments conceptually and normatively through an empirical lens.

From this vignette, Ann's students understand that Polly is frustrated by the narrow viewfinder of mainstream frames and their prioritisation of economic values, voices and interests. The tangible example of Polly's experience gives Ann's students a setting to explore how certain voices and non-economic interests are silenced in orthodox, neoliberal discourse, and then how an ESL can offer an alternative framework in which myriad interests and values can be accommodated. Her students can begin to explore the outcomes of interventions such as those designed by Polly and the impact on communities of the language and theories she uses. Ann might develop the vignette of Polly into a mini case study in future years, including more details about her work that Ann can base on her own research and experience to give her students a richer and more detailed contextual narrative for exploring theory.

While images (discussed below) bypass language to engage through perceptions,[15] personas and vignettes sit between the two spheres of communication: based in text but looking to image and imagination. As user-centred, or 'designerly' devices, personas and vignettes make visible relevant people and characteristics in an abstract sense, aesthetically embodying the conceptual.[16] Setting them out on a piece of paper as Ann does is one way of making this abstract concrete, engaging the visible and the tangible to show rather than tell. In this way, personas and vignettes engage the aesthetic to complement the traditionally rational approaches of mainstream legal theory. In engaging the emotive and the subjective, they access the 'non-rational other' just as narrative or fiction might, relying on the imagination of the audience to bring the content to life.

Zooming out to our first level of analysis, we can appreciate that, as an embodiment of an empirical instantiation of theory, personas and vignettes acknowledge the sociological turn in legal theory that responds to the mainstream, doctrinal focus on laws as written rules. Lenses like ESL remind us that law must be studied as a social institution, with visible, concrete elements but also as a site of shared expectations where meaning is attributed and intention, or Weber's *verstehen*, is created and applied.[17] This phenomenological dimension requires us to understand law as a communal resource that mediates and moderates relations and resources, but which is in turn re-co-constituted through interactions.[18] A focus on context enables understanding of the contingency, relativity, dynamism, fluidity and variability of social institutions, allowing for explorations of power, privilege, and ways of analysing these in empirical, applied situations. Thus, the creation and use of a persona or vignette responds to calls both from design and from legal theory to interpret the subject contextually.

The visual

As the previous section hinted, the relationship between law and the image has a long history of opposition between, on the one hand, law's supposed 'rationality' and, on the other hand, the 'emotional' aesthetic.[19] 'Art is radically subjective, while law is reasoned and objective. In Hegelian terms, law is the combination of reason and necessity, art of sensuality and freedom'.[20] Modernist approaches, drawing on Kantian categorisation and the later interpretations of Weber and Habermas in particular, adopt 'three areas of enquiry and action, the cognitive, the practical and the aesthetic to develop their own specific, internal rationality, in separate institutions operated by distinct groups of experts'.[21] But rejecting modernism's supposed objectivity and neutrality, Perry-Kessaris updates these taxonomies, suggesting that 'designerly' approaches offer practical-critical-imaginative spaces, encourage us to be experimental, and give us ways of making things visible and tangible.[22] Such 'designerly ways' allow us to explore the visual at the 'boundary between the social system and consciousness', thereby bypassing regular means of communication that rely on vocabularies and grammars and engaging instead through perception.[23]

However, use of the visual in law might seem a radical departure, given that law is usually constructed and communicated through words or text. While words may be originally derived from pictures, symbols and signs, they

> are not like boxcars freighting reality around; they do not simply leave the scene once their load of meaning has been dumped in our minds. The language we use [...] helps to create the reality we live in. And as the means of communication change so too does our sense of ourselves, others, and the world around us.[24]

Thus, as Ann is aware, the language that she uses when describing the relationship between law, economy and society not only defines how she is able to think of these connections, but how she is positioned and constructed as an actor in the process. Additionally, as noted, vocabularies and grammars both reveal and conceal, offering and hiding spaces for imagination. Mirroring ESL's claim that law cannot be purely rational or objective, the visual offers a way to aesthetically 'make and communicate sense'.[25]

While text and image are usually juxtaposed, often their greatest achievements come from their close cooperation. The interlacing of text and image offers new frontiers for approaching epistemological claims and new ways of knowing the law as an aesthetic endeavour. We might imagine a continuum of textual-visual approaches that sees varying degrees of one or the other, with the greatest impact from, and engagement with, the materials lying between the two extremes. Simple captions, labels, and 'alt text' can ground or 'anchor' images and direct the reader, ensuring that synergies are maximised and misunderstandings minimised while simultaneously avoiding text fatigue.[26] While graphical representations of ideas that step beyond language can create 'structured yet free spaces' in which innovation and imagination can occur,[27] communication remains the 'core function' and the aim is not simply to make the text look pretty.[28]

We can identify myriad non-textual visual technologies of narrative spanning 2D and 3D creative approaches and responding to visual and kinaesthetic learning. The most familiar to legal scholars and educators will be diagrams, tables and arrows setting out causation or correlation and outlining connections, links and influence. These tend to be monochrome, however where colour is possible, this can offer an alternative dimension for coding and describing objects, subjects and their (inter-)relations. Mind-mapping graphs and flow charts can (re-)present themes and connections, allowing directionality of both correlation and causation to be graphically displayed.[29] It is important to note the impossibility of rendering concepts in two dimensions without activating natural yet culturally-specific page hierarchies. Emphasis might be attributed differently by students whose native language reads right to left or top to bottom, for example, and this tyranny of two-dimensional hierarchy can be addressed somewhat by the addition of a third dimension (discussed below).

We can also identify forms of graphical representation that may or may not rely on accompanying text in the form of labels or captions. Art and digital art in the form of paintings,[30] illustrations,[31] tableaux, graffiti[32] and photography can be used to spark discussion or can visually depict a situation, establishing the context. Narrative as context can be constructed visually through storyboarding and comics that may use or avoid text-based additions.[33] Such visual tools can be prepared and presented in advance or used as a creative tool to enable synchronous engagement and understanding.[34] Additionally, as we saw with Ann's diagrams, graphic design can be applied to concepts, frames, lenses and theories to engage and communicate, using the basic elements of visual communication to address legal problems.

Then, more technologically-involved forms of visual engagement might include 3D computer modelling,[35] and animation.[36] Augmented reality (AR) and virtual reality (VR) also sit on a continuum of immersive digital experience for the exploration of substantive, procedural and theoretical areas of law, and offer a way of juxtaposing the familiar with the unfamiliar, creating spaces for different perspectives to emerge. Additionally, digital platforms have expanded the scope for non-textual communication,[37] and the use of Serious Games, simulations and multi-user virtual environments (MUVEs) can allow students to explore fictional but relevant environments before encountering such situations in real life, improving both confidence as well as engagement and retention of information.[38] These collaborative, interactive, and transactional learning environments create spaces for knowledge co-production as students engage with the material both synchronously and asynchronously, discovering the content with their peers and reacting both to the material and its interpretation by others, potentially fostering a more experientially-grounded approach to theory in legal education.[39] Finally, modular building (such as LEGO®), or the materiality of found objects can be used as a foundation for kinaesthetic as well as visual engagement, drawing immediate and tangible connections for the student between the law and its embodiment through, and construction throughout, everyday objects.[40]

The visual as illustration

Accessibility of material need not be a barrier to engaging with the core concepts, and Ann is mindful that while some of her students have dyslexia, there is a sliding scale at which point text fatigue will set in for all students. Visual cues, signposts and maps of the field can help focus attention and emphasis, while also directing perspective, contrast and proportion. Once again, context is important, specifically that of the image; textually on the page, subtextually within the material surrounding it, and contextually in the socio-economic, political, psychological and legal climate into which the image is deployed and interpreted. The importance of the image's context(s) speaks to the ability of the audience to interpret the work, drawing on their shared cultural, social and institutional knowledge to construct meaning in any given setting. Design principles note that '[t]he form of an object is not more important than the form of the space surrounding it', and that '[a]ll things exist in interaction with other things'. Moreover, 'perception is an active process' that 'merges what we see with what we know to build a coherent understanding of the world'.[41] Thus, imputed meaning may vary according to the mode of communication used, the space in which it is deployed, and the intended audience making '[l]ayout, whitespace, headings, patterns, designs, and colour [...] important in establishing meaning'.[42] However overwhelming this might initially sound, it is important to note that when communicating in any form, the author, painter or composer can control only what they output, entering into a bargain with the reader or audience who interprets the work according to existing (usually shared) frames of reference, context, and experience. These frames are contingent, and recent movements like Black Lives Matter and #MeToo exemplify how a fluid and shifting cultural and political context can redefine art and its interpretation. For example, campaigns to remove public statutes of those who engaged in the slave trade such as that of Edward Colston, and those who engaged in acts that are no longer deemed tolerable such as Cecil Rhodes have become visible points of friction between changing social preferences and the visual representation of these.[43] At the same time, art or the image can offer a mirror for society to reflect on the voices and interests it chooses to prioritise while simultaneously offering a platform for shifts in attitudes to be displayed and, in turn, reflected on. The discourse surrounding the 'Rhodes Must Fall' campaign in Oxford, UK, and the toppling of Colston's statue in Bristol, UK, demonstrate the reflexivity brought about by engagement with visual representations.

Finally, while the traditional educational setting might be the classroom, the effects of the pandemic might mean that face to face teaching is no longer the norm. The impact of this on knowledge co-production and the interpretation of non-textual materials cannot be overstated given the reduction in synchronous opportunities for verifying interpretation and engagement across a cohort. Additionally, the digital context in which asynchronous connections take place is constantly in a state of flux. Platforms, software and digital access vary across time and space and mean that there is greater competition for the attention of the student as well as variability in what they might eventually see. Thus, until there is a generalised visual literacy along with visual interpretation of text as Peter Goodrich has argued, authors and educators like Ann must be aware of the contexts in which she is deploying images, and the work that she is asking those images to do.[44]

The visual as interrogation

Use of the visual brings methodological benefits for Ann as well as her students. The act of graphically representing concepts (and facts) mandates boiling down the core principles and arguments, offering different perspectives and points of entry. The simple act of thinking graphically can function like a zoom lens on a camera, bringing different features in and out of focus while presenting new connections, interfaces and points of engagement.[45] In addition to letting her step beyond the limitations of language that was explored earlier, Ann may find that, in reimagining her work visually and graphically, she is confronted with different questions and connections than those that had presented themselves through text. Moreover, combining the insights of textual analysis and visual illustration might allow her to differently interrogate both the conceptual frameworks that she is developing and their empirical application, resulting in richer insights.

Conclusions

This chapter has set out three layers of analysis, the first suggesting a broad, general proposition about the use of the visual, personas and vignettes in legal education. These can bypass the limitations of the mental models that have become 'baked in' to existing frames, offering quick access routes to shared sites of meaning while revealing fresh perspectives. Then, in side-stepping law's mainstream ways of doing, talking and thinking, visual approaches can respond to movements like legal aesthetics and ESL in recognising contingencies central to law's (social) construction. Zooming in to the second layer, the chapter introduced Academic Ann who has been exploring ESL in her research and wants to introduce it to her students. Zooming in further to the third layer, the chapter presented some of Ann's class materials, including a diagram of ESL and the persona and vignette of Policy Polly, showing how these might empirically ground and contextualise conceptual discussions, and enhance accessibility and engagement. In combination with text or as a separate resource then, the visual can simplify complexity, reduce text fatigue and create spaces for knowledge co-production, bringing benefits both for Ann and her students.

Notes

1 ESRC-SeNSS Postdoctoral Research Fellow, Kent Law School, University of Kent. I am grateful to SeNSS for their funding and support, and to the editors of this collection for feedback. Errors are my own.
2 For accessibility I use the anglicised plural of persona.
3 This assumes a constructivist understanding of law, as set out in John Gerard Ruggie, 'International Regimes, Transactions and Change: Embedded Liberalism in the Postwar Economic Order' (1982) 36 International Organization 379.
4 This is an oversimplification, but see Stephanie Lee Mudge, 'What Is Neo-Liberalism?' (2008) 6 Socio-Economic Review 703 for further accounts of neoliberalism.
5 Emilie Cloatre, 'TRIPS and Pharmaceutical Patents in Djibouti: An ANT Analysis of Socio-Legal Objects' (2008) 17 Social and Legal Studies 263.
6 Viviana Zelizer, *Economic Lives: How Culture Shapes the Economy* (Princeton University Press 2010); Viviana Zelizer, *The Social Meaning of Money* (Princeton University Press 1997); Greta Krippner and others, 'Polanyi Symposium: A Conversation on Embeddedness' (2004) 2 Socio-Economic Review 109.
7 Roger Cotterrell, 'A Legal Concept of Community' (1997) 12 Canadian Journal of Law and Society 75; Amanda J Perry-Kessaris, 'Anemos-Ity, Apatheia, Enthousiasmos: An Economic Sociology of Law and Wind Farm Development in Cyprus' (2013) 40 Journal of Law and Society 68; Amanda J Perry-Kessaris, 'What Does It Mean to Take a Socio-Legal Approach to International Economic Law?', *Socio-Legal Approaches to International Economic Law: Text, Context, Subtext* (Routledge 2012), https://papers.ssrn.com/sol3/papers.cfm?abstract_id=2085007, accessed 13 March 2017.
8 This constructivist understanding is differentiated from constructivist approaches taken in an education context. See Karen Barton, Patricia McKellar and Paul Maharg, 'Authentic Fictions: Simulation, Professionalism and Legal Learning' (2007) 14 Clinical Law Review 143. Instead, see Donald MacKenzie and Yuval Millo, 'Constructing a Market, Performing Theory: The Historical Sociology of a Financial Derivatives Exchange' (2003) 109 American Journal of Sociology 107. Ruggie (n 3); Andrew Lang, 'Reconstructing Embedded Liberalism: John Gerard Ruggie and Constructivist Approaches to the Study of the International Trade Regime' (2006) 9 Journal of International Economic Law 81; Anthony Giddens, *The Constitution of Society: Outline of the Theory of Structuration* (Polity 1984).

9 Fred Galves, 'Will Video Kill the Radio Star? Visual Learning and the Use of Display Technology in the Law School Classroom' (2004) 195 University of Illinois Journal of Law, Technology & Policy 219; cited in Brian A Glassman, 'In the Mind's Eye: Visual Lessons for Law Students' (2014) 23 Perspectives: Teaching Legal Research and Writing 25, 27.

10 An Jacobs, Katrien Dreessen, and Jo Pierson, '"Thick" Personas—Using Ethnographic Methods for Persona Development as a Tool for Conveying the Social Science View in Technological Design' (2008) 5 Observatorio (OBS*), IBBT Research Group SMIT – Vrije Universiteit Brussel (VUB), Belgium 79, 081.

11 This constructivist understanding of law references Ruggie (n 3).

12 Rhidian Hughes, 'Considering the Vignette Technique and Its Application to a Study of Drug Injecting and HIV Risk and Safer Behaviour' (1998) 20 Sociology of Health and Illness 381.

13 Gourlay et al., 'Using Vignettes in Qualitative Research to Explore Barriers and Facilitating Factors to the Uptake of Prevention of Mother-to-Child Transmission Services in Rural Tanzania: A Critical Analysis', (2014) BMC Medical Research Methodology 14, (21), https://bmcmedresmethodol.biomedcentral.com/articles/10.1186/1471-2288-14-21. See also Hughes and Huby. 'The Construction and Interpretations of Vignettes in Social Research' (2004) 11(1) Social Work and Social Sciences Review 36–51, https://www.researchgate.net/publication/233596831_The_Construction_and_Interpretation_of_Vignettes_in_Social_Research.

14 Asli Kandemir and Richard Budd, 'Using Vignettes to Explore Reality and Values with Young People' (2018) 19.2 Forum: Qualitative Social Research, http://www.qualitative-research.net/index.php/fqs/article/view/2914/4193.

15 Niklas Luhmann, *Art as a Social System* (Stanford University Press 2000) <https://www.sup.org/books/title/?id=1609> accessed 10 March 2021.

16 Amanda Perry-Kessaris and Joanna Perry, 'Enhancing Participatory Strategies with Designerly Ways for Sociolegal Impact: Lessons from Research Aimed at Making Hate Crime Visible in Europe' (2020) 29.6 *Social and Legal Studies* 835–857.

17 Ruggie (n 3).

18 Roger Cotterrell, 'Why Must Legal Ideas Be Interpreted Sociologically?' (1998) 25 Journal of Law and Society 171.

19 See inter alia Andreas Fischer-Lescano, 'Sociological Aesthetics of Law' (2016) 16 Law, Culture and the Humanities 268; Costas Douzinas, 'The Legality of the Image' (2000) 63 Modern Law Review 813; Thomas Giddens, 'Comics, Law and Aesthetics: Towards the Use of Graphic Fiction in Legal Studies' (2012) 6 Law and Humanities 85; Peter Goodrich, 'Rhetoric, Semiotics, Synaesthetics' in Emilios Christodoulidis, Ruth Dukes and Marco Goldoni (eds), *Research Handbook on Critical Legal Theory* (Elgar 2019), https://www-elgaronline-com.chain.kent.ac.uk/view/edcoll/9781786438881/9781786438881.xml; Paul Maharg, 'Democracy Begins in Conversation: The Phenomenology of Problem-Based Learning and Legal Education' (2015) 24 Nottingham Law Journal 94; Paul Maharg, *Transforming Legal Education: Learning and Teaching the Law in the Early Twenty-First Century* (Routledge 2016), https://www.routledge.com/Transforming-Legal-Education-Learning-and-Teaching-the-Law-in-the-Early/Maharg/p/book/9781138248274; Desmond Manderson, 'Desmond Manderson, Beyond the Provincial: Space, Aesthetics, and Modernist Legal Theory, 20 MELB. U. L. REV. 1048 (1996)' (1996) 20 Melbourne University Law Review 1048; Richard Mohr, 'Desmond Manderson, Songs Without Music: Aesthetic Dimensions of Law and Justice. Berkeley: University of California Press, 2000, 316 Pp., Book Review' (2002) 11 Social and Legal Studies 146.

20 Douzinas (n 19) 813.

21 ibid.

22 Amanda Perry-Kessaris, 'Legal Design for Practice, Activism, Policy and Research' (2019) 46 Journal of Law and Society 185.
23 Luhmann (n 15).
24 RK Sherwin, *When Law Goes Pop: The Vanishing Line between Law and Popular Culture* (University of Chicago Press 2000) 27, quoted in Giddens (n 19) 94.
25 Amanda Perry-Kessaris, *Doing Sociolegal Research in Design Mode* (Routledge 2021).
26 For more detail on this, and the pitfalls to be avoided, see Perry-Kessaris, *Doing Sociolegal Research in Design Mode*, Chapter 2, "Enabling Ecosystems" (Routledge 2021).
27 Perry-Kessaris and Perry (n 16) 16.
28 Margaret Hagan, 'A Visual Approach to Law' (2017) Miscellaneous Law School Publications, http://repository.law.umich.edu/miscellaneous/36, accessed 11 March 2021; Margaret Hagan, 'Law by Design' (*Law by Design*), https://www.lawbydesign.co/, accessed 11 March 2021; Perry-Kessaris and Perry (n 16) 10–11.
29 Francina Cantatore and Ian Stevens, 'Making Connections: Incorporating Visual Learning in Law Subjects through Mind Mapping and Flowcharts' (2016) 22 Canterbury Law Review 153.
30 Glassman (n 9).
31 Included here as a separate ontology of visual representation to 'art', with its own theoretical body of work. See Alan Male, *Illustration: A Theoretical and Contextual Perspective* (Bloomsbury Visual Arts 2017), https://www.bloomsbury.com/uk/illustration-9781474263030/.
32 Linda Mulcahy and Tatiana Flessas, 'Limiting Law: Art in the Street and Street in the Art' (2015) Law, Culture and the Humanities, http://eprints.lse.ac.uk/64564/1/limiting%20law%20art%20%20ini%20the%20street%20street%20in%20the%20art.pdf, accessed 11 March 2021.
33 Rachel Ayrton, 'The Case for Creative, Visual and Multimodal Methods in Operationalising Concepts in Research Design: An Examination of Storyboarding Trust Stories' (2020) The Sociological Review 1.
34 Emily Allbon, Tina McKee and Michael Doherty, 'Connecting Legal Education: The Legal Design Edition' (*Association of Law Teachers*, 8 June 2020), http://lawteacher.ac.uk/connecting-legal-education/connecting-legal-education-the-legal-design-edition/, accessed 11 March 2021. Allbon uses 'design sprints' to creatively engage students with the application of legal principles, using visual methods to ensure quick yet accurate communication.
35 Open source (and therefore free yet powerful) software like Blender has democratised 3D modelling and animation.
36 For short animations illustrating socio-legal ethnography, see inter alia Lydia Hayes, *Stories of Care: A Labour of Law* (Palgrave Macmillan UK 2017), https://sites.cardiff.ac.uk/law-lab/people/director-profiles/stories-of-care-a-labour-of-law-gender-and-class-at-work-by-lydia-hayes/; Lydia Hayes, 'Stories of Care', https://sites.cardiff.ac.uk/law-lab/people/director-profiles/stories-of-care-a-labour-of-law-gender-and-class-at-work-by-lydia-hayes/, accessed 14 January 2021.
37 Stephanie Broadribb and others, 'Second Life in the Open University: How the Virtual World Can Facilitate Learning for Staff and Students' in Charles Wankel and Jan Kingsley (eds), *Higher Education: Teaching and Learning in Virtual Worlds* (Emerald Group Publishing 2009), http://oro.open.ac.uk/43632/, accessed 8 January 2021.
38 Gregory Silverman, 'Law Games: The Importance of Virtual Worlds and Serious Video Games for the Future of Legal Education' (2012) Part II—Teaching with Digital Course Materials Legal Education in the Digital Age 130; Paul Maharg, 'Legal Sims: From Everquest to Ardcalloch (and Back Again)' (2004), https://strathprints.strath.ac.uk/708/, accessed 12 March 2020; Maharg, *Transforming Legal*

Education: Learning and Teaching the Law in the Early Twenty-First Century (n 19); Daniela Ahrens, 'Serious Games—A New Perspective on Workbased Learning' (2015) 204 Procedia—Social and Behavioral Sciences 277; Jane Reeves, *Training Child Protection Professionals through Gaming and Simulation* (2016), https://www.youtube.com/watch?v=KE5jtt2f10Y, accessed 5 February 2020.

39 Maharg, *Transforming Legal Education: Learning and Teaching the Law in the Early Twenty-First Century* (n 19).

40 Amanda Perry-Kessaris, 'The Pop-Up Museum of Legal Objects Project: An Experiment in "Socio-Legal" Design' (2017) 68 Northern Ireland Legal Quarterly 225; Perry-Kessaris and Perry (n 16).

41 Ellen Lupton and Jennifer Cole Phillips, *Graphic Design: The New Basics: Second Edition, Revised and Expanded* (Princeton Architectural Press 2015), Kindle Edition, Loc.1092.

42 Fleming, cited in Glassman (n 9) 25.

43 Michael Race, 'Decision over Future of Oxford's Cecil Rhodes Statue Delayed' (5 January 2021), https://www.bbc.co.uk/news/uk-england-oxfordshire-55549876, accessed 5 April 2021.

44 Goodrich (2014) Legal Emblems and the Art of Law, in Piyel Haldar, 'Review Essay: A Gesture: A Review of Peter Goodrich, Legal Emblems and the Art of Law: Obiter Depicta as the Vision of Governance' (2014) 8 Law and Humanities 304; See also Glassman (n 9).

45 This mirrors the call for a language of design patterns for contracts. See Helena Haapio and Margaret Hagan, 'Design Patterns for Contracts', https://papers.ssrn.com/sol3/papers.cfm?abstract_id=2747280, accessed 5 January 2021.

4 Objects and visual devices in teaching for peace in Colombia

Narrowing the gaps between social sciences and law

Ximena Sierra-Camargo[1]

Introduction

This chapter explores how objects and visual devices can be used as part of formal assessment, especially in courses that are interdisciplinary in approach and that address sensitive or contested topics. It draws on my own practice teaching a course in 2019 and 2020 that critically explores the policies implemented within the framework of the peacebuilding process in Colombia as part of the MA in Peacebuilding programme at Los Andes University in Bogotá, Colombia.

The course is especially meaningful because the peace agreement signed between the Fuerzas Armadas Revolucionarias de Colombia (FARC) and the Colombian government has entailed multiple challenges, many of which academics have contributed to overcoming. For example, they assisted with the interpretation of the agreement; proposed how it ought to be implemented in practice; anticipated how it will impact local communities and territories, both positively and negatively; and facilitated reconciliation between all the parties involved and affected by the armed conflict. The course is also especially challenging to teach due to the diversity of the students, and the sensitivity of the subject matter.

The students came from different parts of the country and the world, and had very different political positions from each other; and some had themselves played various roles in the peace-building process in Colombia. This led to very enriching discussions on the different topics discussed in the course. However, opportunities for discussion were constrained by the diversity of political positions and of the knowledge fields in which each student was embedded. Some held very firm positions on certain issues, and more generally found it difficult to be open to other perspectives and views on the peace process, especially where such openness might force them to question ideas that they had developed through experience. Following the classification suggested by Florian Hoffmann, it seemed that their perception about the peacebuilding process was more defined by their 'conscience' on human rights than by an official or 'neutral' human rights discourse,[2] because their perception was subjective and apparently unmodifiable. This meant that each

DOI: 10.4324/9780429021411-5

student gave his or her own interpretation on the peacebuilding process—interpretations which were sometimes opposed to each other, sometimes apparently irreconcilably so. In this sense, one of the questions that arose in the course was whether using creative tools and languages, more closely aligned with the fields of Art and Design than of Law and of Social Sciences, could close the gap between the different students' positions or even generate empathy—to put ourselves in the place of the others, perceive what others may be feeling and to connect us with the pain of the others—towards diametrically opposite understandings of the peacebuilding process.[3]

Furthermore, the students came from a wide range of disciplines—not only lawyers, but also social scientists such as sociologists, anthropologists, political scientists, social workers and educators. Likewise, the course was attended by diplomats, public officials, judges, members of the military forces, activists, militants from different political parties, ex-combatants, members of NGOs, etc. This diversity made the debates very interesting, but in some cases, it was also difficult to create a bridge that would allow the different positions expressed in class to be brought closer together, which in turn were supported by the very specific language of the scientific or social field in which each one was embedded.

I decided to tackle these challenges through visual and material methods.

As part of the course assessment, the students were required, firstly, to submit a final essay focusing on a case study framed in the peacebuilding process in Colombia; and, secondly, to represent it in the form of an object or a visual device. Specifically, they were asked to select an existing object, or to make an object, to represent the case study which they had analysed in the essay.[4] The selected object was to be accompanied by a short text explaining the relationship of the chosen object or artefact with the case analysed.

In devising this method of assessment I was influenced by the pop-up collection methodology developed by Amanda Perry-Kessaris through the Pop-Up Museum of Legal Objects—a 'crowd-sourced accessible, legally curated, infinitely expandable collection of legal objects from museums all over the world'.[5] It developed out of a series of events in which participants were invited to select an item from a public curated collection which seemed relevant to their legal research and to prepare a commentary about that object as well as a model of it; and Perry-Kessaris has gone on to use the same methodology with postgraduate research students studying research at Kent Law School. I encountered this methodology during the IEL Collective inaugural conference at Warwick Law School in 2019. The IEL Collective is a collaboration of academics and practitioners from across the world who aim to work inclusively to "stimulate conversations about plurality, representation and criticality" in the field of International Economic Law.[6] As Perry-Kessaris explains:

> It is only by bringing diverse conceptual frames, empirical examples, and normative agendas into the same space that we can really respect, understand,

> and use them in practical, critical, and imaginative ways. Collaborative mindsets, tools, and processes are not part of traditional legal scholarship and practice. Might they be introduced though model-making? This was the question that motivated me to propose the co-production of an IEL Pop-Up Collection.[7]

The IEL Collective conference delegates, who came from all over the world, were invited to bring with them an object or image that they felt was in some way relevant to how they approach or understand International Economic Law, and to exhibit it as part of an IEL Pop-Up Collection during the conference.

I realised that this methodology was could help me to address some of the above-mentioned challenges associated with teaching my course on peacebuilding in Colombia. Firstly, by requiring students to make a visual representation I could encourage them to socialise their case studies—to create a bridge for more direct communication of ideas between students, across divides of discipline and of lived experience. Secondly, I could encourage the dissemination, in an accessible form, of the case studies to people within academia and beyond who might be interested in knowing different peacebuilding experiences in Colombia and challenging the semantic codes used by each of them in the different argumentative exercises. An important result was that students reported that the visual devices allowed them to better communicate their own ideas, and to better understand the various perspectives from which other students had analysed the selected cases.

According to Nohora Blanco and Zulma González, students of the MA in Peacebuilding programme, watching the visual representations made by their classmates allowed to them to identify and to understand various interpretations explained in the course regarding some peacebuilding policies in Colombia. They explain that the exercise based on the pop-up collection methodology was 'an incentive to analyse and to propose other ways of understanding the selected case studies from originality and creativity lens'. They also argue that it was challenging because it led them 'to rethink worldviews in contexts far from their daily lives' and 'to open key spaces for discussion and dialogue on the topics and theories addressed in class, contrasting them with real situations'.

In this regard, student Juan Roberto Rengifo states that the visual representations were able to sensitise and to attract the open public to the implications and challenges of the peacebuilding process in Colombia. Rengifo argues that the space created to make and to spread the visual representation is 'an emancipatory space, not only because of its symbolic content, but because it manages to tell other unofficial and often silenced stories of those who have suffered the war in Colombia'. Moreoever, he remarks that those representations are adjusted to the way of producing new digital content in this era.

Finally, Mariana Valderrama, Meyda Tafur and Natalia Ruiz state that the exercise on visual representations meant 'an opportunity to translate a successful story on peacebuilding in Colombia to a visual, creative and alternative level'. They argue that this type of exercise allows them 'to understand better the views of other classmates on the peacebuilding process' and 'to reach a broader audience, since the methodology used for the creation of visual representation invites and draws attention much more than a descriptive text, especially for a public that is not necessarily close to the peacebuilding field from a theoretical approach'. The students also mentioned that 'It was an enriching experience but at the same time challenging, since it was necessary to imagine a representation easy to understand but that at the same time has a meaningful content and honours the magnitude and depth of the represented case'.

The following sections highlight three of the most outstanding representations, each of which were published via Twitter @peacebuilding4. In each visual representation we can see three elements alluded to by Perry-Kessaris: the practical, the critical and the imaginative.[8] The objects and visual devices used in each of the representations allow anyone, both within the academia and outside it, a practical, accessible, entry point to understanding peacebuilding experiences, in particular by exposing their main features, and by highlighting those aspects that are especially problematic. Furthermore, in the elaboration of each of the 'visible' and 'tangible',[9] the authors also revealed their critical approach to peacebuilding. Finally, they deployed their imagination through the particular materials, objects and visual devices used, and in so doing allowed external observers in turn to deploy their own imagination, as well as to understand the complexity and importance of the cases represented, including their limitations, scope and challenges.

Visual representations of the challenges of peacebuilding in Colombia

'The marginal road in the jungle': the tensions between development and environment in the peacebuilding process.

In the representation entitled 'The marginal road of the jungle' ('La carretera marginal de la selva'), Zulma González and Nohora Blanco[10] showed the importance of incorporating an "integral" approach in the peace-building processes and taking seriously the dynamics of the local communities and their territories, their cosmogonies and needs vis-à-vis the interests of other actors who, like the State, participate in this type of process. González and Blanco explain that the objective of their representation is to show the phases through which a territory could transit in the framework of a peacebuilding process in cases where the specificities of the dynamics of the territory and the local communities are not taken into account.

Specifically, the authors analysed a case in the Department of Guaviare where some actors aimed to build a 381-kilometer highway in the middle of the jungle that connects the Amazon area with the Colombian 'Orinoquía'.[11] Thus, through their representation, González and Blanco aimed to show what

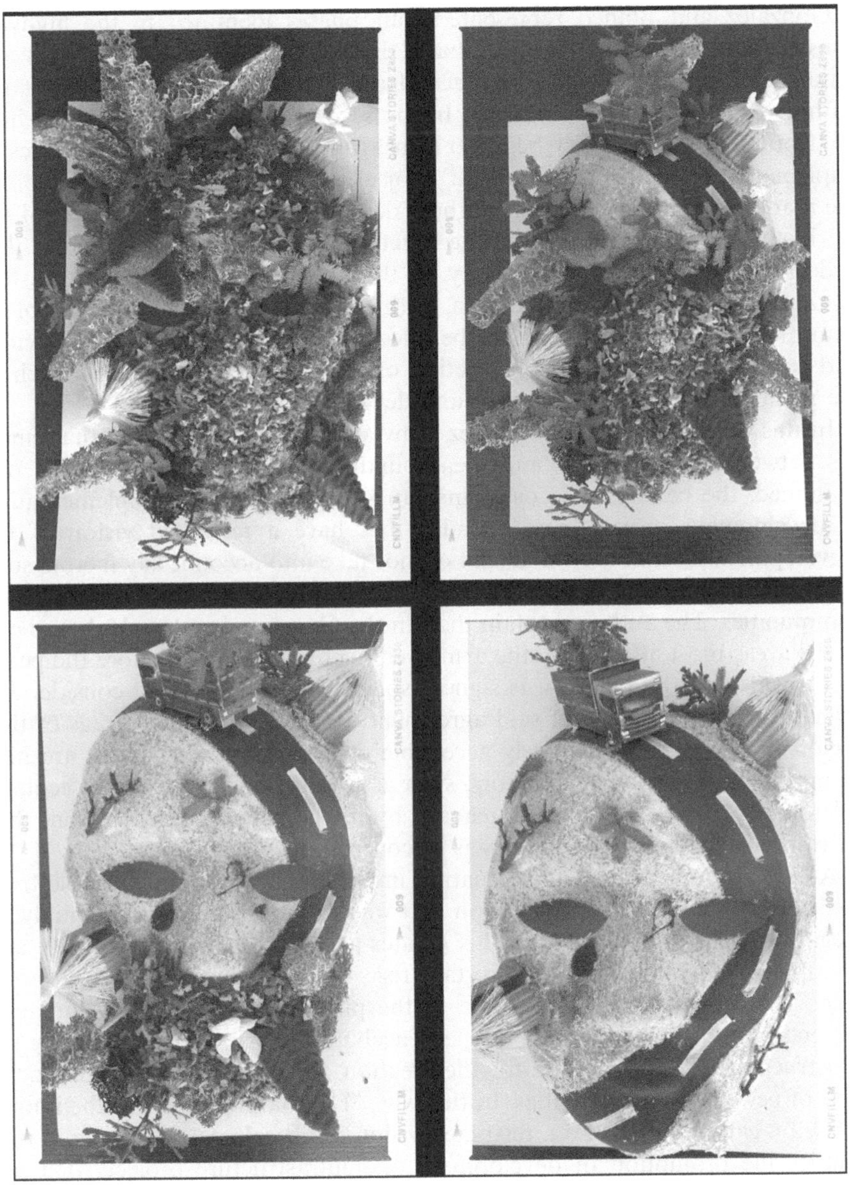

Figure 4.1 Visualisation of 'The marginal road in the jungle' by Zulma González and Nohora Blanco. Image by creators 2020. Reproduced with permission.

could happen if a dialogue between the different actors involved was not implemented before the construction of the said project was carried out, which, in turn, is framed in a development project as part of the peacebuilding process in the region.

González and Blanco represented four phases identified in the highway construction project. In the first phase, they showed a territory full of vegetation, still unexplored, and with social and natural characteristics that the authors call 'the other Colombia'. In the second phase, they illustrated how the features of the territory begin to transform from the preliminary stages of implementation of the 'development' project whose axis is the construction of the road. In the third phase, the authors demonstrated that the progress of the work causes a greater impact on the vegetation of Guaviare, to the point that it decreases by 30 per cent. Finally, in the fourth phase, a radical transformation of the territory can be seen, with the alteration of its use and of its natural cycles. This in turn could be affected by the new economic activities and consequences that the construction of the highway would bring, such as the planting of monoculture crops and deforestation.

In this way, Blanco and González draw attention to the tension that emerges between 'environment' and 'peacebuilding' when, in cases like the one examined, the balance of ecosystems can be affected by the implementation of development projects and agendas that have a restricted vision of the 'development' notion itself and that do not take into account key factors such as the interdependence between ecosystems and the cosmogony of local communities. The authors explain that, in the Guaviare jungle, which was one of the areas most affected by the armed conflict in Colombia before the peace agreement with the FARC was signed, some dynamics changed considerably after the implementation of said agreement. For example, some areas of that region that were not previously accessible due to the conflict itself, are now being known by non-armed actors, such as tourists who want to do 'ecological tourism', biologists, and in general, by researchers. For this reason, they affirm that until now 'the country is discovering the Guaviare'.

As the authors explain, this situation implies a paradox, since people from civil society can now access a region that was previously controlled mainly by illegal armed groups. However, this greater access to the region for new and multiple actors may also imply certain risks for the same biodiversity in the area. These risks also increase due to the promotion of new 'development' projects within the framework of the peacebuilding process, which imply the construction of infrastructure for the creation of new jobs and for the inclusion of new economic activities. In this way, 'The marginal road in the jungle' is itself a call to go beyond a restricted vision of liberal peace,[12] which in turn implies the promotion of development and infrastructure projects that can lead to environmental degradation and change in land use and the dynamics of the territory and local communities.

'Embroidering a future of peace, from coca to banana': creating new legal and sustainable means of livelihood from a bottom-up approach.

In the visual representation entitled 'Embroidering a future of peace, from coca to banana' ('Bordando un futuro en paz, de la coca al plátano') Natalia

Ruiz, Meyda Tafur and Mariana Valderrama,[13] used embroidery to illustrate an example of the policy of substitution of crops considered of 'illicit use' in Colombia. Specifically, they analysed the policy implemented in the area of the municipality of Tame (Arauca) on the substitution of coca crops for banana crops, taking into consideration that coca is considered one of the key factors that has caused the intensification of the armed conflict in Colombia.[14] In this sense, the authors made an analogy between embroidery and the policy of substitution of crops for illicit use in the framework of the peace-building process.

In this regard, they explain that like the embroidery technique, which requires 'patience, dedication and the adaptation of the type of stitch', depending on the objective to be achieved, the substitution of the so-called illicit crops policy in Tame (Arauca) was an arduous process that required the stitches of the different actors involved, to ensure that the substitution was gradually adapted to the territory in which said policy was implemented.

The region has been one of the areas most affected by the armed conflict in Colombia, in part due to the large areas of coca crops there. In this regard, Ruiz, Tafur and Valderrama explained that coca was one of the main means of subsistence for local communities, so the government authorities implemented different measures to eradicate this sort of crop by such means as fumigation and aerial spraying with glyphosate. However, these types of measures ended up affecting other agricultural crops, causing serious social

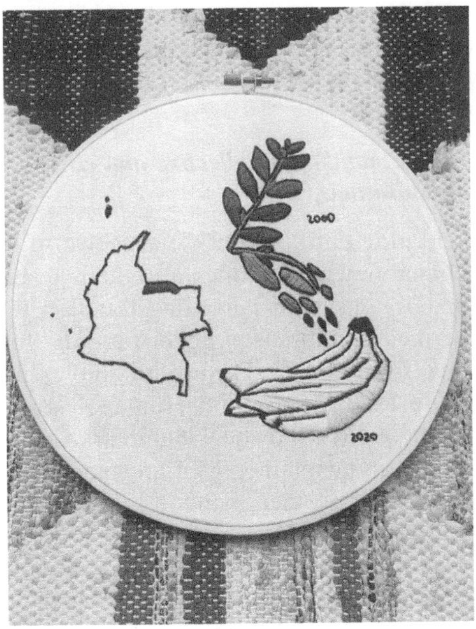

Figure 4.2 Visual representation of 'Embroidering a future of peace, from coca to banana'. Image by creators 2020. Reproduced with permission.

and economic impacts, and generating a relationship of mistrust between local communities and state authorities that promoted those crop eradication policies.

The authors explained that this situation led local communities to rethink new ways of carrying out the substitution of coca crops, with fewer adverse effects on the land and on the population itself. New measures were promoted to eradicate illicit crops 'by hand', to preserve the fertility of the land and to plant other products than coca. Although new illegal armed groups entered the territory after the signing of the peace agreement, Ruiz, Tafur and Valderrama still perceived the peacebuilding project to have been as success because significant advances in the reduction of illicit crops had already been made. This in turn allowed the inhabitants of that area to begin to export the new agricultural crops and to participate in other market chains. In addition, it is also important to mention that it was not only national and international actors that participated in said policy, but that the participation of local actors was also meaningful.

Finally, the authors explained what they had represented in the embroidery: firstly, the map of the territory in which the policy of substitution of coca crops was implemented, and, secondly, the transition from coca towards banana crops. To do this, they used a colour palette that ranged from duller shades such as coffee to more vivid colours such as yellow and green. Likewise, when illustrating this transition in embroidery with the selected colour palette, the authors explained that they also wanted to show the alternatives of socio-economic development for coca producers in a post-conflict context, and the importance of articulating local initiatives with the national policies within the framework of the peace-building process.

'Let's make love to fear': building a collective and critical memory from grassroots women organisations.

In the visual representation entitled 'Let's make love to fear' ('Hagámosle el amor al miedo'), Diana Jimena Ordóñez and Juan Roberto Rengifo[15] analysed the case of the 'Organización Femenina Popular' (OFP) in the municipality of Barrancabermeja (Santander), understanding this as an outstanding case of peace-building 'from below'. The authors represented the construction of the 'Museum-House for Memory and Human Rights of Women' ('Casa Mueso de la Memoria y los Derechos Humanos de las Mujeres'), better known as 'Casa Museo', and explained its importance in the conflicts that the population, and in particular, women living in that region, had faced since the second half of the twentieth century.

Ordóñez and Rengifo highlight some of the overlapping elements in their representation, such as the 'black suits', the 'community pots' and the 'keys' and explain that these elements are symbols of the local communities' polyphonic voices that have promoted peace-building projects with a bottom-up approach. This is the case of the Museum-House, whose main objective was

Figure 4.3 Visualisation of 'Let's make love to fear' by Diana Jimena Ordóñez and Juan Roberto Rengifo. Image by creators 2020. Reproduced with permission.

the construction of a collective and critical memory, mainly aimed at exalting the stories of the present and the future of women, to transcend the violent past they lived, and recognising the central role that women have as key actors in the construction of this type of memory.

The authors explained that the Museum-House, and the actions promoted by the OFP through that space since it opened in 2019, is a symbol of resistance against past violence faced by the local population as a consequence of a development model based on hydrocarbon extraction. Moreover, Ordóñez and Rengifo pointed out that the Museum-House offers the possibility of the symbolic reconstruction of the social fabric at the national and local levels, insofar as it ensures that the people who have been victims of the armed conflict in the oil port of Barrancabermeja are not condemned to oblivion.

The representation 'Let's make love to fear' also emphasises the historical importance of the Museum-House in the peace-building process in Colombia. In this regard, Ordóñez and Rengifo explained that the OFP originated in the second half of the twentieth century as an initiative of a group of priests who were part of the well-known 'Theology of liberation'. Thus, the OFP initially emerged as part of a series of 'clubs' attended by housewives to train them in sewing and dressmaking activities and to empower them financially.[16] However, a few decades later, the OFP became an autonomous and independent entity, and joined other social movements whose work has been essential in Colombia to make visible the differentiated effects of the armed conflict on women.

In this regard, Ordóñez and Rengifo stated that the OFP, which was originally conceived as a house in which a group of women met to sew, today is perceived by local communities as a museum. However, the new institutional identity of that space also implies certain challenges, which could also 'blur' the essence of the Museum-House as a local space of collective and heterogeneous resistance. Finally, the authors pointed out that the OFP, with other women's organisations, has resisted pressure from different illegal armed groups in Colombia, and has insisted on the importance of a 'negotiated' and non-violent solution to the armed conflict and on the guarantee of rights to the truth, to justice and to reparation of the victims, and especially of the women who have suffered the effects of the conflict.

Building a bridge between social sciences and law for peace.

In the representations described above, the students used different objects and visual devices to illustrate the selected peace-building cases. In the first case, in the work entitled 'The marginal road in the jungle', Zulma González and Nohora Blanco used a mask as a symbol of the 'face' of the Guaviare jungle, which in turn was altered with different materials to show the transformation that the region could undergo if the construction of the road was carried out as part of the development project that was being promoted within the framework of the peace-building process. The mask was modified on four occasions to represent each of the phases identified on the project. Likewise, each of the modifications was photographed to show the metamorphosis of the face of Guaviare.

In the first photograph, that represents the first phase of the project, it can be seen that the mask, or the 'face' of the Guaviare, is completely covered with a green material that simulates the typical vegetation in that region. In the second photograph, the mask is still covered with the green material that represents the jungle vegetation, but another less vivid colour is already glimpsed; an opaque colour that is beginning to gain ground and that represents the aridity and deforestation of the territory. Likewise, it is possible to observe an initial path of the road. In the third photograph, the percentage of vegetation is further reduced and most of the mask or 'face' of the Guaviare can be seen uncovered, painted in a sandy colour and crossed by the road. Finally, in the fourth photograph, vegetation is no longer visible and the mask is completely uncovered. In this fourth phase, the sand colour can be observed over the entire mask, which, in turn, is crossed from top to bottom by the road and on which a truck can be observed circulating.

In the second representation entitled 'Embroidering a future of peace, from coca to banana', Natalia Ruiz, Meyda Tafur and Mariana Valderrama used the embroidery technique to represent the transition in the municipality of Tame (Arauca) that occurred between coca crops and banana crops within the framework of the peacebuilding policy. To do this, they wove three figures on the white background of the canvas that is stretched on the fabric frame. On the left side of the frame, a map of Colombia was woven with black thread, with violet thread highlighting the location of the region where this policy was carried out. In the upper right part of the frame, they wove green leaves and brown seeds to represent the crops that are part of the transition policy. Finally, in the lower right part of the frame, they wove the bananas with black and yellow threads, which were the fruits that produced the new crops in the region as a result of the implemented policy.

Finally, in the representation entitled 'Let's make love to fear' the authors made a mock-up of the OFP Museum-House, which in turn was recorded. In the video, can be seen some elements that symbolise the collective resistance that local communities, and in particular women, have exercised from that space for the construction of memory. Some of the outstanding items are: a key, a black suit and a community pot. In this last object, around which women usually congregate to share food, the words 'resistance' and 'autonomy' can be read.

Other objects also can be observed in the model, such as a machine that extracts oil from a well, better known as a 'rod pump'. This element symbolises the extraction of hydrocarbon, which is in turn an activity that has been at the centre of the armed conflict that the population, and in particular, the women of the region have had to resist. These elements, some illustrated in black, others in purple and gray tones, are located in front of the house that has a sign that says 'Popular Women's Organization'. At the entrance of the purple house, can be observed open doors, and inside you can see two chairs. The house itself, which due to its architecture reveals the high temperatures of the region, is perceived as a welcoming place to which people are invited to enter.

In the front yard, next to the community pot, an elderly black woman is also seen standing, representing the women who participate in that space. Moreover it is striking that the objects that stand in the front garden vastly exceed the scale of the house and the woman. These objects, which stand out for their scale, give us some clues, on the one hand, about the dimension of the conflict that the women of the OFP have had to face, and, on the other hand, about the greatness of their resistance actions in a place that has been historically affected by the different armed groups involved in the armed conflict.

The three regions in which the peacebuilding projects have been carried out differ in terms of their geographical, natural, economic, social and cultural features. Not only have the three regions been seriously affected by the armed conflict in Colombia, but the different development projects that have been promoted in each of them have mainly impacted local communities. In this sense, the three representations show the importance of taking seriously the voices of local communities,[17] particularly in the design, formulation and implementation of development projects within the framework of the peacebuilding process.

For example, the case of the road building in the department of Guaviare shows how an infrastructure project associated with an economic development model in a peacebuilding scenario could cause serious impacts, especially due to the jungle nature of the area and its biodiversity. This representation draws attention to the possible transformations of the territory with the arrival of 'peace' and the economic activities and visions of development[18] that the peacebuilding policies imply. The transformation of this territory is represented using a mask that undergoes a metamorphosis, as the implementation of 'peacebuilding' and 'development' projects progresses. It shows the contradictions and challenges of the peacebuilding process in Colombia, as well as the various visions of development, which are articulated in turn with different notions of peace that range from a liberal peace to a hybrid or local peace.[19] In this sense, the representation by Zulma González and Nohora Blanco, demonstrates the importance of building peace from a bottom-up approach,[20] taking into account the particularities of each territory, and its economic, social, cultural and environmental dimensions.

For a second example of what these representations can tell us about development planning we can look to the representation entitled 'Embroidering a future of peace, from coca to banana', by Natalia Ruiz, Meyda Tafur and Mariana Valderrama, which shows the importance of including the voices of local communities in the projects of economic development promoted within the framework of the peacebuilding process, and of designing and implementing such projects from a local view. The authors explained that the success of the peacebuilding policy they analysed relies on the fact that the concerns of the communities were taken seriously, learning from past experiences and previous policies to eradicate illicit crops.

In this sense, the new policy of substitution of crops 'by hand' was supported by the communities themselves, who argued that it was less detrimental for the territory and for the population. Moreover, this policy also resulted in new forms of economic sustainability, not associated with the illicit crops that exacerbated the armed conflict.

Finally, in the representation entitled 'Let's make love to fear', Diana Jimena Ordóñez and Juan Roberto Rengifo, highlighted the importance of a genuine participation of social movements in peacebuilding policies[21] and, in particular, of grassroots women organisations. The authors showed how local communities have resisted the threats and attacks from different armed groups and have consolidated a space of resistance to build a memory from a bottom-up approach and to redefine the past. In this sense, the Museum-House is understood as a space of resistance 'from below', in which women are the main architects of memory. For this reason, it is an outstanding sample of peacebuilding, that challenges the hegemonic policies that tend to establish 'official truths' that do not take seriously the stories and experiences of local communities, to resist oblivion and to resignify through memory the violations suffered by the victims and their families in the context of the armed conflict.

Final remarks

The visual representations made by the students of the MA in Peacebuilding demonstrate, on the one hand, the importance of creating spaces in education and socio-legal research in which lawyers are able to be practical, critical and imaginative,[22] and, on the other hand, the importance of building communication bridges to interact with scholars and professionals from other fields like social sciences, who are immersed in other scientific languages.

They draw on different theoretical and methodological influences, mainly from the social sciences, to explore how the peace agreement legal framework in Colombia has been implemented on the ground, and how such norms impact on the lives of local communities as well as on the natural and social cycles of the territories. Through visual representation they socialise the case study and their approach to it—making them more accessible and understandable to others within academia and beyond. In these ways they begin to combine socio-legal research with activism: exposing problems associated with peacebuilding policies and drawing attention to the limits and scope implied by the policies.

In response to the question posed by Amanda Perry-Kessaris: 'What can design do for the law?',[23] we can say that visual objects and devices can generate more accessible and direct forms of communication about controversial norms and policies especially where they are complex, and/or are the subject of intense debates, challenges and tensions. In this way they can contribute to better understanding, more consistent thinking, more persuasive arguments, more imaginative and critical thinking both among those who participate in the design and implementation of such norms and policies, and among those who suffer their effects.[24]

However, it is important to mention a common challenge present in the representations explained in this chapter: The importance of carrying out peacebuilding policies 'from below'; of taking seriously the voices of local communities. Indeed, the visualisations produced by the students directly highlighted the fact that there are multiple visions of development[25] as notions of peace,[26] and that each actor and population, according to individual context and the particularities of each territory, can provide a different meaning to a peacebuilding policy and to the development projects that derive from it. Furthermore, each visual representation could also communicate different meanings to different people, depending on their own perspectives and experiences. The fact that spectators also end up participating in some way in the visual representations by interpreting the artefacts shows how important, and yet how difficult, it is to build bridges between actors who are embedded in different epistemological fields, and who interpret the world from different points of view and semantic codes. In this sense, visual representations can work as a communication channel between actors from different fields such as law, peace studies and social sciences. In this way, design would be both the objective of communicating more directly and the method itself to achieve this.

To sum up, the visual representations examined in this chapter illustrate the importance of strengthening the law–design relationship through experimentation and the use of visual objects and devices to create tangible artifacts that allow not only lawyers but also interdisciplinary actors to communicate their ideas more easily and directly, mainly through visual language, and to synthesise ideas that may involve a certain level of complexity. In this sense, the cases explained above represent in themselves a form of activism, insofar as they constitute an effort by key actors in the peacebuilding context in Colombia to create a consciousness on the implementation of the norms and policies framed in the peacebuilding process, highlighting, in turn, its challenges and difficulties, and the situations of inequality that may result, if the limitations evidenced by the authors are not taken seriously.

Notes

1 Catalyst Fellow, Osgoode Hall Law School, York University.
2 Florian Hoffmann, 'Human Rights, the Self and the Other: Reflections on a Pragmatic Theory of Human Rights' in Anne Orford (ed), *International Law and its Others* (Cambridge University Press 2006) 221–242.
3 Jimena Sierra-Camargo, '¿Qué son las estéticas legales? Una aproximación a la noción de arte y derecho' (2014) Revista Derecho del Estado 32, 57–76.
4 Peace Agreement between the guerrilla group Fuerzas Armadas Revolucionarias de Colombia—FARC and the Colombian Government, 2016: 'Acuerdo final para la terminación del onflict y la construcción de una paz estable y duradera', 24 November, 2016, https://www.jep.gov.co/Normativa/Paginas/Acuerdo-Final.aspx.
5 The Pop-Up Museum of Legal Objects can be viewed at https://amandaperrykessaris.org/collections/pop-up-museum-of-legal-objects-2017/. See further: Amanda Perry-Kessaris, 'The Pop-up Museum of Legal Objects Project: An Experiment in "Sociolegal Design"' (2017) 68.2 *Northern Ireland Legal Quarterly* 225–44; and https://warwick.ac.uk/fac/soc/law/research/centres/globe/ielcollective/newsevents/conference2019.
6 IEL Collective, 'Disrupting Narratives and Pluralising Engagement in International Economic Law Scholarship, Teaching and Practice', https://warwick.ac.uk/fac/soc/law/research/centres/globe/ielcollective/about/.
7 Amanda Perry-Kessaris, 'Making Sociolegal Research More Social by Design: Anglo-German Roots, Rewards and Risks' (2020) 21.6 *German Law Journal* 1427–1445, 1442.
8 Amanda Perry-Kessaris, 'Legal Design for Practice, Activism, Policy and Research' (2019) 46.2 Journal of Law and Society 185–210.
9 ibid.
10 Nohora Blanco and Zulma González, 'La carretera marginal de la Selva', https://twitter.com/peacebuilding4/status/1341916473095282688.
11 Andrés Liévano Bermúdez, 'La carretera amazónica que tiene aterrorizados a los científicos colombianos' Revista Semana (Bogotá, 2 January 2018), https://sostenibilidad.semana.com/medio-ambiente/articulo/carretera-marginal-de-la-selva-amenaza-la-biodiversidad-amazonica/39199.
12 Roger Mac Ginty, 'The Liberal Peace' in *International Peacebuilding and Local Resistance. Hybrid Forms of Peace* (Palgrave Macmillan 2011) 19–46.
13 Natalia Ruiz, Meyda Tafur and Natalia Valderrama, 'Bordando un futuro de paz, de la coca al plátano', https://twitter.com/peacebuilding4/status/1341921313821249536.
14 María Alejandra Medina, 'Arauca: la estrella en la producción de plátano' *Diario El Espectador* (Bogotá, 27 August 2020), https://www.elespectador.com/noticias/economia/arauca-la-estrella-en-la-produccion-de-platano/.

15 Diana Jimena Ordóñez and Juan Roberto Rengifo, 'Bordando un futuro de paz, de la coca al plátano', https://twitter.com/peacebuilding4/status/1341926480570441729.

16 Wilson Lozano, 'La historia tras la ONG de mujeres más antigua en Colombia' *Diario El Tiempo* (Bogotá, 1 June 2017), https://www.eltiempo.com/politica/proceso-de-paz/historia-de-la-organizacion-femenina-popular-en-barrancabermeja-92106.

17 Gustav Rudd and Hanna Leonardsson, 'The Local Turn in Peace Building: A Literature Review of Effective and Emancipatory Local Building' (2015) 36.5 Third World Quarterly Journal 825–839.

18 Arturo Escobar, *La invención del Tercer Mundo. Construcción y deconstrucción del desarrollo* (Grupo Editorial Norma 1996) 33–42; 52–100.

19 Roger Mac Ginty, 'Hybridity' in *International Peacebuilding and Local Resistance* (Palgrave Macmillan 2011) 68–90.

20 Gustav Rudd and Hanna Leonardsson, 'The Local Turn in Peace Building: A Literature Review of Effective and Emancipatory Local Building' (2015) 36.5 Third World Quarterly Journal 825–839.

21 Sona Dilanyan, Aia Beraia and Hilal Yavuz, 'Beyond NGOs: Decolonizing Peacebuilding and Human Rights' (2017) Local Transformation 158–173, https://caucasusedition.net/beyond-ngos-decolonizing-peacebuilding-and-human-rights/.

22 Amanda Perry-Kessaris, 'Legal Design for Practice, Activism, Policy and Research' (2019) 46.2 Journal of Law and Society 185–210.

23 ibid.

24 ibid.

25 Arturo Escobar, *La invención del Tercer Mundo. Construcción y deconstrucción del desarrollo* (Grupo Editorial Norma 1996) 33–42; 52–100.

26 Oliver Richmond, 'A Genealogy of Peace and Conflict Theory' in Oliver Richmond (ed), *Peacebuilding. Critical Developments and Approaches* (Palgrave Macmillan 2010) 14–38.

5 Psychologically-Informed Design in Legal Education

Sarah Stein Lubrano[1]

Introduction

I am not a lawyer, nor even a student of law. But I was, once, a 19-year-old college student tutoring inmates in a correctional facility. Past the metal detectors, I learned three things in fairly rapid succession. Firstly, the women for whom I served as a tutor were perfectly capable of learning mathematics, especially with the right visuals and metaphors. Secondly, despite this, many of the women did not *believe* they could learn fractions and were not sure why they would need to. They struggled not due to issues of ability but because what I was teaching seemed irrelevant. And third, many incarcerated people are functionally illiterate. These three realisations are excellent examples of the subject of this chapter: the role of pedagogy and learning psychology in making legal systems accessible—that is, comprehensible—to expert lawyers and other non-expert users.

Legal education, like most academic education, reflects its origins in a time when printed information was expensive, and the formal study of the psychology of learning had yet to begin. So, lecturers might simply stand at the front of a classroom and read directly from a book, and a high premium was placed on memorisation. Paolo Friere refers to this traditional style of education as the 'banking' model in which the teacher 'issues communiqués and makes deposits' which students are obliged to simply 'patiently receive, memorize', file, store, retrieve 'and repeat'.[2] There is no two-way process of communication. This model is psychologically inaccurate and promotes poor pedagogy—for example, it assumes one central source of knowledge and expertise, and it instils inflexible and often unhelpful power dynamics in the classroom. And yet, although we can now access seemingly infinite quantities of information from a phone, education still too often relies on such traditional practices. Some law teachers and professors will object at this point, arguing that they are not relying on the banking model, but instead are teaching students legal analytical skills, the art of 'finding' the law in a text or, as the character Charles W. Kingsfield Jr. puts it in the film *The Paperchase*, 'how to think like a lawyer'. This includes acquiring the ability to apply 'the law' to 'the facts'; and also a deeper, more complex and perhaps intuitive

DOI: 10.4324/9780429021411-6

ability to recognise ambiguities in the law and how it can be changed—an ability that must be constantly honed over the course of a lifetime.[3] And certainly, to the extent that they focus on this kind of more dynamic and evolutionary learning, law schools are ahead of the pedagogical curve. However, legal educators face a number of obstacles that are the legacy of the 'banking' system, including students' assumptions about how to read legal texts, and the emphasis placed by the professional bodies on exams that privilege information retention.

The remainder of this chapter explores insights from psychology that might be used to improve legal communication within the education system, legal practice and the wider world public, in particular by activating emotions and visual cognition to improve the communication, comprehension and retention of information. It first considers the role of affect, then the importance of navigating what psychologists call cognitive load, and finally questions of accessibility.

Target affective context

Perhaps the most important cause of ineffectiveness in traditional models of education is misconceptions around relationships between information and memory. The mind does not record information in the same way that books and electronic devices do. Indeed memories only relate to *information* in a secondary way. For example, in a 1974 study with John Palmer, pioneering psychologist Elizabeth Loftus[4] showed subjects footage of car crashes, then questioned them about what they had seen. The study revealed, firstly, that memory is highly susceptible to retrospective influence. For example, if the interviewer asked about how fast the cars 'bumped' into one another, participants estimated slower speeds; whereas if the interviewer used the word 'smashed', subjects tended to recall higher speed crashes. Indeed Loftus eventually discovered that she could convince a minority of subjects of entirely false memories.[5] Secondly, the study revealed that memories are not 'recalled' from a banked 'deposit' or log of experiences. Our minds only retain and encode a skeletal, affective trace of the emotional and bodily associations that an event, experience or idea has inspired. The details of what we colloquially term 'memories' are reconstructed after the fact, accurately or otherwise. Moreover, we tend to best retain those memories and associated information that relate to our personal concerns.

We are not empty receptacles. We come to learning situations with preexisting concerns to which we must tie any new ideas or information that we wish to incorporate into our understanding of the world.[6] As those who rely on mnemonic devices to commit large quantities of information to their memory instinctively know, in order for something to be important enough to be retained, it need not be highly emotional, in the sense of being a very traumatic, nor a hugely joyful experience. Indeed some of our concerns may in fact sound mundane to others. It must connect with our affective context.[7]

So learning theorist Nick Shackleton-Jones notes in describing his Affective Context Model of Learning that while '[m]achine code is written in 1s and 0s, human code is written in feelings. We are coded with care, so to speak'.[8] To teach well we must access this code in our students—their feelings, cares and concerns—and occasionally we must seek to alter them. So for example, legal educators might use a combination of pre-session surveys and ongoing online chat areas to gain a sense of what affective points of contact exist among their students and use those insights when choosing which legal issues to discuss, and to choose real world examples or craft bespoke stories. For example, Emily Allbon's 'Coltsfoot Vale' project consists of a navigable virtual online village in which students can learn the principles of land law through stories, giving legal concepts a deeper significance and relevance.[9] Drawing on these insights from psychology we can say the role of a good communicator is to lead students from what they already know and care about to a map of related information, and onwards to an understanding of the relationship between these pieces of information.

The same principles apply to all legal communications in legal practice and in the wider world. A client seeking advice will best retain information if the information or request for action is related to, say, their biggest worry about the issue at hand, or their hope for how it is resolved, rather than as a series of principles and possible outcomes.[10] So, for example, lawyers might invest more in small talk with legal clients to better understand and target their affective context.

Beware cognitive overload

Law is a highly text-centric discipline and many pedagogical models retain the banking model assumption that the goal is for the learner to read and retain as much information as possible. For example, conversations with recent legal graduates suggest to me that they are given too much reading with too little context. Some indicated that they prefer to ease themselves into a subject using 'nutshell' summaries, other told me they would have preferred to be taught about law more 'like a story'. These observations point back to the above arguments in favour of targeting affective context in the sense that stories have high affective potential, and summaries can make the affective stakes more visible. But they also suggest that traditional legal teaching methods risk overwhelming students with cognitive overload.[11]

Psychologist John Sweller developed the term 'cognitive load' in the 1980s to capture the implications of his discovery that human short-term memory tends to be generally limited to around seven items. This is where information is stored when it is first discovered—for example when someone reads you a phone number. Daily experience teaches us that our working memory is limited, which is why we may repeat a phone number until we can find a place to write it down. For information to be permanently retained it must be carried from short term memory into our longer-term memory. This tends to happen once we apply the information in some way—for example, by repeatedly dialling the phone number. Research on cognitive load suggests that learners such as law students should receive new important information in these kinds of small, manageable chunks and be allowed to think about and process them—thereby moving them into longer-term memory—before engaging with more information. Related research demonstrates that cognitive load be further reduced by providing students with 'schemas'—for example, by sorting and defining concepts, and by gathering information into subgroups.[12] This is why we often break down a phone number into smaller chunks, remembering, for example, twenty-eight instead of two and then eight. Such groups are also central to mapping arguments discussed below.

Authors and publishers of legal educational texts can, and increasingly do, bear these considerations in mind when planning the structure and layout of their publications. Carefully phrased introductory sentences, regular headings, bolded key terms and ideas, bullet points as well as white space can all enhance visual clarity, especially for those with learning disabilities.[13] Rather than develop wildly new ways of visually representing information, then, a great deal of important work can often be more easily and fruitfully accomplished by reformatting existing texts so that they are easier to visually parse. Expertly designed and/or beautiful visuals may well add value in many cases. But what is most important is that, firstly, visual differentiation and organisation of information happens in all key texts and methods of communication; and, secondly, this is done very clearly, mapping the most crucial ideas and information in a way that allows participants to understand the relation between them.

More specifically such adjustments can facilitate scan reading that is essential to complete a high volume without reaching cognitive overload.[14] A related, necessary pedagogical move is to shift from the understanding of the 'good' student as a *completionist* reader, attracting all the risks of cognitive overload and affective disconnect indicated above, to one who is a *strategic* reader. Strategic readers learn the common structures of texts, they know where the argument tends to get laid out, they look for which sections are examples and which are summaries, and they focus their reading on the most relevant parts and on drawing a relationship between key ideas within the text. Law students are taught how to parse the common structure of legal texts, such as where to look in the document for the key issues, who the judge was and so on. But they are rarely taught the broader skill of strategic reading—perhaps it is assumed that they either already have this skill, or perhaps there is a sense that suffering through this kind of confusion is what previous generations of lawyers have had to do and the current generation should struggle in the same way. Explicitly teaching for strategic rather than completionist reading prepares students for a lifetime of reading within a particular tradition such as statutes, cases and other forms of legal writing. This kind of strategic reading can be taught top-down by a legal educator. It can also be learned by doing, and in a less hierarchical or Socratic context, through students' study groups of the kind that are common in law schools in the US. Here texts are divided among students, each of whom studies one part in detail and then relays it back to the group. To encourage the development of strategic reading skills in such a group context one might, for example, ask students to analyse and share the type and format of argumentation deployed in their section of text, in addition to the content. They might do this individually or collaboratively. Any collaboration might be synchronous or asynchronous, and might use commonly available cloud-based document annotation systems such as Googledocs, or more specialist software such as hypothes.is,[15] to allow for different schedules and reading proficiency.

In asking students to read closely in this way, and to share their strategic understanding with one another, it is good practice to create guidelines for the kinds of questions that they might ask of one another, which can also have the effect of improving students' oral communication skills.

Evidence suggests that asking students to visually express what they have learned about the structure of legal argumentation can aid comprehension, especially for students who are struggling to understand argumentation. So another important intervention in this text-heavy discipline might be to focus on the practice of mapping—that is, graphically representing ideas, cases, concepts, rules, events and so on in relation to each other. Legal educators engage in mapping all the time, asking students to identify patterns in a series of cases and drawing from them a sense of the law as a whole, before applying the law back to a particular case. As noted above, research into memory suggests that information on its own is very unlikely to be retained. But visualised information, especially of the kind that emulates a geographic landscape, is more 'sticky'. Furthermore, because mapping emphasises relationships, visualisations can also generate or nurture higher-order levels of understanding. Legal educators might make a spatial map, timeline or similar graphical representation themselves and distribute them to students. Alternatively educators might start a map and ask students to complete and extend it. Such maps may take any form from hand drawn to digital, and a number of online tools exist to enable remote and asynchronous participation.[16]

It is often when we begin to teach something that we come to fully understand it,[17] and mapping can also be useful for legal educators in learning their subject, and determining how best to approach it with students. Many educators rely on dense textual slides, that are designed more to serve their own need to have presentation notes than to serve the needs of their, almost certainly overloaded, students. In my own courses on pedagogy, I ask practitioners to take 15 minutes or so to draw out appropriate visual aids to support their next teaching session without referring to their usual notes. We then spend time in small groups comparing these visuals, drawn from memory, to those upon which they usually rely in their teaching. Generally there are two key takeaways. Firstly, the visual aids that practitioners draw from memory tend to be far more sparse, including only the most significant details. I encourage them to redesign their visual aids with the insight in mind that whatever details have escaped their expert memory ought not to clutter a visual aid as they are even less likely to be retained by their students.[18]

Make communication accessible

The previous sections have introduced some of the ways in which a text-heavy tradition can make legal learning and communication inaccessible for the kinds of students who are traditionally anticipated, and that will also benefit those more recently anticipated students such as those for whom the language of instruction is less familiar, and those who have dyslexia. This section considers some wider questions of accessibility, in particular how legal communication practices may be disabling to those with those whose needs are less common, and so less often anticipated, understood and addressed; and how by addressing those needs we can improve accessibility for all.

Many contemporary break-throughs in relation to designing for accessibility are owed to the work of the disability rights community. When the attention of designers is called to the need to design inclusively, we all tend to benefit. As designer Paul Boag puts it, you might ask:

> How could you justify spending money on a podcast transcription when you don't even know if you have any deaf users? But good accessibility (or inclusive design) benefits all. Take the transcript example. A transcript has many benefits. It is great for search. It allows people to scan content which is hard in audio. It makes referencing content easier. It provides access to those unable to listen to audio because of disturbing others (e.g. in an office) … .[19]

What Boag captures here is the essence of the principles of universal design—a practice which is geared toward making products and services easy to use for the greatest possible number of people.[20] Digital accessibility means, for example, including alt text for significant images, and formatting and coding text to make it legible to reading software. But accessibility can also mean, for example, creating an audio textbook, and such advances improve accessibility more generally, including for those who, for example, wish to listen while commuting, exercising or doing household chores.

Many pedagogical issues can be reframed in terms of accessibility. In the same essay on accessibility in design, Paul Boag writes, 'People rarely consider those with a cognitive disability… In fact, we all have moments of cognitive disability! We are distracted, in a rush or otherwise engaged. We might have dyslexia or not speak English as our first language'. There is one such cognitive disability that affects everyone and that is particularly relevant in the legal tradition, especially for members of the general public: stress. Repeated studies show that those who experience moderate, short-term stress are often better able to take in information, while stress over a longer period of time, or extremely high levels of stress, can impede subjects' ability to learn.[21] Stress that is too intense or that goes on for more than a short burst effectively functions like a cognitive impairment and makes learning or absorbing new ideas highly unlikely. Legal communications should therefore be geared towards the worries people might have: anything from how much a process will cost (financial stress) to whether they will have to see their ex in person (interpersonal stress) to what might happen if something goes wrong with the process (stress that is about the legal outcome). It may be, for example, that meetings with clients who face difficult cases, for example, should be kept short, especially if the client appears to be becoming more distressed; and public legal education materials should be kept bite-sized, allowing subjects to regulate their own stress levels, as well as to avoid cognitive overload.[22]

While avoiding extremes of stress is very important in order to enable learning, research also suggests that stress in moderate and short bursts can be helpful if it emulates the kind of stress that we will have to undergo again in the future. In essence, it prepares us for future stressors, if taken on intentionally, and in a trauma-informed way. For example, someone who will be called as a witness should be prepared in a way that involves the same emotional stressors they will experience on the stand—perhaps a test audience of relatively stony-faced people, or at least a discussion of what it will 'feel' like to be a witness. So, legal educators might consider to what extent the stress that is produced by their chosen form of assessment emulates the kinds of stress that their students will face in future; and, if not, whether those assessments are doing more harm than good. Such a practice would mark yet another departure from the banking model of education, which focuses primarily on information transfer and regurgitation, and towards a more dynamic, student-centred approach.

Conclusion

The invention of many new online education tools, no doubt accelerated by the coronavirus crisis, has created an important opportunity to rethink education. A more diverse group of learners presents yet another opportunity to change the learning model for the better. To do this effectively, however, it will be important to not only innovate in terms of technologies but also in terms of the educational model itself. By focusing on learners' affective context, managing cognitive load, mapping concepts and thinking about a broad concept of accessibility, those wishing to teach and communicate the law more effectively can build on the existing focus on skills in the legal area, transcend the 'banking' model of education and improve not only how law is formally taught, but also how it is communicated to members of the public.

Notes

1 Learning designer, content strategist, and doctoral student, University of Oxford.
2 Paulo Freire, *Pedagogy of the Oppressed* (Herder and Herder 1970).
3 Rebecca Huxley-Binns, 'Tripping over Thresholds: A Reflection on Legal Andragogy' (2016) 50.1 The Law Teacher, 1–14, DOI: 10.1080/03069400.2016.1147310.

4 EF Loftus and JC Palmer 'Reconstruction of Auto-Mobile Destruction: An Example of the Interaction Between Language and Memory' (1974) 13 Journal of Verbal Learning and Verbal Behavior 585.

5 D Strange, S Clifasefi and M Garry, 'False memories' in M Garry and H Hayne (eds) *Do Justice and Let the Sky Fall: Elizabeth F. Loftus and Her Contributions to Science, Law, and Academic Freedom* (Lawrence Erlbaum Associates 2007) 137–68.

6 See further J Panksepp, *Affective Neuroscience: The Foundations of Human and Animal Emotions* (Oxford University Press 1998); P Hertel and D Reisberg, *Memory and Emotion* (Oxford University Press 2005).

7 There are many ways to demonstrate this; perhaps the most rigorous are the meta studies detailing the poor retention that occurs under traditional methods such as lecturing, compared to more effective methods like active learning. For just two meta-analyses, see Michael Prince, 'Does Active Learning Work? A Review of the Research' (2004) 93.3 Journal of Engineering Education 223–231, and Scott Freeman et al., 'Active Learning Increases Student Performance in Science, Engineering, and Mathematics' (2014) 111.23 Proceedings of the National Academy of Sciences 8410–8415.

8 See Nick Shackleton-Jones, *How People Learn: Designing Education and Training that Works to Improve Performance* (Kogan Page 2019) 28.

9 See further, https://tldr.legal/resource/a-day-in-coltsfoot-vale.html.

10 For one statistical measurement of this, see this study, in which medical students retained more of lectures when those lectures pertained to clinical cases in which they had been recently involved. BS Malau-Aduli et al., 'Retention of Knowledge and Perceived Relevance of Basic Sciences in an Integrated Case-Based Learning (CBL) Curriculum' (2013) 13.1 BMC Medical Education 1–8. For a longer, philosophical discussion of why this might be and what it implies about learning as a whole, see Joseph D Novak, 'Learning Science and the Science of Learning' (1988) 15.1 Studies in Science Education 77–101.

11 A book full of suggestions for how people can individually manage their cognitive load is Richard Saul Wurman, *Information Anxiety* (DoubleDay 1989).

12 See J Sweller, 'Cognitive Load Theory: Recent Theoretical Advances' in JL Plass, R Moreno and R Brünken (eds), *Cognitive Load Theory* (Cambridge University Press 2010) 29–47.

13 The pattern that has been measured with online reading is often termed the 'F shape pattern' where subjects scan the first line or two at the top of a page, and then quickly scan down the page, moving briefly across the top line of each new paragraph. See Robert Waller, 'Graphic Literacies for a Digital Age: The Survival of Layout' (2012) 28.4 The Information Society: An International Journal 236–252; Connie Malamed, *Visual Design Solutions: Principles and Creative Inspiration for Learning Professionals* (John Wiley & Sons 2015).

14 https://www.nngroup.com/articles/f-shaped-pattern-reading-web-content/.

15 See https://web.hypothes.is/, and particularly the example of work done by Matthew Roberts at https://web.hypothes.is/education/examples-of-classroom-use/. As Roberts put it to me in correspondence, 'Asking students to annotate an opinion with their questions and then answer each others' questions helps to create the sense that everyone is reading a common text [when learning happens virtually and face-to-face discussion while holding the same text isn't possible]. Questions appear in context and can be answered in context—instead of simply being references and quotes cited in a discussion board' (19 April 2021).

16 Two popular examples at the time of writing are Google's Jamboard and the software Miro. These are offered not as recommendations but merely as referents.

17 This is probably because it engages teachers in their own process of retrieval, forcing them to recon with what they know, fill gaps and organise their own

knowledge. See: Aloysius Wei Lun Koh, Sze Chi Lee, and Stephen Wee Hun Lim, 'The Learning Benefits of Teaching: A Retrieval Practice Hypothesis' (2018) 32.3 Applied Cognitive Psychology 401–10.

18 This exercise is drawn from Garr Reynolds, *Presentation Zen: Simple Ideas on Presentation Design and Delivery* (New Riders 2011).

19 Paul Boag, 'Accessibility is Not What You Think', https://boagworld.com/accessibility/accessibility-is-not-what-you-think/.

20 See further, CL Bennett and DK Rosner, 'The Promise of Empathy: Design, Disability, and Knowing the "Other"', CHI 2019, 4–9 May 2019, Glasgow, Scotland, UK, https://dl.acm.org/doi/10.1145/3290605.3300528 and William Lidwell, Kritina Holden and Jill Butler. *Universal Principles of Design, Revised and Updated: 125 Ways to Enhance Usability, Influence Perception, Increase Appeal, Make Better Design Decisions, and Teach Through Design* (Rockport 2010).

21 Susanne Vogel and Lars Schwabe, 'Learning and Memory Under Stress: Implications for the Classroom' (2016) 1.1 npj Science of Learning 1–10.

22 This fits in with 'trauma-informed' approaches, which I cannot do justice to here.

6 Service design comes to Blackstone's tower

Applying design thinking to curriculum development in legal education

Michael Doherty[1] *and Tina McKee*[2]

Introduction

This chapter outlines how service design methods were used as the framework for a major curriculum re-design of an undergraduate law degree.[3] It was, to our knowledge, the first time that design thinking was applied to planning how the foundations of legal education are delivered, rather than to introduce a legal design elective element into a law programme. Our aims for the chapter are quite practical: to explain what service design tools we used and why, and to share our experience of implementing them in a legal education project.

The law degree curriculum re-design at Lancashire Law School

A detailed curriculum redesign for a new version of Year 1 of a law degree at Lancashire Law School (LLS), University of Central Lancashire (UCLan), UK,[4] in 2018–19 provided an opportunity to re-think approaches to teaching, learning and assessment. The re-validation was the most significant change to the core law programme at LLS for over 40 years. It was prompted, in part, by proposed changes in the qualification route for solicitors in England and Wales by the Solicitors' Regulation Authority.[5] The Year 1 team also saw this as an opportunity to address a wider range of challenges in legal education and in UK higher education, including:

- The siloed nature of many HE programmes consisting of an agglomeration of individual modules that do not easily connect to, or build upon, each other. This can result in gaps, overlaps and incoherence. Individual teacher perspectives of a degree programme often focus on their particular contribution to it, but this is not the broader student perspective. The aim was to produce a more connected curriculum that consistently builds towards explicit programme-level outcomes.[6]
- Recognition of the need to address issues of inclusion, with a specific focus on the ethnicity attainment gap.[7] This is highly relevant in LLS as the law programmes have a demographic intake of around 50 per cent students from a BAME (Black, Asian and Minority Ethnic) background,

DOI: 10.4324/9780429021411-7

predominantly from local Asian heritage communities. Previous research within LLS identified that students from BAME backgrounds achieved lower marks and had less positive experiences of their studies than their counterparts from white backgrounds.[8]

- The increasing problems across the sector around attendance and engagement. There are a host of possible reasons for this disengagement; more commuting students, part-time work, the increase in student mental health and wellbeing issues, the availability of recorded materials.[9] Digital distractions do not just keep students away from class but reduce their sense of presence when they are in class. This sense, almost one of alienation, may contribute to increasing isolation and anxiety across campuses.[10]

The curriculum design had to create learning outcomes for the whole degree, plan the structure of class contact, set the balance between skills development and substantive legal content, and develop assessment and pedagogic approaches.

Much of the work of academic legal designers so far has involved going outside the walls of the law school and finding legal problems, such as impenetrable contracts or daunting court processes, to address through design thinking.[11] When academic legal designers do design work within their academic institutions, they normally focus on jams, sprints, and short courses that empower law students to apply design thinking to legal problems—*education in legal design.*[12] The focus of this project was somewhat different—*the service design of legal education*. It sought to use design thinking and service design methods to create a curriculum for a mainstream law degree. The areas covered in the first year (Legal Method, Public Law, Contract Law, Criminal Law) have their equivalents as foundations of general legal education in law degrees around the world.

Institutional and personal context

A key feature of service design is its focus on the specific users of particular services; that is, the context is important. Any lessons drawn from our experience will need to be applied with a suitable regard for different contexts. In our case, LLS was part of an established teaching-focussed (and research-active) post-92 university, with a Year 1 law degree intake of around 180 students. The cohorts are from a diverse range of educational backgrounds, and most originate from the North-West of England, with many commuting rather than living on campus.[13] A high percentage are first generation to university and many students are from economically and educationally disadvantaged backgrounds.[14]

In discussing this project with colleagues from other institutions, including beyond the UK, the most common question is not why we used design thinking but, how (on earth) were we able to get permission to do so, and how did we get staff buy-in? The leading practical guide to doing service design from Stickdorn et al. suggests that in the sometimes delicate process of introducing service design into an organisation for the first time, design teams should 'try to speak a common language, understand [the organisation's] current goals and challenges' and translate the project details into its overall business strategy.[15] Similarly, Perry-Kessaris suggests that where design practice is directed towards social change, i.e. the adaptation or replacement of existing conventions, the designer should seek to 'unsettle without alienating'.[16]

For our project, the particular make-up and experience of the design team was relevant to securing support from the School management team.[17] We had a track record of working together on educational development projects within the School, a shared interest in pedagogic innovation and a deep commitment to the development and success of our students. There was some, albeit limited, experience of doing legal design within the team, and our existing base of trust in each other meant that we were willing to take an experimental approach to this challenge. We had both some formal authority and some soft power within the School, and the belief from the Head of School that we knew what we were doing. This experienced insider and authority status meant that we already spoke the 'common language' of the organisation and understood its goals and challenges. It was easier for us to unsettle existing working practices without alienating colleagues.

Not all readers of this chapter will be in this position, but there are wider opportunities. For the project in LLS we consciously went 'all in' on design thinking, but this is not the only route for design to interact with legal education challenges. Jay Mitchell, who leads the transactional clinic at Stanford Law School, has written on the benefits of picking and choosing from the design toolkit and how academics can seek to support student professional development 'through modest refinements in practice inspired by design methods and mindsets'.[18] Similarly, for colleagues who are in a different teaching and learning environment than that described above, it may not be realistic to seek to radically change whole School approaches via a full-on design project, but there is scope for experimenting with some of the individual methods outlined here for more defined teaching and learning developments.

Rationale for use of legal design

Design thinking and service design tools were appropriate for this legal education project because many of the challenges it addresses, such as encouraging student engagement and enhancing attainment, have the character of 'wicked problems'.[19] That is, they are ill-formulated, with confusing information, and have stakeholders with conflicting values. The solutions to wicked problems are neither true nor false, only good or bad, and there is no exhaustive list of admissible operations or solutions. Problems are unique and, interesting to note in an educational context, 'The wicked problem solver had no right to be wrong – they are fully responsible for their actions'.[20] As Buchanan argues, design is fundamentally concerned with *the particular* and there is no science of the particular.[21] We can see this in the contextualised nature of education projects and in the observation that 'the problems educators face in practice are complex, diverse and often difficult to address'.[22]

Legal design has many facets including product design, systems design and visual projects, but we drew on the methods of service design and design thinking more generally. That is, 'a general human-centred approach to problem-solving, creativity and innovation' that is abstracted from designers' ways of thinking and doing,[23] and from their mental strategies for working on a project.[24] We are happy to conceive of higher education as a service, but not as a consumer service based on a purely bilateral vendor and purchaser relationship. Other stakeholders or 'users' within our user-centred design include the academics delivering the programme, the systems for ensuring quality and standards in what is still (directly or indirectly) publicly funded education, and even the wider social dimension of the society that higher education takes place in and contributes to.

Although the project was a very practical one, the role of a conceptual model of design thinking was important. We used the Stanford d.school Design Thinking Process which structured the specific tools we used and provided a landscape and rationale for our development activities.[25]

On reflection we could just as easily have used the Design Council's double-diamond, or the HCD model (Hear, Create, Deliver),[26] particularly as we would be the 'deliver' team as well as the 'design' team. A key principle of design thinking models is that the stages are not consecutive. A project team may start at some place other than the beginning and loop back to different stages as the project progresses. This was certainly our experience, not least because we had to balance the need for structure and direction with the practicalities of undertaking the activities outlined below around a range of existing teaching, administrative and research commitments.

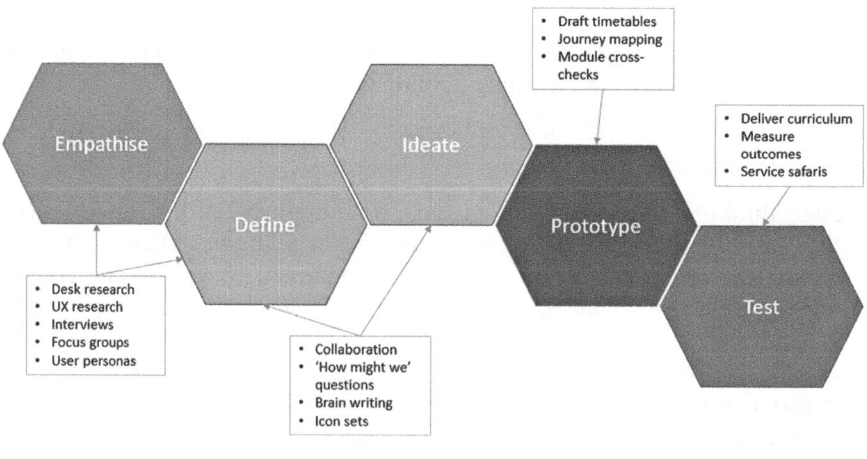

Figure 6.1 Stages of UCLan design process presented in terms of the Stanford model (original diagram © Stanford University).

Our main resource on the detailed practical methods for the project (within the framework established by the Stanford model) was *This is Service Design Doing* by Stickdorn et al. which provides a comprehensive toolkit for service designers.[27] We could not have undertaken a hands-on service design project without a resource such as this.

As mentioned above the activities were not all sequential, but the following sections organise them around the key headings of the Stanford model.

Empathise

Empathising involves data collection to provide insight into user needs. Grant and Berry explain that 'the necessity of others is the mother of innovation'[28] and this perspective—a deliberate effort to understand what others need – is at the heart of design thinking.

Existing knowledge and desk research

We had ongoing research interests and projects within the team that were relevant e.g. on inclusive learning, addressing the BAME attainment gap and diversity barriers.[29] We needed to consciously question and critique our assumptions, but we did have existing insight into our students with well over 100 years' experience in LLS between us in teaching and student support, both academic and pastoral. We supplemented this knowledge by desk research, i.e. the collection and review of existing research on issues such as connected curricula and the mental resilience of undergraduate law students.[30]

User Experience (UX) research

Higher education is increasingly awash with data. Qualitative and quantitative information comes from module evaluations, attainment and attendance data, the National Student Survey and now from highly granular metrics on student engagement with virtual learning environments and recorded lectures. It is necessary to be familiar with these existing data, but they are often intended for different purposes (ranking, overview and audit) and often do not get under the skin of the lived experience of students. We commissioned *in-depth UX interviews* with a small number of Year 1 students.[31] The staff–student power relationship would have distorted the openness of these interviews, so we hired a third-year undergraduate to undertake them. The questions were around things we felt we did not currently fully understand, such as the students' initial interest in law, their motivations for undertaking a law degree, the social connections they made at law school, and the relationship between their studies and the rest of their lives, including family and friends. We were searching for what are known within service design as 'pain points'—in our context this means blockages in students' engagement with their studies, and triggers for enhancing feelings of connection to the school, the programme and each other. There were some rich insights from the research, for example on the importance of kindness in staff/student interactions and revelations of the difficulties that some students from families with no history of participation in higher education faced from unsupportive and even obstructive family members.

The project also drew on ongoing research from two team members on the experience of BAME students in legal education.[32] This focus on inclusion utilised a further research method commonly used by service designers to explore user experience—*focus groups.* These involved a series of informal discussions between an academic and a group of postgraduate Black and South Asian heritage students. Many explained that the social, cultural and family experience of undertaking study for them was very different from what they perceived as the dominant paradigm derived from young white students living away from home. This user research was very insightful, but we felt that we lacked some broader conceptual understanding of how to respond to this information via our teaching practices. We invited an external consultant on de-colonising the curriculum to work with a key group of staff.[33] This is a movement that has gained some traction in the UK, the US and South Africa, which argues that university curricula are strongly conditioned by colonial and Western-centric world-views leading to feelings of marginalisation and alienation for BAME students and which recognises that university environments can be structurally racist. This forced us to consider representational issues—did we overuse Western European names in our problem scenarios and white faces in our slides and images? It also led us to question our reading lists and to think more creatively about the topics we discussed, introducing a stronger focus on issues of social justice and positive examples of effective legal approaches from across the world. Broader approaches to inclusion[34] also inspired us to redesign our classroom activities and dynamics to promote a 'friendly classroom' approach where we provide structured opportunities for students from different backgrounds to work together both within and beyond the classroom.

User personas

The software designer Alan Cooper developed the concept of personas as a design tool, and explained that 'Personas are not real people, but they represent them throughout the design process. They are hypothetical archetypes of actual users, [often] defined by their goals'.[35] Pruitt and Grudin argue that their strength lies in their usability; as a conduit for conveying a broad range of data not covered by other design methods.[36]

We worked with students, through drafting, consulting and re-drafting, to co-create three user personas to represent a range of educational and social/family backgrounds, demographic characteristics, career goals and personal interests. We kept the personas as constant reference points and test cases by placing the one-page persona documents in the middle of the table during weekly meetings. Because each persona has a name, a face and a realistic background, they very quickly became authentic to us. We became emotionally invested in how our design decisions on timetabling, or pedagogy, or academic support would work for Terri, Nazir and Karen. The benefits were at least three-fold. First, they helped us shift perspective from a teacher to a student view of issues. As Cooper says, designers often have a vague or contradictory sense of users and so revert to scenarios based on people like themselves.[37] Second, they provided diversity, not only in their demographics, but also in their life circumstances and different priorities outside of their studies.

Third, the personas acted as 'boundary objects'. Pruitt and Grudin argue that a great value of personas is in providing a shared basis for communication.[38] When a team member used the phrase 'our first years' there were, inevitably, at least six different mental images of what we were talking about, derived from our different assumptions and experiences. The personas will not have eliminated this effect but should have reduced the disparities in our thinking. This is indicative of a wider benefit of some of the prototyping outlined below—that when we get information, views and assumptions out of our heads and into some form of written/visual representation, we develop a better shared understanding.

Define and ideate

Defining involves data synthesis and coming to a refined problem understanding whilst ideation aims at suggesting multiple, alternative and diverse ideas to address the problem; an opportunity 'to drive in variance'.[39] In line with the fluid nature of design thinking, it is difficult to unpick what we did and put it into separate define and ideation stages. The UX research and the idea creation activities, for example, generated ideas and information relevant to the empathy, definition and ideation phases.

The team were experienced in curriculum development but were not used to the process of deep collaboration. We scheduled an hour a week together (plus occasional longer sessions) so that we could co-create, e.g. the programme-level learning outcomes, using the ideation methods outlined below. This helped to define our project goals and actions, which we captured and monitored through Gantt charts.

In theory, this was quite a simple part of the process, but in practice it was difficult to schedule times when all team members were available. It also felt like an unusual way of working. Many of our prior experiences in higher education involved working in isolation and then reporting back to colleagues, often with fairly detailed and developed drafts and proposals. This often led to a need to reassert or clarify the parameters of the particular project. There could also be a reluctance to unpick the work of colleagues or conversely an invitation to act like archetypal lawyers in, according to Hagan, making 'a sport out of shooting down ideas as quickly and thoroughly as possible'.[40]

1

Curriculum Design Project – Persona A

Terri Jackson

Age: 19

From: Wakefield, Yorkshire; going to live in IQ Halls of Residence

Educational Background: BTEC in Business, DD; 8 GSCEs Grades A-D

Work: Terri thinks she will try to get a job working in a bar for e.g. two nights a week.

Goals: Terri currently thinks she wants to qualify as a solicitor but is not 100% sure and she is also attracted to a career in teaching. She aims to enjoy her time at University and, despite her social anxiety, hopes to make some good friends.

Interests: Terri is vegan and is interested in environmental issues. She is looking forward to learning about criminal law and human rights.

Social Background: Terri has had a chaotic family life. She was bullied at school and developed social anxiety. At times, this has developed into depression. She has a good relationship with her GP in Wakefield but hasn't registered with a GP in Preston. She is a bit overawed by the size and scale of UCLan and university life.

Figure 6.2 User personas developed for the UCLan law curriculum project.

In contrast, this co-creation method meant that we often did not know who had proposed a particular idea. It was just as likely to come from an interaction as from a single person, which chimes with Berg's observation of 'the primal mark', that the beginning of a creative process shapes the end and that new ways of working affect the outcomes.[41] Our experience also accords with Johnson's thesis that good ideas are more likely to be generated by networks and collaboration, especially if this is structured as time alone, followed by focussed time together.[42] On reflection, we could have explored ways of more directly involving students in the collaboration process beyond the interviews, user personas and other informal consultations. The process, though, was a bit of a stretch for the project team. We were already out of our comfort zones. With such an interactive process where we needed to feel that we could be very open with each other, including on existing shortcomings, it may have been difficult to bring in students to all meetings without negatively affecting the dynamic.

To ideate we used 'How might we ...?' questions and brain writing techniques (a process where participants sit in silence and write as many ideas as possible, one idea per sticky note). This opened a space for us to think differently about our educational approaches and for all team members to contribute ideas. We felt that it allowed us to postpone the usual legal/academic processes of critique, review and defence until we had generated a wider range of ideas. We used sticky notes, idea clustering, and voting to prioritise ideas and actions.

Some team members found it genuinely difficult to undertake the brain writing task, not because they could not generate ideas but because they struggled to do so in silence. As lawyers, and teachers, they were used to verbalising ideas as they went along, together with rationalising, amending and examining consequences. One example of an output generated by these methods was a visualisation idea. We adopted a uniform icon set to highlight the key skills and learning outcomes developed across modules, e.g. research, legal reasoning, and employability. Staff use the icons in lecture slides and other learning materials to show students the connections between modules, and how their educational development is an iterative, virtuous spiral process.[43]

Prototype

Prototyping involves quickly and inexpensively developing 'tangible and experienceable representations of ideas',[44] and is a central feature of design practices. We prototyped what a typical week of overall contact time would look like for a Year 1 student—how many classes, how long, when scheduled, and the gaps between them. This enabled us to account for the different needs and demands on our students, as derived from UX research and kept visible via the user personas.

We also had a more detailed *journey map* of the first semester. This enabled us to draw connections between modules in greater depth than we had previously been able to. The module leaders for Legal Method and Public Law (the first semester modules) were able to sit together and see week by week the range of learning activities that students would be undertaking. This allowed us to eliminate repetitions and to develop coherence in the programme design. Again, this seems like a simple step, but it was the first time, to our knowledge, that this detailed user view of student experience across modules had been done within our school.

We had planned to do a full user experience journey mapping exercise for the whole year. We envisaged this as a desktop exercise with a wider audience including students, professional services staff and the head of school, so that we could see the student journey through the year and obtain insights from a wider group. This did not happen due to time constraints and was indicative of a broader difficulty (or critical self-reflection)—that we had been too ambitious in the scope of changes that we wanted to introduce in a single year and the design methods we intended to use to develop them. A consolation was the design notion that everything is a prototype, and the teaching principle that delivery is improved by iteration and reflection.

Test

Testing involves trying out new solutions with users. Our first cohort of students 'tested' the new course from September 2019, and we were pleased to have the new curriculum structure, together with the supporting timetable adjustments and detailed module content, in place in good time. Despite the project co-ordinator changing institutions, the project team remained committed to the ethos and implementation of the project and progress continues.

It has been challenging to test and measure the effect of the curriculum redesign, as we are still in the early phases of implementation. The waters have also been somewhat muddied by overlapping institutional initiatives and the effects of the coronavirus pandemic, which suspended our plans for formal qualitative evaluation of staff and student experience of the new curriculum. However, we believe that our innovative service design approach has led to innovative changes. Examples of this include our adoption of 'bridging task' activities where students work in small groups on interactive tasks outside the classroom which 'bridge' into the following workshop; and our thematic embedding of social justice and decolonisation across all modules. Early indications also suggest positive outcomes for our students; module pass and attainment rates have improved, and student withdrawal rates have fallen, but the huge changes to delivery modes, assessment methods and progression and award criteria precipitated by the Covid-19 crisis make direct comparison with previous years impossible.

Initial student feedback highlighted both positive experiences and areas to address in future iterations. Students really appreciated the greater classroom interaction and the opportunity to work in groups on a broad range of learning tasks but (the perennial issue of) inconsistent student experiences across different classes was a concern. We also trialled an innovative example of a UX service design method, *'service safaris'*, as part of our testing phase. This involves a researcher shadowing users throughout the course of a full day and can be used in the 'empathise' or 'testing' phase of a project, offering rich insights into the lived experience of users. The team member who conducted the service safaris fed back suggestions for improving our next iteration e.g. specific learning activities that needed further development. Many of these changes have been incorporated for the 2020 cohort and seem to be going well.

Our reflection on the curriculum re-design process acknowledges that some key aspects will take time to embed as they involve a real shift in practice e.g. moving from didactic to more active learning approaches, introducing social justice themes and de-colonising the curriculum. These changes require staff 'buy-in', training and thoughtful integration into module content—it can never be a quick fix. However, ongoing dialogue and sharing of ideas is leading to further progress in module content and delivery in the current academic year.

The overall picture so far is that the structures and approaches we developed in design mode have passed proof of concept and survived contact with the real world. They work as a curriculum and a pedagogical ethos. However, design theory is not a 'one-stop-shop'. We recognise that the ambition and scale of our foundational goals in redesigning our law curriculum will take time to become embedded, and we will return to design mindsets and tools in evaluating the programme and further developing it. We also acknowledge the ongoing value of design theory as we continue to use service design methods to evaluate changes to date and to influence changes to come.

Conclusion

Herbert Simon, a founding figure of design as a discipline, argues that 'everyone designs who devises a course of action aimed at changing existing situations into preferred ones'.[45] This is precisely what any team of curriculum developers, or anyone starting a practical pedagogic project, aims to do. This being the case, this chapter has argued that design thinking and service design provide not a template, but a valuable framework and toolkit, that can be applied outside of 'legal design and innovation' programmes, in order to help re-envisage the delivery of general foundational law programmes. It is not a short-cut or a panacea, and it involves at least as much work as more traditional approaches, but in focussing more on the whole experience of the student and in drawing on the collective creativity of teams it opens up spaces for different ways of thinking about learning in law.

Notes

1 Professor of Law and Associate Head of the Law School, Lancaster University.
2 Senior Lecturer, Lancaster University.

3 The reference in the chapter title is to the classic account of the English law school in William Twining, *Blackstone's Tower* (Sweet & Maxwell 1994).
4 Now subsumed with other social sciences and policing into the School of Justice, UCLan.
5 Solicitors Qualifying Examination, https://www.sra.org.uk/sra/policy/sqe/, approved by the Legal Service Board in November 2020 (last accessed 3 November 2020).
6 Dilly Fung, *A Connected Curriculum for Higher Education* (UCL Press 2017), https://discovery.ucl.ac.uk/id/eprint/1558776/1/A-Connected-Curriculum-for-Higher-Education.pdf.
7 Jane Berry and Gary Loke, *Improving the Degree Attainment of Black and Minority Ethnic Students* (ECU and HEA, 2011), https://www.advance-he.ac.uk/knowledge-hub/improving-degree-attainment-black-and-minority-ethnic-students-0. See also the work of the Kaleidoscope Project (University of Kent) on inclusion and decolonial thought, https://research.kent.ac.uk/sergj/kaleidoscope-network-decolonising-the-university/ (last accessed 10 March 2021).
8 The Participation Puzzle 2016–18, a mixed methodology research project exploring issues of attendance and attainment in LLS, led by Tina McKee and Rachel Nir, UCLan.
9 Rachael Field, James Duffy and Colin James (eds), *Promoting Law Student and Lawyer Well-Being in Australia and Beyond* (Emerging Legal Education 2016); Natalie Skead et al., 'If You Record They Will Not Come—But Does It Really Matter? Student Attendance and Lecture Recording at an Australian Law School' (2020) 54.3 *The Law Teacher* 349–367.
10 Emma Jones, *Emotions in the Law School: Transforming Legal Education through the Passions* (Routledge 2019).
11 See, for example, Helena Haapio, 'Contract Clarity and Usability through Visualization', in Francis Marchese and Ebad Banissi (eds), *Knowledge Visualization Currents: From Text to Art to Culture* (Springer-Verlag 2013) 63–84; Margaret Hagan, 'A Human-Centred Design Approach to Access to Justice: Generating New Prototypes and Hypotheses for Intervention to Make Courts User-Friendly' (2018) 6 Indiana Journal of Law and Social Equality 199–239, 208, https://papers.ssrn.com/sol3/papers.cfm?abstract_id=3186101.
12 There are many existing initiatives in legal education to enhance design and innovation skills, including *inter alia*, at short courses and clinical legal education activities at institutions such Stanford, Northeastern University, Vanderbilt Law School, and the Universidad de los Andes. The only full Masters programme focussing on legal design, rather than legal tech, appears to be at Laurea University of Applied Sciences, Finland.
13 45 per cent of undergraduate students live in their parental/guardian home and 25 per cent live in their own home rather than on campus—UCLan HESA Return 2018/19.
14 Almost double the national average are from 'POLAR4 Young HE' lowest participating neighbourhoods (13 per cent compared with 7 per cent national average) and 41 per cent are from areas in the most deprived 'Indices of Multiple Deprivation' quintile (national average 30 per cent)—UCLan data from HESA Return 2018/19; national data from HESA, 'Who's studying in HE?' (2018/19), https://www.hesa.ac.uk/data-and-analysis/students/whos-in-he (last accessed 8 October 2020).
15 Marc Stickdorn, Markus Hormess, Adam Lawrence and Jakob Schneider, *This is Service Design Doing* (O'Reilly 2018) 457, 'make clear that service design works in your organisation, in your structures, in your culture'.
16 Amanda Perry-Kessaris, *Doing Sociolegal Research in Design Mode* (Routledge 2021).
17 The design team comprised Michael Doherty (Academic Lead—Student Experience), Tina McKee (Year 1 Course Leader), Andrew Harries (Academic Lead—Quality),

Rachel Nir (Reader in Legal Education and Inclusion), Linda Chadderton (Deputy Year 1 Course Leader), Kim McGuire (Criminal Law Lead).

18 Jay Mitchell, 'Outlooks, Techniques and Words: Product Design, Practising law and Engaging Students in Legal Practice' (2020), https://medium.com/legal-design-and-innovation/outlooks-techniques-and-words-ddcf49e3b46d (last accessed 16 February 2020).

19 Developed by Horst Rittel in the 1960s, but the leading account is from Richard Buchanan, 'Wicked Problems in Design Thinking' (1992) 8.2 Design Issues 5–21.

20 This is Rittel's final characteristic of wicked problems, cited in Buchanan, ibid 16.

21 ibid 17.

22 Danah Henriksen, Carmen Richardson and Rohit Mehta, 'Design Thinking: A Creative Approach to Educational Problems of Practice' (2017) 26 Thinking Skills and Creativity 140–153, 140.

23 Lisa Carlgren, Ingo Rauth and Maria Elmquist, 'Framing Design Thinking: The Concept in Idea and Enactment' (2016) 25 Creativity and Innovation Management 38–57.

24 Katja Tschimmel, *Design Thinking as an Effective Toolkit for Innovation* (2012) Proceedings of the XXIII ISPIM Conference: Action for Innovation: Innovating from Experience.

25 See e.g. Stanford d.school, Design Thinking Bootcamp, https://dschool.stanford.edu/executive-education/dbootcamp (last accessed 12 December 2019).

26 Design Council, What is the Framework for Innovation?, https://www.designcouncil.org.uk/news-opinion/what-framework-innovation-design-councils-evolved-double-diamond (last accessed 16 September 2020); IDEO, The Human Centred Design Kit, https://www.ideo.com/post/design-kit (last accessed 16 September 2020).

27 Stickdorn et al. (n 15).

28 Adam Grant and James Berry, 'The Necessity of Others is the Mother of Invention: Intrinsic and Prosocial Motivations, Perspective Taking and Creativity' (2011) 54 Academy of Management Journal 73–96.

29 Tina McKee et al., 'The Fairness Project: Doing What We Can, Where We Are' (2018) Journal of International and Comparative Law 181–216; Tina McKee et al., 'The Fairness Project: The Role of Legal Educators as Catalysts for Change. Engaging In Difficult Dialogues on the Impact of Diversity Barriers to Entry and Progression in the Legal Profession' (2020) The Law Teacher, https://doi.org/10.1080/03069400.2020.1796061.

30 For example, Fung (above n 6); Lydia Bleasdale and Sarah Humphries, *Undergraduate Resilience Research Project* (2018) Leeds Institute for Teaching Excellence, https://teachingexcellence.leeds.ac.uk/wp-content/uploads/sites/89/2018/01/LITEbleasdalehumphreys_fullreport_online.pdf (last accessed 16 February 2020).

31 The original intention was to interview ten first year students but, ultimately, we were only able to secure five.

32 McKee et al (n 29).

33 Dr Deborah Gabriel, Founder and Director of Black British Academics, https://blackbritishacademics.co.uk/ (last accessed 7 December 2020).

34 For example, the Kingston University Inclusive Curriculum Framework, https://www.kingston.ac.uk/aboutkingstonuniversity/equality-diversity-and-inclusion/our-inclusive-curriculum/inclusive-curriculum-framework/ (last accessed 7 December 2020).

35 Alan Cooper, *The Inmates are Running the Asylum: Why Hi-Tech Products Drive Us Crazy and How to Restore the Sanity* 2nd edn (Sams 2004) 124.

36 John Pruitt and Jonathan Grudin, 'Personas: Practice and Theory' (2003) Proceedings of the Conference on Designing for User Experiences, https://www.microsoft.com/en-us/research/wp-content/uploads/2017/01/personas-practice-and-theory.pdf (last accessed 18 December 2020).

37 Cooper (n 35).
38 Pruitt and Grudin (n 36).
39 Grant and Berry (n 28).
40 Hagan (n 11) 208.
41 Justin Berg, 'The Primal Mark: How the Beginning Shapes the End in the Development of Creative Ideas' (2014) 125.1 Organizational Behaviour and Human Decision Processes 1.
42 Steven Johnson, *Where Do Good Ideas Come From: The Natural History of Innovation* (Penguin 2010).
43 See the RACER project at City Law School, London, for further examples of using consistent visualised information across a law programme, https://tldr.legal/resource/the-racer.html (last accessed 10 March 2021).
44 Lisa Carlgren, Ingo Rauth and Maria Elmquist, 'Framing Design Thinking: The Concept in Idea and Enactment' (2016) 25 Creativity and Innovation Management 38.
45 Herbert Simon, *The Sciences of the Artificial* 3rd edn (MIT Press 1969) 130.

7 Teaching innovation in the age of technology

Educating lawyers for digital disruption using visually-oriented legal design principles

Lisa Toohey[1], Monique Moore[2] and Sara Rayment[3]

Introduction

As Diane May wryly and rightly observes:

> In the age of technology, sometimes it just seems right to have students sit down together, grab a pencil, and scratch their heads,
> In the age of passivity, sometimes it just seems right to have students sit down together, grab a pencil, and scratch their heads,
> In the age of complexity, sometimes it just seems right to have students sit down together, grab a pencil, and scratch their heads.[4]

In 2018, Newcastle Law School became the first law school in Australia to offer students a dedicated course on Legal Design Thinking. We did so in response to the changing legal environment, with the intention of helping students to understand the role of innovation in a 'disrupted' legal world. At the same time, we were aware of the transformative potential of the three activities that May alludes to in the quote above—collaborative, human-focussed approaches; practical, experiential learning; and the value of tackling big complex challenges.

This chapter reports on our experiences of deploying this initiative in the university context, reflects on our own design decisions in constructing the course and explains the skills and attributes that were developed through formal Design Thinking instruction to help facilitate innovation. We also explore the design choices that we made in creating the Legal Design Thinking course, some of the benefits and challenges of our approach, and what we have identified as future directions for our research in this area. Our discussion is based on a range of sources—our own reflections on the teaching experience, the extant literature and qualitative data that we have collected as part of a broader project examining lawyer engagement with innovation.

The chapter begins by explaining how contemporary legal industry discourse about innovation, technology, and the future of law—led particularly

DOI: 10.4324/9780429021411-8

by the Law Societies—has shaped views of legal education in Australia, and how it shaped our course in particular. The final form of the course was the culmination of concerns and challenges that had engaged us as legal educators over several years, as well as specific dilemmas that we encountered once we started planning and teaching the course. While the course was borne out of a wish to focus on the impact of technology on the changing practice of law, our research-led approach to the course led us to intentionally focus on analogue and visual elements and resist an emphasis on technology, which we explain below.

The chapter then explains the structure and approach of the course, and how our ongoing empirical and secondary research in legal innovation has informed and enriched our course design, and continues to do so. We also explain, conversely, how our teaching of the course has revealed other important issues for further research, and hypotheses for our ongoing exploration of the nature of legal innovation. Our conclusion, somewhat paradoxically, is that a course in legal design that focusses primarily on non-digital approaches, and which emphasises visual, analogue experiences, is an important foundation for future lawyers to develop the skills to work in the age of technology.

Flip it, innovate it: the transformation debate in Australia

In the years leading up to the creation of our Legal Design Thinking course, the country's two largest Law Societies, the Law Institute of Victoria and the Law Society of New South Wales, undertook substantial investigations into the future needs of the legal profession and produced reports on how the Australian legal community needed to position itself to remain relevant and competitive.[5] As we explain below, these reports were influential in Australian law schools, and resulted in increasing interest in how topics such as technology and innovation could be incorporated within the curriculum.

The larger of these reports was the 'FLIP Report', produced by the Law Society of New South Wales following an extensive Commission of Inquiry, with terms of reference seeking to 'identify and understand the changes affecting the profession'.[6] After receiving evidence from over one hundred witnesses, the Inquiry produced a detailed report with ten chapters addressing different dynamics impacting the practice of law, including globalisation, changing client needs, technology and legal education. Smaller in scale, the Law Institute of Victoria's work ('LIV Innovation Report') focussed more specifically on innovation, based on interviews with over 40 experts, and was designed to identify how legal practice would change by 2025, and how lawyers could best adapt and innovate to meet the challenges of change.[7]

The overall tenor of these reports reflects the concerns raised by the well-known (but often critiqued) futurist Susskind about the changing competitive dynamics in legal practice, including its commoditisation and the disruptive effects of technology.[8] While the emphasis and conclusions of these reports differed slightly from one another, both overwhelmingly adopted Susskind's predictions of dramatic change in the profession, and sought to make recommendations accordingly. Both highlighted the importance of fostering innovation within the sector, developing knowledge and cultures that support innovation, and ensuring that lawyers have a better understanding of the potentially transformative effects of emerging technologies. As explained below, the practical orientation of Australian law schools has meant that these two reports were of great interest to Australian law schools and closely considered by those interested in legal education and curriculum reform.

The Australian legal education context

In the wake of these reports, and notwithstanding a dynamic academic debate that challenges and critiques aspects of the 'Susskind prophecy',[9] law schools around Australia have revised their curriculum offerings, especially elective (nonmandatory) courses.[10] Their objective is to better equip graduates with the skills, attributes, and knowledge to be effective in their future practice of law. This has led many law schools to introduce courses on coding or app building, as well as courses on technologies such as blockchain and artificial intelligence.[11]

Australian law schools tend to have a strong emphasis on integrating legal skills into the curriculum, generally with the aim of enhancing graduate employability and producing graduates who are well prepared for legal practice. While this approach is not without significant criticism of this 'vocational' emphasis,[12] this remains a dominant narrative in Australian legal education.[13] Law schools were therefore very attuned to the recommendations of both the FLIP Report and the LIV Innovation Report that encouraged universities to teach skills necessary for innovative practice[14] and for students to 'receive training in the skills necessary to create novel ways to communicate legal information and provide legal services'.[15] The FLIP Report in particular highlighted the importance of technology, with its recommendations including that '[c]onsideration needs to be given to whether aspects of technology need to be included in core courses ... and whether new subjects such as coding for lawyers are needed'.[16] However, because of the nature of professional regulation in Australia, these Law Societies, while influential, are not directly responsible for prescribing what is required for admission to practice in Australia, or for shaping the core requirements of qualifying law degrees.[17]

An additional dynamic is the fact that graduates of Australia's legal education have never been destined exclusively for careers as lawyers. In some law schools, barely a majority of students may aspire to practice law. This stands in stark contrast with the United States (US), where the curious concept of 'JD advantage jobs' is a recent term coined to describe law graduates who deploy their skills outside of legal practice.[18] In Australia, law graduates have long sought careers in consulting, government policy and corporate positions, and use their legal knowledge as an additional skills base. It is expected that an increasing proportion of graduates will seek careers in innovation, knowledge management, process re-engineering, data science and technology roles, both inside and outside of law firms. Such issues have become increasingly topical in Australian discussions about the future of law because it identifies the growing need for legal education to offer transferrable skills.

The sum of these dynamics is to present something of a dilemma for the curriculum designer and the law teacher. There are competing conceptions about the relative importance of various future-oriented skills within the curriculum, and while influential recommendations exist, there are no mandated requirements. It is therefore up to each law school, and often each academic, as to how to best equip their diverse student cohort with the skills and knowledge necessary. At the same time, neither Susskind nor others offer a clear path towards the 'innovation' that is required in a changing legal environment, as very little research has been undertaken on how to promote innovation in the legal environment or how best to teach innovation skills to lawyers.[19]

Being cognisant of these dynamics, we set about to offer an elective course to develop the capacity of our students to confidently innovate, and to navigate their future careers in which technology will play an ever-increasing role. Along the way, we needed to make several design decisions, which (unsurprisingly) profoundly shaped the final shape of the course. We explain these decision points in more detail below.

Technology-informed, but not technology-focussed

We intentionally sought to avoid a technology focus in our course for a range of philosophical and pedagogical reasons. Firstly, we were keen to avoid a lawyer-centric narrative that focusses on how technology helps or harms lawyers through the 'commodification of the practice of law'.[20] As Susskind points out, the same 'disruption' that makes lawyers uneasy about the future of the profession also brings with it the possibility of better access to justice for those who cannot currently afford legal advice.[21] A lawyer-centric narrative is also at odds with the value that we, and many members of the legal profession, see in a human-focussed and client-focussed approach.

Secondly, the evidence suggests that the pace of technological change has advanced more slowly than predicted. While there is no doubt that disruptive technologies will transform the role of the lawyer, automating many tasks that have been the 'bread and butter' of legal practice such as many aspects of litigation, due diligence, contract drafting and review, the core of lawyering remains. In the foreseeable future, much of the 'higher value' work, particularly that requiring complex reasoning and skilful understanding of human nature, will remain the domain of humans. Deloitte Access Economics argues that demand for these 'soft skills'—problem solving, teamwork, critical thinking, innovation, emotional judgment and communication—will increase to account for up to 80 per cent of jobs by 2030.[22] While rapid technological evolution means that what students learn in class about 'tech' can quickly become obsolete, what they learn about innovation skills is both enduring and translatable into different contexts.

Thirdly, and most importantly, by centring technology in the innovation process, we risk implying that innovation necessarily involves technology. This is a common misconception for many within the legal profession. Empirical research recently undertaken by our team reinforced this false assumption, with one interviewee lamenting:

> It's interesting because often when I do a lot of public speaking on this, there is a bit of a perception in the market that often innovation equals technology. I always say if people come with that mindset, it is destined a failure. It is not technology. In fact, I have seen many organizations think that technology is going to solve their problems, and they don't do any person's work beforehand. As a result, they only make the problem that much worse because they are applying technology to it.[23]

A strongly technology-focussed view of the future legal profession is both unhelpful and potentially harmful. As Graben argues, law schools are uniquely positioned to instil in future members of the justice system the ability to both promote and critique the use of technology, and yet the 'paucity of analysis on the effects of technology on law's production stands in stark contrast to disruptive technologies already being introduced to the market'.[24] In other work, we have explored the ease with which technology can be deployed to be deeply harmful to the justice system and impede rather than promote access to justice.[25] Such conclusions helped to inform our teaching approach. What we discovered was that design thinking, executed with rigour, is an effective approach 'to ensure [that] technological solutions are designed from the outset to meet the needs of end users of legal technology, and not just the needs as they are perceived by system experts such as lawyers and policymakers'.[26]

With these considerations in mind, we selected Design Thinking as a methodology on which to centre our course. We adopted the Stanford d. school five step model of empathise, define, ideate, prototype, test[27] because it is a commonly-used model, as exemplified in Margaret Hagan's 'design-driven approach to law'.[28] As we have explained in a previous article, the benefit of Legal Design lies largely in its process of structured innovation:

> Legal Design offers a structured method to encourage an iterative and user-focused process of law reform and innovation that allows for miscalculations and mistaken assumptions to be made and corrected before a purported solution is released to an end user. It offers the ability to integrate methods of information delivery that suit a range of users, for example through the integration of visual law.[29]

Such observations offered a unique opportunity to make an important (and symbolic choice) to design a more human-centred rather technocentric course. In summary, our approach could be described as technology-informed, rather than technology-focussed.

Course structure

The current Legal Design Thinking course begins with an introduction to the concept of law as information, focussing on the tangible problems that people experience when they try to access legal services.[30] It then introduces the design thinking methodology, highlighting how it differs from mainstream legal thinking, and focusses on students approaching a group 'innovation challenge'.

When identifying suitable challenge scenarios, the teaching team drew on the insights of staff at the University of Newcastle Legal Clinic (Legal Clinic). The Legal Clinic has direct contact with the community and with local lawyers, and therefore has invaluable insight into current community legal needs. Our selection of challenge scenarios was also created with reference to common student experiences with the legal system, so that our class of students would hopefully have some pre-existing understanding of the context and underlying legal principles. Some of the actual challenge scenarios included: 'How can we make insurance more comprehensible?'; 'How can we help people report workplace bullying?'; and 'How can we assist international students to understand their work rights in Australia?'

We found that the choice of scenario was extremely important. Where scenarios were too legally complex, or broached unfamiliar areas of law, students would lose focus on the Design Thinking process as they became preoccupied with understanding the underlying legal doctrines and legislation that applied to the scenario. We also rejected scenarios that were the topic of present law reform debates, as our objective in the course was to work with law as it presently exists.

Most of the face-to-face time was allocated to stepping students through the stages of Design Thinking methodology. This included helping them to work towards their own group challenge and offering smaller 'mini challenges' to help them develop the skills required for each stage of the methodology. These mini challenges used templates, patterns, and exemplars such as the Visual Law Library,[31] the Graphical Advocacy Project[32] and the Contract Pattern Design Library.[33] We asked students to model some of these patterns in these smaller tasks, such as a visual redesign of a section of Apple®'s Terms of Service, to build their confidence with these techniques before considering them in the prototyping phase.

We found it important to delay the discussion of technology until after we had established the Design Thinking methodology as the fundamental concept of the course. Therefore, rather than opening and framing the course with a discussion about technology and disruption, such as artificial intelligence or blockchain, we focussed on a discussion of access to justice concerns along with community challenges related to grasping complex legal information and processes. Only once students had completed the ideation phase and were part-way through prototyping, then technology aspects were introduced. This avoided students being pre-disposed towards technological solutions and instead focussing squarely on end user needs. Consequently, the students tended towards creating more feasible, user-focused solutions, instead of being inclined towards complex technology or 'apps' that were not necessarily the best solution.

Assessment in the course required the group to submit a refined version of their prototype, together with a portfolio that showed the evolution of their work and research undertaken, and a reflection on the group's experiences. This offered evidence of the iterative nature of the design process, as well as highlighted the role of experimentation. We expressly encouraged students to include evidence of their rejected or failed ideas. The remainder of the course assessment included a class participation mark and a research essay on a topic based on the course readings of the student's choice.

The section above may give the misconception that many of these features were present in the initial course offering. We would like to stress that, like the design process itself, our course evolved iteratively, where we reflected on the sequencing and structure, and experimented with changes. For example, when we first offered the course, we introduced technology quite early in the piece. We soon found that the students were keen to propose blockchain solutions to a range of scenarios, at the expense of analogue, lower cost initiatives. Subsequent revisions of the course addressed the sequencing issue, as explained above, with better results. In a future iteration of the course, we plan to expressly instruct students to create both an 'analogue' and a 'digital' solution and compare the advantages and disadvantages of each in their portfolio.

Research-led course design

Supporting the evolution of our Legal Design Thinking was our research agenda. Commencing in late 2019, we established a qualitative project based on phenomenographic principles to explore how the Australian legal ecosystem has responded to the changing nature of legal practice and calls for innovation.[34] Our study involved 48 participants from a range of backgrounds, including practising lawyers, consultants, academics, students and people working in innovation roles in law firms. Interviewees were asked about a range of topics, including their views of legal industry trends and challenges; their definition of an approach to innovation, the skills and capabilities might facilitate innovation, and how best to aid law student's development of innovation capacity.

Several findings evolved from our research which has confirmed and further informed our Legal Design Thinking course. These include a focus on: (1) the visual; (2) process and method; (3) working with experts; (4) connecting with empathy; and (5) normalising challenge, failure, and ambiguity. The remainder of this chapter will draw on the observed experiences of developing the Legal Design Thinking course and research findings.

A visual focus

Lawyers in our empirical study have reported that some of their most effective innovations have come from non-technological initiatives that pay attention to the visual. While visual approaches are a corner stone of 'designerly ways', they do not always come naturally to lawyerly types.[35] US-based research on law students reinforces what many educators intuit, and which our interviewees identified – that on average, law students are less oriented to visual sources and tactile kinaesthetic learning than the general student population and show stronger preferences towards writing and speaking.[36] These insights are important in a Design Thinking context, as lawyer-designers may tend to underestimate the preference of the general population for visual and tactile learning methods.

Often lawyers underestimate a client's preference for visually oriented flowcharts, graphs, or other pictorial elements and overestimate their willingness to digest complex written or verbal information. One in-house lawyer at a banking institution confirmed this view. It was shared that even though the banking institution operated in a traditional manner, brevity was critical. Brevity was best achieved using easy-to-digest visual displays (like flow charts). This helped to reduce information asymmetries between the legal department, other professionals and clients. Lengthy legal responses coupled with verbose legalese were viewed negatively as increasing unnecessary costs, while visual manifestations of the same information were viewed positively as offering value.

Another lawyer reported that their firm had systematically reviewed all client facing documentation, resulting in the firm converting letters that had previously been three to four pages into single-page infographics. They then measured responses identifying an increase in positive client feedback.[37] An interviewee from one of Australia's largest firms commented that visual approaches were being sought by clients seeking 'much more streamlined and visual contracts' and 'want[ing] whatever we give them to be immediately digestible … there are really complex things that we're trying to get across, but they want them simplified and they want the visual'. They lamented that in their experience, law graduates were ill-equipped to support these client needs:

> [G]rads come out of university writing and conveying [written] messages. They've got some very formalized techniques that they use … . We have to then retrain them, and we have to retrain them with partners who have been doing it the same way their whole lives. It's a really slow reskilling.[38]

Integrating these insights into our teaching practice, we observed that reskilling our students was a worthwhile process. It was helpful for students to have access to a range of physical materials to develop their visual representation skills. We also observed that it was important to provide opportunities for non-visually-inclined people to develop these skills even if they were initially reticent to do so. To encourage physical rather than computer-based experimentation, we provided the students with blank scrapbooks, making art materials available, along with a range of props such as paper money, LEGO®, plasticine and foam boards. Students that remained highly resistant to drawing or using physical materials were instead encouraged to start with more familiar programs like PowerPoint®, visually displaying ideas using icon sets or clipart.

A focus on process and method

We found that students responded positively to clear processes and methods to assist them in the "messy" work of innovation. Social problems of law and justice are inherently complex and non-linear, standing in contrast to the simplified and compartmentalised problems that students experience in black letter scenarios presented in traditional classroom-based contract or tort problem-solving. Through innovation challenges and interacting with users, students come to utterly understand the way in which legal problems become actual social problems. This process often involves gaining insights from key stakeholders like end-users and multiple disciplinary experts who may be involved in Design Thinking. As one law dean interviewee explained when asked about what makes a good lawyer:

> It's about being able to understand a complex problem from a complexity of points of view which is what people find, and again, find so incredibly frustrating.[39]

One of the strengths of centring the course around Design Thinking was that it offers a structured and practical step-by-step method to innovate and entrenches a human-focussed perspective. Few people would expect that a lawyer is going to understand how to run a case or undertake legal analysis simply by being told to do it. Instead, lawyers are given instruction in principles, context, method, and strategy, both during formal study and in the workplace. Critical to this is grasping context, for without context, laws cannot be crafted.

We found that applying similarly structured approaches to innovation gave both students and practising lawyers the confidence to both experiment and to trust the method. This process prevented teams from diverging from their problems. We also found that trust in the method increased when we spent time focussing on the intellectual history of Design Thinking, summarising and explaining the research, both in law and from other disciplines, and on having guest speakers join by Zoom to present short case studies illustrating the successful application of principles across the full justice spectrum.

In the second iteration of the course, we spent additional time explicitly discussing the different types of reasoning—specifically abductive reasoning—that underpins Design Thinking, and how it differs from standard legal reasoning. A hallmark of this mode of reasoning and problem solving is that there is no fixed concept of a solution reached through the reasoning process. This was something that students found particularly challenging. This was overcome by reassuring students that Design Thinking is initially inherently ambiguous, predicated on resolving 'wicked' or difficult to resolve problems, rather than undertaking rational 'black letter' legal analysis. Also, such difficulties and difference can often yield innovative results mainstream legal analysis may not be capable of achieving.

Working with experts

Another value we wished to communicate during the course was to reinforce respectful boundaries between lawyers and other professionals. This was another reason we encouraged students to produce messy prototypes and wireframes rather than finished products. Too often, in our opinion, lawyers are falsely given the impression that they can grasp the fundamentals of complex technologies and high-level skills such as coding or graphic design in a single course.[40] We tried to reinforce the idea that a lawyer can create a prototype, which can then be developed with more rigorous testing in collaboration with graphic designers, programmers or other appropriate experts.

According to some researchers, the ability to work well in teams, and respect different disciplinary expertise is at least, in part a generational attribute, with millennials (born 1982–1998) noted as being strong at teamwork compared to previous and subsequent generations. A disinclination towards teamwork has been a striking characteristic of legal practice, particularly where senior lawyers need to collaborate with graduates or law students.[41] Law firms are replete with terminology that downplays the role of experts from other disciplines—particularly seen in the term 'non-lawyer':

> Law firm talent wars today seem myopically focused on lawyers. The challenge of recruiting top legal talent pales in comparison to hiring top AI and data science talent. Both fields are growing explosively but the talent is not. Firms that want to win the war for that talent—even for consulting support—must eliminate the caste system. They must banish not just the term 'non-lawyer', but also the thinking behind and projected feelings from it.[42]

In our course, we tried wherever possible to introduce law students to experts—particularly from fields such as graphic design and IT. Such experts were invited to speak to the class about multi-disciplinary collaboration and how to develop practices that foster trust-building, clear communication, conflict resolution and extract value when working with experts from differing backgrounds to achieve outcomes.

Connecting with empathy and emotions

Critical to effective design thinking is the ability to distil possible solutions from the designers' genuine and deep understanding of the end-user's needs. Data about those needs are collected through the step often referred to as 'empathy'—so called because its objective is for the designer to be able to 'walk a mile' in the end-user's shoes. This end-user focus revolves around listening first, as opposed to developing instant solutions. This requires a flexible, open-minded approach by a designer capable of absorbing a broad range of practical, emotional and conceptual information.

Gaining end-user and stakeholder views, and iteratively weaving those into the prototyping process has the effect of making the design process non-linear. The process explicitly avoids definitive solutions during the stages of the design thinking process, focussing instead on prototypes to elicit further feedback. The consequence is that Design Thinkers must be willing to sit with frustration because solutions are not clear from the outset. There is no reverse engineering. Both the uncertainty and the demands for empathy are often challenging for those with legal analytical tendencies.

Few of these skills receive attention in the mainstream legal curriculum. In fact, the dominant view of 'professionalism' is to train students on how to distance themselves from emotional connections and avoid empathetic approaches to information. As the managing partner of a major law firm observed in a newspaper interview, 'To be innovative, we needed to first tap into our lawyers' empathy'. In a similar vein, Inglis explains:

> Innovation is about challenging the status quo with a mindset that embraces change, interrogates the root cause of a problem and then thinks creatively to solve that problem. It's essential to have the right attitude – be curious, authentic, empathetic and have fun. If and when you incorporate these things into your legal practice, you will become an innovative lawyer and will be set up for an interesting and innovative legal career.[43]

We found that many students are naturally inclined to skip the 'empathy' stage—perhaps because they wish to rush to solutions. Often, they may prefer to develop their own ideas to solutions rather than listening to what end-users and stakeholders tell them. Others expressed frustration with speaking to end-users, observing it is both challenging and uncomfortable. Insisting upon use of the Design Thinking methodology was one tool that helped us to ensure that the students adequately addressed end-user experience. We often reiterated the similarities with qualitative research and the importance of concepts such as saturation. At a practical level, we also reinforced the importance of empathy work through the assessment requirements—and required evidence of their primary research with end-users to be featured in their portfolios.

Normalising challenge, failure and ambiguity

Finally, we believe that there are many aspects of the Design Thinking process that can facilitate resilience for those who learn the method. Tang has undertaken extensive exploration of law student resilience, and believes that this can be facilitated by a model of lawyering that advocates for 'collaborative, relationship-based models that emphasize mobilizing hope and optimism, active client involvement, … and helping clients mobilize their own intrinsic intelligence for solution-finding'.[44] There is striking resonance between Tang's model and the Design Thinking method—not just in their emphasis of an engaged end-user, but also in their collaborative, human-focussed approach, and even for the capacity to mobilise hope and optimism.

Design Thinking allows law students to believe that they can make meaningful contributions to address 'wicked problems'—and equally that they are not required to solve the unsolvable, but rather to improve the experience of the end-user. We believe this is capable of inculcating students with a sense of hope and optimism.

At the same time, the iterative nature of the Design Thinking process emphasises failure as a normal and essential part of the process, something that is required rather than something that is to be avoided. Law students, like lawyers in practice, are less accustomed to failure, and generally poorly disposed to seeing the advantages of failure. However, it is well acknowledged that failure is an important part of innovation—meaning that if lawyers are not willing to fail, they are unlikely to succeed at innovation. As one former student, now practising lawyer interviewee observed, when asked what they found most challenging about innovation:

> Learning that it's okay to fail and learning from those mistakes. That's definitely the hardest thing to get used to because every failure will be different, like you haven't experienced it before. It's hard just trying to get used to the process of failure and learning from it.[45]

Much has been written about lawyer personality, although the research tends to be quite outdated, US-focussed, and the results not overly consistent. However, the general findings are that lawyers tend to have much higher rates of cynicism, pessimism and perfectionism when compared with other populations.[46] While these are clearly generalisations, and perhaps more applicable to the average law student than to one that voluntarily enrols in an innovation course, we nonetheless noticed the difficulties that many students had sitting with 'messy' data, with making rough prototypes, with seeking and receiving feedback, and facing setbacks and failures. We also found that, at times, we struggled with allowing students to fail—and in subsequent iterations of the course, became more adept at not intervening when students went off course, letting failures happen and then coaching them to reflect and correct.

The research is overwhelmingly clear, both in Australia and elsewhere, that law students and lawyers as a cohort have particularly poor levels of wellbeing.[47] Considering how best to improve law student outcomes, Tang explains the benefits of better understanding law student's subjective experiences, understanding and supporting them to make changes.[48]

Having taught the Legal Design Thinking course across several iterations to law students, and having also delivered parts of the course to practising lawyers, we are convinced of the potential for Design Thinking to benefit lawyer and law student wellbeing through its ability to raise self-awareness and metacognition, decreasing perfectionism and increasing comfort with navigating failure and uncertainty. We believe that law students who experience the challenges of a Design Thinking class are more emotionally capable of managing every day and future challenges in practice. Furthermore, we propose that the positive, human-focussed nature of Design Thinking promotes legal student and practitioner wellbeing because it offers hope to all practitioners (the new and old guard) that all can contribute positively to difficult problems evolving in law and justice regardless of technological or creative propensity. As we have flagged, these are starting propositions that we believe offer opportunity for further formal research.

Conclusion

Our case study serves to illustrate the benefits of incorporating both Design Thinking and visual law into the law curriculum, as well as some of the decision points and challenges. It provides insights into how teaching Design Thinking can help students relate to the wider world of lawyering in an age of technological change. The case study also reveals aspects of Design Thinking in the law curriculum that warrant further, more detailed evaluation and research.

This chapter opened with a quote from Diane May about the values of working in groups to physically 'nut out' complex problems.[49] This quote encapsulates so much about our impetus for opting to use a more unorthodox analogue—and visually-focussed, legal design thinking course. Critical to this decision was the realisation that students need to be better equipped to navigate change, disruption, and failure for an emerging 'future law' century. Teaching Design Thinking to law students has been both a challenging and an immensely rewarding experience. While the term 'Design Thinking' was not in Susskind's lexicon, he nonetheless advocates for a human-centred approach:

> One person's disruption can be another's salvation. There is a lesson here for lawyers that reaches beyond the issue of disruption—always give thought to the recipient of your services. When considering some kind of innovation, put yourselves in the shoes of those you are meant to be helping. What will it mean for them?[50]

In our experience, many lawyers, especially more recent graduates, can readily understand the tasks that are being asked of them—to be innovative and to be client-focussed—but are not equipped with the skills and methods to reach these innovative needs. Our experience in teaching this course, coupled with our research, identifies the importance of teaching Design Thinking to legal graduates to enhance innovative capabilities of tomorrow's lawyers. More specifically, our experience highlights the benefits that can be gained from 'dialling back' an emphasis on technology in favour of an emphasis on design thinking methods.

Notes

1 Professor of Law, University of Newcastle, Australia.
2 Doctoral researcher, University of Western Australia.
3 Founder, Inkling Legal Design and Adjunct Associate Professor, University of Newcastle, Australia.
4 Diane May, 'Using Scaffolding to Improve Student Learning in Legal Environment Courses' (2014) 31.2 Journal of Legal Studies Education 233, 233.
5 Katie Miller / Law Institute of Victoria, *Disruption, Innovation and Change: The Future of the Legal Profession* (2015), https://www.liv.asn.au/Flipbooks/Disruption–Innovation-and-Change–The-Future-of-t.aspx, accessed 23 January 2021 ('LIV Innovation Report'); Law Society of New South Wales, *The Future of Law and Innovation in the Profession* (2017), http://lawsociety.com.au/ForSolictors/Education/ThoughtLeadership/flip/index.htm, accessed 23 January 2021 ('FLIP Report').
6 FLIP Report, above n 5 at 10.
7 LIV Innovation Report, above n 5 at 6.
8 Richard Susskind, *The End of Lawyers? Rethinking the Nature of Legal Services* (Oxford University Press 2010); Richard Susskind, *Tomorrow's Lawyers: An Introduction to your Future* (2nd edn, Oxford University Press 2017).
9 The 'Susskind prophecy' is our own term, but for development of the critique, see, for example, Lisa Webley, John Flood, Julian Webb, Francesa Bartlett, Kate Galloway and Kieran Tranter. 'The Profession(s)' Engagements with LawTech: Narratives and Archetypes of Future Law' (2019) 1 *Law, Technology and Humans* 6; Kate Galloway, Julian Webb, Francesca Bartlett, John Flood and Lisa Webley, 'The Legal Academy's Engagements with Lawtech: Technology Narratives and Archetypes as Drivers of Change.' (2019) 1 *Law, Technology and Humans* 27.
10 The qualifying law degree in Australia takes two forms—either a Bachelor of Laws (LLB) or a Juris Doctor (JD). An LLB is an undergraduate course that students take in conjunction with a second degree such as business, arts or science. Most Australian law schools also offer a Juris Doctor (JD), which is a standalone graduate entry degree. Both qualifying law degrees incorporate a mix of compulsory law courses and elective courses.
11 See, for example, Ashley, Kevin, Jaromir Savelka and Matthias Grabmair, 'A Law School Course in Applied Legal Analytics and AI' (2020) 37.1 *Law in Context* 1.
12 For explanation and critique of this 'vocational' narrative, see NJ James, 'More Than Merely Work-Ready: Vocationalism Versus Professionalism in Legal Education. (2017) 40.1 *University of New South Wales Law Journal* 186.
13 Kate Galloway, 'Disrupted Law Degree: Future Competencies for Legal Service Delivery' (17 July 2017). Available at SSRN: https://ssrn.com/abstract=3082486.
14 LIV Innovation Report, above n 5 at 33.
15 FLIP Report, above n 5 at 77.

16 ibid 78.

17 See also Margaret Thornton, 'The New Knowledge Economy and the Transformation of the Law Discipline' (2012) 19.2/3 *International Journal of the Legal Profession* 265.

18 Susan D Carle, 'The Current Anxiety About JD Advantage Jobs: An Analysis' (2020) 57 San Diego Law Review 675.

19 See, however, the ground-breaking work by Michele DeStefano, *Legal Upheaval: A Guide to Creativity, Collaboration, and Innovation in Law* (American Bar Association 2018). Our own research (forthcoming) examines the question of how to facilitate innovation amongst Australian lawyers.

20 Margaret Thornton, 'Towards the Uberisation of Legal Practice' (2019) 1.1 Law, Technology and Humans 46.

21 Richard Susskind, *Tomorrow's Lawyers: An Introduction to your Future* (2nd edn, Oxford University Press 2017).

22 Deloitte Access Economics, *Soft Skills for Business Success* (2017), https://www2.deloitte.com/au/en/pages/economics/articles/soft-skills-business-success.html, accessed 15 February 2021. See also Kate Galloway, 'Disrupted Law Degree: Future Competencies for Legal Service Delivery' (2017), https://ssrn.com/abstract=3082486> or http://dx.doi.org/10.2139/ssrn.3082486, accessed 24 February 2021.

23 Interview with Cara (pseudonym), Lawyer, Commercial Law Firm (Sydney, Australia, April 2020).

24 Sari Graben, 'Teaching Emerging Technologies as Legal Systems: Proposals for a Changing Law School Curriculum' (2020), http://dx.doi.org/10.2139/ssrn.3339363, accessed 15 February 2021. See the amended and published version: Sari Graben, 'Law and Technology in Legal Education: A Systemic Approach at Ryerson' (2021) 58 Osgoode Hall Law Journal 139.

25 Lisa Toohey, Monique Moore, Katelane Dart and Daniel Toohey, 'Meeting the Access to Civil Justice Challenge: Digital Inclusion, Algorithmic Justice, and Human-Centered Design' (2019) 19 Macquarie Law Journal 133.

26 ibid 134.

27 Hasso Plattner Institute of Design / Stanford University, *Bootcamp Bootleg* (2010), http://dschool.stanford.edu/wp-content/uploads/2011/03/BootcampBootleg2010v2SLIM.pdf, accessed 16 February 2021.

28 Margaret Hagan *Law By Design* (undated), https://lawbydesign.co/.

29 Lisa Toohey, Monique Moore, Katelane Dart and Daniel Toohey, above n 25 at 154.

30 See further, Lisa Toohey, Jonathan Crowe, Rachel Field, Helen Partridge and Lynn McAllister, 'Understanding the Legal Information Experience of Non-lawyers: Lessons from the Family Law Context', (2018) 27 Journal of Judicial Administration, 137; Stefania Passera, Beyond the Wall of Contract Text: Visualizing Contracts to Foster Understanding and Collaboration Within and Across Organizations (2017 PhD Dissertation, Aalto University).

31 https://www.legaltechdesign.com/visualawlibrary/category/civil-procedure/.

32 https://www.graphicadvocacy.org/work.

33 https://contract-design.worldcc.com/.

34 This study was approved via Human Research Ethics Committee (HREC) at the University of Newcastle, Research reference number HREC H-2019–0339.

35 See further Amanda Perry-Kessaris, 'Legal Design for Practice, Activism, Policy, and Research' (2019) 46.2 Journal of Law and Society 185 at 190–191.

36 Robin Boyle, Jeffrey Minneti and Andrea Honigsfeld, 'Law Students Are Different from the General Population: Empirical Findings Regarding Learning Styles' (2009) 17.3 Perspectives: Teaching Legal Research and Writing 153, 158. Note this is based on self-reporting of preferences.

37 Interview with Lea (pseudonym), lawyer and consultant (Sydney, Australia, April 2020).

38 Interview with Leslie (pseudonym), innovation manager in a law firm (Melbourne, Australia, May 2020).

39 Interview with Erica (pseudonym), Dean of an Australian law school (location withheld for confidentiality, May 2020).

40 See also our discussion on this point below.

41 Susan Daicoff, 'The Future of the Legal Profession' (2011) 37.1 Monash University Law Review 7, 29–30.

42 Ron Friedmann, *A Multidisciplinary Future to Solve Legal Problems* (2018), https://prismlegal.com/a-multidisciplinary-future-to-solve-legal-problems/, accessed 22 February 2021.

43 Rose Inglis, 'What is an Innovative Lawyer?' (2019) Law Institute of Victoria Young Lawyers Blog, https://www.liv.asn.au/Staying-Informed/Young-Lawyers-Blog/Young-Lawyers-Blog-2019/October-2019/What-is-an-innovative-lawyer-, accessed 27 February 2021.

44 Arthur C Bohart, 'The Client is the Most Important Common Psychotherapy' (2000) 10 Journal of Psychotherapy Integration 127, quoted in Stephen Tang, 'Valuing Persons and Communities in Doing Wellness for Law Well' in Rachael Field, James Duffy and Colin James (eds), *Promoting Law Student and Lawyer Well-Being in Australia and Beyond* (Routledge 2016) 27, 39.

45 Interview with Cam (pseudonym), former student and practising lawyer (Newcastle, April 2020).

46 Martin E P Seligman, Paul R Verkuil and Terry H Kang, 'Why Lawyers Are Unhappy' (2001) 23 Cardozo Law Review 33.

47 See Paula Baron, 'The Persistence of Distress' in Rachael Field, James Duffy and Colin James (eds), *Promoting Law Student and Lawyer Well-Being in Australia and Beyond* (Routledge 2016) 57, 59–60.

48 Arthur C Bohart, 'The Client is the Most Important Common Psychotherapy' (2000) 10 Journal of Psychotherapy Integration 127, quoted in Stephen Tang, 'Valuing Persons and Communities in Doing Wellness for Law Well' in Rachael Field, James Duffy and Colin James (eds), *Promoting Law Student and Lawyer Well-Being in Australia and Beyond* (Routledge 2016) 27, 39.

49 Diane May, 'Using Scaffolding to Improve Student Learning in Legal Environment Courses' (2014) 31.2 Journal of Legal Studies Education 233, 233.

50 Richard Susskind, *Tomorrow's Lawyers: An Introduction to your Future* (2nd edn, Oxford University Press 2017), 44.

8 Teaching IT Law through the lens of legal design[1]

Rossana Ducato[2] *and Alain Strowel*[3]

Introduction

Law curricula are often accused of being too theoretical and knowledge-based, and of not preparing students adequately for practice and the challenges of the legal professions. A number of developments over the last few years have sought to address this perceived gap between academia and practice, including individual initiatives by professors to tailor-made courses on legal skills, the blossoming of legal clinics and moot courts to curricular internships as part of the study plan, and student associations enterprises to the launch of European projects aimed explicitly at modernising legal education.[4]

These initiatives integrate the learning experience with practical skills, advocacy, problem-solving thinking, and communication ability. However, there is a growing demand for further educational needs beyond the 'think like a lawyer' framework. The legal professions are evolving rapidly, in particular, due to the technological turn.[5] Many practitioners have to deal daily with complex problems that often require a multidisciplinary effort, and a subset of those are involved in the co-creation of innovative services that are quite distant from the traditional legal opinion.[6] In a way, the 'lawyer 4.0''s work tends to resemble the activity of the legal researcher: they need to navigate the complexity of the technological environment, be inclined towards life-learning, open to interdisciplinary collaborations, able to organise and manage projects to offer innovative legal services.

To cover these additional needs, legal education should provide graduates with a solid knowledge of the law, legal skills, and a *forma mentis* that will allow them to communicate and collaborate with experts in other fields. This is the idea behind the 'T-shaped' curriculum. The latter is not something completely new, but nor is it yet fully embraced.[7] Among the disciplines that can contribute to the T-shaped lawyer's horizontal segment of expertise, design and design thinking figure prominently.[8] Today, only a small number of courses integrate designerly thinking in the toolkit of the law student, but the labs and initiatives in the field are growing and showing some interesting achievements.[9]

DOI: 10.4324/9780429021411-9

This chapter introduces the teaching and learning experience developed within the 'European IT Law by Design' (EITLab) module at UCLouvain.[10] The module has been awarded an Erasmus+ Jean Monnet grant for EU studies, and it aims at introducing the students to Information and Technology (IT) Law at the European level by combining a theoretical analysis of the current legal issues raised by artificial intelligence with a more practical approach, based on 'legal design'.

Legal design is a growing field of research, practice, policy, and activism in which design's human-centred approach is applied to the world of law.[11] It is increasingly accepted that design methods and processes can contribute to opening new legal (and extra-legal) pathways for testing and improving the legal system. Examples of legal design applications include not only the representation of legal texts (contracts, privacy policy, legislation, criminal and civil evidence) through visualisation, but also access to justice, access to legal information, provisions of new legal services, citizens' empowerment.[12]

The following sections present the course structure, goals, and learning outcomes, showing the strategies and tools that might provide insights into building interdisciplinary courses at the crossroad of law and design.

Course structure and learning outcomes

The EITLab runs for eleven weeks. It is offered as an optional module to the students of the Master in Law and the Advanced Master in European Law, and to postgraduates from the certificate in 'Gestion des droits intellectuels et pratiques numériques' ('Management of intellectual property rights and information technology'). It aims to support an interdisciplinary learning journey through IT law using a series of activities that promote academic excellence, critical thinking, acquisition of soft skills and active citizenship.

More specifically, the students are called to work collaboratively to solve a legal problem in the field of IT Law through the lens of human-centred design. In so doing they must integrate legal knowledge, legal skills and design methodologies to develop innovative services or solutions. The course is therefore constructed primarily as a 'learning by doing' experience. The following sections introduce the core pedagogical components of the course: 'Foundations of IT Law' and 'Legal Design in Action'. It is important to note that these pedagogical components are complemented by a series of interactive 'Conversations on Legal Design' in which guest scholars, lawyers and experts present their work in the field of legal design to students.

Foundations of IT law

This first part of the EITLab introduces students to contemporary issues in the regulation of information technology and artificial intelligence (AI). IT Law is a highly technical area with which most students are not familiar, so this series of thematic sessions provides basic knowledge of relevant legal frameworks, such as privacy, data protection, consumer law, e-commerce and so on that are to be applied during the second part of the course. This part of the course presents some of the current challenges brought by the developments in the field of AI, explores the legal framework applicable to it, exposes the gaps of protection caused by AI-based tools, and how the law reacts (or not) to them.

This part of the course, which is in principle more theoretical, is meant to provide the principal coordinates of the relevant legal disciplines, i.e. their rationale, structure, fundamental principles and relationship with other branches. The lectures, however, include an interactive session where students are immediately called on to elaborate on the concepts and notions just presented. This critical thinking activity is developed through individual and collective exercises which encourage students to use visual tools.[13] Here we highlight two such activities that we have developed and experimented with over the past three years: the Data Protection Canvas and the Jigsaw Seminar.

The Data Protection Canvas is a paper-based tool we provide to students for their first exercise during the lecture on data protection. The class is divided into pairs, and each of them has to solve a basic data protection case. The canvas, which contains the key points to address—such as material and territorial scope of application of the General Data Protection Regulation, actors involved in the processing, potential violation, and solution—is meant to support the understanding of the facts and legal implications of the given

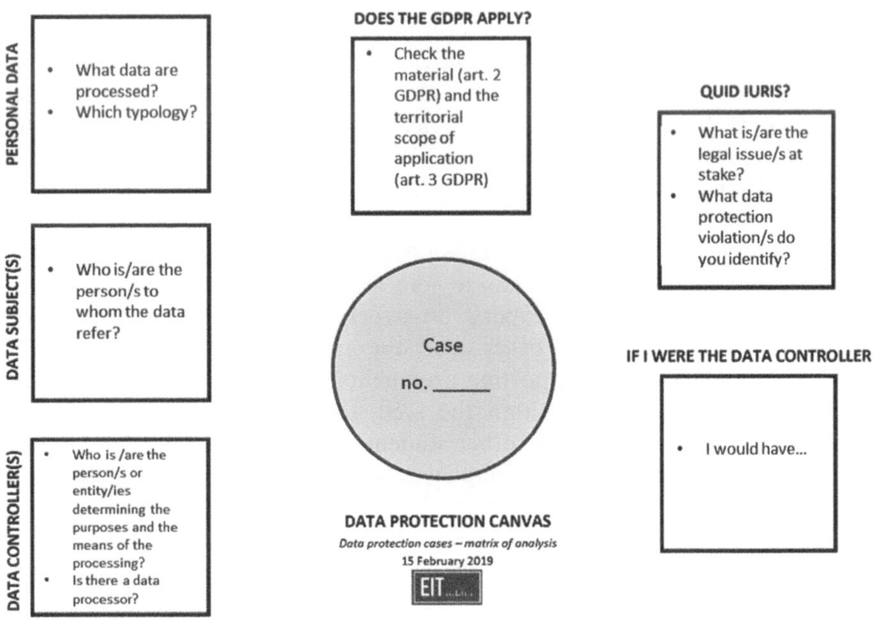

Figure 8.1 Data protection canvas—mind map. The students annotate their answers (in the form of keywords) on Post-it® notes which are then applied on the different squares.

data protection scenario. Students have to visualise such key elements and use the canvas to present their solution in front of the rest of the class. Therefore, the canvas helps students structure the legal reasoning, reach significant conclusions and communicate such outputs.

The Jigsaw Seminar (see Figure 8.2) is an example of the flipped classroom—that is, a student-centred approach based on active learning.[14] More specifically, the jigsaw activity is a co-creative knowledge-building exercise that can be imagined as a puzzle: each student has to add their piece to complete the picture for the whole class's benefit. In 2019/2020, we decided to use the jigsaw seminar technique to address the right to explain automated decision-making processes in the General Data Protection Regulation (GDPR).[15] The issue is topical in the contemporary debate on artificial intelligence and its regulation, and it gave rise to different positions in the literature. We, therefore, selected a few seminal scientific papers (that were also equivalent in terms of length) and assigned one of them to each student.[16] All students had to read and analyse their article before the seminar. In particular, they had to identify the core thesis or theses of the contribution, the arguments supporting each thesis and critically engage with the paper. On the day of the seminar, the activity is articulated in four main steps:

1 In the first part, the tutor explains the jigsaw seminar's instructions and briefly introduces the topic at stake (automated decision-making and the right to explanation under the GDPR in our case), re-capping the relevant points or provisions to take into account.
2 After this introduction, the students are grouped with the peers who received the same paper. Within this group (so-called 'seed group'), the students have to discuss the article and their individual preparatory work's main outcomes. To support this activity, the students are asked to visually represent the structure of the paper's arguments in the form of a mind map.
3 Following this first group discussion, each student (now indicated as the 'expert', e.g. on paper 1) has to join a newly formed group ('post-seed' group), which includes experts on papers 2 and 3. Each expert has to briefly introduce to the other peers the article they analysed, presenting the main claim and supporting arguments. The expert can also show the mind map elaborated within the seed group discussion. After the first round of presentation, the other students can ask questions to each other about the papers, find convergences and divergences among the works and highlight the points of strength and weakness of each argument.
4 After this second group discussion, the tutor reconvenes everyone for the plenary session. With the whole class's inputs, they outline each paper's key points, emphasises the tensions and the concurring opinions, adds further insights from the literature, leads the discussion and encourages a fair debate among students.

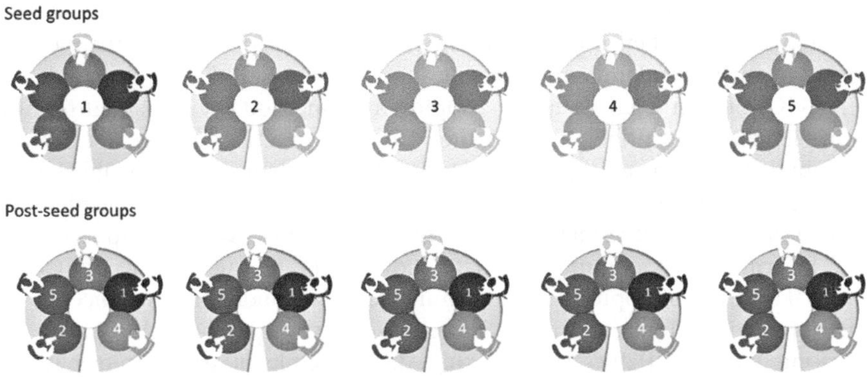

Figure 8.2 Papers and groups allocation in the jigsaw seminar. From top to bottom, representation of the seed groups and the post-seed groups, where the number indicates the paper.

This type of seminar is particularly interesting to perform with a law class because it allows students not only to acquire theoretical knowledge about one topic but also to train several legal skills, such as analytical, critical and communication abilities. The use of mind maps and graphs in such seminars can contribute to strengthening the above-mentioned skills. The visualisation exercise can help students 'see' the structure of a scholarly opinion, thus facilitating identifying the relevant aspects, such as the main theses and the hierarchy of arguments, comparing the different positions and discerning potential gaps or contradictions more easily.[17]

Legal design in action

The second block of the course is fully dedicated to developing a project in the field of legal design and is modelled on the legal design cycle successfully experimented in other Universities.[18] It integrates human-centred design and designerly thinking into legal studies, inviting students to create innovative services and solutions to prevent or solve legal problems.

The focus area of legal design labs varies across countries and research expertise: from access to justice to legal activism, from contract design to legal visualisation and legal tech. The specific approach taken at the EITLab derives from our research experience and the willingness to transfer this research-based knowledge immediately into teaching. This virtuous exchange is valuable not only for the students, who can access the latest developments in the field, but also for the whole research and academic environment: on the one hand, the lecturer can continue challenging their assumptions and research results with the students; on the other hand, being introduced to some basic research methodologies, the students will be more prepared to engage with their final dissertation.[19] Furthermore, getting in contact with the research context, they might 'test' their willingness to continue their career development in academia and consider applying for a PhD.

At UCLouvain legal design is adopted as a method for investigating how to implement legal principles (and their ratio) in practice.[20] More specifically, we found the design toolkit particularly valuable when the law establishes an information duty but leaves its concrete development to the obliged party. Design offers a set of principles, instruments, and processes for improving the way information is communicated to individuals, taking into account their needs. This kind of approach has been indirectly seconded, for instance, in the data protection domain. In its Guidelines on transparency, the Article 29 Working Party (WP29)[21] stressed that the principle of transparency in the GDPR is 'user-centric rather than legalistic'.[22] Thus, when providing information to the data subjects, if accountable controllers are

> uncertain about the level of intelligibility and transparency of the information and effectiveness of user interfaces/notices/policies etc., they can test these, for example, through mechanisms such as user panels, readability testing, formal and informal interactions and dialogue with industry groups, consumer advocacy groups and regulatory bodies, where appropriate, amongst other things.[23]

These tools and procedures are paradigmatic of the legal design cycle, which itself is modelled on the design process. The latter is variously presented in the literature, and several authors stress that the process should be adapted depending on the project.[24] Despite the use of slightly different models and frameworks,[25] the basic outline of the design process aimed at problem-solving can be represented in few iterative steps, as those popularised by the UK Design Council in the well-known 'double diamond' matrix: 1) Discover; 2) Define; 3) Develop; 4) Deliver.[26]

In approaching a project, the designer should first understand the problem, explore the situation from the target user's perspective, and investigate the state of the art (Discover). The results gathered from this phase are then conveyed in the definition of the problem and the outline of its concrete challenges (Define). Once the problem is identified, the designer has to explore a range of potential solutions to that, and develop and test them on a small-scale (Develop), finally refining and implementing the solution that proved to work (Deliver). The double diamond graphically represents such stages and the alternation between an expansive-thinking session (to investigate, understand and create as much as possible) and a synthesis session (definition of the problem, delivery of the outcome).[27] All of these stages are characterised by a set of methodologies (from brainstorming techniques to user journey maps and prototyping) to support the project's development.

This kind of design cycle has been subsumed, with adaptations, in the legal design practice. One of the first examples of adopting the design process in the legal field is the Stanford legal design lab, directed by Margaret Hagan.[28] The design cycle framework, used by the students and the fellows in the activities of the lab, is centred on a participatory methodology and structured around five main steps (Discovery–Scoping–Building–Experimenting–Evolving).[29] By integrating design methodologies into legal education, the Legal Design Lab pioneered a series of initiatives for policy and social change and is now focusing primarily in the field of access to justice.[30]

The second part of the EITLab ('Legal Design in Action') drew direct inspiration from this model. The module is organised in six stages, which also take into account what learning outcomes are reasonable to achieve given external constraints (credits, time and workload).

The 'Legal Design in Action' is the core part of the learning by doing exercise. It starts from a challenge, i.e. the legal problem on which the students are going to work for the rest of the course. Students are assisted by a team of interdisciplinary tutors (lawyers, designers, social scientists, etc.) during the legal project's development phases. The challenge is formulated by the teaching team, based on our research expertise, or presented by external partners who bring concrete issues they face in their practice (e.g. hidden advertisement by social media influencers, GDPR's data protection icons, provision of privacy notices by voice assistant technologies, understandability of privacy policies, etc.).[31]

The class is then divided into small working groups of 4–5 students, ensuring the gender and age balance, which begin investigating the legal and design aspects of the topic (phase 1—Discover). They investigate the legal framework applicable to their challenge, identifying the relevant legal provisions, interpreting them, and extracting the legal requirements to be taken into account. At the same time they investigate the design aspects of the challenge: Who is the potential target affected by the corresponding legal problem(s), and what is the state of the art (for instance, how the law—or social norms or technology—is already addressing the challenge). At this stage, they are introduced to some design tools, such as the 'persona', i.e. a

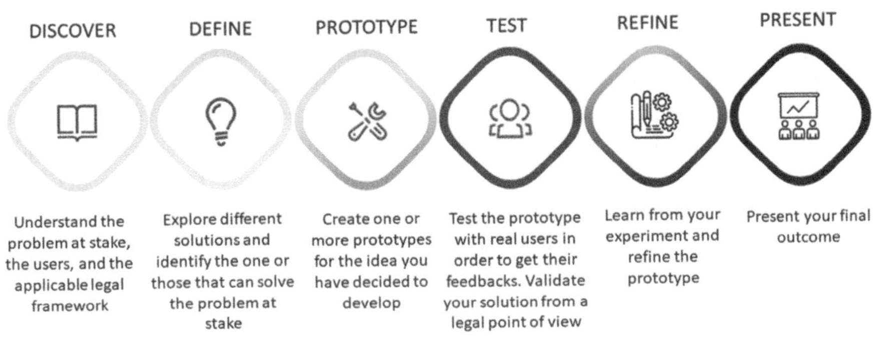

Figure 8.3 EITLab's Legal Design cycle.

realistic representation of the typical user of the product or technology to be tested, and the 'user journey', which is a map to visualise the persona experience when facing the legal challenge. These are examples of tools meant to favour empathy towards the people affected by the problem at stake. To complete their persona or user journey, the students are then introduced to quantitative and qualitative research. In particular, the focus is on the methodology for conducting interviews and observations.

All the data gathered in the 'Discover' phase is then used during the second step ('Define'). Here, the students are guided through strategies for defining the case's core aspects and, ultimately, their research question. Once this general framework is set, the groups engage in "ideas generation" using techniques such as brainwriting and brainstorming. As in the design process, the sparkle of creativity convergences into a moment of synthesis, where the teams will have to select the solution or the group of solutions that might be more promising in terms of efficacy, efficiency, user empowerment, legal compliance.

In the third phase ('Protoype') the groups learn how to develop the primer of their solutions, and, in phase 4 ('Test') how to set the experiment to verify whether their idea will work in practice or how it can be improved. Results of this phase are used to refine the prototype into something that can be piloted (phase 5—'Refine').

Finally, they receive training on argumentation and public speaking techniques, including for online formats, to prepare them for their final presentation before the exam commission (phase 6—'Present').

Methods of evaluation

Two formative assessments are used to support the students' metacognitive process and capability of self-reflection to involve them in their learning and evaluation journey.[32] The first type of assessment is an individual reflective report, where each student has to examine their learning experience and engage with each session's content. The second formative assessment is a group exercise leading to the redaction of the research notebook. The latter contains a brief report of the steps taken during the 'Legal Design in Action' and explains the decision taken. The notebook reflects a good practice adopted in labs and research teams: especially in long-term projects, it is important to be in the condition to easily trace back the data and motivations behind a certain research path. This procedure is a way not only to ensure accountability but also to speed up the retrieval of the relevant information when needed. Furthermore, the research notebook is a tool for the instructor to follow students' progress, see how they motivate certain choices and take on board critiques and suggestions during the regular feedback group sessions with the tutors.

The students are then graded based on two summative assessments. A written assignment, e.g. preparing a scientific blogpost, intends to evaluate the theoretical knowledge acquired during the first part of the course (Foundation of IT Law), the students' ability to perform research independently, and present legal arguments in a well-structured and persuasive way. The second assessment consists of a group presentation of the legal design solution at the end of the course. For this task, each team has to show the final result, but it must also guide the commission through their research experience. In particular, they should critically address the limitations of their project and outline the possible future lines of investigations, including long-term strategies for the product/service evaluation. In their final presentation, the students can also formulate recommendations and policy proposals based on the observations and preliminary results of their project.

Concluding remarks

In the university's safe environment, this kind of course allows students to discover and experiment with alternative ways to know and practise the law, mirroring what could be the experience in the professional context. To achieve this balance the EITLab uses a hybrid model that combines the acquisition of basic knowledge about the subject matter with a project-based approach. The latter proves to be particularly useful to gain multi-dimensional knowledge and skills, which are usually underdeveloped in the traditional law curriculum.[33] Through their project development, students learn and train a different set of abilities, such as empathy, teamwork and collaboration, time management, communication and presentation, self-discipline and self-motivation. The iterative process teaches them how to deal with critiques and build on them to improve their work. The interactions with experts in different fields and the seminars with visiting scholars also strengthen their networking skills.

The EITLab course does not have the ambition to form 'designers' nor 'empirical legal researchers', rather to introduce students to different methodological perspectives from design and the social sciences, and to help them understand how they can use them in their future career, whether they decide to become solicitors, judges, legal technologists, policy consultants, researchers, academics. Nor does the course intend to replace the traditional lecture-based courses, which still play an important role in legal education. Rather it aims at complementing the core law curriculum with an additional block to form the 'T-shaped' lawyer.

Notes

1 The publication of this chapter has been made possible by the EU's co-funding within the framework of the Erasmus+ Jean Monnet Program. The European Commission's support for the production of this publication does not constitute an endorsement of the contents, which reflect the views only of the authors, and the Commission cannot be held responsible for any use which may be made of the

information contained therein. We thank Helena Haapio for her generous support in mapping the legal design courses and initiatives in Finland.

2 Lecturer of IT Law and Regulation, School of Law, University of Aberdeen.

3 Professor of Law, UCLouvain and University Saint-Louis, Brussels. Avocat at the Brussels bar.

4 Jeff Giddings and Jacqueline Weinberg, 'Experiential Legal Education: Stepping Back to See the Future' in Catrina Denvir (ed), *Modernising Legal Education* (Cambridge University Press 2020); Ian Walden and Patrick Cahill, 'Skills Swap?' in Catrina Denvir (ed), *Modernising Legal Education* (Cambridge University Press 2020). With reference to the European projects, see, for example, the recent Erasmus+ Partnerships 'Modernising Legal Education', https://mele-erasmus.eu and 'DiGinLaw', https://diginlaw.com.

5 Richard E Susskind, *Tomorrow's Lawyers: An Introduction to Your Future* (Oxford University Press 2017). For an interesting development, see also the role of legal technologist that the Law Society of Scotland has recognised: https://www.lawscot.org.uk/members/career-growth/specialisms/areas-of-specialism/accredited-legal-technologist/.

6 Interestingly, a recent survey among solicitors in England and Wales shows that 40 per cent of the respondents are already working in multidisciplinary teams. See, Mari Sako, John Armour and Richard Parnham, 'Lawtech Adoption and Training. Findings from a Survey of Solicitors in England and Wales' (University of Oxford 2020) available at: https://www.law.ox.ac.uk/sites/files/oxlaw/oxford_lawtech_adoption_and_training_survey_report_18_march_2.pdf. Thus, it appears important to provide additional support for training students on teamwork and collaboration.

7 The European Commission has been advocating for this turn in higher education at least since 2009: 'Curricula should be "T-shaped": rooted in the specific academic discipline while at the same time interacting and cooperating with partners in other disciplines and sectors'. See, Communication from the Commission to the European Parliament, the Council, the European Economic and Social Committee and the Committee of the Regions—A new partnership for the modernisation of universities: the EU Forum for University Business Dialogue {SEC(2009) 423 SEC (2009) 424 SEC(2009) 425} /* COM/2009/0158 final, point 3.1. Many authors have also underlined the importance of the T-shaped model for Law Schools. See, Giovanni Pascuzzi, *Giuristi si diventa. Come riconoscere e apprendere le abilità proprie delle professioni legali* (2 edizione, Il Mulino 2013); R Amani Smathers, 'The 21st Century T-Shaped Lawyer' (2014) 40 ABA Law Practice Magazine 32; Václav Janeček, Rebecca Williams and Ewart Keep, 'Education for the Provision of Technologically Enhanced Legal Services' (2021) 40 Computer Law & Security Review 105519.

8 Anna Carpenter, 'Developing "NextGen" Lawyers through Project-Based Learning' in Catrina Denvir (ed), *Modernising Legal Education* (Cambridge University Press 2020); Janeček, Williams and Keep (n 7). Some law firms have already embedded a design mindset in their innovation programs. In 2017, Baker McKenzie announced the adoption of design thinking at a large-scale ('First Law Firm to Apply Design Thinking on Global Scale' (*Global Compliance News*, 12 April 2017), https://globalcompliancenews.com/first-law-firm-to-apply-design-thinking-on-global-scale-20170410/, accessed 18 March 2021. Many others are also offering legal design as a specific service to their clients, e.g. Dot in Finland (https://dot.legal), Amurabi in France (https://www.amurabi.eu/en/), LCA in Italy (https://www.lcalex.it).

9 See, for instance, the Legal Design Lab in Stanford (https://law.stanford.edu/organizations/pages/legal-design-lab/), the NuLawLab at the Northeastern University (https://www.nulawlab.org), the Comic Book Contract initiative at the University of Western Australia (https://www.comicbookcontracts.com), the course 'Legal

Innovation and Design' at the University of Newcastle—Australia (https://www.newcastle.edu.au/course/LAWS6116), the research group in 'Law, Technology, and Design Thinking' at the University of Lapland (https://www.ulapland.fi/FI/Kotisivut/Law,-Technology-and-Design-Thinking-Research-Group), the course "Legal Design" at the University of Vaasa (https://www.univaasa.fi/fi/opiskelijat/opinto-oppaat/kauppatieteiden-opinto-oppaat), the study module 'Legal Design and expertise' at Laurea, University of Applied Science—Finland (https://ops.laurea.fi/index.php/en/68096/en/209760).

10 www.eitlab.eu.

11 Paraphrasing Amanda Perry-Kessaris, 'Legal Design for Practice, Activism, Policy, and Research' (2019) 46 Journal of Law and Society 185. See also, CR Brunschwig, 'Visualisierung von Rechtsnormen—Legal Design [Visualization of Legal Norms]' (PhD Thesis, Doctoral Thesis Zürcher Studien zur Rechtsgeschichte 2001); Margaret Hagan, *Law by Design*, https://www.lawbydesign.co (evolving book since 2013); Gerlinde Berger-Walliser, Thomas D Barton and Helena Haapio, 'From Visualization to Legal Design: A Collaborative and Creative Process' (2017) 54 American Business Law Journal 347; Stefania Passera, *Beyond the Wall of Contract Text—Visualizing Contracts to Foster Understanding and Collaboration within and across Organisations* (Aalto University 2017); Helena Haapio and others, 'Legal Design Patterns for Privacy', *Data Protection/LegalTech Proceedings of the 21st International Legal Informatics Symposium IRIS* (2018); Marcelo Corrales, Mark Fenwick and Helena Haapio, 'Digital Technologies, Legal Design and the Future of the Legal Profession', *Legal Tech, Smart Contracts and Blockchain* (Springer 2019); Arianna Rossi and others, 'When Design Met Law: Design Patterns for Information Transparency' (2019) Droit de la Consommation = Consumenterecht 79; Michael Doherty, 'Comprehensibility as a Rule of Law Requirement: The Role of Legal Design in Delivering Access to Law' (2020) 8 Journal of Open Access to Law 1; Margaret Hagan, 'Legal Design as a Thing: A Theory of Change and a Set of Methods to Craft a Human-Centered Legal System' (2020) 36 Design Issues 3; Amanda Perry-Kessaris, 'Making Socio-Legal Research More Social by Design: Anglo-German Roots, Rewards, and Risks' (2020) 21 German Law Journal 1427; Colette R Brunschwig, 'Visual Law and Legal Design: Questions and Tentative Answers' (2021) Tagungsband des Internationalen Rechtsinformatik Symposions IRIS 179; Helena Haapio, Thomas D Barton and Marcelo Corrales Compagnucci, 'Legal Design for the Common Good: Proactive Legal Care by Design' in Corrales Compagnucci and others (eds), *Legal Design: Integrating Business, Design and Legal Thinking with Technology* (Edward Elgar 2021).

12 For an overview, see Perry-Kessaris (n 11).

13 On the pedagogical value of visualisation for legal education, see Colette R Brunschwig, 'On Visual Law: Visual Legal Communication Practices and Their Scholarly Exploration' in Erich Schweihofer and others (eds), *Zeichen und Zauber des Rechts: Festschrift für Friedrich Lachmayer* (Bern, Editions Weblaw 2014) 899; Elizabeth G Porter, 'Imagining Law: Visual Thinking Across the Law School Curriculum' (2018) 68 Journal of Legal Education 8; Vincenzo Zeno-Zencovich, 'Through a Lawyer's Eyes: Data Visualization and Legal Epistemology' in Cécile de Terwangne and others (eds), *Law, Norms and Freedoms in Cyberspace* (Larcier 2018); Emily Allbon, 'Changing Mindsets: Encouraging Law Teachers to Think beyond Text' (2019) 7 Journal of Open Access to Law 1.

14 On flipped classrooms and their positive effects on the learning experience, see Jalal Nouri, 'The Flipped Classroom: For Active, Effective and Increased Learning—Especially for Low Achievers' (2016) 13 International Journal of Educational Technology in Higher Education 1; Carl Reidsema and others, *The Flipped Classroom Practice and Practices in Higher Education* (Springer Singapore 2017); Yanjie

Song and Manu Kapur, 'How to Flip the Classroom—"Productive Failure or Traditional Flipped Classroom" Pedagogical Design?' (2017) 20 Educational Technology & Society 292; Michael Sailer and Maximilian Sailer, 'Gamification of In-Class Activities in Flipped Classroom Lectures' (2021) 52 British Journal of Educational Technology 75.

15 Rossana Ducato is thankful to Professor Anne-Lise Sibony for having introduced her to this technique. The jigsaw seminar has been adopted in the EITLab course after participating in a session specifically tailored for law students and organised at Sibony's course 'Law and Behavioural Science' (KULeuven, academic year 2019/2020). On the method for jigsaw activities in general, see Nathan Hensley, 'Exploring Complexities of Energy Options Through a Jigsaw Activity' in Loren B Byrne (ed), *Learner-Centered Teaching Activities for Environmental and Sustainability Studies* (Springer International Publishing 2016).

16 The papers were Sandra Wachter, Brent Mittelstadt and Luciano Floridi, 'Why a Right to Explanation of Automated Decision-Making Does Not Exist in the General Data Protection Regulation' (2017) 7 International Data Privacy Law 76; Gianclaudio Malgieri and Giovanni Comandé, 'Why a Right to Legibility of Automated Decision-Making Exists in the General Data Protection Regulation' (2017) International Data Privacy Law 243; Lilian Edwards and Michael Veale, 'Enslaving the Algorithm: From a "Right to an Explanation" to a "Right to Better Decisions"?' (2018) 16 IEEE Security & Privacy 46.

17 Although in a different sector (policy drafting), legal provisions' visualisation proved to help spot gaps or contradictions. While preparing the White Paper 'Toward a New Format for Canadian Legislation. Using Graphics Design Principles and Methods to Improve Public Access to Law" (2000), Berman and his team discovered some inconsistencies in the legislation thanks to the preparation of flow chart diagrams of some of the statutes. As reported by Stefania Passera and Helena Haapio, 'Visual Law: What Lawyers Need to Learn from Information Designers' (*VoxPopuLII*, 2013), https://blog.law.cornell.edu/voxpop/2013/05/15/visual-law-what-lawyers-need-to-learn-from-information-designers, accessed 19 March 2021.

18 See, for instance, https://law.stanford.edu/organizations/pages/legal-design-lab/.

19 In Belgium, the final dissertation is a mandatory step to complete the Law Degree.

20 See, for instance, http://www.rosels.eu/research/research-project-iop/; http://www.rosels.eu/research/proseco/; http://www.rosels.eu/research/shine/. We are expanding such a perspective, including other notable examples coming from speculative design and foresight studies.

21 The WP29, now European Data Protection Board (EDPB), is an independent EU body formed by representatives from all the national data protection authorities and the European Data Protection Supervisor. The EDPB promotes the consistent application of the GDPR, and to this end, it can issue guidelines, recommendations, best practices, and opinions. See, Articles 63–76 GDPR.

22 WP29, 'Guidelines on Transparency under Regulation 2016/679 (Wp260rev.01)' (2018), point 4.

23 ibid. point 9. See, also point 25.

24 See, for example, Marc Stickdorn and others, *This Is Service Design Doing: Applying Service Design Thinking in the Real World* (O'Reilly Media, Inc 2018).

25 The framework may vary from three main steps (Kathryn Best, *Design Management: Managing Design Strategy, Process and Implementation* (AVA publishing 2006)) to five or seven (see, for example, the Stanford d.school process: empathise-define-ideate-prototype-test, https://web.stanford.edu/~mshanks/MichaelShanks/files/509554.pdf).

26 Jonathan Ball, 'The Double Diamond: A Universally Accepted Depiction of the Design Process' (*Design Council*, 1 October 2019), https://www.designcouncil.org.

uk/news-opinion/double-diamond-universally-accepted-depiction-design-process, accessed 16 March 2021.

27 However, the design cycle framework does not have to be interpreted as a rigid and linear model. As Buchanan pointed out (expanding on Rittel's work), design deals primarily with the so-called 'wicked problems'. The latter are indetermined problems, i.e. issues with no definitive conditions or limits. The indeterminacy, however, does not imply that the object of design remains undetermined: it can be made concrete and specific through working hypothesis for exploration and further development (what Buchanan calls "placements". See, Richard Buchanan, 'Wicked Problems in Design Thinking' (1992) 8 Design Issues 5).

28 https://law.stanford.edu/organizations/pages/legal-design-lab/.

29 As described in Margaret Hagan, 'Design Comes to the Law School' in Catrina Denvir (ed), *Modernising Legal Education* (Cambridge University Press 2020).

30 http://justiceinnovation.law.stanford.edu/courses/prototyping-access-to-justice-courses/. See, also: Margaret Hagan, 'A Human-Centered Design Approach to Access to Justice: Generating New Prototypes and Hypotheses for Interventions to Make Courts User-Friendly' (2018) 6 Indiana Journal of Law and Social Equality 199; Daniel W Bernal and Margaret D Hagan, 'Redesigning Justice Innovation: A Standardised Methodology' (2020) 16 Stanford Journal of Civil Rights & Civil Liberties 335.

31 http://eitlab.eu/legal-design-challenges/.

32 The template for both formative assessments is provided by the instructors in advance.

33 On the relevance of project-based learning to acquire multidimensional knowledge and skills, see Carpenter (n 8).

9 Making a racism reporting tool

A legal design case study

Andy Unger[1] *and Lucia Otoyo*[2]

This chapter describes a project by student volunteers to build a racism reporting tool for a local charity, The Monitoring Group (TMG).[3] It grew out of two final year modules at London South Bank University that are taught and assessed together: Law and Technology, which we have been running for law students since 2018/2019, and ICT Project Management in Practice which is run for Computing Sciences students. The modules aim to introduce students to the increasing impact of technology on the professions and professional careers, particularly in the field of legal services, and to help them develop and demonstrate new core skills that are likely to be in demand from employers. In the first few weeks, we explore LawTech, Legal Design and Project Management. Students engage in a short design project, rethinking how to present social media contracts to users. They then work in multi-disciplinary teams to design a digital Access to Justice resource for a real client. To date these have included members of our Legal Advice Clinic[4] team, as well as local lawyers, charities and organisations. Students are assessed by an individual piece of self-reflection entitled Careers, Skills and Personal Development Planning; and a group work report, which includes a recorded demonstration of the working prototype of their proposed resource.[5]

It has always been our ambition to see potentially viable prototypes taken on and developed for use in the local community, but the Law and Technology module is too short for this to be a realistic outcome. The volunteer project for TMG that we describe below was our first step towards realising our goal. In the long run, we hope to establish a LawTech clinic to create further opportunities for our students and support for local access to justice initiatives.

The project

The Monitoring Group is a grassroots organisation established in Southall in the early 1980s by community campaigners and lawyers who wished to challenge the growth of racism in the locality. It has grown to become a national anti-racist charity that promotes civil rights. Their aims are: to promote good race relations; to advance race relations by means of education and awareness

DOI: 10.4324/9780429021411-10

raising; and to relieve the needs of those who are distressed or suffering violence or harassment. They specialise in 'family-led empowerment and justice campaigns' which focus on casework, research and campaigns, including helping the families of, for example, Kuldip Singh Sekon, Ricky Reel, Michael Menson, Stephen Lawrence, Zahid Mubarek and Victoria Climbie.[6]

The Law Division of London South Bank University has worked with TMG for a number of years, including hosting joint conferences. At one such conference, in October of 2018, which focused on State Racism, Collusion and Resistance,[7] we agreed to explore developing a tool to enable victims to report incidents of racism to the TMG online. Presently, TMG receives over 1,000 calls a year to its Help Line from people suffering racial violence, religious hatred, sexual violence and state neglect or misconduct. They do not have the resources to staff the helpline 24 hours a day, 7 days a week and are aware that many incidents go unreported and unaddressed. So, we agreed that an online reporting tool would be useful.

As an initial step, two senior Monitoring Group staff members, Suresh Grover and Dorothea Jones, volunteered to act as clients for groups of students taking the Law and Technology module. Their groups were asked to develop a racism reporting prototype for their assessed project work. Students consulted them to understand the needs of potential users and to test potential designs for the proposed reporting tool. After the students submitted their work, the projects were reviewed by TMG and it was agreed that together we had a good understanding of what was needed.

The team

In December 2019, we began the process of recruiting a group of student volunteers to help build a Minimum Viable Product (MVP) for The Monitoring Group to adopt, test and develop further. Students were invited to submit a one-page application letter outlining their motivation, skills and experience. Completion of the Law and Technology module was not a prerequisite. From those applications, Lucia and Andy recruited three law students and three computing students. The three law students were Gloria Feudjo-Tepie, Victoria Heidt and Jasmine Upton and they worked on content and design. The three computing students were Juan Carlos Blanco Delgado, who was the technical mentor and advisor, Nasir Cujaj, who was responsible for the frontend development, and Vittorio Rinaldo, who was responsible for the backend development.

We were also very fortunate to recruit Alex Hamilton from Radiant Law[8] as a mentor. From the teaching team, Andy Unger, who knew the client and their problem well, acted as an internal client and Lucia Otoyo was the Scrum master/project coordinator.

The approach

We used an 'agile' project management framework known as Scrum[9] for our project. The goal of this framework is to promote flexibility and to allow the design process to continue throughout the lifetime of the product's development, incorporating regular reviews by the team and the clients. This was necessary for our project because, although we knew what we wanted to build, many questions about how best to achieve our goals remained unanswered. The project was planned as a series of fortnightly Scrum sprints—that is, development iterations—each aiming to develop and test a selection of the product's features. We held weekly internal mid-sprint meetings to review progress and solve problems, and fortnightly end-of-sprint meetings with clients to get their feedback. One of the key Scrum practices is the end-of-sprint 'retrospective' meeting, during which the whole team takes part in discussing what went well and what can be improved going forward into the next sprint. We also had the commitment and availability of all internal team members to work in close collaboration, which is the key requirement for this approach to work successfully.

Since not all team members were familiar with this way of working, Lucia trained us on Scrum methodology at the outset and then continuously coached on Scrum practices during the project. We started with weekly meetings at LSBU and then moved online when the coronavirus pandemic intervened. Our main tools were MS Teams for online meetings, Google Docs for sharing documents, WhatsApp for instant communication, Jira[10] for managing the project development, Easy Retro[11] for weekly sprint retrospective meetings and MockFlow[12] for creating the designs. Tasks were created and assigned to team members during weekly Scrum planning meetings based on team members' skills. Each team member updated progress on these tasks during each sprint on the JIRA board. We met at the end of each sprint and every team member demonstrated what they had developed or produced and feedback was provided which then fed into the next sprint. At the end of the meeting we held the sprint retrospective.

The process

To begin with, we reviewed our understanding of the requirements of good legal design, particularly by reference to the work of Margaret Hagan and her three fundamental design principles: be user-centred, be experimental and be intentional. She outlines a five-stage design process: discover; synthesize; build; test; and evolve (see Law By Design[13] and Design Comes to Law School).[14] To be user-centred, legal designers are encouraged to engage extensively with stakeholders at the discovery stage and to create detailed user personas for a range of specific imagined users at the synthesis stage. The consequent design brief is then explored and experimented and finally built in an iterative way, allowing for thorough testing with users and planned evolution, based upon practical operational experience and feedback. We also reviewed the design work of the Law and Technology students who had already worked on a TMG racism reporting tool for their assessed coursework. These students kindly assigned their intellectual property rights to TMG and allowed us to benefit from their work.

We were then ready for an initial meeting with Suresh Grover, TMG Director, to establish the project brief. Suresh spoke directly on behalf of potential TMG advisors and administrators and indirectly, based on his experience, on behalf of members of the public who might use the tool to report racist incidents. Suresh first helped the team to understand the typical concerns and potential vulnerability of people who seek help from TMG, including fears for their personal safety, anxiety about provoking further incidents, previous negative experiences with the police,[15] language barriers and, sometimes, irregular immigration status.[16] Consequently, Suresh explained, it was important to establish that TMG can be trusted and will deal with the issue promptly. He identified key messages to communicate, particularly: we understand your problem; we want to ensure you are safe; we understand it is not your fault; even if it is minor, we understand the impact; and, we will do everything we can do to help you.

Secondly, Suresh emphasised that the proposed tool is intended to supplement the TMG office hours Help Line and will be used for out of office hours emergencies, as well as more general advice and emotional and legal support. He advised that in an emergency, it is best to ask the minimum number of questions. Based on TMG practice, the key initial questions to be asked are 'Are you safe?' and 'Have you reported the incident to the police?'. Victims in immediate danger needed to be advised to contact the police immediately. He also explained that, as is common in the advice sector, vulnerable clients may fail to continue to seek help if their initial effort fails for whatever reason.[17] For this reason, all users need to be given an option to leave their minimum contact details and to request TMG to get back to them urgently, rather than making a full online report.

These insights led the team to identify the following 'minimum viable product' features and associated 'user stories':[18] a client can report an incident out of hours; TMG will be alerted to incoming reports so they can respond as soon as possible; a client can access initial information and advice online; TMG can allocate reports to advisors to follow up; and, the developed system has to be secure, as TMG has been the subject to cyber-attacks in the past. The following desirable additional features were also identified: TMG can search and compile reports from the same client to be used as an incident diary to assist reporting and prosecution in cases of repeated acts of harassment and abuse and TMG can analyse report data collected to identify trends and hotspots of racist activity.

The detailed user stories we created are shown below (Table 9.1). Each user story captures the role of a particular type of user, what they want to achieve and why. Once we started discussing these user stories it became evident that as a team we didn't have a common understanding of how the key function – report incident – should work, so we undertook a group exercise led by Victoria involving Post-it® notes and discussion[19] to establish our first version of the process and required information needed for this feature (see Figure 9.1 left).

Table 9.1 Minimum viable product user stories

User	*Stories*
Victims of Racism	I can call 999 through the app. I can call TMG through the app. I can complete a short contact form (out of hours). I can submit a detailed racism report (including video/picture). I can read the latest TMG news/posts. I can get online resources (list of sites and their support type). I can get online help (content provided by TMG).
TMG Staff	I can update the latest news report. (Create, Read, Update, Delete) I can delete/approve forum posts. I can update the online help section. (Create, Read, Update, Delete) I can see report stats. (Number of cases, regions, timetable etc.) I can filter the reports. After Report Submission: Automatic email is sent to the 'victim' with Case ID. Send a link to guide users to "self-service page". TMG receives a message that a case is submitted. TMG team reads and contacts the victim. TMG updates case information for that victim. After Emergency report submission: TMG team is notified immediately. TMG calls back the victim asap.

The next step was to start thinking of how the information will be organised within the system, in particular the page layout. The first draft was made by Nasir during one of our meetings (Figure 9.1 right), which we then revised over several iterations until we decided on the number of pages we needed and roughly what information we wanted to present on each.

Having had a good enough understanding of the key features and the page layout, we started to create User Interface (UI) designs. Our first few versions

Figure 9.1 Clarifying the report racism feature (left) and discussing the first version of the page layout (right).

were created using Google slides, but then we switched to using a professional UI planning tool MockFlow,[20] which allowed us to use pre-built components (such as material design) that can be re-used by our development team and thus speed up the implementation. Figure 9.2 shows early designs of the report racism feature which underwent several feedback and review iterations. Gloria took these with her on a Black Lives Matter march to get instant feedback from fellow protestors and wrote up all their responses in a Design Report (Table 9.2) which we shared with TMG.

What we built

The application we have built allows users to make detailed reports of racist incidents or simply request TMG to contact them. They are alerted to contact the police if they are in immediate danger. TMG can monitor and manage

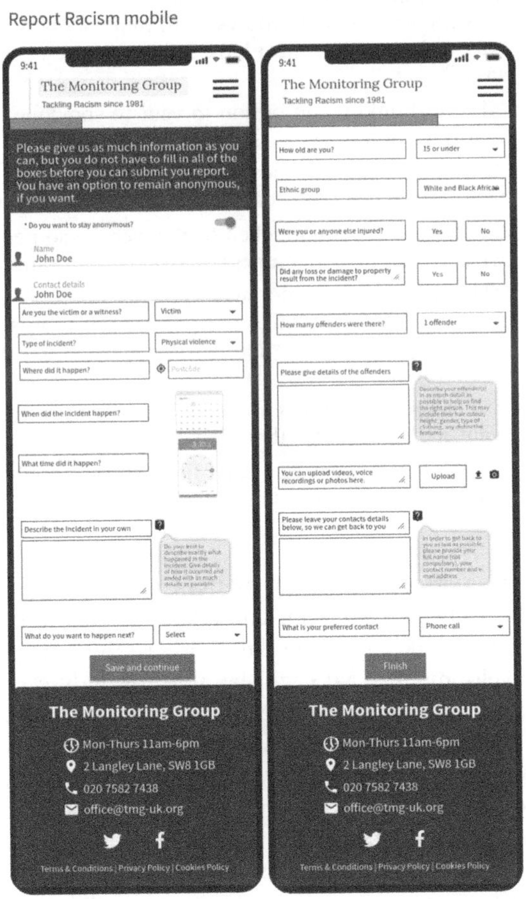

Figure 9.2 Early design of the 'report racism' feature.

Table 9.2 Examples of feedback from Black Lives Matters protestors extracted from the Design Report

Protestors	*Feedback*
Helena, 17	"… the best thing you could make is a website that tells you other people's experiences and from that you can see how they dealt with it and go from there. I am tired of people who do not look like me telling me how to handle situations as they do not know how it feels like to be in my position."
Joelle, 44	"… this website would need to ensure that if I report to them, they do something about it."
Jess, 20	"… like now I have reported our abuse now what? What will you do with my data, I'm tired of speaking and not being heard."
Mo, 19	"… offer useful legal information when I do report to you. That's important."
Jay, 21	"I would like a website that if I report I can also browse through valuable information. I do not know my rights and laws and lawyers are expensive. If you want to make a good app you will find a way to help people who have suffered abuse to know what steps to take."
JC, 12	"There should be an option to vent to someone, but also … a report section."
Nathan, 19	"I think it would be nice to have a website where we can share our views on things that's happened and also comment on others."
Hanniyah, 19	"… have helplines attached to the website so people can know where to go if the comment section is not doing it."
Justine, 21	"The main goal should be to show users on the website that other people are going through what they went through. On Twitter you can find people discussing their experiences but they are lost in the other topics."
Helena, 17	"… looks professional and nice but I don't really get what you want me to do other than donate to the charities."
Hanniyah, 19	"… it's very triggering I can't lie. I think it needs to be more about helping us deal with racism than give reasons for us to be angry."

reports. They are alerted to urgent matters and can allocate and review reports for further action. TMG can compile individual reports into a log of incidents for anyone making a complaint or seeking a legal remedy. In the next stage of development, TMG will be able to analyse reports to identify significant patterns and trends of racist incidents over time and across the country.

The Scrum methodology we followed supported early and iterative development. As soon as we had a good enough understanding of the requirements, our technical team started the technical review to research and select suitable technologies to implement the system. It was decided to build a progressive web application (as opposed to a native mobile app) that will allow users to access the site on any device without the need to download it, which was an important consideration for our user demographic. The application was split into two main parts from the development point of view. Firstly, there is an outward-facing frontend, built using React.js[21] with Material UI React Framework, for members of the public to submit reports, access information and get online support (see Figure 9.3).[22] Secondly, there is an inward-facing backend, originally built using WordPress CMS[23] and MySQL[24] database, for TMG administrators to view and manage submitted reports. Each of these parts was responsible for different key features of the application, but all of them were linked, so close collaboration between the developers of each part was essential. WordPress was initially selected to

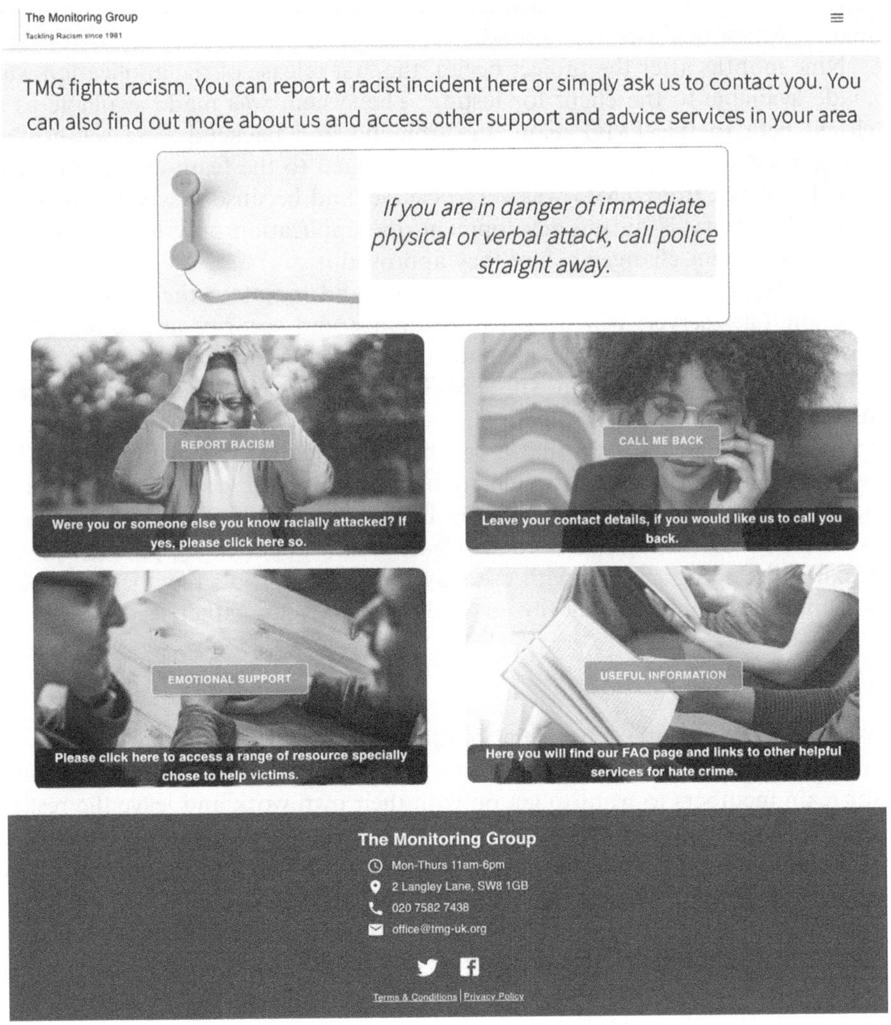

Figure 9.3 'Frontend' desktop view of the racism reporting tool homepage.

develop the backend due to its out of the box features that allow for fast development. However, after several sprints we realised it did not have enough flexibility to allow us to implement the required features to an acceptable standard of user experience. There were too many compromises we had to make because we couldn't design and label the frontend exactly as we wanted. Juan Carlos, our most experienced developer, undertook another technical review to find a suitable alternative. On his advice, we chose Directus v8, a Data-First Headless CMS & API Management platform,[25] which proved to have the flexibility and all the required features to implement the backend. Once we completed the backend implementation, the founder of Directus asked us, as one of the active contributors to the new release of Directus, for permission to mention our project within one of their testimonials,[26] which made us very proud.

Nine months after the project began, the first release of the application was made available to the client for testing. The system was made available as a closed beta to the TMG team, the frontend and backend were self-hosted using a VPN as a docker-machine that belonged to the team during the project. Feedback from TMG was very positive, and because they were involved at regular intervals during development, the application only required minor editorial content changes before they approved it.

Alex Hamilton has allowed us to deploy and maintain the backend on a Radiant Law server, which provides stability and security and saves TMG costs. The application is now a standalone system.

After further consultation with TMG and Alex, we decided to undertake a further reimplementation, this time of the frontend. We decided to use form.io[27] instead of React.js, so that it can be integrated directly within the TMG website. This decision was made to help improve the user experience and avoid visitor confusion by having two different sites with overlapping content. At the time of writing, the second release is still under development. We are seeking direct engagement with users by asking grass roots members of TMG to submit test reports using this first release so we can gather feedback.

Lessons learned

We learnt the value and potential of intentional legal design and good teamwork and project management. It is important to gently resist any tendency for team members to want to get on with their own work and leave the rest to others. Everyone needs to be aware of what everyone else is doing, otherwise you may end up with difficult problems when you come to assemble the application from its parts. Our biggest problem, inevitably for a volunteer project, was time. The project lasted over 9 months, and throughout that time the students had significant work, study and family commitments, quite apart from the stress and disruption of the pandemic. At a certain point, we had to recommit to following the agile Scrum methodology because whenever someone skipped reporting on their progress, we found ourselves drifting, sometimes in the sense of not making progress but often in terms of drifting apart, meaning that we all ended up working on slightly different projects. Not only was there a tendency to design/build what was easy rather than what was needed, but it became clear several times that we were all working to our own personal templates of what the tool would look like and do. In hindsight, despite our best intentions, we rushed the discovery stage of the design process.[28] This was in part because the onset of the coronavirus pandemic prevented a planned visit to observe a TMG advice session and in part because limited time led us to rely on Suresh's experience rather than investigate further ourselves. In the end, we do not think this impacted negatively on our final design, but greater time spent involving the whole team in the creation of user personas might have helped to prevent the problem of us all working towards slightly different visions of both what the tool was for and how it would work. To address this, we appointed Andy as the internal client to speak for TMG when they were not present, and Juan Carlos as a mentor/supervisor of the technical team. Scrum methodology facilitates and encourages this kind of intervention through retrospectives and the flexible allocation of roles for each sprint. The most encouraging lesson was that none of us could have built the tool on our own; it is a product of our combined work, expertise and creativity and a testament to the power and importance of teamwork, greatly assisted by agile methodology.

Conclusion

For us the project has been a success and encourages us to continue with our ambition to involve students in building LawTech resources for use in the local community. Initial feedback from TMG is also very positive but we will not really know if the tool is useful until it has been used and tested by TMG and users in real cases. We were very grateful to receive the support of Alex Hamilton at Radiant Law, who not only gave us valuable advice and feedback but stepped in at the end to solve some key problems in setting up the tool in a safe, sustainable and affordable way by giving us access to the time and resources of the firm. Feedback from our volunteers has been very positive. They were very impressed with the work of TMG and were glad of the opportunity to contribute to their fight against racism. They developed a deeper understanding of the importance of design, project management, communication and teamworking skills and the impact of technology on access to justice and legal services. They enjoyed the creativity and fun of teamworking and missed our weekly meetings once the coronavirus pandemic forced us to meet online. Finally, they have built something they are proud of and can include in their career portfolios.

Notes

1 Associate Professor of Law and Head of the Law Division, London South Bank University.

2 Senior Lecturer and Deputy Head of the Computer Science and Informatics Division at London South Bank University.
3 See The Monitoring Group website, http://www.tmg-uk.org/.
4 For more information about the LSBU LAC, see https://www.lsbu.ac.uk/study/study-at-lsbu/our-schools/law-and-social-sciences/subjects/law/legal-advice-clinic.
5 For more information about the module, see Legal education meets computer science: an interdisciplinary approach to teaching law, Chapter in K Gledhill and A Thanaraj, *Teaching Legal Education in the Digital Age* (Routledge 2020).
6 See The Monitoring Group website, http://www.tmg-uk.org/.
7 http://www.tmg-uk.org/state-racism-collusion-resistance/.
8 Radiant Law specialise in applying LawTech solutions to commercial contracting, see their website for more information, https://radiantlaw.com/.
9 See https://www.scrumguides.org/ and https://www.atlassian.com/agile/scrum.
10 For project management, see https://www.atlassian.com/software/jira.
11 Formerly FunRetro, for our weekly retrospective reviews of our progress, see, https://easyretro.io/.
12 To visualise and collaborate on our frontend designs, see https://www.mockflow.com/.
13 See Hagan, M., Law by Design – https://www.lawbydesign.co/
14 See Hagan, M. Design Comes to The Law School in Denvir, C. (Ed), Modernising Legal Education (2020), Cambridge University Press.
15 The HMICFRS Report Hate Crime: What Do Victims Tell Us (2018) reported that victims would like the police to be better at recognising hate crime, to be better trained in dealing with it and to be provided with clear and accessible information about support services. See https://www.justiceinspectorates.gov.uk/hmicfrs/wp-content/uploads/hate-crime-what-do-victims-tell-us.pdf (accessed 19 February 2021).
16 See also, Challenge it, Report it, Stop it: The Government's Plan to Tackle Hate Crime (March 2012), para 3.2, review of reasons victims are reluctant to report hate crime. See https://assets.publishing.service.gov.uk/government/uploads/system/uploads/attachment_data/file/97849/action-plan.pdf (accessed 19 February 2021).
17 See for example Pleasance, P., Balmer, N. & Sandefuron, J., Paths to Justice: A Past, Present and Future Roadmap, Report prepared under a grant from the Nuffield Foundation (AJU/39100), August 2013 – https://www.nuffieldfoundation.org/sites/default/files/files/PTJ%20Roadmap%20NUFFIELD%20Published.pdf
18 See, for example, Agile Alliance: What are User Stories – https://www.agilealliance.org/glossary/user-stories/
19 As recommended by Wavelength Law and others – see https://www.wavelength.law/blog/legaldesign3
20 https://www.mockflow.com/
21 See https://reactjs.org/
22 See https://material-ui.com/
23 See https://en-gb.wordpress.org/
24 See https://www.mysql.com/
25 https://directus.io/
26 See https://directus.io/open-source/
27 https://www.form.io/
28 See section 3. Design Process for Lawyers in Hagan, M., Law by Design – https://www.lawbydesign.co/

10 Teaching comic book contracting

Camilla Baasch Andersen[1]

Introduction

This chapter introduces a unique design-based method of teaching and assessing students' abilities to engage in collaborative contract innovation, which emerged out of the Comic Contracting Project at the University of Western Australia.

For the past four years, I have had the privilege of being one of the pioneers at the forefront of innovations in contract visualisation as part of the Comic Contracting Project at UWA. This project aims to improve contract law and its practices by helping industry to create new approaches to humanising legal services with the inclusion of images, and it has generated many fascinating lessons especially around the different perspectives that disciplines offer on law, the importance of diversity in skills sets and much, MUCH more. The power of visuals in this innovative area of law is becoming better understood through ground-breaking work carried out by scholars such as Stefania Passera, Helena Haapio, Collette Brunschwig and others.[2] The Comic Contracting project has not only contributed to this emerging knowledge around comprehension, engagement and perceptions of visualised contracts,[3] but also provided a number of methods for developing specific behavioural drivers with visuals in the creation of these contracts.[4]

As the Comic Book Contracts project took off and began to change many aspects of law and lawyering in Australia,[5] fostering a new industry of visual contract services[6] and even gaining recognition by being exhibited in the Queensland Supreme Court,[7] I lost focus on one important aspect of innovation—namely, teaching it to our students. The project findings were shared in multiple conference presentations in a small teaching pack, but it was not until the 2020 redesign of the UWA Business Law in Practice unit (hereinafter affectionately referred to as BLIP) that the project moved beyond teaching students *about* the project and began to share sufficient methodologies to allow students to try their hand at contract innovation themselves. BLIP is a final year compulsory unit on the Business Law Major undergraduate programme at UWA. It focuses on developing students' abilities to apply knowledge and skills to solve a series of specific portfolio challenges. These

DOI: 10.4324/9780429021411-11

challenges are addressed from the perspective of fictitious commercial entities which students design and role play running throughout the semester. They are assessed both on their ability to meet the challenges as a group, and on individual reflections on the challenges. This combination of assessment allows insight into their applied knowledge and personal engagement with the individual portfolios. There are five portfolios throughout the semester, the third which requires students to design an innovative contract format for a crucial aspect of their imagined business. The following sections describe that challenge, including underpinning resources, and the responses from students. First, however, a brief exploration of the power of visuals in legal practice and legal education.

The power of visuals in contracting and in teaching

Effective communication is a corner stone both for effective legal practices and for effective legal education. It is well-established in education research that using pictures to illustrate a text strongly improves comprehension. According to Levin and Mayer,[8] there are seven principles underpinning the effectiveness of visually enhanced comprehension. In summary, pictures make the text more: focused, by directing a reader's attention; concise or compact, in the sense that 'a picture is worth a thousand words'; concrete, due to their representational function; coherent, because they organize information; comprehensible, in the sense that they facilitate interpretation; correspondent, in that they tend to relate unfamiliar text to a reader's prior knowledge; and easy to remember, because they assist the mnemonic function. Multiple studies have demonstrated that individuals typically learn better from a combination of text and pictures, compared to text alone.[9] For example, Eitel et al. have found that the global spatial information that is extracted from a picture may be used as a mental scaffold to help better facilitate comprehension and mental model constructions.[10]

Focusing on a legal context, Passera et al. compared levels of comprehension between traditional, text-only contracts, and a version of the contract that included diagrams to complement the text. They found that when diagrams were integrated into contracts, there was an increase in both speed and comprehension in the results, and that this benefit was consistent with both native and non-native English speakers.[11] Likewise, two year longitudinal psychometric surveys completed as part of the Comic Contracting Project demonstrated the efficacy of visuals when compared to text based contracts in three main categories: comprehension, engagement and perception (see Table 10.1). In all three categories, users demonstrated a significant preference for visual contacts across all age groups and socioeconomic groups. As will be seen below, these insights served as an important point of reference in designing the teaching that underpinned Portfolio Three.

Despite the overpowering evidence above, law has not generally been very good at embracing the power of visuals in its own professional communication.

Table 10.1 Data from the Comic Contracting Project, UWA Law School, funded by Aurecon

	Text	*Comic book contract*	*Weighted % difference*	*Points difference*
Total	61.75 (68.61%)	72.49 (80.54%)	+ 11.93	+ 10.74
Comprehension	20.95 (69.83%)	23.70 (79%)	+ 9.17	+ 2.75
Engagement	20.80 (69.33%)	24.77 (82.57%)	+ 13.24	+ 3.97
Perception	20.01 (66.70%)	24.56 (81.87%)	+ 15.17	+ 4.55

However, in legal education, it is increasingly accepted that a combination of many different forms of communication come together to form effective frameworks for legal understanding.[12] For example, Skead and Offer note that 'effective communication is an exercise in aural and visual multi-tasking and requires the identification and interpretation of the explicit and implicit messages embedded in the "larger-than-life communication" of both the sender and the receiver'[13]; and the Law School at UWA has long been engaged in visual teaching and learning.[14]

Teaching and assessing visual contract innovation

As part of an undergraduate 'capstone' unit, the innovative contracting challenge known as Portfolio Three had to include a combination of independent research and more structured content, such as required reading, lectures, workshops and tutorials.

We had hoped to run workshops face to face and to encourage smaller group work face to face but, because of the ongoing COVID19 pandemic, we were restricted to using online platforms throughout most of the teaching period. This forced us to rethink the nature of the student collaborations and, interestingly, to redesign the unit again in light of our experience. For example, we are eliminating the larger group workshops for future years, and focusing solely on smaller group deliveries, which were much better received by students both online and in the (rare) instances of face-to-face teaching.

Teaching was provided via pre-recorded lectures—a pandemic-initiated shift which will be retained in future; live online workshops—to be replaced with face-to-face as soon as possible; and, when conditions made it possible, mixed online and face-to-face small group tutorial 'consultations' focusing the fictitious entities. The initial lecture consisted of a reminder of contract law basics that they had covered in their first year. Subsequent shorter lectures were supported by PowerPoint slides with embedded audio emphasising key messages. The first sets of lectures set out the context of innovation, contracting and business; later lectures focused on the current issues of concern in contract law and some possible innovative solutions. The challenge for their entities was entirely structured around having to design an innovative contract. The outcome was extremely gratifying.

The following sections set out the key messages which students responded to in relation to embracing the unique challenge, and sets out the main material used to communicate the messages.

Step 1: I told them law was broken

After four years of seeing the impact of my own research, this was not difficult to do. I deliberately tailored the material and the online lecture in order to provoke them, making clear that I was being overly dramatic—but I maintained that I was only visualising what they already knew, emphasizing experience-based learning.

The message was pressed home with bespoke images illustrating the downsides of using legalese in a modern society, as well as with academic and contemporary sources. Teaching and learning was structured around the key themes of engagement, comprehension and perception from the research findings set out in Table 10.1. However, those themes were translated it into experiences: engagement was translated into actually reading contracts, comprehension into actually understanding them and perception into actually liking them. In this way the assessment was transformed into a subjective examination of their own attitudes to contracts. Figure 10.1 shows images used to discuss the theme of broken law, some of which originated at the 2017 Comic Contracting conference,[15] couched in questions about engagement, comprehension and perception.

Audio embedded in the slides gave examples and in depth explanations of the problem—including prompts for the students to think honestly about how often they did not read their own contracts. A poll was taken in the first online workshop on zoom, showing that the vast majority of students were willing to admit they often did not read but simply agreed or signed. Their willingness to be frank was (according to several admissions in reflective logs) reinforced by the pop-culture references in articles such as Hunt's article on Amazon terms,[16] and Hern's iconic article on how he nearly died reading all the small print in his life.[17]

Interestingly, however, students reported in their reflective logs that although the subjective self-interrogation was effective in making them re-think the efficacy of traditional contracts, it was the so-called 'Herod clauses' which really shook them. A 'Herod clause' is inserted in a contract, usually humorously or for research purposes, which is assumed not ever to be read by the other party as it would never be accepted. The name is taken from one of the original clauses, which signed over a users' first-born child in exchange for Wi-Fi.[18]

It seems the evidence-based approach of demonstrating real contracts with real clauses which showed clearly that no one read them, was more convincing than a subjective self-determination, however honest.

Figure 10.1 Images by Louis Silvestro used by the author in BLIP lectures on contract innovation and to illustrate (a) the impact of legal jargon (left) and (b) and the question 'Does anyone actually read them?' (right). Copyright Camilla Baasch Andersen.

Having cemented the message that traditional legal language was not satisfying the requirements of modern contracting, we then went one step further.

Step 2: Expand on the virtues of relational contracting

In a nutshell, relational contracting can be defined as contracts which focus on values and relationships between parties, emphasising trust and the implied framework of the relationship. It is hard not to be enamoured with the concept; it forms an easily digestible step on the ladder of rethinking traditional contract forms and comes with a Nobel prize[19] and a glut of literature and case studies on the virtues of the concept. Ian Macneil was an early advocate in the 1960s,[20] and a recent white paper by the World Commerce & Contracting (WCC, formerly known as IACCM) espouses the important steps to relational contracting in practice, the first and foremost being: 'Focus on the relationship, not the deal'.[21] It is taken further by J Kim Wright, who has reimagined her own brand of relational contracting with her humanizing brand of law termed 'Conscious Contracting', part of the integrative law movement making law more values based.[22]

Students reported finding this very convincing—it is a concept which is difficult to dislike. Moreover, by simplifying the concept using the nine principles of relational contracting isolated by the WCC (then known as the IACCM) it is rendered collaborative and practical. In their reflective logs, many students commented that it was surprising not all contracts were relational—demonstrating their open mind-sets, preparing them for the next message.

Step 3: Show them the data on comic contracting, including how hard it is to get right

At this stage in our Comic Contracting Project, we can demonstrate dozens of different contracts with thousands of users—and we can still pride ourselves on complete dispute elimination. With several of our contracts attracting prizes for business communication (Golden Quill award for the UWA Aurecon project in 2019) and innovation awards (IQ award nomination for the UWA project in, 2017 and Hiil grant for Robert de Rooy in 2019) the stats on comprehension, engagement and perception no longer stand alone. Dozens of student reflective logs commented that the data were convincing them that this is a better way forward for law, but many also acknowledged the evidence-based case studies. A fair few also relied on the authority of the former Chief Justice, who commented favourably on the contracts in 2017.[23] A significant portion of the teaching material ensured care was taken to communicate the pitfalls of legal visualisation as experienced by my research team on actual comic contracting projects, and the importance of interdisciplinarity and interpretational clarity. This message seems to have been taken well on board at step 6, below.

Finally, it may be cheating, but sharing a *Law Review* article entirely in comic book form (possibly the first of its kind?), expanding on the positive aspects of the work as well as hints and tips on how to do it right, clearly also helped build the understanding students reflected within their logs.[24]

Step 4: Show them some actual comic contracts

One of the main advantages of research-based teaching is the ability to showcase your own research even before it becomes public. Before the Aurecon contract was released for public viewing,[25] I was still permitted to show it to my students for teaching purposes—and in many ways, seeing really IS believing. Many students reported the same thing as we have found in focus testing: namely that while comic contracting sounds 'weird' to many it is not as uncomfortable once you see it applied in context and experience an example of a well drafted contract with cartoon visuals. Students reported a clear 'seeing is believing' response in their own learning reflections, which was certainly assisted by the data mentioned above, but still identifiable as an individual factor in convincing them of the feasibility of the project (see Figure 10.2).

Figure 10.2 'Of course comic contracts are binding'. Image by Stuart Medley and Bruce Mutard used by the author in BLIP lectures on contract innovation.[26] Reproduced with permission.

Step 5: Get lucky with a fresh-off-the-press UK case on the virtue of visuals

Napoleon Bonaparte allegedly once espoused the virtues of 'lucky generals' in battle.[27] And, certainly, the timing of the Altera case[28] was most fortunate in this particular battle for this particular general. In this case, a judge was asked to balance the significance of visuals in contract negotiation, where these were in direct conflict with a traditional fine print terms in the contract. The visuals are given precedence in the case, as specific examples of how the parties intended the contract to play out. Released *while* we were teaching Portfolio Three, the 7th and final online lecture explains how the UK courts highlighted the significance of visuals, reinforcing an earlier case which leaned in a similar direction, the Starbev case.[29] I was thrilled to include it in their curriculum—but much to my surprise, very few students indicated it had been instrumental in changing their perspective. I suspect it may have had a subtle effect, but it is worth remembering that the students in this class are undergraduate major students in a Business Law Major and NOT law students, so their commitment to the significance of precedents may not be as ingrained as that of students on an actual legal qualification degree.

Step 6: Make them do it themselves

The portfolio challenge for this section of the unit was to draft an innovative contract in an area significant to their businesses:

> 'Considering what goods/services your company provides, and how it operates, consider what kind of contract you want to draft to ensure your entity report demonstrates your engagement with the challenge. Your choices are: [1] Employment contract—you are hiring new employees and want to offer a new and exciting and approach to commercial hiring, starting with an innovative employment contract for innovative people. Consider strengths and weaknesses of different approaches … [2] Contract for Goods/Services—you want to offer an innovative and exciting way to sell/provide your goods/services and need to ensure your "boiler plate" terms are engaging and innovative … [3] Something else/ wild card—you are welcome to choose to draft *any* other contract in relation to your entity's business operation'.

Students were supported through two online workshops in which they were given general information and some individual support in break out groups, and their concepts and ideas were discussed. They then had one hour of individual tutorial support to discuss their concepts. Generally, aside from the general information they were given, they were given minimal guidance.

Although many propositions could not be developed and completed—indeed, it was made clear this was not expected in the challenge description—the majority of the 10 entity groups developed impressive visual contracts, several of which my research team would have been proud of had they been produced for a sponsor! For example, one group pushed the brief further and developed an audio contract accessible to those with visual impairments; another created a contract entirely composed of memes; and a third created a video contract. The creativity and exploration of visuals and solutions to visual challenges such as avatar design was generally exceptional.

Conclusion

Set in the wider context of an interactive and immersive course, Portfolio Three provided a unique opportunity for students to reflect on their own responses to visual learning as well as innovations in contract law.

The systematic incorporation of visuals, as well as an evidence-based understanding of their power, into the BLIP unit, changed the minds of a number of students whose reflective logs reveal that they went from openly rejecting the idea that visuals or comics could improve professional legal communications, to advocating comic contracting. Perhaps one potential long term, wide-ranging and desirable outcome of the unit is that BLIP graduates might become advocates for an increased emphasis on visualisation as they move into legal practice.

Collectively, in their reflective logs, more students reported a passionate engagement with the topic than in any other portfolio on the BLIP curriculum. Of the 170+ logs, the vast majority also reported a very strong change in their position on the feasibility of the concept, outlining the steps above as important moments in their re-thinking of the feasibility of comic contracting. I will not discount the human tendency to write what their teacher may have wanted to hear—so it is not, arguably, a sound empirical study of the convincing nature of the comic contracting research. Nevertheless, others may enjoy the way it was taught and the lessons learned.

But as a law educator, the most interesting aspect of this was the quality of the reflections themselves. With significantly better, and consistently more, introspection and reflection on subjective engagement with learning in this portfolio above the others, it became clear that the provoking nature of the topic and the changing of mind-sets throughout the teaching triggered a much more subjective engagement. They were provoked, prodded and felt it—and it made them engage more deeply and more subjectively with the material and their own reflective writing.

The final conclusion: rocking the boat of established convictions makes for great teaching experiences! At the very least—fun for the educator…;-)

Notes

1 Professor of Law, The Law School, University of Western Australia.

2 See, for example, Stefania Passera, *Beyond the Wall of Contract Text* (Aalto University 2017) and Helena Haapio, *Next Generation Contracts: A Paradigm Shift* (Lexpert Ltd 2013) and Collette Brunschwig, 'Humanoid robots for contract visualisation' (2020) 6.1 UNIO – EU Law Journal 142–160. Retrieved from https://revistas.uminho.pt/index.php/unio/article/view/2703. See also the 2019 Special Edition of the UWA Law Journal dedicated to comic book contracts available at: https://www.able.uwa.edu.au/centres/uwalr/issues/2019-volume-46,-issue-2 with key articles on the comic contracting project and its feasibility (based on the inaugural 2017 Comic Book Contract Conference).

3 For an analysis of the genesis of the project, see: Camilla Baasch Andersen and Adrian Keating, 'A Graphic Contract: Taking Visualisation in Contracting a Step Further' (2016) 2.1–2 Journal of Strategic Contracting and Negotiation 10; see more recently Camilla Baasch Andersen, 'Musings on the Comic Book Contract Project and Legal Design Thinking' (2020) Journal of Graphic Novels and Comics, DOI:10.1080/21504857.2020.1731563. Specific projects are outlined in Andersen and de Rooy, 'Employment Agreements in Comic Book Form—What a Difference Cartoons Make' and Andersen and Hsien Lee, 'Facilitative Contracts with Visuals and Comics; Access to Justice and Steps for the Future' both available in Haapio, Corrales and Fenwick (eds), *Research Handbook on Contract Design* (Edward Elgar 2020), and C Andersen and J McGuire, 'Improving Aurecon's Employment Contracts through Visualisation' (2019) 46.2 The University of Western Australia Law Review 218–236.

4 See C Baasch Andersen and A Keating, 'Engineering Visual Contracts: Using If–Then Thinking to Develop Behavioral Drivers for Imaging' (2020) Journal of Open Access to Law (21 February).

5 See the official project website at www.comicbookcontracts.com.

6 See, for example, the commercial venture springing from comic contracting available at www.alternativecontracting.biz.

7 See the 2020/2021 'Graphic Justice: Pictures Worth 1000 Words' exhibit at the Legal Heritage Centre at the Queensland Supreme Court Library, partially available here: https://legalheritage.sclqld.org.au/comic-book-contracts.

8 JR Levin and RE Mayer, 'Understanding Illustrations in Text' in BK Britton, A Woodward and M Brinkley (eds), *Learning from Textbooks* (Erlbaum 1993) 95–113.

9 See, amongst many others, AM Glenberg and WE Langston, 'Comprehension of Illustrated Text: Pictures Help to Build Mental Models' (1992) 31.2 Journal of Memory and Language 129–151; WH Levie and R Lentz, 'Effects of Text Illustrations: A Review of Research' (1982) 30.4 ECTJ 195–232; JR Levin, GJ Anglin and RN Carney, 'On Empirically Validating Functions of Picture in Prose' in HA Hougton and DM Willows (eds), *The Psychology of Illustrations, Vol. 1: Basic Research* (Springer-Verlag 1987).

10 A Eitel, K Scheiter, A Schüler, M Nyström and K Holmqvist, 'How a Picture Facilitates the Process of Learning from Text: Evidence for Scaffolding' (2013) 28 Learning and Instruction 48–63.

11 S Passera, A Kakaanranta and L Louhiala-Salminen, 'Diagrams in Contracts: Fostering Understanding in Global Business Communication' (2017) 60.2 IEEE Transactions on Professional Communication 118–146.

12 See for example Jojappa Chowder, 'The Nonverbal Dimensions of Presentation' (2013) 1.4 Research Journal of English Language and Literature 1; Peter Andersen, *Nonverbal Communication: Forms and Functions* (Waveland Press, 2nd edn, 2007); Janine Driver, *You Say More Than You Think* (Crown Publishers, 2010); Loretta Malandro, *Nonverbal Communication* (Newbery Award Records 1989), 8.

13 Natalie Skead and Kate Offer, 'Learning Law through a Lens—Using Visual Media to Support Student Learning and Skills Development in Law' (2016) 41 *AltLJ* 186.

14 For example, in 2017, a number of law staff began a (still ongoing) experiment to use amateur videos filmed on campus to showcase legal issues: See Carruthers et al., 'Enhancing Student Learning and Engagement in the Juris Doctor Through the Rich Tapestry of Legal Story-Telling' (2017) 10 Journal of the Australasian Law Teachers Association 26.

15 See https://www.comicbookcontracts.com/the-2017-conference for a day-by-day tour and information on the conference.

16 Elle Hunt, 'Amazon Kindle's Terms "Unreasonable" and Would Take Nine Hours to Read, Choice Says' *The Guardian* (15 March 2017), www.theguardian.com/australia-news/2017/mar/15/amazon-kindles-terms-unreasonable-and-would-take-nine-hours-to-read-choice-says, accessed 8 December 2019.

17 Alex Hern, 'I Read All the Small Print on the Internet and it Made Me Want to Die' *The Guardian* (15 June 2015), www.theguardian.com/technology/2015/jun/15/i-read-all-the-small-print-on-the-internet, accessed 8 December 2019.

18 https://www.theguardian.com/technology/2014/sep/29/londoners-wi-fi-security-herod-clause.

19 Economic Sciences Nobel Prize awarded to Hart and Holmstrom in 2016 for their contract theories on more practical and cooperative/relational contracting and design, see https://www.nobelprize.org/prizes/economic-sciences/2016/press-release/.

20 IR Macneil, 'Whither Contracts?' (1969) 21 Journal of Legal Education 403.

21 'Unpacking Relational Contracts: The Practitioner's Go-To Guide for Understanding Relational Contracts' (2016) Vested Way, see Kate Vitasek's analysis of the white paper at https://www.vestedway.com/relational-contracting-overcoming-the-paradox/.

22 See generally http://consciouscontracts.com and J Kim Wright *Lawyers as Changemakers—The Global Integrative Law Movement* (ABA Publishing 2010).

23 See Hon Robert French, 'Closing Address, Comic Book Contracts Conference' (2019) 46.2 UWA Law Review 268–271, available at https://www.law.uwa.edu.au/__data/assets/pdf_file/0011/3442655/8.-French-Closing-Address.pdf. Bruce Mutard and Stuart Medley in their fully illustrated article 'Applied Comics

for Law and the Avatar Brainstorming' (2019) 46.2 UWA Law Review 252–258, available at https://www.law.uwa.edu.au/__data/assets/pdf_file/0009/3442653/6.-MutardMedley.pdf.

24 Mutard and Medley, *ibidem.*

25 Available in full now at https://www.comicbookcontracts.com/aurecon-contract.

26 See Stuart Medley and Bruce Mutard (2019) 'Applied Comics for Law and the Avatar Brainstorming' (2019) 46.2 UWA Law Review 252–258.

27 Some claim Napoleon never said this, and attribute it to Mazarin, see https://www.warhistoryonline.com/instant-articles/famous-things-napoleon-said.html. That is not important here—what is important is the convenience of luck!

28 Altera Voyageur Production Ltd v Premier Oil E&P UK Ltd [2020] EWHC 1891 (Comm) (17 July 2020), available at https://www.bailii.org/ew/cases/EWHC/Comm/2020/1891.html.

29 Starbev GP Limited v Interbrew Central European Holdings BV [2014] EWHC 1311 (Comm).

Part II

Public Legal Education

11 Using human-centred design to break down barriers to legal participation

Gráinne McKeever[1] *and Lucy Royal-Dawson*[2,3]

Introduction

Since 2016, the *Litigants in Person in Northern Ireland* (LIPNI) project has been exploring the experiences of litigants in person (LIPs) in civil and family cases in the jurisdiction. The first phase of the research focused on understanding whether going to court without a lawyer has an impact on the right to a fair trial under Article 6 ECHR.[4] In addressing this question, the research prioritised the concept of legal participation. The ability to participate is a basic feature of access to justice. It is not only a procedural tool for engaging in the proceedings but it is also related to perceptions of 'fairness' that access to justice demands as part of the social contract between citizens and state.[5] We found four main barriers to participating in legal proceedings: intellectual—not understanding the process; practical—not being able to access help or support; emotional—the process itself generating frustration, fear and anger on top of on-going stress around the reason for the litigation; and attitudinal—being stereotyped as difficult to deal with by other court actors. One of the greatest problems was that LIPs were expected to educate themselves on what they were required to do for each stage of their legal proceedings. Their inability to do so was seen as a failure on their part rather than an acceptance of their lack of familiarity with the system and the lack of available information or support.

It would be possible to assume that simply filling the information gap for LIPs would lead to better informed litigants who could participate adequately in court processes. Yet, the empirical evidence does not support this assumption. In our initial study, we gave free procedural advice to a number of LIPs, tailored to their cases. Even though the LIPs found the support helpful and felt better equipped and more confident than before, they did not always act on the advice they received and were not always given opportunities to participate in court on an equal footing with legal representatives.[6] The assertion that 'information is power' ignores the existing power relationships in the legal system: effective participation depends on the sharing of power with those who do not have it and not just the provision of information. Without accompanying attitudinal changes to how LIPs are seen and treated, the provision of information alone is unlikely to facilitate effective participation.

DOI: 10.4324/9780429021411-13

In this second phase of the research, we are using human-centred design to achieve two objectives: to create litigant support materials to improve LIP participation in court hearings and generate attitudinal change. Our hypothesis is that creating public legal information for LIPs through a co-productive process, which centres the LIP as the user, has the potential to develop a foundation for cultural change in how LIPs are supported that can in turn help break down intellectual, practical, emotional and attitudinal barriers to participation.[7] We contend that identifying with the perspective of the litigants may bring about a deeper appreciation both of why support is important and of their needs.

This chapter explores our experience so far of facilitating a human-centred design (HCD) process that tests our hypothesis. We begin with an outline of how we understand HCD, then set out our methodological approach within the stages of HCD and the experiences arising from the execution of this approach. We use the reflections of the diverse group of legal stakeholders, users and professionals to understand how HCD enables collaboration, empathy and experimentation to develop. Our conclusion is a positive endorsement of the HCD process to both identify suitable supports for LIPs and to modify how stakeholders and professionals see and feel about LIPs in the justice system.

Empathy, collaboration and experimentation

HCD is not a new approach to either research or development, although its application to wicked legal problems is relatively recent.[8] The logic of HCD is to approach the design of services and products from the perspective of the user. The principle is straightforward: designers work with potential users of the products or services which are being developed so that the end product or service matches the needs and preferences of the users.

Three main principles can be seen to underpin this method of design: empathy, collaboration and experimentation.[9] Empathy is critical in ensuring that the solution researchers and designers seek is directed at the human experience of services or products. Placing that human experience at the centre of any solution-focused thinking requires the designers to respond to the human needs that the product or service must meet. The solution is intended to remove or alleviate the elements of the user experience that cause unnecessary pain or friction. This is done by understanding the human experience of any obstructions and so designing the product or service deliberately to avoid these pain points occurring. The collaborative principle of HCD is perhaps the most obvious feature. Designers and researchers apply their knowledge and expertise of system design and development to the problems and experiences of the users, informed by what the users see as the potential solutions, and collaboration allows these distinct but critical experiential perspectives to elide. The experimental principle enables breathing space for solutions to go through cycles of development and failure until an optimal solution is reached. There is scope here for multiple ideas to be developed and explored, with the iterative process of experimentation guiding the decisions on what solution best fits the users' needs.

The two research objectives of our study are: 1) to assess whether the HCD process can facilitate a diverse group of stakeholders to identify the support needs of LIPs within a legal system that sees their existence as an aberration; and 2) to assess whether the HCD process has a positive impact on stakeholders' attitudes towards LIPs so that they recognise their support needs. This chapter therefore examines the outputs of the HCD process with regards to the supports identified and whether the stakeholders were able to articulate any change in their attitudes towards the problems faced by LIPs.

Mentors for learning about HCD

Our lodestar for planning the HCD process were the innovations in the field of legal design employing user-focused methods, such as Margaret Hagan's 'Law by Design' (2018) and Lorne Sossin's 'Designing Administrative Justice' (2017), but it was from the work of Kari Boyle and Jane Morley at the British Columbia Family Justice Innovation Lab that we took our greatest inspiration.[10] The description of their journey of discovery and learning using HCD techniques in the access to justice field gave us the confidence to begin our own journey. Their account of the development of the Family Justice Innovation Lab revealed the power and potential of HCD in family court reform. Our aim for attitudinal change aligned with their on-going work to challenge hardened perspectives and orient people to not just see things from a different point of view, but to reflect on their own perspectives through empathy with others.

We included Boyle and Morley in our project planning from the outset which meant we had the resources necessary for them to mentor us, supporting and challenging our thinking on how we would develop the process.

Our approach to HCD

We took the five design principles described by Hagan as the framework for our methodology:

1. Discover—what is the landscape? This means a thorough understanding of the challenges and the stakeholders involved.
2. Synthesise—what is your mission? This means defining the problem and the people for whom you will be designing.
3. Build—what ideas may work? This means generating possible solutions for the problem and prototyping them.
4. Test—are the ideas worthwhile? This requires testing prototypes with the users and in live situations.
5. Evolve—how to move forward? This is the iterative process of feedback, improving the design and re-testing.

Mentored by Boyle and Morley, we designed a series of workshops to cover these five principles. The postponement of workshops in response to COVID-19 has meant we have not yet reached the Evolve stage. This chapter reflects primarily on phases Discover to Synthesise.

Discover

The Discover principle required a thorough understanding of the challenges faced by LIPs in family proceedings in Northern Ireland and their reasons for self-representing. This came from the first phase of the research and provided the context and detail for us to produce personas to use in the HCD process with the Design Group.

Personas are a device that places humans at the centre of the design process. They are descriptions of fictitious users, in this case LIPs, which represent real experience and behaviour.[11] They are used in HCD to enable product or service developers and users to focus on a common user journey. They also offer a means of equalising the status between participants and removing links to actual individuals. Our personas were compilations of the experiences of several LIPs we met in the study. Boyle and Morley advised us to put ourselves in the shoes of the Design Group participants and make the persona journeys digestible so they would be easy to relate to yet leave room for participants to use their imagination to develop more detail. They advised that participants tend to get very attached to their persona, and therefore to make them as real as possible. On their advice, we used a template to structure the information to include a photo, background information, their goals for the family case, a summary of the litigation journey so far and quotes to reflect the persona's thoughts and feelings at different stages of their journey.

To ensure sufficient exposure to different characteristics and journeys, we developed four personas and journeys as shown in Figure 11.1:

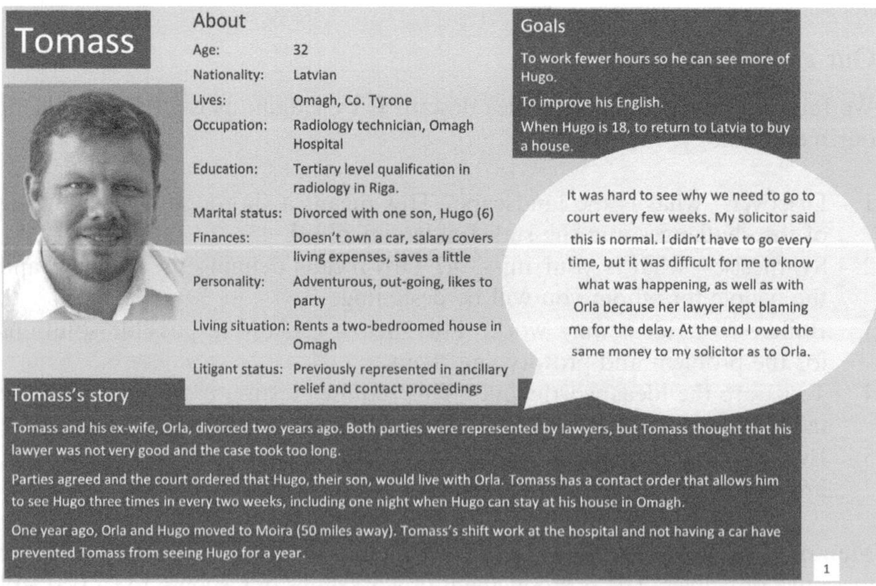

Figure 11.1 Example of persona template used in the Human Centred Design process. Image: authors.

Synthesise, build and test

To enable us to implement the design principles of synthesis, build and test, we held a series of workshops with a Design Group constituted specifically for this project. We envisaged the co-production of supports for LIPs as the work of a group of stakeholders from both sides of the court service counter—users and providers. In all, 33 people from the major stakeholder groups agreed to join the Design Group, as shown in Table 11.1, many of whom the research team had made connections with through the first phase of the project, while others were identified on the basis of gaps in expertise or perspective within the group.

The Design Group participants were invited to a series of workshops to facilitate their understanding of a LIP's journey using the personas as the stimulus for the design process. Table 11.2 shows the main activities of each workshop and how they map onto the design principles.

The first three workshops were held in November and December 2019 at Ulster University. The choice of the neutral location, not aligned to any one of the LIP or justice sector stakeholder groups, and the participation of the Department of Justice and court service personnel as equals in the process and not as gatekeepers of it, added legitimacy to the process. The fourth workshop was due to take place in March 2020, but industrial action at the University forced it to be postponed to later in the month. It then fell victim to COVID-19 restrictions and was postponed, resuming in November 2020 as an online workshop.

Table 11.1 Design group members

Stakeholder groups	*No.*	*Label used in quotations*
Department of Justice senior managers	2	Court personnel
NICTS senior managers	6	Court personnel
Court Children's Officer	1	Practitioner
Therapeutic counsellors	2	Other professional
McKenzie friend	1	Practitioner
Voluntary sector—women, family mediation, children, mental health, human rights	6	Other professional
Family barristers	2	Practitioner
Family solicitors	2	Practitioner
LIPs	7	LIP
IT specialist	1	Other professional
Retired judge	1	Practitioner
Change management specialist	1	Other professional
Observer	1	Other professional

Table 11.2 Workshop activities mapped onto the human-centred design stages

Workshop	*Content*	*Human-centred design stage*
Workshop 1 November 2019	Introductions. Context of LIPs in Northern Ireland. Purpose and goals of Design Group. Introduction to reflective diaries. Introduction to human-centred design approach in family justice. Break into groups to 'step into the shoes' of the personas. Map the persona's litigation journey. Identify persona's pain points. Develop 'How can we' questions to alleviate the pain points.	DISCOVER SYNTHESISE
In between	Research team synthesised the 18 'How can we' questions produced by the groups down to five for Workshop 2.	
Workshop 2 November 2019	Group presentations on their persona, pain points and 'How can we' questions. Presentation of five 'How can we' questions and groups choose one that would help their persona the most. Divergence stage—ideation (groups brainstorm ideas) to address the 'How can we' questions. Convergence stage—each idea is placed on axes of high/low impact and easy/difficult to implement. Groups select one or two high impact/easy to implement concepts to take forward. Group presentations on the chosen concepts. Feedback and vote on each concept. Concept with the most votes is 'Information for LIPs'.	SYNTHESISE
In between	Research team identify any additional supports/ expertise needed for the groups to work on the chosen concept.	
Workshop 3 December 2019	Review chosen concept 'Information for LIPs.' Rapid introduction to design. Groups flesh out the concept into a tangible design; focus on alleviating pain points. Group presentations of the tangible designs. Feedback on all designs.	BUILD
In between	Research team chose two concepts to take forward to prototyping: a website on family proceedings in Northern Ireland and an online pathfinder to guide litigants given their circumstances.	BUILD
Workshop 4 November 2020	Share participants' COVID-19 realities. Introduction to prototyped concepts: website and pathfinder.	TEST

At Workshop 1, we introduced the Design Group to their personas. To 'get into the shoes of their persona,' the participants mapped the litigation journeys on rolls of paper stuck on the wall, using coloured pens and sticky notelets to mark events, as Figure 11.2 shows. This process of trying to understand how the personas navigated this journey, and how they would be thinking and feeling at different points, allowed the group to synthesise the problems and understand the people at the centre of the design process.[12]

A further element of synthesising was the identification of 'pain points' on the personas' journeys; that is, particularly difficult experiences or interactions they had in their court proceedings.

The final element to synthesising was using these pain points as a trigger to possible solutions by asking 'How can we [avert pain point X from happening to Persona again]?' The production of 'How can we' questions formed the basis for the next stage of the design process.

At Workshop 2, the groups worked on ideas and concepts that would prevent their persona's pain points from arising. This ideation process starts with divergence in which the participants generate dozens of possible ideas, then converge the ideas according to selected criteria. We used impact and ease of implementation as our selection criteria. Groups selected the idea with the highest impact and that was easiest to implement.

Workshop 3 entered the Build stage of the HCD process. Armed with stationery and tips on designing, the groups fleshed out their selected concept into a prototype. See Figure 11.3 for one example.

They presented their designs to the whole group, and everyone fed back. Using this feedback, we selected two designs which we could build fully given

Figure 11.2 Persona litigation journey mapping example. Image: authors.

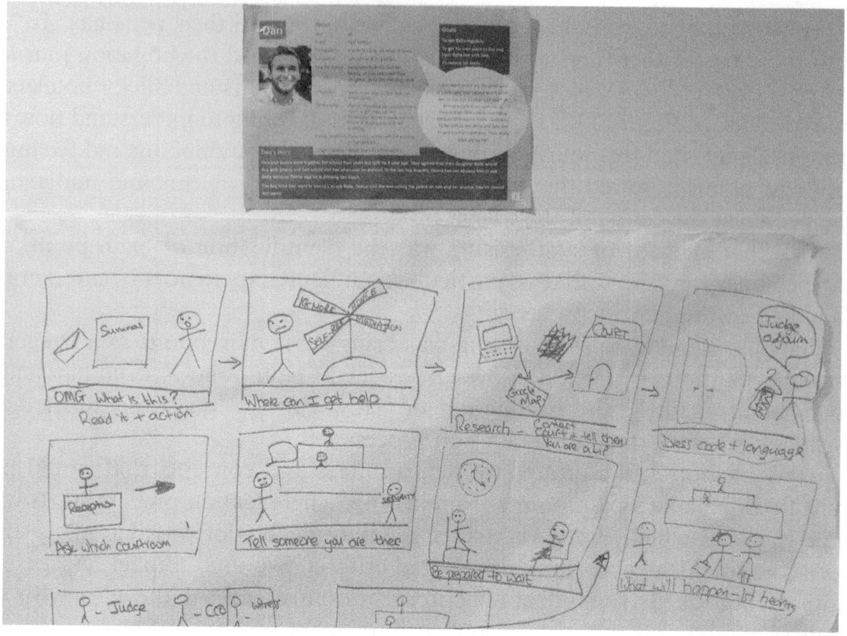

Figure 11.3 Example of a design concept fleshed out into a prototype. Image: authors.

our budget, time and resources: a website of information on family proceedings in Northern Ireland and an online pathfinder to guide litigants based on their circumstances.

We postponed the next workshop due to COVID-19 restrictions. In the meantime, the research team built the two selected designs. In November 2020, we held the fourth workshop online.

Using HCD to break down barriers to legal participation—the findings so far

At the workshops, we asked the participants to write reflective diaries to generate qualitative data on their emerging reactions and reflections on attitudes to working in a diverse group in a HCD process.[13] The participants wrote entries prompted by questions about their expectations and more general views of the process, their personal goals and the experience of working in a group of diverse stakeholders, such as:

> Were there different perspectives around the table that impacted on your thinking?
>
> What are your reflections on how the method made you view the court system from the point of view of a LIP?

We used NVivo to code their reflections and used thematic analysis to answer two research questions:

> Can the HCD process facilitate the diverse group to identify the support needs of LIPs?
>
> Did the HCD process have a positive impact on stakeholders' attitudes towards LIPs?

Even though we are only part-way into the project, we report here some findings on these two questions.

Can the HCD process facilitate the diverse group to identify the support needs of LIPs?

There is clear evidence from the fleshed-out designs that the Design Group participants were collectively able to identify the support needs of their personas. The caveat to this is that they were pre-disposed to wanting to see change and improvement to the court system. At the outset, the majority of them wanted specific improvements for LIPs, such as accessible, available and suitable information for LIPs, for LIPs to have a better experience at court, and for LIPs to be less anxious and more confident or be on an equal footing in the court process with other court actors:

> Changes that I would like to see are mainly in the sphere of information accessibility—primarily shaped by service users.
>
> (Other professional)[14]

> Some effective support for LIPs as well as improving the whole LIP experience in the court with personal support.
>
> (LIP)

The workshop activities gave ample opportunity to mine this pre-disposition, capitalising on the diverse mix within the group. The Design Group reflections acknowledged that the exposure to different perspectives from group members was critical in being able to challenge their own thinking and develop their understanding and empathy:

> By being able to listen to [other group members] I have been able to 'slow down the process' and ask questions—this has really helped me understand.
>
> (Other professional)

> Listening to other people's perspectives of the LIP helped me think of things that I hadn't thought of before.
>
> (Court personnel)

The group largely embraced a positive attitude to the process, acknowledging the potential for conflict but not necessarily seeing this as irreconcilable. The curation of the group's membership may have made this consensus inevitable but there was still a healthy degree of scepticism and honesty, where negative prior experiences and likelihood of tension were acknowledged as the starting point:

> Anticipating tension given wide range of perspectives before common threads & co-operation emerges.
>
> (LIP)

> My experience of LIPs has been entirely negative. LIPs do not follow court procedure, professional courtesy and generally are impossible to negotiate. Disrespectful to the court. Quick to complain to governing bodies about opposing solicitor.
>
> (Practitioner)

The practitioner here who reported negative experience of LIPs later added that listening to others made him reflect on what he takes for granted, suggesting a shift in his own thinking. The HCD process provided the way to test whether the group could overcome these tensions to focus on the needs of their personas, developing empathy and working collaboratively to identify LIP-focused solutions.

Indeed, collaboration is a critical feature of the HCD process. It gave Design Group participants freedom to come up with multiple solutions from the pragmatic, such as a process map with clear explanations, to the wishful, including a virtual reality friend supporting you through the court experience. The solutions could then be narrowed down to those high impact, low cost possibilities. This meant that the supports we envisaged as capable of prototyping were something that the group endorsed. The use of personas specifically was essential to the process:

> Concentrating on the personas took out the 'heat' from any personalisation … the de-personalised approach was very effective.
>
> (Court Personnel)

> Makes it more real to use a persona. Highlights some of the problems in the system: delay, lack of legal knowledge.
>
> (Legal professional)

There was broad support for HCD as an enjoyable and engaging method to producing supports for LIPs. This was particularly heartening to hear given that the members attended the workshops voluntarily in their evenings:

> Very easy to generate ideas … [O]ur group was mixed & able to come up with a range of concepts. Very enjoyable, we are making progress … Human-centred design process needs to be a priority for judicial system.
>
> (Other professional)

> Very useful as it identified the areas which needed to be addressed.
>
> (Practitioner)

It was a significant aspect of maintaining equal status between members that there was no hierarchy of ideas; the focus was not on generating one or 'the best' idea, but on as many as occurred to the group, who were reassured that there were no 'bad' ideas:

> I found coming up with different ideas somewhat of a challenge initially but it got much easier as I felt safe enough to have a go.
>
> (LIP)

It was vital to address concerns that the focus would be mainly on the needs of the court system, losing sight of the human at the centre of the design.

The complexity of the litigation procedure and marshalling the amount of information that LIPs need were challenges to the design process:

> What appeared to be a simple exercise quickly became complex when we realised the amount of information that would need to be contained.
>
> (Other professional)

> We can't design support that will match a legal degree & qualification but we can make progress. Citizens have a fundamental right to use the justice system.
>
> (Court personnel)

The group remained conscious of the practical constraints including cost and the need for additional resources to implement design solutions, as well as the need to balance expectations against concerns that nothing would change:

> My concern would be that a lot of this work is in vain if the court system simply puts the findings on a 'shelf', pays lip service to it and only implements the recommendation they are comfortable with.
>
> (LIP)

There were also suggestions for ways in which the process could be improved, including greater involvement by the judiciary and bringing political representatives into the group. The former was our intention but the latter was not something we had considered. For some participants, the process was initially seen as being too protracted, described by some participants at the end of the first workshop as self-indulgent, muddled and long-winded, while for others it was just another means of arriving at the obvious answer:

> It was thought provoking and good to have different viewpoints. However, I think the results would have been able to be arrived at in another way as well—we knew change was needed.
>
> (Court personnel)

Overall, however, reflections were positive, with initial scepticism, frustration and impatience being replaced by an awareness that the slower pace made sense, that the process was moving towards tangible solutions and an acknowledgement that Boyle and Morley were right to encourage them to 'trust the process'.

In Workshop 4, we were able to show more developed designs of the two supports that we are progressing, but as yet, the Design Group participants have not been able to test them thoroughly or consider how they would suit their persona. Group members were positive that the website and pathfinder tool would be useful, but their comments were based on limited exposure. Nonetheless, the objective of a stakeholder group arriving at supports for LIPs was met.

Did the HCD process have a positive impact on stakeholders' attitudes towards LIPs?

The process of listening to other perspectives while mapping the persona's litigation journey and identifying their pain points to identify needs enabled participants to develop ideas to support the persona. In getting to this point, group members reflected on transformations in their thinking, rooted in empathy:

> Working through [persona's] perspective reminds me of people that I have worked with and their complete frustration. I am reminded of the reality that I don't know what I don't know and this is especially pertinent when it comes to the language. If I am a 'native' speaker in any given language then I will understand … nuance. If I am not a 'native' speaker of 'legal-eeze' then I am immediately disadvantaged without even knowing.
>
> (Other professional)

> Useful to hear from other participants—a lot of concerns around how the persona felt, underlined the emotions that someone attending court deals with—sympathy, and felt that some of the things which upset LIPs and compounded their fears could have been resolved.
>
> (Court personnel)

'Stepping into the shoes' of their persona and exposure to different perspectives appear to have been successful in producing some profound cognitive or affective shifts in some of the participants.

> [Persona] has changed my perspective, ie made me think about their motivations … I have been periodically thinking about them during the week and ways the situation could be improved.
>
> (Court personnel)

> Learning about family court changed my view on issues I realised I had quite a fixed view on beforehand.
>
> (LIP)

These self-reported shifts in perspective are important markers that the HCD method can produce individual realisations. Whether they remain as permanent attitude-change is hard to say at this stage. As a method for producing supports, the reflections tell us that the HCD stages of ideation and designing a prototype evoke a sense of progress towards a result, which in itself resulted in a positive reaction to the process of change generally:

> Inspired to keep going—positive that something will change and improve.
>
> (Court personnel W2)

> End of night I was hopeful that tonight was the start of a journey that would end in equality of arms and effective participation.
>
> (Practitioner W2)

The critical question posed by Perry-Kessaris' research is "whether designerly ways are resulting in … policy-making environments, that avoid, expose, and remedy biases and inequalities".[15] The HCD process offers a positive step towards achieving this.

Conclusions

Our research started from the position that there was a need for LIPs to participate effectively in their court hearings. Our initial research, based on a two year qualitative and quantitative study in the civil and family courts in Northern Ireland, identified the nature of participative barriers, where LIPs did not understand the legal process, were unable to access help, were distressed by the process and were seen as the problem by other court users. The challenge was not just to provide support materials that could help tackle the intellectual, practical and emotional barriers to legal participation, but to reorient the perspectives of those for whom LIPs were problematic trespassers rather than legitimate court users. The task of cultural change is considerable and yet HCD offered a way to consider how to change the mindsets of some, as a way of moving towards changing the mindset of others. The process has allowed us, and others amplifying the LIP experience, to challenge the perspectives of some of those engaged or working within the legal system, creating subtle but significant shifts in attitudes. The need to lift the eyes of a range of people beyond their own professional and personal circumstances, to be comfortable with rather than riled by the position of others, while still connecting them to tackling complex problems in the legal system was our main aspiration.[16] In doing this, we hoped to simultaneously develop innovative ideas that were centred around resolving the problems experienced by LIPs.

The HCD process was itself a challenge to deliver—time-consuming, resource-intensive, intricate and intimidating. Our own intellectual, practical and emotional difficulties were evident. While there is often no substitute for learning-by-doing, learning from others can help ensure that a new approach has a greater chance of success. Like the participants in the Design Group, the research team were impatient to plough on towards the end goals, particularly where time seemed too precious to waste on building rapport and creating space for trust to develop. Our mentors, Boyle and Morley, kept us focused to trust the process, to shake ourselves free of the rigidity we found ourselves defaulting to, requiring us to put our Design Group's needs at the centre of our thinking rather than to keep a low gaze on deadlines, 'efficient' meetings and quick outcomes. With them, we found a clearer direction through the stages of HCD that yielded the core outcomes we had sought.

What emerged strongly from our findings was the theme of empathy, with participants acknowledging the differing perspectives within the Design Group and the insights brought by the 'others', seeing these as both challenge and opportunity. Participants reflected on the 'humanity', the generosity and the commitment evident within the group in what was a demanding schedule of evening workshops. They worked through their frustrations, trusting in the researchers initially and then the HCD process itself. At the time of writing, we have not finished the prototypes under development, which will evolve through the next stage of the research when they are made available to LIPs in family courts in Northern Ireland. But what has led us to this point, starting with the focus on participation and power, has been the HCD process. The frustrated, isolated, confused and upset LIPs who feature as our personas have found a collective voice of support from those who now identify with the problems in their litigant journeys. Support materials—designed specifically for their needs—are now under development as a result of those with power, authority, knowledge and expertise collaborating to provide it. And the Design Group has itself acknowledged its own journey, from scepticism to optimism, impatience to awareness. From this we move from fear to hope that change initiated by this process can grow.

Our final reflection is on the unplanned lessons from COVID-19. In some ways, the pandemic arrived at the right time—advice for LIPs in a remote justice system is now part of our focus as the need for accessible online materials has become even more evident.[17] A nine month delay in getting to the next workshop, the need to convene online and the additional demands on the time of over-burdened court service staff, among others, resulted in difficulties in regrouping our Design Group members. What emerged was a smaller Design Group who immediately stepped back into the shoes of their personas, noting that "it all came flooding back" (Other Professional). Their commitment and passion to bring life to the design proposals has invigorated our trust in the process, reminding us of what patience can achieve and setting us up for the Evolve stage of HCD that will determine how to move forward.

Notes

1 Professor of Law and Social Justice, School of Law, Ulster University and Co-Director of the Ulster University Law Clinic.

2 Research Associate, School of Law, Ulster University

3 Our thanks to Kari Boyle, Jane Morley and Priyamvada Yarnell for helpful comments on an earlier draft of this work, and the Nuffield Foundation for funding this research.

4 G McKeever, L Royal-Dawson, E Kirk and J McCord, 'Litigants in Person in Northern Ireland: Barriers to Legal Participation' (2018), www.ulster.ac.uk/__data/assets/pdf_file/0003/309891/179367_NIHRC-Litigants-in-Person_BOOK___5_LOW.pdf, accessed 6 January 2021.

5 J Thibault and L Walker, *Procedural Justice: A Psychological Analysis* (Hillsdale 1975).

6 McKeever (n 4) ch10.

7 By 'co-productive' we mean active participation in the design process by users (those for whom the system is designed) and by the various 'insiders' (professionals, court staff and other stakeholders) as common in participatory research. See for example S Kemmis and R McTaggart (eds), *The Action Research Planner* (3rd edn, Deakin University 1988); P Park, 'People, Knowledge and Change in Participatory Research' (1999) 30 Management Learning 141; J Bergold and S Thomas, 'Participatory Research Methods: A Methodological Approach in Motion' (2012) 13 Forum: Qualitative Social Research Art 30.

8 S Passera, 'Flowcharts, Swimlanes, and Timelines—Alternatives to Prose in Communicating Legal-Bureaucratic Instructions to Civil Servants' (2015) 32 Journal of Technical and Business Communication 229; M Hagan, 'Law by Design' (2016), www.lawbydesign.co, accessed 6 January 2021; J Morley and K Boyle, 'The Story of the BC Family Justice Innovation Lab' (2017) 34 Windsor YB Access Just 1; A Perry-Kessaris, 'Legal Design for Practice, Activism, Policy and Research' (2019) 46 Journal of Law and Society 185.

9 Hagan (n 8); IDEO, 'The Field Guide to Human-Centred Design' (2017), www.designkit.org/resources/1, accessed 6 January 2021; L Sossin, 'Designing Administrative Justice' (2017) 34 Windsor YB Access Just 87.

10 Hagan (n 8); Sossin (n 9); Morley and Boyle (n 8).

11 M Hagan, 'A Human-Centred Design Approach to Access to Justice: Generating New Prototypes and Hypotheses for Intervention to Make Courts User Friendly' (2018) 6 Indiana Journal of Law and Social Equality 199.

12 See C Corrigan, 'The Chaordic Stepping Stones: A Planning Tool for Designing Participatory Processes' (2016), www.chriscorrigan.com/parkinglot/wp-content/uploads/2015/01/Chaordic-Stepping-Stones-1.pdf, accessed 11 January 2021.

13 C Robson, *Real World Research* (2nd edn, Blackwell Publishing 2006).
14 Quotations from participants' reflective diaries are labelled to show their stakeholder role.
15 Perry-Kessaris (n 8) 206; A Perry-Kessaris and J Perry, 'Enhancing Participatory Strategies With Designerly Ways for Sociolegal Impact: Lessons From Research Aimed at Making Hate Crime Visible' (2020) 29 Social and Legal Studies 835.
16 A Perry-Kessaris (n 15).
17 See also G McKeever, J McCord, L Royal-Dawson and P Yarnell, 'The Impact of COVID-19 on Family Courts in Northern Ireland' (2020), www.ulster.ac.uk/courtsurvey, accessed 20 February 2021.

12 Judging by appearances

Isobel Williams[1]

With Covid-19 British justice is, to quote Bob Marley, jammin'. The courts are improvising. And signal jams mean a frozen screen.

This is a kaleidoscopic look at the visual side of courts during the onset of the pandemic, contrasted with some pre-virus experiences. I write as an occasional unofficial sketcher having mildly hallucinatory courtroom sensations for my blog about drawing in different places. I see what the public sees but am free to present it in an idiosyncratic way, paying attention to the negative space, the bits in between.[2]

After the courts close the public sees precious little, so to set the scene here are four people on the legal front line whom I invited to write about their experiences: a campaigner, a judge, a barrister and an official court artist (see Box 1). Then I report on the illegality of courtroom drawing, rifle through artists'

Figure 12.1 During the first lockdown, the all-party law reform and human rights organisation Justice experimented with mock Crown Court trials online, to assess their workability and fairness. In one crucial innovation, people in the virtual public gallery could see non-confidential court documents displayed on the screen: transparency campaigners would like this to continue in court.

DOI: 10.4324/9780429021411-14

travelling kit and peer at the UK Supreme Court. I end with a pre-pandemic meditation on a visually unique courtroom experience, the Naked Rambler in the dock, and what that exposes about the justice system. A constant underlying theme: when you look at an image, believing your eyes is never the best policy.

First lockdown

Poor concentration, patchy sleep. Life becomes filtered, vicarious. Measured out in pixels. The courtroom migrates to the screen. Transmissions can be barnacled with time-wasting glitches. You look where the fixed camera says you must. You can't scan the room, subconsciously pick up the pheromones of a panicked QC, spot a bored instructing solicitor scrolling down Facebook, or hear the gentle breathing of the stranger asleep beside you in the public seats.

On the other hand, if you're watching at home, you can eat and drink in your dressing gown; file your nails with your Swiss army knife rather than surrender it to security; shout obscenities at the screen or split it with your Tesco order; decode taste in décor (the higher up the food chain, the greater the chance of an oak-beamed ceiling).

But first you must get permission to watch the virtual spectacle. It feels as if the public gallery has been junked for the duration, despite pious official assertions to the contrary. I don't want to eavesdrop on telephone-only cases, but my requests to watch video-streamed civil hearings meet unexplained refusals or no reply. Regrettably, things open up once I start to drop a name or two. (The lack of information about whether hearings are recorded and how to access recordings is beyond the scope of this chapter.)

Box 1 Lockdown experiences

Campaigner

Those checking on how the law is administered need more than a camera lens. Penelope Gibbs, a former magistrate, focuses her campaign on fairness, transparency and a humane approach. In 2012 she set up the charity Transform Justice which generates research and informs the public, legal practitioners and politicians. She reports on loss of access:

> 'Covid-era criminal courts were for a period closed courts. Many hearings were done virtually with no public access to lists or to the hearings themselves. The first month after lockdown started on 23 March 2020 was the worst. I spent it trying to gain virtual access to criminal court hearings, with no success. I also tried to work out whether it was legal to visit one of the magistrates' courts which was open. It was not at all clear whether travel to a court simply to observe constituted 'essential travel'.
>
> In the end the Minister Chris Philp suggested that the public could legitimately visit magistrates' courts. So I started with my local—Highbury in

North London. The experience of getting in was not straightforward. I was rebuffed by court security there and at other courts, but insisted on my right to enter.

Once inside, the court was open as usual. Many seats in the public gallery were taped up to enforce social distancing, but very few people were watching. The challenge in some courts was in getting a good view of the defendants since they usually appeared virtually from police custody suites. They appeared on screens which were at an angle to the public gallery, so anyone watching got a distorted view.

I subsequently gained virtual access to two magistrates' courts via the Cloud Video Platform. I was one of the few non-journalists to observe magistrates' courts during the pandemic. It is a pity that so few people accessed these hearings. The normal justice rules were not followed at the peak of the pandemic and as a consequence I believe many defendants' rights were ignored. No research was conducted on criminal justice in the crucial months'.[3]

Judge

Robed or not, the judges trapped in their virtual doll's house squares evoke Francis Bacon's screaming popes. The stifled command, the confinement, the frustration with the bundles. Above the Master of the Rolls, grid lines of polystyrene ceiling tiles recede to infinity, echoing the painted popes' geometric cages.

But away from my flights of fancy, here is a measured look at reality from one judge:

> 'My overall impression is that remote hearings and mediations can work very well. I did my first remote mediation using the brilliant Microsoft Teams which allows you to put the different parties in entirely separate rooms, with no risk of anyone hearing anyone else (not something the Ministry of Justice's preferred platform, Kinly CVP, allows you easily to do). Counsel for one of the parties said his client preferred this form of mediation to the conventional kind, because there is absolutely no risk that you have to see or meet the other side.
>
> You certainly need two screens, if not three, to allow you to have documents and emails open on one, while you conduct the hearing/mediation on the other. Again, being able to email at the same time is very useful, not least to warn people that you are about to pop into their space (or I might resort to using a bell!) but also to exchange documents, plans and so on.
>
> My sense is that remote mediations might be easier and more popular than remote hearings, but it is too early to tell. In a courtroom, of course, a judge has an overview of what is going on, and can learn a

great deal from the reaction of parties and witnesses to evidence being given, which you simply do not get in a remote hearing (of course, no reference is ever made to any such clues in any judgment!). The other obvious point is that so much depends on the quality of your broadband or internet. I can well imagine that there will be many cases where the parties will not be able to take part, or will do so in a frustrating way. For me, the ability to work at home, and not to have to commute, is wonderful. I am sure that even when life goes back to 'normal' we will continue to use remote hearings and to conduct remote mediations'.[4]

In an aside, the judge comments about the visual side of arts events, but this chimes with what I see in virtual courtrooms too:

> 'I have been watching any number of remote talks and interviews: all the literary festivals have gone digital, and I am astonished that even really well established ones often have poor connectivity and, more strikingly, seem to give no guidance to speakers on background, height of webcam or distance from the screen. The best background is an entirely neutral one, but that is not always possible'.[5]

Barrister

Catherine Rowlands of Cornerstone Barristers gives the inside track from the early days:

> 'Remote hearings are inventing themselves as we go along. It's working well, because it's being developed by those of us who are actually doing it, rather than having a working party designing the system in the abstract and telling us what to do. Our processes work for us because they work for us, and the systems reflect the people who are adopting them. It's not surprising, then, that the visual aspects of our hearings are more casual and homespun than was initially intended. We were given stern advice about our backgrounds: they should be as plain as possible, they should not distract from our submissions, they should be appropriate and clean.
>
> It didn't last long. We have backgrounds with books and with children's pictures and with fine art. We have clutter and mysterious blanket-covered heaps. We have shelves of files or shelves of spices. I've seen people in their bedrooms, even in their beds, in their living rooms with glimpses of the real world through their windows, and in anonymous, blank rooms that may be closets or bathrooms re-purposed but which are as distracting as a cluttered library as you wonder where they are.
>
> We were supposed to behave as if we were in court. That didn't last long, either. Some behaviour is better: people interrupt less, knowing

that it's hard to manage. Some is less formal (worse? I don't say that). Judges swig coffee or tea (we assume) from mugs. I can't bring myself to do that, but I am acutely aware of how I look on screen—the bags under my eyes, despite wearing more make-up than if I were in 'real court' (and I always wear perfume!) and what faces I am pulling as I speak.

It's the closeness of the judge that is the shock. It's a lesson in advocacy writ large—you can read the impact of your submissions on the judge's face. That was a good point, and elicited a smile. A wince tells you that was a bad point. A raised eyebrow leads you to elaborate and explain your point—most judges have mobile, expressive eyebrows. The flicker of a judge's eye becomes all-important; a cloud across it, a twinkle in it, mean far more than they ever can in the courtroom. The distance is gone; you're close enough to share a smile of complicity.

And what about my expression as my opponent makes her submissions? I am not consciously trying to look sceptical or shocked or amused, but I read those emotions on my own face—a new experience, this, watching the spill-words write themselves across my features.

The one expression you can't afford to allow is boredom or distraction. You must gaze at the screen like a mother watching her sleeping child, never wavering. It's tiring; it's difficult. You can't let the background distract you, even when you notice something interesting. You start to worry about what your background tells others about you.

But the closeness also engenders familiarity. When the judge is sipping her tea, why not crack a joke? The screen is no barrier. When your opponent is so close you can see where he missed a spot shaving, why wouldn't you tease him a little? You do your best to treat it like a formal hearing but the façade soon slips. You're in someone's house—they're in yours—you must be friends, surely? This is not necessarily a good thing. Perhaps seeing the picture of the judge's kids behind him on the wall is stepping too close to intimacy. Perhaps the formality of the courtroom helps with respect. Image matters'.[6]

Court artist

I cover the point in more detail below but let's get this clear: in the UK it is illegal to draw or photograph court proceedings even if you are not in court but watching them on a device. Official court artists draw from memory. Here Elizabeth Cook describes that process:

'One of the earliest prominent cases after lockdown began was the libel hearing *Duchess of Sussex v Associated Newspapers*. The news agency PA Media commissioned me to draw the pre-trial hearing from home on 24 April 2020.

I would always prefer the interaction and close scrutiny that a live sitting would allow, but I can concentrate intently to the degree that I can memorise all I need to reproduce a good likeness. So the constraints I worked under for this hearing were no different from my normal modus operandi. I watched proceedings for about 10 minutes memorising the figures on screen, made brief notes re clothing and moved to an area out of sight and sound of the laptop to start the drawing. In fact, for a few years now, some defendants have appeared in pre-trial hearings on video screens in court, so the concept is not new to me. It is an advantage sometimes, in that I get a front view of the defendant rather than an awkward side view in a crowded courtroom.

Attending a trial is fascinating for any observer but for an artist concentrating intently on expression, mood, reaction and so on, it is very dramatic. I'm looking to convey all of these emotions in a single drawing. The interaction between the prosecuting barrister and the defendant is usually full of tension—there may be tears, an outburst, anger or indignation. Listening to the unfolding evidence, observing courtroom etiquette, running through the marble halls of the Old Bailey and planning the drawing while setting up my drawing board in a corner of the press room all provide a buzz of excitement. This was rather a contrast with the arrangement surrounding the Duchess of Sussex hearing, where I didn't have to catch the 5.50am train to London, squeeze on a rush hour Tube, go through security checks nor join the long queue to get into the courtroom and find a seat on the press bench with a good view.

If it's a warm and bright day it's nice to draw outside on a step near the court or a low wall. Passers-by stop and comment or watch for a while, surprised that I am able to draw a detailed scene from memory—they imagine a court artist draws in court.

When my drawing is finished I take it outdoors, photograph it on my phone and email it to PA Media who distribute it to the press nationally and often internationally within minutes. If a TV news company has commissioned me there will be a camera operator waiting outside to film it.

For the Duchess of Sussex hearing I drew exactly what I saw on screen. Disappointingly the screen was divided in four, with one quarter blank. There was no detail, just the head and shoulders of judge and counsel for the defence and prosecution in suit and tie. No paperwork was visible and the backgrounds were plain. My drawing would have been so much more interesting had there been a microphone visible or the back of a leather chair, files or books, a carafe and glass, or had participants worn wigs and robes'.[7]

Banned images

As highlighted by the court artist's account in Box 1, Section 41 of the Criminal Justice Act 1925 rules out drawing and photography in courts (excluding the UK Supreme Court) and their undefined precincts in England and Wales. Restrictions also apply in Northern Ireland and Scotland.

Technically, such activity is illegal only if it is 'with a view to publication', but no court usher in the land would give you the benefit of the doubt. Tom Keating, the notorious art forger, was allowed to get away with sketching from the dock at his trial in the Old Bailey, but didn't create a precedent.

This ban is particularly galling when people around you in the public gallery may be tweeting any old defamatory rubbish unobserved. While it is right that court artists have to leave juries and vulnerable participants out of the picture, such deliberate mystique is not helpful.

The ban was broadly to do with official distaste when newspapers published illicit photos of sensitive scenes—such as a poisoner attentive in the dock at the Old Bailey as he is sentenced to death by the black-capped judge.[8]

In 2018 the Court of Appeal was permitted to live-stream certain proceedings on YouTube, but such moves to make more court footage available have been hamstrung by Covid-19. The UK Supreme Court is the only court to put footage of all hearings (live and recorded) on its website and to post judgment summaries on YouTube. Established under the Constitutional Reform Act 2005, this court is able to take transparency seriously.

Making images

One day I saw a court artist working in the UK Supreme Court. As far as I am aware, this was the only time that a news agency had commissioned one to draw there: perhaps an editor with little experience of the dryness of Supreme Court appeals had hoped for some through-the-keyhole copy. It was *Bull v Hall*, a sex discrimination case about a same-sex couple in a civil partnership who were denied a room in a B&B.

The artist had a suitcase containing masses of well-used pastels and sheets of thick, tawny, parchment-type paper, 3' by 2', one of which she draped over her lap. She quickly blocked out a picture in outline and then, in a controlled frenzy to meet the deadline, drew the scene largely—it seemed—from memory. On paper, she moved the five justices closer together, pushed the appellants Mr and Mrs Bull apart, and redistributed anyone blocking the view. That way, she choreographed a compact dramatic tableau. A TV camera's lens could wander across it, picking out faces. It was not meant to be the equivalent of a photograph. (Nor was Laura Knight's depiction of the Nuremberg trials in 1946, a patchwork of portrait studies she had made over weeks in the courtroom and then copied for her oil painting.)

But how true to life is a photograph, anyway? On 4 November 2016 *The Times* ran a photograph of the Lord Chief Justice, the Master of the Rolls and Lord Justice Sales standing together in solidarity. This was after they had been described as "enemies of the people" by the *Daily Mail* in response to their Divisional Court ruling that Parliament had a right to vote on triggering Article 50, leading to Brexit. Just one snag: if you look closely at the photograph (in the hard copy edition, not the online version),[9] you observe that they are not standing together at all. Only one of them—the judge with a shadow—is in the room. The other two, hovering above cloned stretches of carpet as shadowless as Peter Pan, have been added by someone using software.

Matériel

Court artists in England generally use pastels to cover a lot of ground quickly. Artist Richard Cole—who, in a flak jacket, was the only accredited artist at the Abu Ghraib prison abuse courts martial in Baghdad—is one of those who prefer the portability of pencil and watercolour, which he points out has the drama of still drying in front of the cameras.

One of the most prominent court artists, the American Howard Brodie (1915–2010), got by with a few crayons. Artist Victor Juhasz describes on his blog how, as a newbie sweating with nerves at the start of the trial of Ronald Reagan's would-be assassin John Hinckley, he spotted his idol, Brodie:

> 'Where are all his art supplies? I came loaded for bear. Where are the million and one colored chalks, and brushes, and pens? He's got his drawing pad open, 18" × 24", like me. That's cool. But all he's got are some Prismacolor pencils—three colors—Tuscan red, black, and a dark blue. My attention is drawn to his lightning fast gestural marks setting his characters in place. With Zen-like jottings and jabs, he establishes the basic structure in black pencil and then brings in the red and blue to fill in and add weight. The energy is startling and the confidence is unmistakable'.[10]

I am normally snooty about drawing with software, which to me has a dead, second-hand look, a plodding line and a flattened limitation of colour. I like organic materials with a mind of their own which show friction, the passage of time, the body's movement. But, away from the courtroom, I have to make an exception for *Nursing Story* by Oh Young-jun in South Korea. He became a nurse after art school and volunteers for hardship postings in the intensive care unit. His electronic rapid reportage sketches of the nurses' endurance and exhaustion during the Covid-19 onslaught are on Facebook (@nursingstory) and Instagram (@nursing_story). No grand set piece could say as much as a simple drawing of an ICU nurse giving herself a coat-hanger drip so that she can slog on. And the caption to a seemingly ordinary picture of a nurse says that she is not being protected from radiation while deploying a mobile X-ray unit.

In the UK Supreme Court

I have been an occasional sketcher in the public seats (with the court's permission) but there is of course no point in drawing here, since everything is filmed, so why do it at all? To quote Lord Neuberger, former President of the Supreme Court, wildly out of context: "In many cases, quick and dirty justice would do better justice than the full majesty of a traditional common law trial".[11] I argue that there is also a place for quick and dirty drawing, my favourite kind.

The three courtrooms are sometimes sparsely populated, generally busy, and on rare occasions packed and febrile, as during the emergency hearings about the illegal prorogation of parliament in 2019. In terms of creature comforts the building is a softer option than some of my other drawing gigs which have included:

- Fetish clubs. Compared with courts, they have more rules, a stricter dress code and a less inclusive door policy.
- Occupy protest camps and squats. In a court, two opposing sides are represented. Occupy contained far more than two.
- Next to a flyover on Portobello Road. Great personnel, poor air quality.

In the court, my paper must be no more than body-width, an exiguous limit for me, especially when there are nine or even 11 judges instead of the usual five. I use nothing that would leave dust on the magnificently bright Peter Blake carpet (pastel, charcoal). Nothing splashy (ink) or noisy (swooshes of hard Conté stick on textured paper). I have trusty Japanese cartridge pens, felt-tips (sorry), pencils, crayons. Some watercolours, a manga pen and a plastic waterbrush all in a cute box (the Kuretake Little Red Gift Set), although it's more grown-up to make your own miniature set. And I leave my preferred kit at home because it requires a tank of ink: bedraggled goose quills, bamboo pens, wooden coffee stirrers, calligraphy brushes, balls of sheep's wool and (my most cherished souvenir of Occupy) the tip of a white man's dreadlock which led to a court case.

I offer a commentary on my solipsistic blog about live-drawing (drawing on location, not to be confused with life-drawing, depicting the naked figure). A random Miss Flite, I try to decode the courtroom theatre and show people at work. I can look for human details such as the anxiety of a QC on his feet, rapidly clenching and unclenching his hand behind his back while presenting a bold front to a row of Justices.

I am not here to caricature. The robust tradition of political lampooning—an important indicator of a democracy's health—would be misplaced in court. Our justice system is too precious for that.

Spectators come and go, staying for minutes or hours. It's a site for spotters, purists and lovers of cool legal abstractions, not for the *tricoteuses* who frequent the Old Bailey for murder. There is no age limit but a noisy toddler might attract a hard stare from the bench. Some of the casual tourists (and a few lawyers) are clearly unnerved by a primitive fear of what is in the room: the relentless apparatus of a judicial process leading to finality, with roots trailing to an unknown past of human sacrifice. Sometimes there's an inescapable *Wicker Man* vibe, even in civil actions.

The Supreme Court is democratically flat,[12] with the bench on the same level as everyone else. This goes with the lack of pomp and paraphernalia—Justices reserve gowns for ceremony and advocates are hardly ever robed—but it restricts the sightlines, while Justices and staff, even if I can see them through intervening heads, can seem far away across the howling tundra. How do you deal with that? Sometimes I experiment with transparent outlines to show more people.

My main tip: don't get noticed. My most unsettling court experience was in the Cour d'appel in the Palais de justice in Paris: a man with an actual gun—one of a team of gendarmes roaming the courtroom, indifferent to the appeal—loomed over my sketchbook and, worst of all, called me *tu* after I dropped a pencil, the sound of which reverberated around the court for about half an hour.

Despite the low profile, sometimes I have to field questions from others in court. Most common are:

a "Did you draw me?" (That'll be a QC.) Possibly, but maybe not in the conventional heroic guise.
b "Who's going to win?" (That'll be a tourist.) Search me—but don't read too much into whether the bench is fractious, purring or non-committal. The tone of judicial interventions can have more to do with the conduct of the case than the state of the law or any killer argument.

Finally, visitors to the court's cafeteria are subject to the benign but probing gaze of souvenir teddy bears representing the Supreme Court and the Judicial Committee of the Privy Council, which sits in the same building. The bears begin to infiltrate my drawings and this ends up as an illustrated book, *The Supreme Court: A Guide for Bears*, in which the earnest ursines explore their Art Nouveau Gothic habitat.[13]

The Naked Rambler in the dock

My drawing worlds collide in 2015: a nude invades the courtroom in the shape of Stephen Gough, the Naked Rambler. Just one snag: this is Winchester Crown Court, so I will have to draw afterwards, from memory.

I nearly have a wasted journey. Just before the off, Steve's brief, Matthew Scott, kindly warns me that I won't be able to see the dock from the public gallery, which is directly above it. Many courts are designed to lay out their contents like a royal flush for the sole benefit of the bench. I blag my way airside.

Figure 12.2 Some of the negative space in *The Supreme Court: A Guide for Bears*—in this book I point out that there is no jury in the court.

Figure 12.3 Lynn Shellfish Limited and others v Loose and another, UK Supreme Court, 9 February 2016.

Steve is a former Royal Marine trained in the Arctic, so tramping around the UK in nothing but boots, socks, a chunky watch and a rucksack doesn't bother him. I feel that his struggle is concerned not with some right to be publicly naked, but with a compulsion to challenge authority, and that he uses nudity as a fig leaf. This has led him to the highly controlled environment of prison. Does he seek this control? Does he wear HM Prison Winchester like a garment?

When Enid Blyton played tennis in the nude, no one called the cops. Context is all. Sightings of an unclothed Steve have riled the courts to such a degree that he is now saddled with his own tailor-made Anti-Social Behaviour Order. You and I can be legally naked in public unless we commit a chargeable offence, but the bespoke ASBO permits Steve no such luxury. This leads with lumpen logic to a potential infinity of jury trials (I am at his fourth) and custodial sentences.

As Matthew Scott has pointed out, "The problem is with an Anti-Social Behaviour Order that turns an eccentric into a criminal, and a prosecution system that could easily turn a blind eye, but which prefers instead to try to break the will of a harmless and astonishingly courageous man".

As I try to memorise Steve's appearance, life modelling comes to mind. In class or in the artist's studio, the naked model commands the space, clothed by custom and authority. No one is allowed to touch you. As a life model I have felt as armour-plated and anonymous as any judge in wig and robes. Like a judge, you see everything, you keep an eye on the time, you can give orders pertaining to your comfort and safety, no one is going to contradict you (or if they do, they have to be super-tactful in the veiled way of an experienced advocate), and as long as your physical pain is just about endurable you hide it.

The person horribly exposed in class is the artist, whose soul is revealed by every line committed to paper. And in Winchester Crown Court today, Steve's nudity seems almost irrelevant. Splayed out for public scrutiny is the inflexible legal system which has kept him in solitary confinement for some ten years at a public cost of about £400,000.

Steve's prison-pale body is hardy, bone and sinew, gently softening with time. It is the blank parchment on which other people can impose their own interpretation—hero, mischief-maker, victim of injustice. His skin has something of parchment's dry sallowness in the harsh downlights of the dock. He would have been seized by any self-respecting Renaissance painter as the weather-beaten model for another persecuted outsider, John the Baptist. As it is, this former soldier has something of the vulnerable warrior in *Descanso de Marte* ('Mars resting') by Velázquez (1640) and also of *Prometheus* by Gustave Moreau (1868), tormented but philosophical as his self-renewing liver is permanently devoured by an eagle—Steve's predicament indeed.

He is shielded by a wooden screen below, security glass above. He gazes up to heaven like a grizzled terrier or leans forward, straining to hear, his nose against the glass.

(And let's just put the dock in the dock for a moment. Much has been said about whether it should exist at all. Its separateness says "guilty as hell". Take the design in Westminster Magistrates' Court: the dock has a big red panic button. Detained defendants emerge from the lower regions through a door at the back. Those who have not been detained are shown into the dock by the usher who locks its glass door and takes away the key. Microphones give judges and advocates an authoritative resonance. The person in the dock speaks from a dull acoustic, as if masked.)

This morning, Steve has abruptly decided to represent himself, so Matthew Scott must swiftly cast off wig, gown and status. Now he is the one who is officially naked. To the evident relief of the judge he remains as an *amicus curiae* ("friend of the court", a non-party who offers information and arguments).

But you can't defend yourself if you are not allowed in the courtroom at the same time as the jury. Steve won't promise to remain seated and hide his genitals from the jury's sight—he insists on the proper protocol of standing when he is addressed by the judge—so he is forbidden to appear before the jury and banished to the cells. Throughout, an official sits with a plastic-wrapped grey marl prison-issue tracksuit on her lap.

Steve is remanded in custody. This is a memory-drawing gig so on the train home, surrounded by squaddies, I start sketching in pencil in an A5 sketchbook from John Purcell Paper (wholesale fairyland in South London). At home I recreate it with a Platinum 3776 Century pen (soft fine nib) and watercolour.

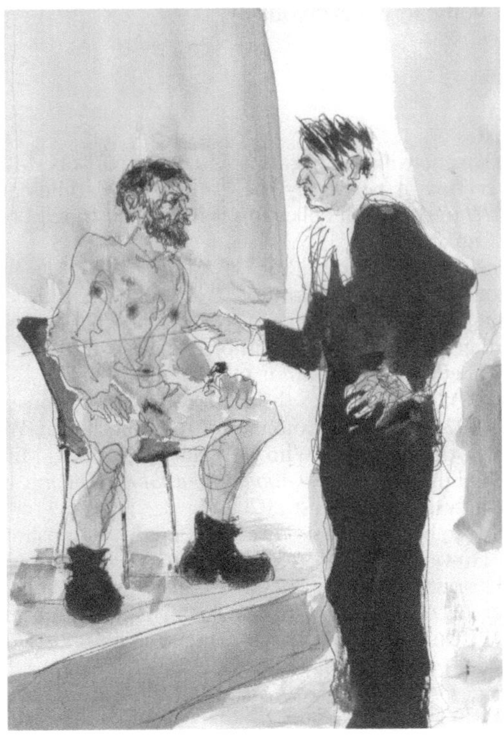

Figure 12.4 The Naked Rambler and his brief, Matthew Scott. The lower part of the dock is not transparent, being made of wood, but I have met and drawn Stephen Gough before, in a private house, so I cheat for the sake of the drawing.

At the sentencing hearing a couple of months later, the same judge sighs, "Do you want to say you're sorry?"

"I'm not sorry," says Steve, his breath misting the glass in front of him. Even so, he gets away with what sounds like the minimum sentence. At the time of writing, Steve is a free man.

Nothing but the truth?

Some kinds of drawing—in the technical fields of surgery or archaeology, for example—augment photography. They represent three dimensions in an objective, sometimes diagrammatic fashion. But in court you are not drawing a motionless anatomical specimen or the strata of a dig. Nor can you draw the concept of legal truth.

Drawing is autobiographical. The artist intervenes between the subject and you. Magritte's 1929 painting *La Trahison des images* (the treachery of images) says *Ceci n'est pas une pipe* (this is not a pipe). Correct. It is a picture of a pipe. Time passes, events unfold. If there is natural light, it changes. A drawing advocates a point of view. A photograph can be just as manipulable as a drawing. Consider how far you can believe your eyes.

Notes

1 Writer and artist.
2 Website: https://isobelwilliams.org.uk. Blog: http://isobelwilliams.blogspot.com. Some of her versions of poems by the Latin poet Catullus are in the anthology *New Poetries VIII* and her full collection is in her illustrated book *Catullus: Shibari Carmina* (both Carcanet, 2021).
3 Email from Penelope Gibbs to author (10 August 2020).
4 Email from anonymous judge to author (6 August 2020).
5 Email from anonymous judge to author (6 August 2020).
6 Email from Catherine Rowlands to author (26 August 2020).
7 Email from Elizabeth Cook to author (19 August 2020).
8 Professor Linda Mulcahy explores the ban in 'Revolting Consumers: A Revisionist Account of the 1925 Ban on Photography in English and Welsh Courts and its Implications for Debate About Who is Able to Produce, Manage and Consume Images of the Trial' (2018) 4 *International Journal of Law in Context*, http://eprints.lse.ac.uk/89510, accessed 23 August 2020.
9 *The Times*, 4 November 2016, 10–11, picture credit 'Photoshot'.
10 Victor Juhasz, 'Howard Brodie 1915–2010' (*Drawger*, 19 September 2010), https://drawger.com/victorjuhasz/?article_id=11315, accessed 23 August 2020.
11 Lord Neuberger of Abbotsbury, 'Justice in an Age of Austerity' (JUSTICE, 15 October 2013), https://justice.org.uk/wp-content/uploads/2015/02/Justice-in-an-age-of-austerity-Lord-Neuberger.pdf, accessed 23 August 2020.
12 See L Mulcahy, *Legal Architecture: Justice, Due Process and the Place of Law* (Routledge 2011) 7.
13 For more about the building: *The Supreme Court of the United Kingdom: History, Art, Architecture*, a handsome illustrated book edited by Chris Miele, from the court and bookshops (Merrell 2010).

13 Designing to dismantle

Hallie Jay Pope[1]

When we employ design processes and visual design tools to increase access to a legal system or process, our approach likely falls on a spectrum between two opposing viewpoints. On one end is the view that the system to which we seek to increase access is capable of producing just outcomes, but is failing to do so because of some combination of flaws addressable through reform. On the other end is the view that the system produces unjust outcomes by design in order to preserve power for an elite few, and increasing access is a stopgap for minimising harm that flows inherently from the system, as well as a step on the path to building the power needed to ultimately dismantle the system.

This division between designing for reform and designing to dismantle is undoubtedly much more nuanced than my crude description suggests. I would not be surprised to learn that current applications of legal design methods to these two viewpoints overlap more often than they diverge. But design is about problem-solving, and ultimately, not all of us are trying to solve the same problems. I feel a sense of urgency in exploring these divergences now, while the field of legal design is still young. As the practice and study of legal design continues to burgeon, we can expect norms within the field to solidify into a reflection of dominant perspectives, excluding, marginalising and even co-opting divergent perspectives. I often hear that legal design is about improving existing systems and processes, making them more effective, more accessible. This framing sits comfortably with prevalent perspectives in the wider field of design, in which 'the majority of design treatises still maintain a fundamental orientation that is technocratic and market centered, and do not come close to questioning design's capitalistic nature'.[2] Fair to say, then, that designing for reform—rather than for radical, movement-based transformation—is the default approach … for now.

Legal design efforts to increase access to law undertaken within this dominant framework have helped and will continue to help people in meaningful ways. But at this moment when our field is still so open and new, it would be a mistake to limit ourselves to this approach. Angela Davis cautions us that 'frameworks that rely exclusively on reforms help to produce the stultifying idea that nothing lies beyond'.[3] In this ever-accelerating era of climate and social crisis, we face an 'irrefutable need' to engage in 'elimination design …

DOI: 10.4324/9780429021411-15

of the structures of unsustainability that maintain the dominant ontology of devastation', and to create 'new, nonexploitative forms of life'.[4] If we can break out of dominant design mindsets, we can use legal design as a tool for this kind of radical dismantling and transformation.

We don't have to start from scratch. 'Design has developed a new sensitivity to the environment and to human predicaments, and is more attuned to its ability to contribute to creating a better world …'.[5] Existing and emerging design practices offer us many tools that we can apply to anti-oppression work, including participatory, community-centred processes and visual design methods for effectively sharing legal knowledge. But all design methods, even those few born of radical political goals, can serve to perpetuate oppressive power structures if we apply them uncritically.

In the next section, I'll briefly lay out one vision for using legal design tools to share legal knowledge, build movement power and ultimately dismantle exploitative systems. Then, I'll identify three points in this process that—in my experience—put radical design visions at risk, and explore three corresponding strategies for moving beyond reform to dismantling: 1) When we define our design problem, we must situate ourselves in solidarity with collective movements; 2) when we facilitate participatory design processes, we must approach oppositional viewpoints with openness but not neutrality; and 3) when we communicate law visually, we must deliberately amplify counternarratives.

Sharing knowledge, shifting power

Anyone concerned with dismantling systems of subordination is concerned with building and mobilising collective power. For lawyers—the gatekeepers of legal knowledge, processes, and systems—power-building is recast, at least in part, as power-shifting: relinquishing our own structural power and shifting it to subordinated communities.[6] How do we do this? The practice of community lawyering, or 'lawyering against subordination',[7] identifies knowledge-sharing as a crucial power-shifting endeavour:

> Lawyers must relinquish our monopoly on legal knowledge by educating the clients and communities we work with; at the same time, we 'must open [our]selves up to being educated by all those with whom [we] come into contact, particularly about the traditions and experiences of life on the bottom and at the margins' (López, 1992, p. 37). This two-way flow of information remakes the traditional lawyer-client relationship into a partnership in which lawyers, clients, and communities 'share power and combine their overlapping practical knowledge of the world in order to solve problems of subordination' (Ancheta, 1993, p. 1364).[8]

My work as a legal information designer at the Graphic Advocacy Project is motivated by this theory. We strive to facilitate participatory design processes, designing informational resources with the communities that will ultimately use them and fostering the two-way flow of knowledge so critical to shifting power.[9] In doing so, we draw from design methods that have gained traction in the legal field among reformers and dismantlers alike, including:

- Design thinking: problem-solving mindsets that focus on the human needs behind a solution[10]
- Co-design: a design framework that 'rejects a hardline distinction between professional designers and users,' facilitating space for 'stakeholders to give feedback and engage in the creation of solutions'[11] throughout the design process
- Visual design: the use of visual elements—like typography and illustrations—to convey information

These methods have promising applications to anti-subordination legal work. As anthropologist Arturo Escobar observes, 'the great popularity gained by design thinking outside the design professions stems precisely from the perception of design's real or potential contribution to addressing "wicked" … problems, and of design as an agent of change.' But, he warns, 'the vexing question of the relation between design and the making of deeply unequal, insensitive, and destructive social orders seems to remain design's own "wicked problem"'. These design tools are not inherently opposed to exploitative structures; we must imbue them with that purpose.

Defining the problem: designing in solidarity

Design thinking urges us 1) to understand and address the root causes of a problem rather than just the symptoms, and 2) to view problems holistically from a systems perspective.[12] Applied to legal problems, these two principles require us to expand our understanding of a problem beyond the individual to the collective, beyond the process to the system, beyond the law to life as a whole. For designers concerned with dismantling oppressive systems, this call to approach problems with depth and breadth is a promising jumping-off point. But these inquiries, even when rooted in a participatory design process, will not necessarily situate a legal problem within broader collective movements against subordination.

This isn't so much a tension with methods like design thinking and participatory design as it is an insufficiency. As Norwegian participatory design pioneer Kristen Nygaard observed, design is '"merely a technique," a vehicle rather than the core of' political movements.[13] Defining the problem is our first opportunity in the design process to explicitly commit to building movement power, or, conversely, our first exposure to the risk of losing sight of 'what lies beyond'[14] our current political reality. When we agree to address the root causes and not just the symptoms of a problem, we must name capitalism, racism, imperialism and other intersecting structural oppressions as root causes, as well as the more concrete systems of law and power that uphold them.[15] 'The power to define certain problems as legitimate for research' tends to stem from the very forms of dominance we seek to destroy.[16] Of course, we are not going to dismantle these oppressive systems with one legal design project. But we can position ourselves within the vast ecosystem of ongoing movements against these systems. 'Successful movements exist'[17]; we must approach each legal design project as an opportunity to position ourselves in solidarity with them.

I can think of several times when I have failed to do this. One was a pamphlet about bail bonds that I created with a legal aid organisation. The problem we set out to tackle was the prevalence of predatory bail bond schemes. We hypothesised that at the point of decision-making, people lacked clear information about what a bail bond actually is, and that those who ultimately did decide to contract with a bail bond agent were largely unaware of the legal protections available to them and therefore vulnerable to abusive practices. We ended up creating a short illustrated pamphlet (Figure 13.1), which the legal aid organisation distributed through community clinics.

I'm very proud of this project; indeed, it's one that I regularly show off to students and potential collaborators. The feedback we received from the community was overwhelmingly positive. Although I haven't managed to collect any follow-up data on the resource's effectiveness, I would very much like to believe that it helped people. But looking back, I can't help but fear that we missed an organising opportunity. The pamphlet gestures at the idea

Figure 13.1 Detail from the pamphlet 'Bail Bonds', a collaboration between Iowa Legal Aid and the Graphic Advocacy Project (2019).

that cash bail is a fundamentally unjust practice, but it leaves undisturbed the notion that incarceration is an inevitable fact of life. It does not provide readers with any outlets to join ongoing movements against the systems that have allowed a practice like bail bonds to flourish, of which predatory lending is an inevitable symptom. It reinforces the status quo instead of tapping into design's potential to facilitate 'social dreaming', a collective imagining and articulation of 'alternative ways of being'.[18]

If I had the chance to do this project again, I would push to include abolitionist organisers as co-designers throughout the process, particularly at the moment of defining the project's scope. That's not to say that the inclusion of these partners would have necessarily affected the outcome in a particular way. When the immediate goal of a project is to convey clear and concise information to alleviate a harmful legal pain-point, attempting to mobilise broader action using the same resource is not without design tradeoffs. Maybe we would have sidelined that goal even if we'd pursued it in the first place and appraised ourselves of the movement landscape. But conversely, maybe the ways in which we chose to address the specific issue of bail bonds damaged ongoing collective efforts in ways we could have avoided had we been intentional about bringing in movement voices. Furthermore, the co-design process itself would have been an opportunity to build collective power by creating relationships and facilitating knowledge-sharing between the legal aid organisation, organisers and the community. For all of these reasons, we should take care to design in solidarity.

Facilitating participation: being open but not neutral

A crucial part of any human-centred design project is collecting insights and feedback from people impacted by the problem. Those of us concerned with shifting power to subordinated communities will likely—and indeed, should—be drawn to more participatory forms of this process like co-design, through which designers 'aim to share power throughout the process of making'.[19] Whatever solution they produce, participatory design processes can themselves be a tool for sharing knowledge and redistributing power to the people impacted by a systemic legal problem. But '[a]s research has shown ... "participation" is not a sufficient condition for changing power relations: forms of participation exist and presently thrive that do not question, but further, dominant power patterns'.[20]

Interestingly, foundational participatory design methods grew out of efforts to build worker power. In the early 1970s, Scandinavian trade unions sought to promote workplace democracy by increasing opportunities for workers to understand and shape the computer systems governing their work.[21] These efforts marked the emergence of Participatory Design, a practice that served as the foundation for contemporary co-design methods.[22] Participatory Design's roots were explicitly political; its early adherents aimed not only to democratise the workplace through systems design, but to democratise the design process itself.[23] But perhaps these original political goals were not sufficiently integrated into the Participatory Design approach. In 2002, educational scientist Eevi Beck observed that '[t]he term [Participatory Design] itself, originally "owned" by the politically radical, has more recently appeared as a slogan for marketing and other purposes'.[24]

In what ways are Participatory Design methods vulnerable to this kind of co-optation by existing power structures? Beck hints at one possible answer when she notes that 'in the European Commission's 1995/96 call for Telematics research proposals "user participation" meant the involvement of large corporations in systems development'.[25] It matters who participates, and how. But treating some viewpoints differently than others butts up against a prevalent design-thinking principle: maintaining neutrality. At the beginning of the COVID-19 pandemic, my colleague and I teamed up with a community lawyering organisation in Florida to design resources around high-priority legal issues, including evictions. In a dynamic emergency situation, and with limited resources at our disposal, we conducted a less robust exploratory research phase than we would consider ideal, limited to Zoom interviews with a handful of organisers and service providers working with the community on eviction prevention and other issues. Months later, we wrote an article[26] about the experience and some of the lessons we learned, which I circulated to a few people for early feedback. One responded to our use of the word 'stakeholders' in describing our co-design participants:

> Are you sure you want to embrace this concept? It was developed in the field of business ethics, where it had the progressive effect of leading management to think of 'stakeholders' other than shareholders, like workers and even consumers. It seems to this reader that you're really talking about vulnerable members of a community, or the working class—not 'stakeholders'. For example, you're a hell of a lot more concerned about tenants than landlords, even though both are equally 'stakeholders' affected by problems related to housing.

I was quite persuaded by this perspective. It had never crossed my mind to attempt to engage landlords as co-designers of our eviction resource. If we'd had more time and capacity, I would have focused on bringing more tenants, organisers and service providers into the process; I believed our exclusion of landlords was a matter of strategy, not circumstance. But my colleague—who, unlike me, actually has extensive experience and expertise in facilitating community co-design (in the arena of tenant advocacy, no less)—was less inclined to categorically dismiss the idea that landlord input might have been helpful in some capacity, pointing out that 'understanding a problem requires observing it neutrally from multiple perspectives'.[27]

Clearly this idea of seeking and synthesising varied viewpoints with a lens of neutrality is aimed at a valuable goal. In theory, viewing insights with objectivity allows you to see the problem and potential solutions more clearly, more truthfully, unclouded by your own personal biases. But we should approach this theory with caution, because we aren't just dealing with personal biases: we are surrounded by structural inequalities so pervasive that we might not even see them, much less successfully challenge them, without an extraordinary level of organization and intention. In such a reality, approaching all stakeholder viewpoints with 'neutrality' will preserve dominant viewpoints and entrench the status quo.

If we take the concept of co-design seriously (and we should!), we must share decision-making power with all of our collaborators; this is what distinguishes co-design from less democratic research and feedback methods. But it would be strategically incoherent to share power with those whose oppressive power we seek to eliminate, unless we have good reason to believe they will relinquish it willingly;[28] we must presume that entities with power will seek (consciously or subconsciously) to preserve it.[29] Therefore, when we define our problems in solidarity with ongoing movements, we also define our set of potential co-designers. Our design process should not serve as yet another avenue for interests opposed to our movements to wield their outsized power.

Although we should not give perspectives of oppressive power the benefit of neutrality, neither should we ignore them. Sometimes these perspectives will come from within the community impacted by the legal problem at issue (of course: communities are not monoliths, and the individuals that comprise them will have all sorts of experiences and views). Indeed, design itself plays a role in replicating dominant ideologies and values throughout society;[30] we should not be surprised that such viewpoints are pervasive across lines of systemic oppression. Encountering oppositional perspectives within impacted communities presents an opportunity to deepen our understanding of hurdles to collective intersectional mobilisation.

At other times, movement organisers might make the strategic choice to engage with oppositional interests in a limited fashion to minimise harm. During the exploratory research phase of our eviction resource project, we heard one particularly interesting insight from a housing organiser that highlights the importance of remaining open, if not neutral. This participant told us that while their mobilising efforts typically cast landlords as antagonists, they had backed away from this kind of rhetoric during the early stages of the pandemic, in acknowledgment of the reality that landlords had also been affected by the crisis and might be willing to bargain in ways they otherwise wouldn't. The participant voiced an ongoing need to activate the community around issues of housing justice like rent cancellation, but also pointed to the effectiveness, albeit temporary, of tenants negotiating ad hoc rental payment agreements with their landlords. We heard this stopgap solution echoed in sessions with other community organizers. Ultimately, although our resource necessarily portrayed landlords as having interests in opposition to their tenants, we made an effort to honour this feedback by focusing more on tenants' relationships to the legal system and to each other (see Figure 13.2).

Figure 13.2 Detail from a visual evictions guide created by the Community Justice Project and the Graphic Advocacy Project (2020).

In some situations, fully understanding a problem may require us to actively seek perspectives from oppositional stakeholders. In this case, we should extract the information we need without engaging in mutual knowledge-sharing or conferring any design power. To do otherwise is to risk co-option of our project by the systems we seek to dismantle. We must also examine what we learn with a critical eye. All design research runs the risk of raising the 'say/do dilemma': people don't always do what they say, and so 'say' research techniques like interviews or surveys leave room for the speaker to communicate misinformation (intentionally or unintentionally).[31] The risk of misinformation is surely higher if the participant's interests are opposed to the project's goals. Observational 'do' techniques and generative 'make' techniques can help resolve this dilemma,[32] but it is hard to imagine successfully applying such involved techniques outside of a meaningful co-designer partnership.

How do we distinguish between which 'stakeholders' to invite into the process as co-designers, which to cautiously mine for information and which to actively exclude? We might start by mapping our assumptions about stakeholders' relative power within the relevant legal systems and processes, and their relative alignment with—or opposition to—our power-shifting endeavours. This can be as simple as drawing two intersecting perpendicular lines to form a quadrant matrix, with stakeholders' systemic power represented on the x-axis (increasing in relative power from left to right) and their alignment with movement goals represented on the y-axis (increasing in alignment from bottom to top).

Using GAP's eviction resources as an example, we might have placed tenants and community organisers in the top left quadrant of such a matrix, community lawyers (and ourselves) in the top right, small-scale landlords in the bottom left (but pretty close to the midpoint), and real estate developers in the bottom right. This kind of matrix can help identify and prioritise potential co-designers in the initial stages of a project, starting with stakeholders closest to the top left and relying on their knowledge and lived experiences to move our map away from assumptions and root it in reality. By eschewing neutrality and evaluating stakeholder perspectives through a lens of power and solidarity, we can more effectively employ participatory design methods to build the collective power that will ultimately remake our world.

Communicating visually: amplifying counternarratives

Visual communication is a uniquely effective vehicle for sharing complex information, which is a key component of virtually any design project aimed at promoting access to law, but a particularly crucial means of building collective power to dismantle oppressive systems (as I discussed in the first section).

Visual narratives are an especially fruitful tool in this regard. Look at how this same information, conveyed in descriptive text on the left and as a mini-narrative on the right, transforms from a dry legal definition into a story about workers building power (Figure 13.3):

Figure 13.3 Detail from a comic about multi-stakeholder cooperatives created by Co-op Dayton and the Graphic Advocacy Project (2017).

Humans love stories about humans,[33] and law is all about humans (although most legal documents seem to go out of their way to obscure that fact). Legal informational resources should take advantage of that fact by depicting people impacted by a legal problem and showing their successful navigation of the processes involved. For those of us designing to dismantle, visual narratives pose an additional opportunity to expose the dominant narratives espoused by those systems, and to amplify counternarratives. As legal theorist Richard Delgado puts it:

> Stories, parables, chronicles, and narratives are powerful means for destroying mindset—the bundle of presuppositions, received wisdoms, and shared understandings against a background of which legal and

> political discourse takes place. These matters are rarely focused on. They are like eyeglasses we have worn a long time. They are nearly invisible; we use them to scan and interpret the world and only rarely examine them for themselves. Ideology—the received wisdom—makes current social arrangements seem fair and natural. Those in power sleep well at night—their conduct does not seem to them like oppression.[34]

But this articulation of the promise of narratives also reveals a potential pitfall for designers using visuals in legal resources. As soon as we depict a person, we are telling the reader a story about that person. Look back at two definitions of a cooperative, one conveyed in text and one through a mix of text and images. The text in the two definitions is almost identical, and indeed is sparser in the right-hand version. But we are learning a lot of things about the coffee farmers from the right-hand version that the text alone did not convey. They both appear to be women. One looks white, the other Black. Both appear happy; indeed, the farmer on the right looks rather triumphant, their hand resting confidently on their hip. As the person who created this graphic, I can tell you that while some of these narrative elements were by design, others seemed to simply appear.

When designing to dismantle we must be intentional and thoughtful in our creation of visual counternarratives, lest oppressive dominant narratives creep their way into our designs. I doubt that I have ever managed to create a graphic that doesn't reinforce dominant narratives to some degree. But I have noticed that certain practices go a long way towards resisting this insidious effect.

The cooperative graphic in Figure 13.3 above is from a comic I made with a co-op incubator. The incubator was supporting the creation of a multi-stakeholder cooperative grocery store in a community that was designated as a food desert. In my first version of the comic, I shaded the characters with a colourful mix of jewel tones. I received feedback that, upon reflection, I was embarrassed to have needed in the first place. The community building the co-op was 80 per cent Black people. My racially-ambiguous green, orange and purple people did not reflect that. I had unintentionally perpetuated the harmful dominant narrative that collective efforts to improve material conditions would come from some sort of idealised race-blind coalition rather than from the real people—mostly Black people—living in the community. The fact that this majority-Black community was in a food desert was no coincidence: it was evidence of capitalism and racism working in tandem.

I think my revised depictions more accurately reflect the fact that the co-op effort was Black-led, but I also see room for improvement. Since creating this comic, I have implemented the practice of designing characters based on reference photos of real people in order to avoid visual stereotypes. I have to be particularly rigorous about this when designing characters with experiences and identities different from my own. Just as neutrality in the research and feedback process will perpetuate power imbalances, drawing 'default' characters will likely reinforce dominant narratives about power relationships.

During the bail bonds project I mentioned in the previous section, I unwittingly made room for a different dominant narrative to slip in. As Figure 13.4 shows, originally, the pamphlet followed the story of one defendant and his family.

But during the feedback phase, someone pointed out that the only criminal defendant in the pamphlet was a person of colour, and the only recurring character with institutional power (the judge) was white. This had been a conscious decision on my part to try to reflect the racist reality of our criminal justice system. But because the pamphlet only followed one person's story instead of a group that could serve as a more inclusive representation, the depiction landed as a stereotype. In the final version, shown in the right panel of Figure 13.4, I created three different defendants to share the role of protagonist:

Figure 13.4 The original (left) and final (right) versions of an image for 'Bail Bonds', a pamphlet created by Iowa Legal Aid and the Graphic Advocacy Project (2019).

It is worth noting that, out of over 60 feedback survey respondents, only one voiced the opinion that the original depiction perpetuated race-based stereotypes. But that might just be further evidence of the pervasiveness of these dominant narratives. Ultimately, we were able to find a way to depict a more representative group of defendants that didn't detract from the effectiveness of the visual narrative.

In addition to soliciting community feedback[35] and basing character designs on real human beings, another promising strategy for producing compelling visual counternarratives is to depict real stories told by the people who experienced them. This isn't a fail-safe method for subverting dominant narratives by any means; as Delgado points out, we all internalise dominant narratives about ourselves as well as others. But as co-design counsels us, people are experts in their own experiences, and these real-life counternarratives provide a status-quo-busting dose of reality that is much more difficult to achieve with make-believe. Cartoonist Eleanor Davis and the Bronx Freedom Fund made beautiful use of this technique by illustrating interviews with people for whom the Fund had posted bail.[36]

Counternarratives don't just serve to subvert dominant narratives; they are generative as well as destructive. 'They can open new windows into reality, showing us that there are possibilities for life other than the ones we live'.[37] Visuals enhance this power. If we use them with care and intention, we can breathe life into the 'imagination[s] of alternative ways of being'[38] we seek to facilitate through radical design.

* * *

I began this chapter by defining two opposing ends of a spectrum of design work aimed at increasing access to law: one concerned with reforming unjust systems and the other with building the collective power needed to dismantle them. But whether we intend to or not, *all* legal designers are engaging with structural power. 'We are not free to choose whether our actions carry political meaning. Conforming to a dominant norm—"not raising your head"—also constitutes a statement; also co-constructs society'.[39] We can use design to entrench consolidated power, limiting our efforts to reforms that largely accept our unjust, unsustainable political reality. Or we can design to transcend this reality, to shift power to movements that 'evince the unwavering conviction that another world is indeed possible'.[40] Please join me in imagining what lies beyond.

Notes

1 Legal information designer and cartoonist, founder and president of the Graphic Advocacy Project.
2 Arturo Escobar, *Designs for the Pluriverse* (Duke University Press 2018) 26.
3 Angela Y Davis, *Are Prisons Obsolete?* (Seven Stories Press 2003) 20.
4 Escobar n 2, 6–7.
5 Escobar n 2, 34.
6 See, e.g., Gerald P Lopez, *Rebellious Lawyering* (Westview Press 1992); Angelo N Ancheta, 'Review Essay: Community Lawyering' (1993) 81 California Law Review 1363; Charles Elsesser, 'Community Lawyering—The Role of Lawyers in the Social Justice Movement' (2003) 14 Loyola Journal of Public Interest Law 375.
7 Lopez n 6, 37.
8 Hallie Jay Pope and Ashley Treni, 'Sharing Knowledge, Shifting Power: A Case Study of "Rebellious" Legal Design During COVID-19' (2021) 49.1 Journal of Open Access to Law, https://ojs.law.cornell.edu/index.php/joal/article/view/114/108, accessed 13 March 2021.
9 For a more robust discussion of GAP's work, see Pope and Treni n 8.
10 See IDEO U, 'What Is Design Thinking?', https://www.ideou.com/blogs/inspiration/what-is-design-thinking, accessed 13 March 2021.
11 Pope and Treni n 8, 3–4.
12 See, e.g., Don Norman, 'The Four Fundamental Principles of Human-Centered Design and Application' (*JND.org*, 1 August 2019), https://jnd.org/the-four-fundamental-principles-ofhuman-centered-design/, accessed 13 March 2021.
13 Eevi E Beck, 'P for Political: Participation Is Not Enough' (2002) 14.1 Scandinavian Journal of Information Systems 82 (quoting Nygaard).

14 Davis n 3, 20.
15 See Escobar n 2, 47 ('Radicalizing Design Politics Will Require … Situating Design Squarely in Relation to Inequality, Racism, Sexism, and Colonialism').
16 Beck n 13, 83.
17 Beck n 13, 86.
18 Escobar n 2, 17 (citing Anthony Dunne and Fiona Raby's writing on speculative design).
19 Pope and Treni n 8, 3–4.
20 Beck n 13, 82.
21 Gro Bjerknes and Tone Bratteteig, 'User Participation and Democracy: A Discussion of Scandinavian Research on System Development' (1995) 7.1 Scandinavian Journal of Information Systems 76.
22 Bjerknes and Bratteteig n 21, 76.
23 Pirjo Elovaara, Faraja Teddy Igira and Christina Mörtberg, 'Whose Participation? Whose Knowledge?—Exploring PD in Tanzania-Zanzibar and Sweden' in *PDC '06: Proceedings of the Ninth Conference on Participatory Design: Expanding Boundaries in Design—Volume 1* (ACM Press 2006) 2.
24 Beck n 13, 79.
25 Beck n 13, 79.
26 See Pope and Treni n 8.
27 Pope and Treni n 8, fn. 17. The Creative Reaction Lab's *Equity-Centered Community Design Field Guide*, which succinctly makes the point that 'inequities exist by design, and only intentional acts can dismantle them', also seems to endorse the general principle behind this view, calling for designers to 'ensure a balanced representation across sectors' of a community (including, for example, the business sector). Creative Reaction Lab, *Equity-Centered Community Design Field Guide*, 16.
28 As discussed above, lawyers fall into this category. We must earn an assumption of good faith by sincerely and consistently demonstrating our willingness to relinquish the power we draw from exploitative systems.
29 As just one example, there is 'evidence suggesting that corporations will seek to undermine any proposal that meaningfully shifts power and resources to workers', even while engaging in corporate processes purporting to protect worker interests. Matteo Gatti and Chrystin D Ondersma, 'Stakeholder Syndrome: Does Stakeholderism Derail Effective Protections for Weaker Constituencies' (2012) 100 North Carolina law Review 167.
30 See Joanna Boehnert and Dimeji Onafuwa, 'Design as Symbolic Violence: Reproducing the 'isms' + A Framework for Allies' (Intersectional Perspectives on Design, Politics and Power School of Arts and Communication, Malmö University 2016) 2–3.
31 Elizabeth B-N Sanders and Pieter Jan Stappers, *Convivial Toolbox* (BIS Publishers, 4th edn. 2018) 69.
32 Sanders and Stappers n 31, 69.
33 Scott McCloud, *Making Comics* (William Morrow 2006) 60–61.
34 Richard Delgado, 'Storytelling for Oppositionists: A Plea for Narrative' (1989) 87.8 Michigan Law Review 2411–41.
35 For a more in-depth, practical discussion of how GAP solicits community input throughout the design process, see Pope and Treni n 8.
36 See, for example, Eleanor Davis, 'Makayla' (Bronx Freedom Fund), thebronxfreedomfund.org/Makayla, accessed 13 March 2021.
37 Delgado n 34, 2414–15.
38 Escobar n 2, 17.
39 Beck n 13, 88.
40 Escobar n 2, 16.

14 Taking a co-design workshop online

Emily Allbon[1] *and Rachel Warner*[2]

Liberty is an independent civil liberties organisation which was founded in 1934 and is currently the largest in the UK. They came to us with a challenge: to identify how information design might help to make their web-based legal information and advice more accessible, useful and understandable. In this chapter we explain how we are responding to that challenge by taking a user-centred approach.

We focus on a preliminary workshop and insights made. We share our approach to planning the workshop, the materials generated and the tools used to help those new to using co-design methods in a legal context. The project is still ongoing at the time of writing, so we share our insights and plans for using the insights to plan the future direction of the project. We place special emphasis on the adaptations to the research activities research we made in light of the COVID-19 pandemic.

Legal information at Liberty

Liberty use a variety of methods to champion anyone whose rights come under threat, from Gypsy and Traveller communities to Government whistle-blowers. Here we focus on two ways that Liberty provide information. Firstly, they produce a series of highly accessible text-based online advice guides, provided as web pages on their website, which Liberty draft with the occasional assistance of lawyers at Reed Smith and a professional copywriter. The guides traditionally focus on the topics of police, protest, and privacy rights. For example, when in 2020–2021 the state sought to use a series of rapidly changing regulations to control the behaviour of the population in response to the COVID-19 pandemic, Liberty responded with guides on topics such as 'What powers do the police have under the Coronavirus Act 2020?' and 'What if I'm arrested at a protest during the coronavirus lockdown?'. Secondly, Liberty provide responses to direct queries made by the public. Liberty's Advice and Information team receives queries from the public via a webform, which collects necessary contact details, a description of their query, whether there is a deadline and whether they are represented by a lawyer. Liberty aim to respond within six weeks, a target which gives an indication of the complexity, range and volume of queries that they

DOI: 10.4324/9780429021411-16

receive. For example, in 2020, Liberty received 2,135 queries. They also receive a large number of requests for legal representation or help with legal topics that Liberty cannot assist with; this can amount to fewer than 20 per cent of all enquiries being provided with information and advice.

Together with Liberty we decided to focus on two of their core topic areas of expertise: police complaints and stop and search. We also decided to focus on a third area, immigration, specifically because it is a topic on which Liberty do not offer advice, instead they signpost to other advice services. This afforded us the opportunity to reflect on how the design of information within Liberty's online guides could equip the public with more relevant and timely advice, and signpost them to relevant external information. It is hoped that improvements could lead to Liberty receiving fewer queries, meaning Liberty advisors can spend more time on complex queries less likely to be resolved by written information alone.

A user-centred design approach

We take a user-centred design approach that focusses on users and their needs throughout each phase of the design process. We loosely base our process on the iterative phases of discover, define, develop and deliver from the Double Diamond model,[3] including a 'challenge' and outcome (Figure 14.1). It is loosely based on this model as the activities, such as the kick-off workshop, spans across phases. In the first phase of the design process we look to *understand* or *discover* the user needs—in this case, those who go to the Liberty website for help; and then the next phase is to *define* the problem we are trying to solve—in this case, how might we make legal information within the Liberty materials more understandable? As the diagram demonstrates this is an iterative process involving divergent and convergent thinking across phases.

Within this iterative process we organise co-design activities, whereby insights and solutions evolve from collaboration among stakeholders. The use of co-design activities can be found across research projects focussed on

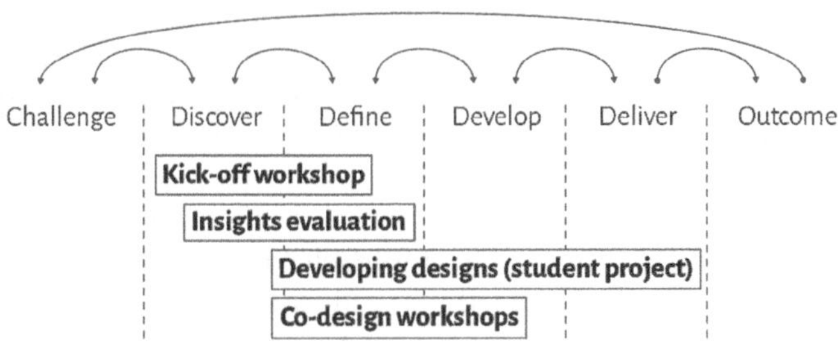

Figure 14.1 A diagram of our design process loosely based on the discover, define, develop and deliver aspects of the Double Diamond model. This chapter focusses on the 'kick-off workshop' and 'insights evaluation' activities within the project.

improving information provided to the public.[4] Noël et al. summarise a co-design process as 'a process of engagement, participation and collaboration'[5] and it is in this spirit that we approach the organisation of our co-design activities for this project.

Co-design activities tend to involve all stakeholders who are involved with the final outcome of a project, such as trained designers who will develop a solution to the end-users who will use it. We recognise the importance of working with users to identify problems, priorities and solutions. This is considered an 'active' involvement of users[6] whereby the importance of 'elevating lived experience' and working with users as 'trustworthy and competent interpreters of their own lives'[7] who play a key role in developing knowledge, ideas, and solutions[8]—is crucial. Indeed, research using co-design methods emphasises a perspective of 'designing with'[9] users who are active partners in a project.

Ideally, we would have worked with some of Liberty's clients, people who use Liberty's information, in the first workshop; however, two factors limited this. Firstly, Liberty differ from many other front-facing legal advice agencies in the access to justice sector in that there is rarely a recurrent relationship with clients. A question is asked by a client, Liberty may or may not be able to assist (depending on the area of law) and a response will be provided accordingly. However, even when they can provide some legal advice in response to an inquirer, this will be provided on a one-off basis and usually that client will go onto their next steps elsewhere. Secondly, given the civil liberties focus of Liberty's enquiries, there is also a risk that unlike someone seeking information on a product, for example, people seeking Liberty's advice often feel limited in how they can interact with services—even those that are there to offer independent help. For example, someone seeking immigration information may not be comfortable identifying themselves within a group setting. Likewise, Liberty staff are aware that some clients may have mental health concerns. This is sometimes the case with queries around surveillance and intrusion by the state.

These factors led us to involve an empathic approach for our first kick-off co-design workshop, whereby Liberty staff who encounter clients seeking human rights information act as 'user researchers'.[10] In this way Liberty staff provide insights from their experiences informing and advising the public on these topics; insights such as how people say they are feeling or the difficulties they face. These insights informed the next activities for our project whereby we plan to organise co-design workshops with end-users during the 'define' and 'develop' phases of our project. The approach for our kick-off workshop acknowledges that using co-design methods with users who might have concerns about interacting with services as described above might be ethically inappropriate,[11] and offers a way of using co-design methods where access to end-users is limited. This approach—combining activities that involve both an empathic mindset and a co-design method advocates a flexible approach to project design whereby resources and contexts may impact plans.

The kick-off workshop

The main aim of the kick-off workshop was to gather insights that would shape the next steps of our project. It was anticipated that these would include considering a range of appropriate visual means for compiling, sharing and presenting information to users to help inform them of their rights.

It was planned around established methods used in user-centred design: empathy maps, personas and journey maps. These would help us gather valuable insights about users such as how information is sought, accessed and used when people confront a legal issue.

Empathy maps are a way of brainstorming how a particular group of people experience a problem. Workshop participants create a 'picture reflecting the thoughts, feelings and emotions about the problem',[12] giving a creative space for the team to focus on what the distinct group are saying, seeing, hearing and thinking. Using an empathy map within our workshop served as a great entry point for the Liberty team, many being new to the process of designing. We also believed the maps would form a rich resource to feed into persona creation: the next method used.

Personas are 'archetypal individuals'[13] constructed during a design process. The act of forming these characters and their narrative is extremely valuable in itself, but then using them within the workshop enabled stakeholders to reflect on how they would likely perceive different experiences and subsequently act. Personas can also be a powerful tool for engaging stakeholders outside of the design process; in the 'Design the Law Nepal' project, Emily worked with colleagues Mara Malagodi and Sabrina Germain alongside the Forum for Women, Law and Development (FWLD),[14] using design to ensure that legal practitioners did not lose sight of the challenges existing for citizens around their reproductive rights. You can see some of the personas created in the 'Design the Law Nepal' workshops for this project at tl;dr,[15] the less textual legal gallery.

Journey maps were the final method used in our kick-off workshop, and they followed on from the personas. Here we asked participants to adopt one of the personas and create a journey map, showing how a person might navigate from A (the point at which the legal problem arises) to B (where they reach a conclusion/possible solution), with all the steps in between.

These activities are extremely interactive; normally taking place via the use of copious pieces of paper, sticky notes, pens and with walls to stick large pieces of paper on in order to collaborate. However, in 2020 Covid-19 put a stop to this tangible experience. So, we headed online. But how?

Adapting to online

In a co-design workshop format, the emphasis is very much on collaboration: everyone in the room (whether physical or virtual breakout) is invited to dig deep within experiences to gain an understanding of user needs, before considering the kind of information materials that might support these needs. Co-design workshops are generally buzzy places to be—lots of ideas flying around and participants sharing thoughts both orally and in scribbles on paper or sticky notes.

To adapt this process from a physical to a virtual space, we needed the following:

- online spaces for breakout groups
- a large area on screen that worked like a physical wall
- digital sticky notes
- ways to collaborate together to develop empathy maps, personas, and journey maps.

How did we do it?

Our breakout groups became Zoom groups

We used the Zoom platform because of the breakout room facility. We needed to split our Liberty colleagues into three groups in order to enable each group to focus on one context each (immigration, stop and search, police complaints), and to be in small enough groups to get the most out of the activities we had devised for them.

Our physical wall became a Padlet Wall and sticky notes became digital Padlet posts

The functionality of sticky notes was a must-have. We looked at a number of options for this, (including Miro and InVision) but in the end went for the simplicity of Padlet's posts functionality. We did not want participants to feel swamped by a big product with lots of extra features other than sticky notes. Padlet offers online 'walls' where groups can easily post their contributions on digital posts (that look like sticky notes) and then move them about on screen. It is not just textual either; participants can post images, links, videos, documents and even voice recordings. The 'walls' come in different kinds to suit the activity you have planned. A *Canvas* allows you to post anywhere and drag posts into your own arrangement, whereas the standard *Wall* format stacks content in a brick-like layout. There are *Maps* and *Timeline* options and then *Shelf, Stream* and *Grid*, which all order content slightly differently again. We'll talk about our choice of walls below.

Our empathy map became a Padlet Canvas

The *Canvas* format on Padlet allows participants complete freedom to move digital posts around; we wanted them to be able to add in their thoughts freely, organising them around the four categories we had set: 'think and feel', 'seeing', 'hearing' and 'say and do'.

Pontis[16] lists examples of questions for each of the categories to help prompt ideas. For *think and feel*, in our workshop participants would be defining what they understood, from their experience advising clients, that people might be thinking, how they feel and how they deal with those feelings when facing a legal issue. For *seeing*, the prompt might be what did the person see or notice? What were they watching or reading? For *hearing* it is determining what they might hear from others (friends, family, colleagues) and for *say and do*, what people might say, to the extent of specific phrases or expressions being of interest. Additionally, they would map what people do when facing a legal issue and what behaviours might be evident whilst experiencing such circumstances.

We asked Liberty staff to consider these four categories in terms of their experiences talking with people who were facing either stop and search, immigration or a police complaints issue, and to assign each thought to one of these contexts. Some thoughts applied to all three. The Liberty staff really threw themselves into this, aiming to get into the mindset of their users. You can see a sample of posts in Table 14.1 below.

Table 14.1 Selected contributions to the empathy map:

	Think and feel	*Seeing*	*Hearing*	*Say and do*
Stop and search	Embarrassed Angry Violated	The police are racist They just want an excuse to criminalise my community	This just happens	Trying to find a way to stop unfair treatment Don't know where else to turn
Immigration	Hopeless Confused Thought we'd be safe here	They don't want me in the UK If I do anything wrong I'll be deported	You don't belong Nothing is certain	Avoid the authorities Don't know who to trust
Police complaints	Victimised Frustration Outraged	The police can't protect me	Don't bother They put hoops for you to jump through, hoping you'll get bored of trying	Want justice for the wrong they have experienced No point reporting, police won't do anything

Our personas became Padlet Shelves

The *Shelf* format on Padlet organises content into columns, enabling participants to organise content in a structured way. This was useful for our kick-off workshop to enable participants to organise their thoughts under key headings associated with developing a persona.[17]Figure 14.2 illustrates a *Shelf* developed for the context of immigration. One *Shelf* was set up for each context and participants were grouped into three, with each group completing a Persona for their assigned context.

Our journey maps became Padlet Timelines

As with the personas above, our participants worked within a context. They had to plot out a likely path that the persona (created on their Padlet Shelf) might take within their given context—essentially taking them from the moment they start to encounter difficulties right through to the end result. The *Timeline* wall provided a format whereby each step along this 'user journey' is plotted out as a digital post—steps can represent moments such as an event, an action taken or contact with a person or organisation. Pontis categorises these as touchpoints, pain points and magic points, where the latter are 'parts of an experience or design that work well for a persona'.[18] In Figure 14.3 you can see an extract from the journey map developed by the team working with the immigration persona. We can see lots of touchpoints

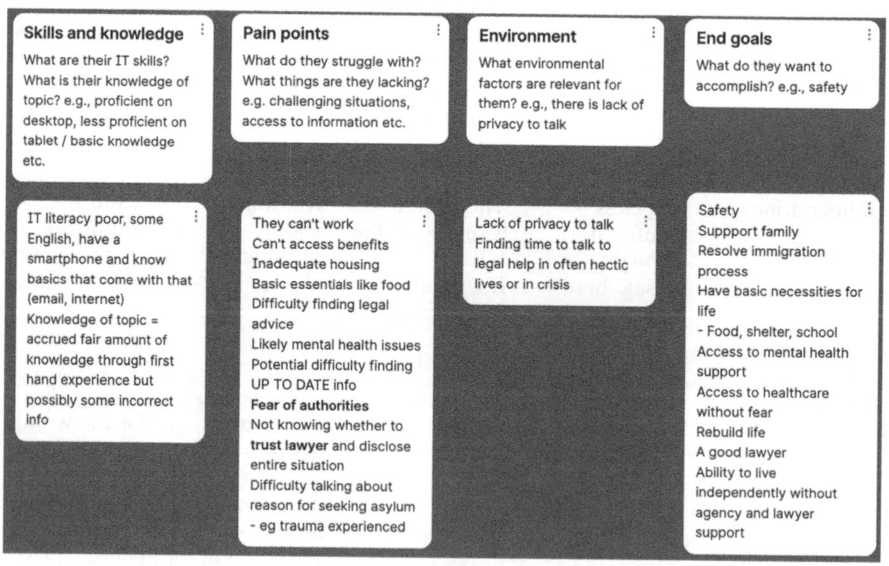

Figure 14.2 Extract from a Persona seeking immigration information and advice. The boxes at the top indicate the headings underneath which are responses from the workshop participants.

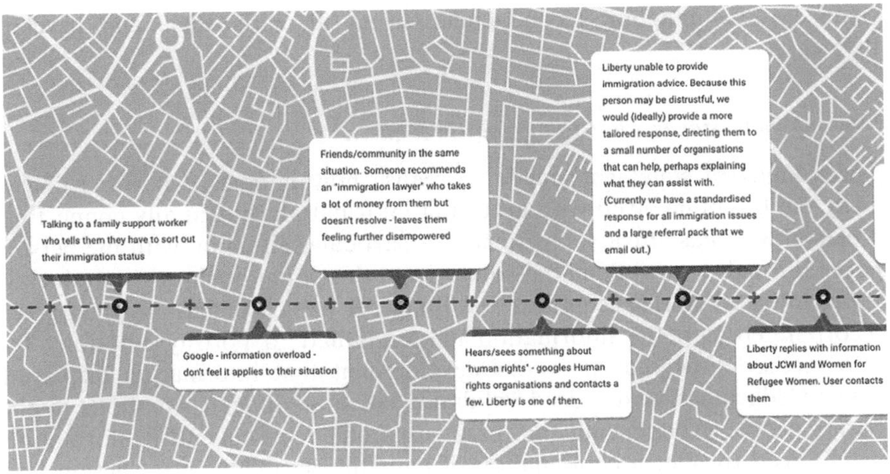

Figure 14.3 Extract of journey map for someone seeking immigration information and advice. Participants add key touch points along the *Timeline.*

(the individual talking to friends, a family support worker, an immigration lawyer…), as well as some pain points (an ineffective lawyer, money wasted…). There is potentially a magic point where Liberty's referral information on other organisations have given some hope and positive direction.

Evaluating insights

After the kick-off workshop we evaluated the workshop insights interpreting the qualitative data that had been generated by Liberty staff. Throughout this evaluation stage (Figure 14.1) we:

- evaluated the insights gathered in the empathy map, personas, and journey maps
- reviewed existing Liberty advice materials
- developed possible routes to take the project forward.

The two of us (Emily and Rachel) collaborated online using InVision. The functionality and flexibility of organising content that InVision provides, although deemed less suitable for a workshop, was suitable for our online collaboration of organising and interpreting workshop insights. The platform offers collaborators an 'endless digital whiteboard' where content (digital sticky notes etc.) can be organised and re-arranged freely and connecting arrows can be included to connect ideas. This suited our method of interpreting the data that firstly took the form of rearranging the empathy map responses into themes (this is akin to using affinity diagrams).[19] From the evaluation of the empathy map, two kinds of statements really stood out and enabled us to pinpoint recommendations at an early stage and develop themes.

'No-one understands what I'm going through ...'

These kinds of statements made us realise how important it was to strip away the layers involved with accessing information, potentially connecting a person who has already experienced a particular situation with the person going through it now. Potential solutions to this could be through producing scenario-based stories using text and image. It was clear that any images we incorporated into the information materials had to portray emotion. We also realised how central to our development that information displayed acknowledgement, and indeed validation, of how difficult situations might be for people experiencing the three situations. Consequently, information would need to offer a combination of empathy, straightforward action and signposting.

'[Feelings of] ... frustration, desperation, mistrust ...'

What these kinds of statement signified was a need for materials to generate a feeling of safety and reassurance. There has to be a real focus on ensuring that users feel there is a human behind the information given, even though it is presented through text and image rather than through one-to-one conversation. For now we are yet to decide how this might be achieved but early thoughts include ideas such as hand-drawn illustrations being a more successful format than computer generated imagery, potentially indicating more care had been taken over the portrayal of actors within any given situation. Outcomes such as these would need to be considered and co-designed with end-users.

We then interpreted the personas and journey maps for each context. Many responses in these activities mapped on to the statements above, strengthening the sense that these are key aspects to address in our outcomes. For the personas and journey maps we scanned the responses for aspects that indicated challenges or issues that the information materials might need to address. For example, a pain point in the persona for someone seeking immigration might be 'fear of authorities', which indicates that the language on a website needs to be mindful of using words such as 'authority' (see the Propositions sections below for overviews of our evaluation of each context).

From all three activities in the workshop, three themes emerged that seemed crucial when considering our strategy for the information materials we would develop:

- connecting experiences
- providing empathy
- showing the human behind the information.

Throughout our evaluation stage (see Figure 14.1) we kept these three themes in mind, as well as the importance of using key design principles and solutions such as:

- clear signposting to information
- use of explainers for official terms
- use of plain language.

For each context we generated propositions about the kinds of information materials, and ways of presenting the information, that might address the information seeking circumstances raised in the workshop. These are explored in the following sections.

Propositions for stop and search information

Findings from the activities in this first workshop around the stop and search context were varied. Key points that came through included the following:

'On the spot' or in-transit information: the information needed would most likely arise shortly after the stop and search procedure had been carried out, with the person on foot, in a car, or on public transport. Thinking about the materials we will develop, this implies that any information solution needs to be easily accessible from a mobile device, or easily understood in a time-sensitive situation.

Pain points might vary: despite the observation above regarding the need for urgent 'at-the-time' information, we acknowledged that there will be additional needs for access to more detailed content after the stop and search event, perhaps when discussing the events with family and friends. There would be different priorities in these materials; the first scenario needing practical explainers that are easily understood when faced with a stop and search event, the second having more scope for aspects such as long-term consequences and links to police complaints procedure or support groups.

People might not know others who have gone through a stop and search experience: there may be a need for seeing other people's experiences. The use of stories from those who have experienced stop and search may help connect experiences and see different sides to a situation.

Feelings: these are likely to be varied; covering the full spectrum from embarrassment to anger and outrage.

Racism: views emerged that there could be a feeling of inevitability to being stopped if you fitted a particular profile, and that the police are looking for an excuse to criminalise the black community. It follows that many may want to find a way to counteract unjust treatment, in which case strong signposting to the police complaints process would be essential.

Media coverage: linked to the issue above would be the dominance of press in the media on the topic of stop and search. We wonder if there is a need for clearer signposting to proven facts and statistics from organisations like StopWatch.[20]

From these insights, potential areas to develop could be information materials that:

- support 'it's happening' (on the spot) scenario;
- support 'it's happened' (after the stop and search) event;
- include 'stories' from lived experiences.

Additionally, we could plan workshops to co-design the above materials with community groups who support young people who have or might experience stop and search.

Propositions for immigration information

As we noted above, one of the crucial aspects of the information that needs to be delivered by Liberty is when the organisation is unable to help. This is why we have included immigration as one of the three areas to be covered; Liberty cannot help with immigration enquiries, they can only signpost. We needed to think carefully about how we would set the user's expectations—as Downe says in their insightful book about service design, 'knowing what to expect helps people to plan and take control of their situation. It gives them power …'[21]. The existing information guide that Liberty provide signposts users to other organisations who may be better placed to help them, but the language feels negative because there are no explanations for *why* Liberty cannot help. It feels like a brush-off. Liberty do not want their users to feel fobbed off, and nor do they want to cause extra anxiety. Here are our more detailed reflections from the workshop insights:

Digital exclusion: users in this category are more likely to have limited access to digital platforms, which prioritises the need for reduced complexity in any digital solutions.

Information overload: people needing help around immigration may be undergoing quite high levels of stress and, consequently, exhaustion. This, combined with the issues around the complexity of information and the fact that the immigration rules change frequently, is likely to make users feel they are drowning in information. To help with this, it is important to be clear at the beginning of any information that Liberty will be signposting a person to another organisation. Yet, it seems important to integrate empathy into Liberty's information resource, acknowledging difficult situations, before going on to signpost to other organisations specialising in this area.

Language: in the current information provided by Liberty there is a reference to 'authorities' when referring on clients to other organisations. This kind of language may well scare such users off, who are likely to be fearful of authorities (as identified in the empathy map). We will need to be alert to the impact of certain vocabulary on this group, and use alternatives e.g. 'not-for-profit organisations', and give explainers of such terms where needed.

Feelings: again, these are likely to be diverse but there could certainly be feelings of uncertainty, fear for themselves and their families, of isolation, not-belonging and the risk of deportation. They might be hearing the negative experiences of those around them and potentially hearing rumours and not knowing what to believe. We feel any future materials could acknowledge these emotions, again adding empathy to the information provided.

Extra materials: through the workshop we learned that Liberty send out a standard response and referral pack to all immigration enquiries. We hadn't seen this pack before so this would be a vital follow-up post-workshop in order to ensure that any online solution also connected to this information and vice versa.

From these insights, potential areas to develop are:

- A review of immigration advice on Liberty web pages, in the referral pack, and the email that is sent to clients to establish where language needs to be reviewed
- Develop explainers where needed
- Develop images (possibly hand-drawn illustrations) that could integrate a feeling of empathy and acknowledgement to complement existing text.

To achieve the work above we hope to work with a community group, who work with asylum seekers, and organise a co-design workshop with potential users and Liberty staff to co-design materials.

Propositions for police complaints information

The main insights that we interpreted from the workshop relating to police complaints contexts were how people might be feeling when making a police complaint and the need for validation.

Feelings: for those seeking to pursue a complaint against the police, it is no surprise that feelings of outrage, victimisation and violation dominated throughout the insights from Liberty staff. A sense that clients may feel defensive and that they are victims of unjust or unfair treatment also came through in the workshop. The persona developed in the workshop was determined to try every angle to get justice, despite feeling the police were 'out to get me'. These insights from Liberty staff's experience of advising their clients imply much attention needs to be paid within the information solution to demonstrating how people can vocalise their points in the process, as well as incorporating information about why perceived 'hoops' are in place. There will be a need for greater transparency and potentially a place for scenarios to be used to clarify what actions amount to successful police complaints.

Acknowledgement and outcome: this insight seems key. There is an argument for the focus to be shifted to helping others uphold their rights by making complaints, such as showing how it can ensure patterns of discriminatory policing are identified. This would imply individuals are carrying out a service to their communities by registering a complaint, not just raising an individual grievance.

We acknowledge that further understanding of the circumstances around police complaints is needed before recommendations for additional information and advice are possible. This will certainly be incorporated into a future workshop.

New information materials to develop include:

- Develop a visual explainer, such as a flow chart, to explain the police complaints process, providing more transparency on what happens throughout the process
- Include in the visual explainer how complaints are used after it has been closed.

Users who might make a police complaint might not be represented by a community group, such as stop and search or immigration contexts. Consequently, we plan to develop prototypes of a visual explainer, and then evaluate and co-design changes to these prototypes in a workshop with members of the public. We plan to work with Liberty to organise appropriate demographics of potential end-users to co-design with.

Next steps

As we have acknowledged, our initial co-design workshop did not include end-users. An aim of our next phase of the project involves co-design workshops with end-users where we co-design and evaluate prototypes of information materials. We plan to approach community-led groups who work with people who are seeking immigration information or those who have experienced stop and search situations, and work with Liberty to organise appropriate demographics to evaluate information materials for police complaints contexts. We have a team of undergraduate graphic communication design students working with us to work on the following:

1 Development of new stop and search information materials
2 A review and development of existing online immigration materials
3 Development of a visual explainer for the police complaints process.

In our future co-design workshops we plan for all participants to be co-designers: the end-users; Liberty staff; student designers; trained designers; and workshop facilitators. Whether these workshops are in person, or using our new online set-up, we are hoping to provide useful information materials that can be easily accessed and used by the public. Wish us luck!

Notes

1 Associate Professor of Law, City Law School, City, University of London.
2 Lecturer at the Typography and Graphic Communication department, University of Reading.

3 Design Council, 'What is the framework for innovation?' (*Design Council*, 18 March 2015), www.designcouncil.org.uk/news-opinion/what-framework-innovation-design-councils-evolved-double-diamond, accessed 13 July 2021.
4 Examples of research involving co-design activities include: Sue Walker, Manula Halai, Rachel Warner and Josefina Bravo, 'Beat Bad Microbes: Raising Public Awareness of Antibiotic Resistance in Rwanda' (2021) 26.1 Information Design Journal 17; Mike Zender, William B Brinkman and Lea E Widdice, 'Design + medical collaboration' in Alison Black, Paul Luna, Ole Lund, and Sue Walker (eds), *Information Design Research and Practice* (Routledge 2017) 655.
5 Guillermina Noël, Thea Luig, Melanie Heatherington and Denise Campbell-Scherer, 'Developing Tools to Support Patients and Healthcare Providers When in Conversation About Obesity' (2018) 24.2 Information Design Journal 131, 134.
6 Mitchell et al., 'Empirical Investigation of the Impact of Using Co-Design Methods When Generating Proposals for Sustainable Travel' (2016) 12.4 Codesign 205.
7 Kelly Ann McKercher, *Beyond Sticky Notes. CoDesign for Real: Mindsets, Methods and Movements* (Beyond Sticky Notes 2020) 46.
8 Elizabeth B-N Sanders and Pieter J Stappers, 'Co-Creation and the New Landscapes of Design' (2008) 4.1 CoDesign 5, 12.
9 Elizabeth B-N Sanders and Pieter J Stappers, 'Probes, Toolkits and Prototypes: Three Approaches to Making in Codesigning' (2014) 10.1 CoDesign 4, 11.
10 Wina Smeenk, Janienke Stum and Berry Eggen, 'Empathic Handover: How Would You Feel? Handing Over Dementia Experiences and Feelings in Empathic Co-Design' (2018) 14.4 CoDesign 259, 260.
11 For more insight into why researching with marginalised groups, or those living with delicate circumstances may require an empathic approach, see Wina Smeenk, Janienke Stum and Berry Eggen, 'Empathic Handover: How Would You Feel? Handing Over Dementia Experiences and Feelings in Empathic Co-Design' (2018) 14.4 CoDesign 259.
12 Sheila Pontis, *Making Sense of Field Research: A Practical Guide for Information Designers* (Routledge 2019) 154.
13 Bon Ku MD and Ellen Lupton, *Health Design Thinking: Creating Products and Services for Better Health* (Cooper Hewitt 2020) 72.
14 FWLD, https://fwld.org/.
15 Tl;dr, https://tldr.legal/home.html.
16 Pontis, *Making Sense of Field Research: A Practical Guide for Information Designers* (Routledge 2019) 156.
17 Ibid. 161.
18 Ibid. 166.
19 Ibid. 151.
20 StopWatch, https://www.stop-watch.org/.
21 Lou Downe, *Good Services: How to Design Services That Work* (BIS Publishers 2020) 69.

15 Designing access to the law

An ethical perspective

Emily MacLoud[1]

Introduction

In exploring the role of design in legal education, a consideration of ethics is crucial because design has the power to fundamentally shift behaviours and perspectives. Visualisation, in particular, is an especially powerful design technique. It has the potential to change the trajectory of legal education in the higher education sphere, the public legal education context and in legal practice. Visuals can be used to help law students understand complex legal concepts, enable citizens to navigate legal information and even make a lawyer's work more satisfying.

Design can also impact the behaviours and perspectives of those who are involved in the design process. The creation of mind maps can help students unpick complex legal concepts, which can foster meaningful learning.[2] The act of co-designing public legal education resources with the communities they seek to serve can enable higher acceptance and usage by those same communities.[3] And the development of diagrams can often help lawyers communicate with each other and their clients more effectively and enable lawyers to think about legal problems in a different way.[4] Therefore, the ethical lens of those involved in the design process is as important to consider as the ethical implications of using design in legal education.

When we use the term 'ethics' we are referring to the systematisation of the concepts of right and wrong, good and bad. In the context of legal education, to design ethically, educators and practitioners should be considering the context of their solutions and asking questions like: What are the intended and unintended consequences of adopting design in legal education? What duties do we owe to our students or clients? How *should* we behave? Rather than answering these questions and spelling out 'right' from 'wrong', this chapter aims to nourish a rich and critical ethical perspective that will enable educators and practitioners to think more deeply about the role of design in legal education. It seeks to strengthen one's ability to exercise ethical judgment and will explore the process of decision-making when faced with an ethical dilemma.

The first part of this chapter will spell out why the questions above are relevant. To begin, it will outline a number of common normative ethical

DOI: 10.4324/9780429021411-17

theories and provide examples that will show how each theory can be used as a lens that can be adopted when making decisions. It will then highlight why an understanding of ethics is important in the context of legal education. The second part of this chapter will explore the ethical implications of adopting design methods in legal education. It will focus on two areas, accessibility and engagement, and highlight the influence that one's ethical lens can have on how these areas are perceived. It will conclude by providing examples of methodologies that support ethical design. Design can influence how students learn, how the public navigate legal content, and how lawyers behave. The discussion that follows hopes to stimulate readers to reflect on the impact of their own ethical lens and how this may influence the way they approach using design in legal education.

What is ethics?

To understand the ethical implications of using design in legal education and what is meant by the term 'ethical lens', we will need to first unpick what ethics is. Ethics refers to the branch of philosophy that concerns morality. Normative ethics is one strand of ethics that contemplates what constitutes good or bad, right or wrong. It should be no surprise that there are several theories that attempt to determine how this distinction is made. These theories have been refined over the years and can help us to justify our actions and enlighten us when someone acts in contravention of what we think is right.

Teleology (commonly referred to as consequentialism) holds that the consequences of one's conduct is the ultimate basis for determining whether that act is held to be right or wrong. Within this class, the most popular approach is utilitarianism. The philosopher Jeremy Bentham first rendered the theory of utilitarianism into the recognisable form we see today. He introduced the *principle of utility*, which requires or permits acts according to the tendency they have to promote happiness and pleasure and forbids acts according to the tendency they have to produce unhappiness and pain.[5] He also brought about the mechanism by which individuals can calculate the moral status of a particular act, based on the pleasure or pain they emit, called the *felicific calculus.* [6] His theory posits that the parameters which are to be taken into account in estimating the *value* of pleasure or pain include its intensity (how strong is the pleasure?), duration (how long will the pleasure last?), certainty (how likely is it that the pleasure will occur?) and propinquity or remoteness (how soon will the pleasure occur?).[7] This same calculus can be used by legal educators and practitioners when determining whether to proceed with a certain action, as we demonstrate later.

The theory was then later tweaked by John Stuart Mill who went on to articulate what is known as the *greatest happiness principle*: the morality of an act is determined by the *aggregate* of the happiness it produces. Under this formulation, aggregate happiness relates to the happiness of all concerned, and does not concern itself with *where* that happiness is distributed. Taken together, these are the key elements of utilitarianism.

With respect to design's role in legal education, this theory supports the view that good decisions are those that maximise happiness. Put in another way, if the consequences of adopting visuals in legal education secures the greatest benefit for the greatest number, this is considered the right thing to do. One notable weakness of this form of ethical reasoning is that it can be used as an excuse for not building accessible solutions. For example, one could use the greatest happiness principle to justify under-serving a small number of students who may have a poor internet connection.[8] This theory is often contrasted with deontology, which we turn to next.

Deontology holds that an act is morally right if it conforms to the moral law, regardless of the consequences. Several approaches have emerged which attempt to define what the moral law is. For example, divine command traditions define the moral law as that which is dictated by a deity. In contrast, philosopher Immanuel Kant conceives the moral law as that which can be deduced through logic and reason. This school of thought is often referred to as *Kantian ethics*. Kant's approach to ethics and moral decision-making was grounded in what he called *categorical imperatives*. [9] These are logical rules which can be applied universally and are independent from an individual's desires. That is, under this formulation, actions are considered morally right if it would be rational if everyone acted in the same way (for example, 'I ought not to lie'). This is in contrast to *hypothetical imperatives*, which can be construed as 'self-serving' (for example, 'I ought to practice the piano if I want to become a pianist').[10] All in all, deontologists tend to view an act as either morally permitted or forbidden on the basis of its conformity with a set of rules, however they are determined.

Accordingly, educators and lawyers who act in compliance with their professional duties can be described as acting ethically, through a deontological lens. This approach has been criticised, for it can result in individuals stopping to think about what's right and, indeed, requires the professional regulatory bodies to keep up with the rapid changes taking place across the sector. For example, in a recent discussion paper issued by the Law Society of England and Wales, it was highlighted that there is 'ambivalence on what ethics means for LawTech and its ultimate effect on risk and compliance'.[11] This example highlights the risk of practitioners adopting a strict deontological perspective and advocates for adopting a much broader ethical perspective. We will now turn to virtue ethics that, unlike consequentialism or deontology, focuses on the person responsible for the act, rather than the act itself.

Virtue ethics is concerned with the condition that an individual is in when they perform an act and what they become through the execution of that act (habituation). It has origins in ancient philosophy and is most commonly associated with the teachings of Aristotle. It was Aristotle who theorised that humanity is driven to pursue *eudaimonia*, which is commonly translated to 'human flourishing' or 'happiness'. In this pursuit, humans are motivated to seek to acquire virtues, like courage and truthfulness. These virtues, Aristotle argues, can be acquired as a result of habit: 'men become builders by building and lyreplayers by playing the lyre; so too we become just by doing just acts, temperate by doing temperate acts, brave by doing brave acts.'[12] Aristotle also posits that, in addition to performing virtuous actions, 'the agent also must be in a certain condition when he does them'.[13] That is, the agent must be fully cognisant of their act and the context in which it is performed.

In the legal education space, this perspective can be demonstrated by the example of an educator who does everything they can to communicate concepts in a way that students can understand because they are motivated not out of a desire to maximize the well-being of their students or because it follows any kind of moral or professional duty, but because it feels like the right thing to do and aligns with how they see themselves as human beings (i.e. generous and courageous). This theory has been criticised for failing to provide a guide as to how one should act in an ethical dilemma given it does not put forward a mechanism for weighing up competing options and is dependent on the individual having the wisdom to know what is right or good.

The above three theories were explored in depth as they tend to be the most dominant in ethics literature. However, there are other ways of framing right from wrong. Care ethics purports that unemotionally weighing up various factors (a consequentialist approach) or deducing the best course of action using logic and reason (a Kantian deontological approach) is male-orientated and loses sight of the interconnected nature of relationships.[14] Care ethics recognises the importance of context when making decisions and the relationship between the relevant parties involved. For example, some educators and lawyers may feel compelled to act, not on the basis of abstract principles or logical reasoning, but rather due to the connection they have with their students and clients.

As demonstrated above, the ethical theory adopted by the lawyer or educator is likely to have a significant impact on how decisions are reached, even if the outcome is the same. Some educators may be motivated to use visuals in their teaching because the benefits outweigh the risks whereas others may feel compelled to do so because they feel duty-bound to serve their students' needs. Some lawyers may feel compelled to communicate using verbal, textual and visual aids out of care for their client, whereas others may feel compelled out of their professional duty as a lawyer. Notwithstanding, these theories should not be treated as mutually exclusive. Those charged with making decisions within the legal education sphere may need to adopt several of these perspectives, depending on the situation they are faced with. Next, we will turn to the reasons why an understanding of the key differences between these approaches is important.

The importance of ethics in an educational context

In the context of legal education, as demonstrated in the previous section, the ethical lens adopted by the educator or practitioner will play a crucial role in influencing how certain activities are approached and what considerations are made. By understanding that different ethical perspectives exist, educators and practitioners are better placed to understand not only their own reasons for making certain decisions but also those of their colleagues. In a recent paper that discussed the different approaches AI practitioners took when deciding whether to sign an open letter banning the development of weaponized AI,[15] the authors highlighted the importance of training in 'multiple complementary modes of ethical reasoning' for this exact reason. Within the legal education space, understanding that multiple ethical perspectives exist will be beneficial as educators and practitioners start to use ethical reasoning to either advance the use of design or discredit its use.

A deeper understanding of ethics can also benefit those who adopt methods and exercises designed to identify and monitor ethical implications of new ideas or new ways of working. For example, when considering an exercise like consequence scanning that is described as 'bringing ethics into the design process' by identifying the intended and unintended consequences of any given strategic decision,[16] it becomes evident that this exercise is biased towards a consequentialist perspective. Other ethics toolkits have been critiqued for being simply 'carefully constructed prompts'.[17] Even though these exercises are well-intentioned and designed to elicit thought provoking discussions, an understanding of ethics is important because it can provide a holistic perspective and illuminate where there may be gaps or perspectives which are missing.

Equipped with a solid understanding of what ethics is and why an understanding of ethics is important, we will now turn to the ethical implications of using design methods in legal education. We will highlight how changing one's ethical lens can change how implications are perceived.

Ethical implications of using design methods in legal education

Introducing design methods, like information design, into the legal education sphere is a relatively new phenomenon. From developing visuals aids for the classroom,[18] to redesigning public-facing legal information,[19] legal educators around the world are using various design methods in their work to improve the way the law can be accessed. In a similar way, lawyers are also starting to recognise the benefits of adopting design methods in their practice.[20] In exploring the ethical implications of this change in legal education and legal practice, two issues stand out: accessibility and engagement. The following sections use these two issues to explore the influence that one's ethical lens can have on the design process and on solutions which are created.

Accessibility

Design methods, and visualisation techniques in particular, can make legal concepts more accessible to a wider audience. In higher education, given the law tends to be very text-centric, design can help those students who may struggle with the volume and complexity of reading. It can also break down the barriers of entry for those students who come to higher education through untraditional routes. For those who are responsible for educating the public about their legal rights, visuals can also be used to make the law less stressful and more inviting, preventing clusters of problems from developing. Yet, these new ways of working can present a number of ethical dilemmas.

To establish whether the approach is right or wrong, a consequentialist may ask: What will be the degree of misunderstanding that occurs? How long will the misunderstanding last? How certain is one that the misunderstanding will occur? How many people are likely to misunderstand? This is very similar reasoning to the *felicific calculus* described above. As a result of this position in which the ends justify the means, the needs of certain minorities (for example, those who will be harmed significantly) may be marginalised.

If one were to adopt a deontological lens, then the same dilemma would be framed according to the relevant ethical guidelines. With respect to using visuals in public legal education, a deontologist may review the web content accessibility guidelines (WCAG 2.1),[21] and determine whether the approach is right or wrong according to how well it meets the criteria set out in those guidelines; that is, the extent to which the legal information is perceivable, operable, understandable and robust.

And finally, if one were to adopt a virtue ethics lens, then they may consider the morally right action to be that which they determine through practical wisdom. Principles, like the Ten Principles for Good Design,[22] may form a critical starting point, but it will be practical experience that will guide the individual to make the ethical choice.[23] Their approach, therefore, is likely to reflect their cultural milieu, which would be influenced by their professional background and the country they reside.

These examples seek to demonstrate the stark differences between these three ethical approaches and show that acting ethically does not always mean the same thing for different people. We will now turn to engagement.

Engagement

The scope, approach and outcome of any design process is impacted by who is in the room and how they are engaged. Research has shown, for example, stark contrasts between concepts developed by co-design teams (which involve users in the design process) and teams of design experts.[24] Decisions relating to engagement are therefore very important in the design process. They can also present significant ethical dilemmas as designers are forced to decide between who is consulted and who is left out. The ethical implications will depend on the level of engagement pursued. Within the legal sphere, the approach to engagement can vary widely. Some projects, such as the redesign of the Lancaster Law School curriculum set out in Chapter 6 of this volume, keep user engagement to a minimum, relying instead on the use of personas.

Others, such as the Legal Design Lab, are more participatory. Examples of their work include gathering feedback through on-site workshops and running co-design jams with former litigants, court staff, and lawyers.[25] These sessions involve the service-users developing new concepts, which the design team then take into the next rounds of design. While the first example raises concerns around the articulation of user needs throughout the design process, the second example raises concerns around issues of negotiation, power balances, and vulnerability.

Methodologies that support ethical design

What methodologies can be adopted by educators and practitioners to ensure that they design ethically?

Rules are just one way to regulate ethical behaviour. For example, research has shown that stories can also act as an effective mechanism to teach us our duties, guide our actions and cultivate our moral sensibilities.[26] By listening to and interpreting people's stories through case studies and other styles of reports, educators and practitioners can gain ethical insight that can complete or substitute for rules or consultations with experts.[27]

Value Sensitive Design is a proactive approach to incorporating values into the design process and is sometimes described as a way to 'frontload ethics'.[28] In order to actively attend to values during the design process, this approach offers a 'tripartite' methodology, which consists of conceptual, technical and empirical investigations that weave together to create value-led designs.[29] It has been used in several design projects, including the redesign of Mozilla's cookie consent mechanism.[30]

Legal Design is the 'application of human-centred design to the world of law'.[31] With respect to working with communities, Stanford's Legal Design Lab has articulated several core principles and mindsets so that Legal Designers can 'set up protocols that abide by ethical best practices'.[32] This includes, but is not limited to: having empathy, being aware of unconscious bias and respecting the community you are working with. These principles act as a good guide, especially when educators and practitioners start engaging with vulnerable communities.

Value levers can also be adopted during the design process to encourage those involved to actively reflect on and discuss areas of concern during their day-to-day practice.[33] An example of a value lever is 'internal testing', which involves those involved in the design process using their own personal data in whichever solution they're developing. The research shows this practice can help designers focus not only on the sensitivity of the data collected, but the possible inferences that could be drawn from the data.[34] Value levers offer a tactical, dynamic way to do ethics.

Several platforms curate resources to help designers act ethically.[35] These tools are designed to help designers think deeply and facilitate thoughtful discussions within design teams around the ethical aspects of the design process.

Conclusion

The use of design methods in legal education is a relatively new phenomenon. As this practice develops, there is no doubt that ethical dilemmas will present themselves as educators and practitioners grapple with decisions relating to accessibility needs, ethical engagement practices and much more. This chapter has sought to draw attention to ethics and the influence that one's own ethical lens can have on how situations are perceived. By providing practical methodologies which can be adopted when using design in legal education, educators and practitioners should now be well equipped to engage in meaningful ethical discourse and understand not only their gut reactions but the behaviours of their peers.

Acknowledgements

I owe special thanks to Angela Tang, Damian Curran and David Massey for your thoughtful comments and helpful perspectives.

Notes

1 Digital Team lead at Law Centres Network.
2 Rossana Deplano, 'Using Concept Maps in Law Schools to Foster Meaningful Learning: Evidence from a Pilot Study' (2018) 1 Journal of Learning and Teaching in Higher Education 125.
3 Emma Blomkamp, 'The Promise of Co-Design for Public Policy' (2018) 77 Australian Journal of Public Administration 729.
4 Damian Curran, 'Why Lawyers Should Use Flowcharts' (*Damian Curran*, 14 October 2018), https://damiancurran.com/2018/10/14/why-lawyers-should-use-flowcharts/, accessed 14 March 2021.
5 Jeremy Bentham, *An Introduction to the Principles of Morals and Legislation* (first published 1789, Clarendon Press 1907) 2.
6 ibid 29.
7 ibid.
8 Morten Rand-Hendriksen, 'Using Ethics in Web Design' (*Smashing Magazine*, 22 March 2018), www.smashingmagazine.com/2018/03/using-ethics-in-web-design/, accessed 10 December 2020.
9 Immanuel Kant, *Groundwork of the Metaphysics of Morals* (first published 1785, Cambridge University Press 1998) 31.
10 Christopher Bennett, Joe Saunders and Robert Stern, in Immanuel Kant, *Groundwork of the Metaphysics of Morals* (Oxford University Press 2019) xv.
11 Law Society, 'Lawtech, Ethics and the Rule of Law: Discussion Paper' (*Law Society*, 13 October 2020), www.lawsociety.org.uk/campaigns/lawtech/news/lawtech-ethics-and-the-rule-of-law-discussion-paper, accessed 13 March 2021.
12 Aristotle, *Nicomachean Ethics* (first published c. 350 BC, translated by WD Ross) Book II.
13 ibid.
14 ibid.
15 Judy Goldsmith and Emanuelle Burton, 'Why Teaching Ethics to AI Practitioners Is Important' (Proceedings of the Thirty-First AAAI Conference on Artificial Intelligence, San Francisco, February 2017).

16 Rob Katz, 'How to Run a Consequence Scanning Workshop' (*Medium*, 28 July 2020), https://medium.com/salesforce-ux/how-to-run-a-consequence-scanning-workshop-4b14792ea987, accessed 13 March 2021.
17 Cennydd Bowles, 'The Limits of Ethical Prompts' (*Cennydd Bowles*, 30 October 2020), https://cennydd.com/blog/the-limits-of-ethical-prompts, accessed 20 December 2020.
18 Emily Allbon, 'tl;dr The Less Textual Legal Gallery' (*tl;dr The Less Textual Legal Gallery*), https://tldr.legal/home.html, accessed 14 March 2021.
19 'The Legal Design Lab' (*The Legal Design Lab*), https://law.stanford.edu/organizations/pages/legal-design-lab/, accessed 14 March 2021.
20 Tim Follett, 'Visualisation in Law: Cutting Through Complexity' (*Legal Business World*, 17 February 2021), www.legalbusinessworld.com/post/visualisation-in-law-cutting-through-complexity, accessed 14 March 2021.
21 Shawn Lawton Henry, 'Web Content Accessibility Guidelines (WCAG) Overview' (*W3C*, 17 October 2020), www.w3.org/WAI/standards-guidelines/wcag/, accessed 14 March 2021.
22 Dieter Rams 'Ten Principles for Good Design' (Vitsœ), https://www.vitsoe.com/us/about/good-design, accessed 14 March 2021.
23 Jan Jacobowitz and Scott Rogers, 'Mindful Ethics—A Pedagogical and Practical Approach to Teaching Legal Ethics, Developing Professional Identity, and Encouraging Civility' (2014) 4 St. Mary's Journal on Legal Malpractice & Ethics 198.
24 Jakob Trischler and others, 'The Value of Codesign: The Effect of Customer Involvement in Service Design Teams' (2018) 21 Journal of Service Research 75.
25 Margaret Hagan, 'Participatory Design for Innovation in Access to Justice' (2019) Dædalus, https://www.amacad.org/publication/participatory-design-innovation-access-justice, accessed 14 March 2021.
26 Hilde Lindemann Nelson, *Damaged Identities, Narrative Repair* (Cornell University Press 2001) 36.
27 Howard Brody, 'Narrative Ethics and Institutional Impact' (1999) 11 HEC Forum 46, 48.
28 Noëmi Manders-Huits, 'What Values in Design? The Challenge of Incorporating Moral Values into Design' (2011) 17 Science and Engineering Ethics 271.
29 Batya Friedman, Peter Kahn and Alan Borning, 'Value Sensitive Design: Theory and Methods' [2002] University of Washington CSE Technical Report 1, 2, https://dada.cs.washington.edu/research/tr/2002/12/UW-CSE-02-12-01.pdf, accessed 9 December 2020.
30 Batya Friedman, D.C. Howe and Edward Felten, 'Informed consent in the Mozilla browser: implementing value-sensitive design' (Proceedings of the 35th Annual Hawaii International Conference on System Sciences, Big Island, USA, January 2002).
31 Margaret Hagan, 'What is Legal Design?' (*Law by Design*), www.lawbydesign.co/legal-design/, accessed 27 December 2020.
32 'Short Book: Ethical Design Engagement with your Community' (*Legal Design Lab*, 8 February 2018), www.legaltechdesign.com/2018/02/short-book-ethical/, accessed 3 August 2020.
33 Katie Shilton, 'Values Levers: Building Ethics into Design' (2013) 38 Science, Technology, & Human Values 374, 374.
34 ibid 381.
35 See 'Toolkit' (*Design Ethically*, 2021), www.designethically.com/toolkit, accessed 14 March 2021; Jet Gispen, 'Ethical tools for designers' (*Ethics for Designers*, 2017), https://www.ethicsfordesigners.com/tools, accessed 14 March 2021.

Part III

Legal Practice

16 Visualisation in contract education and practice

The first 25 years

Helena Haapio[1]

Introduction

> Drawing is a kind of Universal Language, understood by all Nations. A Man may often express his Ideas, even to his own Countrymen, more clearly with a Lead Pencil, or Bit of Chalk, than with his Tongue. And many can understand a Figure, that do not comprehend a Description in Words, tho' ever so properly chosen.
>
> Benjamin Franklin (1749)[2]

Using visual communication to convey complex messages is not new in itself. Contract visualisation—using visual elements to explain, condense, clarify or navigate contracts, contracting or contract law[3]—is not entirely new, either. I started to experiment with it in the 1990s and have been using visuals since, with varying success.

At the time when I started to experiment with contract visualisation this was a somewhat controversial venture, especially among communities who saw themselves as authorities in contract language and drafting. In the early days, contract visualisation was either ignored or called odd and unusual. Who on earth would put pictures in their contracts?

More recently, things have started to change, both within the drafting community and among its clients. In the contracting and legal communities, the availability of new technology tools and the growing interest in designerly ways of thinking and doing have opened up minds and new avenues. In the client community, with the growing number, length and complexity of contracts, many have started to question the value and relevance of contracts to business needs. Seen from the clients' points of view, contract preparation costs too much time and money.

I am no longer alone in calling for a change in the way contracts are designed, communicated, perceived and taught. Increasing evidence proves that contracts are entering a time of major change, which is likely to have a lasting impact on those who craft, review and negotiate them. The UK Government has issued guidance for business on how to help their customers better understand their contracts.[4] Recent articles in magazines such as the *Financial Times, Forbes* and *Harvard Business Review* show that the business

DOI: 10.4324/9780429021411-19

community is ready for a new approach to contracts, even for contracts with pictures in them.[5] Is the legal community ready, too?

The purpose of visualisation is insight, not just pictures.[6] Irrespective of the task at hand, visualisation can help us present our messages better, whether in training, advice or contracting. Visualisation can be used in contract education and at the various stages of the contracting process: from supporting better communication when capturing or negotiating a deal, to documenting its terms, and throughout its lifecycle.

My work has taken me from an in-house legal setting, where contracts are used for business objectives and dispute prevention, to arbitrating cross-border contract cases involving complex factual disputes. I have had the opportunity to facilitate contract training workshops in various parts of the world and across different professions and disciplines. I have seen the power of visualisation in all these contexts.

This chapter illustrates some highlights of my journey and some findings from my research. It explores visualisation in contract education and practice, illustrating what it can offer for future lawyers and those in charge of educating them. The next section addresses the challenges current contracts pose for clients, from their point of view. After presenting the trajectory of contract visualisation from education to practice, the third section illustrates how visuals can be used to respond to those challenges and how they can help teachers, students and practitioners make themselves better understood when explaining contracts and contract law. The final section concludes.

What is wrong with current contracts?

> There are two things wrong with almost all legal writing. One is its style. The other is its content. That, I think, about covers the ground.
>
> Fred Rodell (1936)

These comments were made by Yale Law Professor Fred Rodell in 'Goodbye to Law Reviews', an article published in the Virginia Law Review, in 1936.[7] While the main target of Fred Rodell's critique was law review articles, much of what he wrote also applies to contracts. Reliance on 'tested language' presumed to have a clearly established and 'settled' meaning has led to a writing style that is far from optimal—in fact, documents that many users find incomprehensible and dysfunctional.[8] Moving from legalese to *plain language* certainly helps,[9] yet it cannot alone solve all the problems. A more profound change is required.

Conventional contracts are not fit for purpose, in fact they fall short in many respects; surveys conducted among the contracting community across the globe tell us so.[10] A huge gap often exists between the contract as written ('the paper deal') and the true agreement ('the real deal').[11] The current structure and design of contracts (or lack of meaningful structure and design) overwhelm people. Problems caused by the 'wall of text' and contract complexity have been widely reported.[12] Research has also revealed the current bias of contracts on safeguarding and negatives—something that can seriously harm relationships.[13] Although such contracts might be *legal-friendly*—helping to manage legal risk or win a dispute in court—they are not *user-friendly* or *business-friendly.* [14]

Contract visualisation and contract design have only recently been added to business and legal vocabulary. What most legal scholars and educators have cared about is *contract law*, not *contracts* themselves. The few scholars who have addressed contracts themselves have mostly focused on the formulation and choice of contract clauses around legal concepts, not the needs of clients.[15] Contracts have been *drafted* 'by lawyers for lawyers'—they have not been *designed* to work and be understandable for those who are impacted.[16]

Contracts classes are about *contract law*, you might say, and there is already plenty to cover. But the law is not about content only, it is also about the environment and context in which the law is applied. This is increasingly about matters other than litigation. In order to become successful lawyers and serve their clients well, law students need new mindsets, skills and tools. Adding visualisation to our thinking and teaching toolbox can open up that new path.

The time has come to stop equating *contracts* with *contract litigation.* Apart from being legal tools, contracts are business and management tools. People in charge of negotiating, implementing, managing and monitoring them are mainly business and operational people who do not have law degrees. What they need—and increasingly ask for—is contracts that are not only legally sound, but also easy to work with and act upon. Clients need safeguards and protection, but they also need flexibility and good relationships. Conventional contracts would benefit from a complete overhaul, assuming that they are expected to be read and understood by those whom they are expected to serve: the clients.

Pioneering contract visualisation: experimenting in education and practice

In recent years, a growing number of organisations and lawyers, especially in-house lawyers, have started to see contracts in a more 'designerly' and managerial way. Their focus is not on litigating or winning in court, but supporting business in achieving their objectives and preventing unnecessary problems. The *proactive contracting* approach, founded in the Nordic countries in the late 1990s and early 2000s,[17] started to highlight the *ex ante* promotive and preventive uses of contracts and their managerial functions, putting the users in the centre.[18] The founders, of whom I was one, saw the need to change mindsets and how contracts are designed, communicated, perceived, and taught. Contract visualisation offered a natural way to bring the approach to practice. The early experiments were encouraging, and the enthusiasm of the people who joined in was contagious. Gradually, *proactive contracting* grew into a multidisciplinary stream of research and practice,[19] adopted by scholars exploring topics varying from contract visualisation to functional contracting[20] and from the proactive visualisation of legal information to proactive legal design.[21]

I had the privilege of being part of the early developments of proactive contracting and contract visualisation. Inspired by the work of Colette R Brunschwig, Emily Allbon, Tobias Mahler, Richard K Sherwin, and others,[22] I turned from a pioneering practitioner to a researcher of knowledge visualisation and contract (re)design. The following auto-ethnography illustrates some highlights from my journey, showing how finding and pursuing one's mission and vision can contribute to changing an entire community, in this case the contracting community. I hope it can serve as inspiration for future designerly lawyers, something we should encourage our students to become. In the words attributed to the influential cultural anthropologist Margaret Mead: 'Never doubt that a small group of thoughtful, committed people can change the world. Indeed, it is the only thing that ever has.'[23]

My journey in contract visualisation started with sketching and real-time visualisation in contract training workshops in the 1990s. The first experiments were about helping Contractual Quality and Risk Management workshop attendees see how contracts impact business, how the law interacts with contracts, and how careless contracting can have unexpected consequences. For example, if the parties do not include a notices provision or time limit for making claims, the default rules of the law will determine when and how a party must give notice and whether a claim is time-barred. If the people in charge of sending or receiving those notices or making or responding to those claims do not know the law, how can they comply? In the training, I started to call the default rules that are still read into the contract even though the parties did not expressly include, the 'invisible terms'; I could have called them 'implied terms' or 'terms that are deemed to be part of the contract', but invisible terms seemed to work better in conversations and interactions with the audience.

After meeting Annika Varjonen, a real-time visualiser, who made cartoon-type graphic notes on the spot, it became so much easier to make the invisible visible. Working together we found new ways to verbalise and visualise contract concepts in ways that made them more accessible, even intriguing for the audience. Attendees liked our playful approach to the serious topics. Interviews conducted several weeks after the workshop events revealed that attendees had actually changed their thinking habits and working practices and could still recall the insights they had gained. Many reported that they treasured their visual notes and had shared them with their colleagues.

After receiving the encouraging feedback, I created more workshop hypotheticals and visual metaphors (for example, 'camouflaged contracts') that seemed to work. They became so popular that attendees wanted to know more. So the sketches and visuals moved from flipcharts to handouts and later to contract handbooks, conference papers, book chapters and articles; the era of 'visualisation *about* contracts' had begun. It soon expanded beyond training workshops. In the book on contract risk I co-authored with University of Michigan Ross Business School Law Professor George Siedel in 2013, we dedicated an entire section to visualisation as a tool to simplify and demystify contracts.[24]

The next step was applying visualisation to improve contracts themselves, in order to transform what had been *drafted* 'by lawyers for lawyers' to become *designed* to be understandable for those who are impacted.[25] When I met Stefania Passera, an information designer and PhD student at that time, our lawyer–designer team started to experiment with the research and practice of what we now call 'visualisation *in* contracts': embedding visual navigation aids, such as highlighting and color-coding, and diagrams, such as timelines and flowcharts, in contracts themselves.[26] Through networking, Legal Design Jam events[27] and professional and academic conferences we found colleagues working with visualisation *for* contracts (used in negotiations, contract preparation and deal-design)[28] and visualisation *as* contracts (such as comic contracts)[29].

In hindsight, my work as a pioneer of the proactive and visual approach to contracts appears to have taken place in a designerly way: it was always about experimentation, first with different methods to make contract training and related materials more relevant and engaging and, later, with different ways of simplifying, (re)designing and communicating contracts to make them more useful and usable for everyone, especially the parties themselves. Technology and design started to enable entirely new contract genres, and we started to explore them.[30] We reflected on our projects and reported on our findings. We listened to the users. The journey continued from contract education to contract practice, and after using visuals *in* and *about* contracts we witnessed the use of visuals *for* and *as* contracts.[31]Figure 16.1 illustrates some highlights of my contract visualisation journey and some hallmarks of our thinking and doing.[32]Figure 16.2 is an early example of visualisation in a contract workshop, showing Annika Varjonen's real-time visualisations, graphical notes made on the spot, distilling complex contract and legal topics into images that enable engagement.[33]

Figure 16.3 shows two timelines that I have used in my workshops to illustrate how visualisation might prevent disputes from arising. The image is shared with workshop participants after we have explored a widely cited Canadian dispute[34] concerning the meaning of the following termination clause:

> This agreement shall be effective from the date it is made and shall continue in force for a period of five (5) years from the date it is made, and thereafter for successive five (5) year terms, unless and until terminated by one year prior notice in writing by either party.

In this dispute, one of the parties, Rogers, thought that it had a five-year deal. The other party, Aliant, was of the view that even within the initial term, it could terminate the agreement with one year's notice and increase its fees.

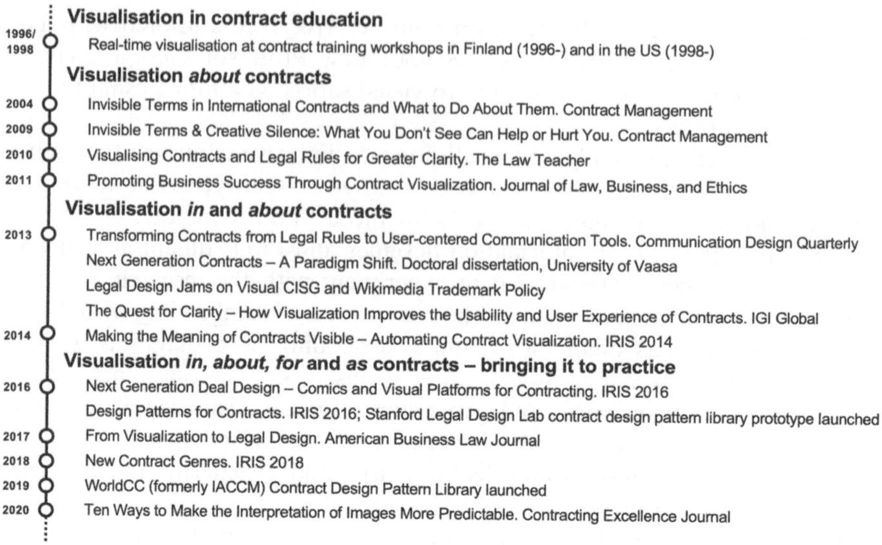

Figure 16.1 A brief chronology of my contract visualisation journey. Image: Author. Reproduced with permission.

Figure 16.2 Sample pages of a 1997 contract workshop visualisation. Images: Annika Varjonen. Reproduced with permission.

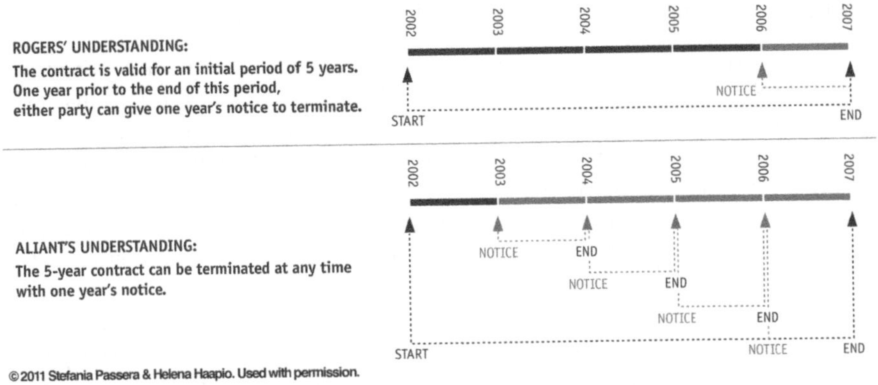

Figure 16.3. Two timelines that make different understandings visible. Image: Author and Stefania Passera. Reproduced with permission.

This is where visualisation enters the picture: simple timelines, as in Figure 16.3, would have shown the parties their different understandings.[35]

A simple timeline drawn on a flipchart would have allowed the parties, during the negotiations, to come to a mutual understanding and remove the ambiguity—or to see that they had no deal and walk away. In the words of Louis M. Brown, the Father of Preventive Law: 'It usually costs less to avoid getting into trouble than to pay for getting out of trouble'.[36]

My 2013 doctoral dissertation, Next Generation Contracts,[37] explored how visualisation can accelerate a paradigm shift in contract thinking and improve the quality, usability and user experience of contracts. As illustrated in Figure 16.1, after having gained experience with the concept, we started to look for ways to spread the word and make it easier for others to apply contract visualisation. We explored ways of presenting complex legal information in other contexts, too—for example, in privacy communication. Design patterns[38] and pattern libraries offered a way to identify, collect, and share good practices across these different contexts. Working with Margaret Hagan of the Stanford Legal Design Lab we developed our first contract design pattern library prototype as part of a co-authored conference paper.[39] After having convinced the leadership of the International Association for Contract and Commercial Management (IACCM; after rebranding, World Commerce & Contracting, WorldCC) of the feasibility of the idea, Stefania Passera and I started to design and build a Contract Design Pattern Library for them.[40]

The work continues. While many welcome contract visualisation, some worry: what would a judge say, or will a visual contract hold up in court? Images and word–image combinations have been researched in language studies and communication sciences for years, yet their scholarly exploration has only just begun for the legal field. In order to promote the practice of contract visualisation, I am currently exploring ways to reduce worries around the interpretation of visuals in contracts.[41]

Towards next generation contracts: the way forward

In recent years, design thinking, simplification and visualisation have gained new proponents, even in the legal community.[42] Even just a glance at various social media platforms shows wide-ranging interest in these topics. Law students and their future clients are likely to be exposed to them. Visual contracts are no longer a remote possibility, they are real: examples are increasingly available, thanks to the early adopters and the WorldCC (formerly IACCM).[43] Law students should know about these developments and resources, and contracts teachers and legal scholars should not ignore them, either.

For information designers, the primary questions always are: what is the context in which the information will be used, and how do we expect people to use it in that context?[44] These are useful questions for those in charge of contract preparation as well. One approach or visual does not fit all contexts, and contract visualisation is not appropriate for every context. The purpose of the contract and the goals of the client need to be considered. To help contract planners and users, it usually makes sense to supplement text with explanatory diagrams and navigation tools. Such tools make it easier for everyone to find the information they need, to understand the information they find, and to use and act upon it.

Lawyer–designer teams and a new breed of contract designers are already joining forces with clients and technologists to improve contracts' functionality, usability and user experience. This requires a new mindset, shifting lawyers from being *unconscious* designers—creating contracts, disclosures, and manuals in conventional ways—to *conscious* designers, with a focus on the users and their needs for more useful and usable contracts and guidance.[45] Visualisation can help change mindsets, too, so the move toward a new paradigm and next generation contracts can begin. Table 16.1 shows what it entails.

Table 16.1 Moving to Next Generation Contracts[46]

From This …	*… To This*
Legally perfect contracts that prepare for failure and seek to allocate all risk to the other party.	Usable contracts that facilitate and guide desired action and help implement what is agreed.
Contracts are purely legal tools, made to win in court: legally binding, enforceable, must cover all conceivable contingencies.	Contracts are also business tools: must be clear and easy-to-use to achieve business goals for a win–win deal.
Contracts allocate risk. They are needed only when things go wrong.	Contracts add value. They enable business success and prevent problems and disputes.
Contracts are text-only.	Contracts can be presented as text, visuals, or hybrids, depending on the needs of the audience. Visual elements can help explain, condense, organise, clarify and navigate text.

Lawyers are increasingly working with other professions, whether they work in business or academia. It is no longer enough for lawyers who work with contracts to master *contract law in books.* They are expected to contribute to *contracts in action*. This often includes helping others—for example technologists developing smart contracts or AI solutions—understand what contracts mean.

Contract visualisation is not just about embedding visual elements in contracts and 'paper deals'. It is also about ensuring that the 'real deal' is captured, represented and implemented as intended. A contract is not the goal, its successful implementation is. A cross-functional team is in the position to make this happen. The processes of *visualising* and *designing* offer ways to respond to the needs and requirements related to the business purposes and managerial functions of contracts. Collaborating with clients and users and applying designerly methods such as customer journeys in those processes, future lawyers may finally be able to bridge the gap between the real (or actual) deal and the paper (or apparent) deal, which generations of conventional lawyers have not managed to do. Moving forward, the new breed of lawyers and law teachers will no doubt develop new tools and techniques to do so.[47]

Future lawyers have been predicted to operate as *transformers*, [48] *transaction engineers* [49] and as *designers* [50]; 'like engineers, [they] want to make something useful that works for their clients'.[51] Many of them will do things 'in designerly ways', with an 'emphasis on communication, experimentation, and making things visible and tangible'.[52] Visualisation can help today's law students be better equipped to take new roles and work successfully as part of cross-professional teams. Visualisation can help law teachers, too, to be better communicators.

Notes

1 Associate Professor of Business Law, University of Vaasa, Finland, Adjunct Professor of Proactive Law and Contract Design, University of Lapland and Contract Strategist at Lexpert Ltd, Helsinki.

2 Benjamin Franklin, 'Proposals Relating to the Education of Youth in Pensilvania' (*The History Carper*, 1 January 1749) note 9, www.historycarper.com/1749/01/01/proposals-relating-to-the-education-of-youth-in-pensilvania/2/, accessed 23 November 2020.

3 In this chapter, I use the concept 'contract visualisation' to refer to using visuals in the context of contract education and practice, the latter covering both the contracting process (from planning and preparation to negotiation, implementation and management) and the contract itself. The concept can also be used more narrowly to refer to contract documents only, for example, 'the use of diagrams, images, and visually structured layouts to make contracts more searchable, readable, and understandable'; see Stefania Passera, 'Bringing Legal Design and Legal Tech to Contracts' (28 March 2018), https://stefaniapassera.com/blog/, accessed 30 November 2020. For different uses of contract visualisation—visuals *in, about, for* and *as* contracts—see Section 3 and Helena Haapio, Daniela A Plewe and Robert de Rooy, 'Next Generation Deal Design: Comics and Visual Platforms for

Contracting' in Erich Schweighofer, Franz Kummer, Walter Hötzendorfer and Georg Borges (eds), *Networks. Proceedings of the 19th International Legal Informatics Symposium IRIS 2016* (Österreichische Computer Gesellschaft OCG 2016).

4 Gov.uk, 'Contractual Terms and Privacy Policies: How to Improve Consumer Understanding' (Department for Business, Energy & Industrial Strategy, 18 July 2019), www.gov.uk/government/publications/contractual-terms-and-privacy-policies-how-to-improve-consumer-understanding, accessed 30 November 2020.

5 See, for example, Kate Vitasek, 'Comic Contracts: A Novel Approach to Contract Clarity and Accessibility' (*Forbes*, 14 February 2017), www.forbes.com/sites/katevitasek/2017/02/14/comic-contracts-a-novel-approach-to-contract-clarity-and-accessibility/#7078e76c7635, accessed 30 November 2020; Bruce Love, 'Can Contracts Use Pictures Instead of Words?' (*Financial Times*, 23 October 2019), www.ft.com/content/032ddcb0-e6b1-11e9-b8e0-026e07cbe5b4, accessed 30 November 2020; David Frydlinger, Oliver Hart and Kate Vitasek, 'A New Approach to Contracts: How to Build Better Long-Term Strategic Partnerships' (2019) 97.5 Harvard Business Review 116.

6 Jessica Hullman, 'The Purpose of Visualisation Is Insight, Not Pictures: An Interview with Ben Shneiderman' (*ACM Interactions Blog*, 5 August 2019), https://interactions.acm.org/blog/view/the-purpose-of-visualization-is-insight-not-pictures-an-interview-with-ben, accessed 30 November 2020.

7 Fred Rodell, 'Goodbye to Law Reviews′ (1936) 23 Virginia Law Review 38, 38.

8 For the causes and consequences, see also Wendy Wagner and Will Walker, *Incomprehensible! A Study of How Our Legal System Encourages Incomprehensibility, Why It Matters, and What We Can Do About It* (Cambridge University Press 2019); Christopher Williams, 'Functional or Dysfunctional? The Language of Business Contracts in English' (2010) XLII.3 Rassegna Italiana di Linguistica Applicata 217; Christopher Williams, 'Functional or Dysfunctional? The Language of Business Contracts in English: An Update' in Marcelo Corrales, Helena Haapio and Mark Fenwick (eds), *Research Handbook on Contract Design* (Edward Elgar forthcoming).

9 See, for example, Joseph Kimble, *Writing for Dollars, Writing to Please. The Case for Plain Language in Business, Government, and Law* (Carolina Academic Press 2012).

10 See, for example, International Association for Contract & Commercial Management (IACCM), '10 Pitfalls to Avoid in Contracting' (20 November 2015), www.worldcc.com/Resources/Content-Hub/View/ArticleId/7847/10-Pitfalls-to-Avoid-in-Contracting, accessed 23 November 2020; IACCM, *The Purpose of a Contract: An IACCM Research Report* (2017), www.worldcc.com/Portals/IACCM/resources/files/9876_j18069-iaccm-purpose-of-contract-a4-2017-11-14-v1-webready.pdf, accessed 30 November 2020.

11 Stewart Macaulay, 'The Real and the Paper Deal: Empirical Pictures of Relationships, Complexity and the Urge for Transparent Simple Rules' (2003) 66 The Modern Law Review 44.

12 See, for example, Stefania Passera, *Beyond the Wall of Contract Text: Visualizing Contracts to Foster Understanding and Collaboration within and across Organizations* (Doctoral Dissertation, Aalto University 2017); International Association for Contract & Commercial Management (IACCM), 'Most Negotiated Terms 2018' (11 June 2018), www.worldcc.com/Resources/Content-Hub/View/ArticleId/9010/Most-Negotiated-Terms-Report-2018-Top-Terms, accessed 23 November 2020; World Commerce & Contracting (WorldCC), 'Most Negotiated Terms 2020' (7 October 2020), www.worldcc.com/Resources/Content-Hub/View/ArticleID/9934, accessed 23 November 2020.

13 Anna Hurmerinta-Haanpää and Sampo Viding, 'The Functions of Contracts in Interorganizational Relationships: A Contract Experts' Perspective' (2018) 4 Journal of Strategic Contracting and Negotiation 98.

14 Helena Haapio and Thomas D Barton, 'Business-Friendly Contracting: How Simplification and Visualisation Can Help Bring It to Practice' in Kai Jacob, Dierk Schindler and Roger Strathausen (eds), *Liquid Legal: Transforming Legal into a Business Savvy, Information Enabled and Performance Driven Industry* (Springer International 2017).

15 Promoters of the *proactive approach to contracting and law* have started to change this, and found allies in the emergence of Contract Design and Legal Design. See, for example, Helena Haapio (ed.), *A Proactive Approach to Contracting and Law* (International Association for Contract and Commercial Management & Turku University of Applied Sciences 2008); Thomas D Barton, 'Re-Designing Law and Lawyering for the Information Age' (2016) 30 Notre Dame Journal of Law, Ethics and Public Policy 1; Helena Haapio, Thomas D Barton and Marcelo Corrales Compagnucci, 'Legal Design for the Common Good: Proactive Legal Care by Design' in Marcelo Corrales Compagnucci, Helena Haapio, Margaret Hagan and Michael Doherty (eds), *Legal Design: Integrating Business, Design, & Legal Thinking with Technology* (Edward Elgar 2021); Thomas D Barton, Helena Haapio, Stefania Passera and James G Hazard, 'Reframing Contract Design: Integrating Business, Legal, Design, and Technology Perspectives' in Marcelo Corrales Compagnucci, Helena Haapio and Mark Fenwick (eds), *Research Handbook on Contract Design* (Edward Elgar forthcoming).

16 See, for example, Thomas D Barton, Helena Haapio, Stefania Passera and James G Hazard, 'Successful Contracts: Integrating Design and Technology' in Marcelo Corrales Compagnucci, Mark Fenwick and Helena Haapio (eds), *Legal Tech, Smart Contracts and Blockchain* (Springer 2019).

17 See, for example, Haapio (ed.), *A Proactive Approach to Contracting and Law* (n 15); George Siedel and Helena Haapio, 'Using Proactive Law for Competitive Advantage' (2010) 47 American Business Law Journal 641; Gerlinde Berger-Walliser, 'The Past and Future of Proactive Law: An Overview of the Development of the Proactive Law Movement' in Gerlinde Berger-Walliser and Kim Østergaard (eds), *Proactive Law in a Business Environment* (DJØF Publishing 2012).

18 See, for example, the resources mentioned in notes 15–17. See also Soili Nystén-Haarala, 'Ennakoivan sopimisen tutkimusmenetelmät' ['Research Methods of Proactive Contracting'] (2017) 115 Lakimies 1015; Anna Hurmerinta-Haanpää, *The Many Functions of Contracts. Empirical Studies on How Companies Use Contracts in Interorganizational Exchange Relations* (Doctoral dissertation, University of Turku 2021); Jouko Nuottila, Osmo Kauppila and Soili Nystén-Haarala, 'Proactive Contracting: Emerging Changes in Attitudes Toward Project Contracts and Lawyers' Contribution' (2016) 2 Journal of Strategic Contracting and Negotiation 150; Helena Haapio, *Next Generation Contracts: A Paradigm Shift* (Lexpert Ltd 2013).

19 Nystén-Haarala (n 18); Hurmerinta-Haanpää (n 18).

20 For example, Passera, *Beyond the Wall of Contract Text* (n 12); Hurmerinta-Haanpää (n 18).

21 For example, Passera, *Beyond the Wall of Contract Text* (n 12); Arianna Rossi and Helena Haapio, 'Proactive Legal Design: Embedding Values in the Design of Legal Artefacts' in Erich Schweighofer, Franz Kummer and Ahti Saarenpää (eds), *Internet of Things. Proceedings of the 22nd International Legal Informatics Symposium IRIS 2019* (Editions Weblaw 2019); Michael D Murray, 'Cartoon Contracts and the Proactive Visualization of Law' (2021) 16 University of Massachusetts Law Review 98; Michael D Murray, 'Diagrammatics and the Proactive Visualization of Legal Information' (2021) 43.3 University of Arkansas Little Rock Law Review 1. See also Haapio, Barton and Corrales Compagnucci (n 15).

22 Colette R Brunschwig, *Visualisierung von Rechtsnormen—Legal Design* [*Visualisation of Legal Norms – Legal Design*] (Schulthess Juristische Medien 2001); Emily Allbon, 'IT'S ALIVE! The birth of Lawbore and the Indispensability of the Law Librarian' (2005) 5.4 Legal Information Management 21; Richard K Sherwin, Neil Feigenson and Christina Spiesel, '*Law in the Digital Age: How Visual Communication Technologies are Transforming the Practice, Theory, and Teaching of Law*' (2006) 12 Boston University Journal of Science & Technology Law 227; Tobias Mahler, 'A Graphical Interface for Legal Texts?' in Dan Jerker B Svantesson and Stanley Greenstein (eds), *Internationalisation of Law in the Digital Information Society. Nordic Yearbook of Law and Informatics 2010–2012* (Ex Tuto Publishing 2013).

23 While often cited, researchers have been unsuccessful in finding the quotation in Margaret Mead's work. See, for example, Garson O'Toole, 'Never Doubt That a Small Group of Thoughtful, Committed Citizens Can Change the World; Indeed, It's the Only Thing That Ever Has' (*Quote Investigator*, 12 November 2017), https://quoteinvestigator.com/2017/11/12/change-world/, accessed 2 December 2020; Wikiquote contributors, 'Margaret Mead' (*Wikiquote*), https://en.wikiquote.org/w/index.php?title=Margaret_Mead&oldid=2899095, accessed 2 December 2020.

24 Helena Haapio and George J Siedel, *A Short Guide to Contract Risk* (Gower 2013).

25 See Thomas D Barton and others, 'Successful Contracts' (n 16).

26 For examples, see Passera, *Beyond the Wall of Contract Text* (n 12) and the resources mentioned in notes 5 and 40. See also WorldCC, 'Contract Design and Simplification', www.worldcc.com/Research-Analytics/Contract-Design-Simplification, accessed 23 November 2020.

27 For example, CISG Legal Design Jam, Information Design Summer School, Syros 30 September – 4 October 2013; Legal Design Jam @ Stanford University, Stanford, 11 October 2013; Legal Design Jam @ The Embassy SF, San Francisco, 12 October 2013—see http://legaldesignjam.com/jams/past-jams/ for details.

28 See, for example, Daniela Alina Plewe and Robert de Rooy, 'Integrative Deal-Design: Cascading from Goal-Hierarchies to Negotiations and Contracting' (2016) 2 Journal of Strategic Contracting and Negotiation 19.

29 See, for example, Robert de Rooy, 'Comic Contracts: Everyone Can Understand Them' *Contracting Excellence Journal* (17 September 2018), https://journal.iaccm.com/contracting-excellence-journal/comic-contracts-everyone-can-understand-them , accessed 30 November 2020; Camilla Baasch Andersen and Robert de Rooy, 'Employment Agreements in Comic Book Form: What a Difference Cartoons Make' in Marcelo Corrales Compagnucci, Helena Haapio and Mark Fenwick (eds), *Research Handbook on Contract Design* (Edward Elgar forthcoming).

30 See Helena Haapio, Robert de Rooy and Thomas D Barton, 'New Contract Genres' in Erich Schweighofer, Franz Kummer, Ahti Saarenpää and Burkhard Schafer (eds), *Data Protection / LegalTech. Proceedings of the 21th International Legal Informatics Symposium IRIS 2018* (Editions Weblaw 2018). In this paper we took stock of the developments and envisioned a future where contracts are designed to contain code, text, sound, visuals, comics and more.

31 Our team coined the continuum of visuals *in, about, for* and *as* contracts, but we were not the first or only persons applying the ideas. Flowcharts, in particular, had already become popular tools. One of the early articles about the topic was Henry W Jones and Michael Oswald, 'Doing Deals with Flowcharts' (2001) 19.9 ACCA Docket 94. See also Henry W Jones, 'Envisioning Visual Contracting: Why Non-Textual Tools Will Improve Your Contracting' (2009) 2.6 Contracting Excellence 27. The first edition of *Contract Law: Flowcharts and Cases: A Student's Visual Guide to Understanding Contracts* by Frank J Doti was published by Thomson West in 2007. Many NEC3 contracts come with guidance notes and flowcharts;

see, for example, NEC, 'NEC3: Guidance Notes & Flowcharts', www.neccontract.com/NEC3-Products/NEC3-Contracts/NEC3-Engineering-Construction-Contract/NEC3-Guidance-Notes-Flowcharts, accessed 30 November 2020.

32 See also Lexpert, 'Contract Visualisation: The Trajectory', www.lexpert.com/our-approach/visualization/, accessed 30 November 2020. The events and resources listed in the Figure not mentioned elsewhere in this chapter are: Helena Haapio, 'Quality Improvement through Proactive Contracting: Contracts are too important to be left to lawyers!' (American Society for Quality ASQ Annual Quality Congress, Philadelphia, 5 May 1998) with real-time visualisations by Annika Varjonen, Visual Impact; Helena Haapio, 'Invisible Terms in International Contracts and What to Do About Them' *Contract Management* (July 2004) 32; Helena Haapio, 'Invisible Terms & Creative Silence: What You Don't See Can Help or Hurt You' *Contract Management* (September 2009) 24; Helena Haapio, 'Visualising Contracts and Legal Rules for Greater Clarity' (2010) 44 The Law Teacher 391; Gerlinde Berger-Walliser, Robert C Bird and Helena Haapio, 'Promoting Business Success Through Contract Visualization' (2011) 17 Journal of Law, Business and Ethics 55; Stefania Passera and Helena Haapio, 'Transforming Contracts from Legal Rules to User-Centered Communication Tools: A Human–Information Interaction Challenge' (2013) 1.3 Communication Design Quarterly 38; Helena Haapio and Stefania Passera, 'The Quest for Clarity—How Visualization Improves the Usability and User Experience of Contracts' in Mao Lin Huang and Weidong Huang (eds), *Innovative Approaches of Data Visualisation and Visual Analytics* (IGI Global 2013); Stefania Passera, Helena Haapio and Michael Curtotti, 'Making the Meaning of Contracts Visible—Automating Contract Visualization' in Erich Schweighofer, Franz Kummer and Walter Hötzendorfer (eds), *Transparency. Proceedings of the 17th International Legal Informatics Symposium IRIS 2014* (Österreichische Computer Gesellschaft OCG 2014); Gerlinde Berger-Walliser, Thomas D Barton and Helena Haapio, 'From Visualization to Legal Design: A Collaborative and Creative Process' (2017) 54.2 American Business Law Journal 347.

33 For real-time visualisations from the Proactive Law conference 'Future Law, Lawyering, and Language: Helping People and Business Succeed' held in Helsinki on 12–13 May 2003, see www.lexpert.com/wp-content/uploads/2015/08/ProactiveLawConference2003-VisualNotesbyAnnikaVarjonen.pdf.

34 For details, see, for example, Ian Austen, 'The Comma that Costs 1 Million Dollars (Canadian)' (*The New York Times*, 25 October 2010), www.nytimes.com/2006/10/25/business/worldbusiness/25comma.html, accessed 30 November 2020; Haapio and Siedel (n 24) 164–68.

35 See also Helena Haapio, 'Contract Clarity through Visualisation—Preliminary Observations and Experiments' in Ebad Banissi and others (eds), *Proceedings of the 15th International Conference on Information Visualisation, IV2011 (London 13–15 July 2011)* (IEEE Computer Society 2011) 339.

36 Louis M Brown, *Preventive Law* (Prentice-Hall 1950) 3.

37 Haapio, *Next Generation Contracts* (n 18). The work examines criteria for 'good' contracts and merges contract design with information design and visualisation, seeking to accelerate a paradigm shift in contract thinking and help implement the new thinking.

38 Design patterns are, in essence, reusable solutions to commonly occurring problems. They are not templates intended to be copy-pasted. See, for example, Helena Haapio and Stefania Passera, 'Contracts as Interfaces: Visual Representation Patterns in Contract Design' in Daniel M Katz, Ron Dolin and Michael J Bommarito (eds), *Legal Informatics* (Cambridge University Press 2021), with references.

39 Helena Haapio and Margaret Hagan, 'Design Patterns for Contracts' in Erich Schweighofer, Franz Kummer, Walter Hötzendorfer and Georg Borges (eds), *Networks.*

Proceedings of the 19th International Legal Informatics Symposium IRIS 2016 (Österreichische Computer Gesellschaft OCG / books@ocg.at 2016); Stanford Legal Design Lab, 'Contract Design Pattern Library', www.legaltechdesign.com/communication-design/legal-design-pattern-libraries/contracts/, accessed 30 November 2020.

40 WorldCC, Stefania Passera and Helena Haapio, 'WorldCC Contract Design Pattern Library', https://contract-design.worldcc.com/, accessed 7 March 2022; to see examples of actual contracts and clauses provided by companies such as Airbus, DXC Technology, Shell and Telstra, go to 'Explore Library', choose a pattern and click on 'Examples'.

41 Helena Haapio, Vesa Annola and Merja Koskela, 'Ten Ways to Make the Interpretation of Images More Predictable' *Contracting Excellence Journal* (5 November 2020), www.worldcc.com/Resources/Blogs-and-Journals/Contracting-Excellence-Journal/View/ArticleID/10987, accessed 7 March 2022; Vesa Annola, Helena Haapio and Merja Koskela, 'Interpreting Images in Contracts' in Marcelo Corrales Compagnucci, Helena Haapio and Mark Fenwick (eds), *Research Handbook on Contract Design* (Edward Elgar forthcoming).

42 For a maturing body of scholarship and practical application of Visual Law and Legal Design, see the 2019 and 2020 Special Issues of the Journal of Open Access to Law (JOAL) and Michael A Curtotti, 'Visualising a Visual Movement—Reflections on a Growing Body of Research' (2020) 8 Journal of Open Access to Law, https://ojs.law.cornell.edu/index.php/joal/article/view/105, accessed 2 December 2020. See also Normactivity, 'Law', www.normactivity.com/law.html, accessed 2 December 2020.

43 In addition to its Contract Design Pattern Library and many other resources, the WorldCC offers a network for members sharing an interest in the topic: see WorldCC, Contract Design—Simplification and Visualisation, www.iaccm.com/gp/ContractSimplification (for members only).

44 David Sless, 'From Semiotics to Choreography' (2017) 23.2 Information Design Journal 173.

45 Helena Haapio, 'Legal Design in Action: From Text-Only Guidebooks to Digital, Visual Playbooks' in Erich Schweighofer, Franz Kummer and Ahti Saarenpää (eds), *Internet of Things. Proceedings of the 22nd International Legal Infomatics Symposium IRIS 2019* (Editions Weblaw 2019). Similarly, Margaret Hagan, 'Law by Design', www.lawbydesign.co, accessed 30 November 2020. For the challenges of using current contracts as training data for machine learning and AI systems, see Helena Haapio and Daniel W Linna Jr, 'Contract Quality and AI: Garbage In, Garbage Out?' *Contracting Excellence Journal* (31 August 2020), https://journal.iaccm.com/contracting-excellence-journal/contract-quality-and-ai-garbage-in-garbage-out, accessed 30 November 2020, with references.

46 Adapted from Haapio, *Next Generation Contracts* (n 18) 41–42 and Rob Waller, Helena Haapio and Stefania Passera, 'Contract Simplification: The Why and the How' *Contracting Excellence Journal* (24 July 2017), https://journal.iaccm.com/contracting-excellence-journal/contract-simplification-the-why-and-the-how, accessed 30 November 2020. Used with permission.

47 For tools and inspiration, see also City Law School, 'tl;dr – The Less Textual Legal Gallery' (City, University of London), https://tldr.legal, accessed 2 December 2020 and Emily Allbon, 'Changing Mindsets: Encouraging Law Teachers to Think Beyond Text' (2019) 7 Journal of Open Access to Law, https://ojs.law.cornell.edu/index.php/joal/article/view/96, accessed 2 December 2020.

48 Stefania Passera, Emily Allbon and Helena Haapio, 'Contract Transformation: Merging Drafting and Design to Meet the Needs of Human Readers' in Marcelo Corrales Compagnucci, Helena Haapio and Mark Fenwick (eds), *Research Handbook on Contract Design* (Edward Elgar forthcoming).

49 See, for example, Marcelo Corrales, Mark Fenwick, Helena Haapio and Erik PM Vermeulen, 'Tomorrow's Lawyer Today? Platform-Driven LegalTech, Smart Contracts & the New World of Legal Design' (2019) 22.10 Journal of Internet Law 3, with references.

50 Hagan (n 45).

51 David Howarth, *Law as Engineering. Thinking about What Lawyers Do* (Edward Elgar 2013) 67.

52 Amanda Perry-Kessaris, 'Making Socio-Legal Research More Social by Design: Anglo-German Roots, Rewards and Risks' (2020) 21 German Law Journal 1427. See also Amanda Perry-Kessaris, 'Legal Design for Practice, Activism, Policy and Research' (2019) 46 Journal of Law and Society 185.

17 How Legal Design is shaping satisfaction, standards and substance in legal practice

Erika Concetta Pagano[1]

Introduction

At its core, good Legal Design enables better understanding, clarity and choice. Our world is changing quickly: developments in globalisation, technology, regulatory complexity and competition are just a few of the forces shifting the way that lawyers, clients, consumers and everyday people make decisions with legal implications. From truly understanding an app's terms and conditions before habitually (and hastily) clicking 'I accept', to communicating what an employee's parental leave rights might be, and to enabling the C-suite to prioritise and action the risks associated with a bet-the-business transaction, Legal Design presents an opportunity not only to meet the needs of tomorrow but to proactively change the future of law, in particular by making it more accessible.

This chapter argues that although these outcomes sound simple and desirable, the process and ecosystem required to make it a reality are anything but. It draws on the experiences of the world's first legal engineering firm, Simmons Wavelength—also home to the first full-time, fully dedicated Legal Design practice housed within a large global law firm, Simmons & Simmons—to examine the present impact and future potential of Legal Design. First, it evaluates why Legal Design is a permanent fixture in the profession. Second, it examines what legal design is and, equally as important, what it is not. Third, it explores the people, processes, and practicalities of Legal Design, asking, for example, 'Who can and should engage in Legal Design?' 'What skills and characteristics are fundamental to a successful Legal Design project?' and 'How does Legal Design actually work?' Fourth it considers the challenges presented by Legal Design including barriers to implementation, understanding and purchasing. The chapter concludes with a forecast on what lies ahead, for both Legal Design as a field and for those involved (or looking to get involved) in it.

Why embrace Legal Design?

No matter how one defines Legal Design (and there are many differing viewpoints!), one truth is universal: Legal Design is rooted in empathy. Drawing on

DOI: 10.4324/9780429021411-20

this human-centred approach, we will begin with one simple question: Why care about Legal Design at all? There are many reasons, and we will highlight three.

First, the world needs it: Consider the following widely quoted statistic: 65 per cent of people are visual learners; that is, they engage in the world through spatial experiences.[2] It is worth noting that this been 'debunked' in various subsequent studies; finding that although the learners have a personal preference for learning, there isn't any evidence that success follows because of that choice.[3] This aside, those who consider themselves visual learners prefer receiving and understanding information through forms and techniques like shapes, diagrams, colour coding and maps. Yet the call to make everything visual is neither simple nor practical. Consider, for example, the growth of assistive technology, such as screen readers that help the visually impaired navigate the digital world, combined with the legal necessity for complex documents, such as complicated financial disclosures. Legal Design is not a magic pill to solve every use case for making law better. However, it is a vehicle to get us incrementally closer to a better experience by communicating in a way that is more aligned with the needs of end users.

Consider another statistic: The average reading age in the US is somewhere between 12 and 14, and 45 million Americans are 'functionally illiterate'.[4] Similarly, in the UK, official guidelines for content on government websites call for a reading age of 9.[5] This is in stark contrast to legal education and practice: As lawyers, we are trained to write in a certain way—we're praised (and paid) for our broad vocabulary, our ability to construct analytical arguments and our powers of persuasion through the written (and spoken) word. Traditionally, we're not taught to use these talents to communicate so that those who count on our advice and work product can confidently understand, rely and act upon it.

In the past decade, there's been a movement in American law schools to teach students to write in 'Plain English', although what that means is neither universally standardised nor clear. One particular anecdote from my first year of law school remains particularly vivid: our legal writing professor asked the class to write a letter to a fictitious client explaining a curtilage issue involving his garden. She said the letter must be appropriate given the client's age, education and occupation. In this case, the client was a high school teacher with a university education. Although we would be graded on our ability to use Plain English, we were not told which words we could (or could not) use, nor were we given a concrete test (for example, the Flesch Reading Ease Score) to understand whether we were writing at an appropriate level. What I didn't know at the time (and what wasn't being taught) was that a clear way to demarcate what was and wasn't appropriate in communicating to this client about his curtilage issue existed, and that the answer to better, more client-centric communication had a name: Legal Design.

If we can't write in ways our clients can understand, then we aren't doing our job. This leads to the second reason to care about Legal Design: regulators demand it. There is a massive push for increased consumer fairness, and an equally forceful willingness to punish bad actors. In 2020, the Financial Conduct Authority issued a fine totalling GBP 26 million—the largest breach of consumer credit rules fine in its history—against a financial institution for a failure to treat customers fairly.[6] While different regulatory authorities have well-established tests for fairness, it is increasingly clear that good communication with customers is more than just a marketing gimmick—in reality, a lack of it presents real reputational, legal and monetary risks. Couple this with an increase in consumer choice, particularly as Millennials move their money to new entrants to the banking space, especially 'fintech' firms, who, for lack of better words, speak their language. For example, UK-based Monzo, a challenger bank with over 5 million customers, puts the user-friendliness of their terms front and centre: 'They're just over 2,500 words, and hopefully nice and easy to follow'.[7] This claim to commercial advantage isn't—and shouldn't—be an exclusive feature of start-ups, unicorns or other tech-forward companies. As the work of Fiona Philipps, Global Head of Digital Legal at HSBC demonstrates, Legal Design can pave the way for even the most established organizations to follow suit.[8]

Third, Legal Design presents a learning opportunity. Despite being a service-oriented profession, most lawyers score below average for emotional intelligence.[9] This is particularly problematic when we're working with clients in mind. Legal Design can be a fantastic remedy: it gives lawyers, legal teams and anyone else involved on a Legal Design project a chance to hone collaboration, problem finding and solving, user centricity and ideation skills. It's also a fantastic way to pick up extra business intelligence. For example, at Simmons Wavelength we have found that clients appreciate the extra value when we can reflect back to them a need, dynamic or trend that we have discovered in our work of which they were not previously aware. In one project, the Legal Department had overlooked the desire of the Customer Service team to input into the written language for a consumer-facing financial product. Including Customer Service into the drafting process provided several benefits, including the birth and development of a new and stronger relationship between the two teams. Such new pathways to identifying and solving challenges can produce stronger lawyers and, ultimately, a better work product.

What Legal Design is (not)

What is Legal Design? Ask ten different people in the legal world for a definition, and you'll get ten different answers. It's easiest to start with some myth busting to understand what Legal Design is not: One of the biggest misconceptions? Legal Design is 'just making things look pretty'. While visual harmony, aesthetic good vibes and the communication of a client's brand, values and ethos are an end result of good Legal Design in action, fixing only the external appearance of a document, playbook, or form is the equivalent of putting a plaster on a water tank leak—a cosmetic fix does not solve the underlying issue, nor does it make a holistic, long-term, value-adding better outcome. Another misconception is what we call 'stick figure syndrome', or that Legal Design's only purpose is to make things as simple as a stick figure could convey. Such a gross oversimplification of the aims and ability of Legal Design to foster increased transparency is a disservice to the discipline and profession as a whole. Take comic contracts (that is, traditional contracts re-designed into comic form) as a prime example: While they are a manifestation of Legal Design principles in practice, they are an appropriate solution in a limited number of circumstances for a very narrow client need.

A broader, more accurate, view is to see good Legal Design as accomplishing three aims—creating better communication, culture creation and empowered information—each of which will be discussed in turn.

First, better communication: Legal Design enables us to ask 'How can we best communicate with others (the wider business, our customers, the world), and how can they best communicate with us?' Consider, for example, how a global automobile corporation shares its compliance and risk policies and procedures with employees who attend a trade show. This guidance is written by lawyers and other stakeholders within the business, and traditionally appears written in legalese and structured into poorly-coloured, narrow-column tables that span multiple pages, and often color-coded in a well-intentioned but garish way. The end result? Employees who should read the guidance don't and, as a result, pose a risk to themselves and to their employer. This is one small example where Legal Design can help: Instead, the information can be better organized into action-oriented checklists. If the guidance is digital, short videos depicting actual scenarios (and the right way to respond to tough or ambiguous situations) help the employees translate policy (or regulation) into reality.

Second, better culture creation: Here, Legal Design enables us to ask 'How can we infuse and promote company values, goals, and change in tangible and intangible ways?' Consider a retail bank customer who is deciding which bank to use for her mortgage. Not only is this a big decision with significant consequences (that is, if she does not meet her obligations, she may, quite literally, lose her home), but the long-term nature of a mortgage means that the relationship between the customer and the bank will last longer than many of our human relationships. The documents she completes during the first steps of the mortgage process will help to form her first impression of the bank: Do they engender trust? Do they make her feel like a valued customer? Are they easy to understand? Can she complete them digitally and with ease? How seamlessly can she get answers to any questions she has? Along this initial foray, any negative experience may incentivize her to take her business elsewhere. This is another example where Legal Design can help: taking a holistic approach to the customer experience so that the customer feels valued and empowered, while also adding value through better business.

Third, empowered information: In a very future-facing way, Legal Design encourages us to ask 'How can we enable better decision making with data and smart design?' Consider a large industrial manufacturer who has some difficult choices to make regarding possible restructuring options. Here, Legal Design focuses on the key parties (in this case, the General Counsel, the Chief Risk Officer, the Board of Directors) and their needs and incentives (in this case, the ability to quickly assess, understand and act on options to ensure the long-term sustainability of the company in a volatile market with significant political pressure). In moments of intense pressure, there is neither time nor willingness to dig through literally thousands of papers of documents—after all, this is a job for the lawyers. But what if the lawyers went one step further and worked collaboratively with data scientists to create an interactive dashboard that visualized the size and priority of the risks, as well as the interdependencies and consequences of those risks based on the possible courses of action chosen? Here, Legal Design can help too: a powerful combination of Legal Design and data science makes for better business sense, enabling a more management information-friendly and board ready way to interrogate, discuss and understand information (and, ultimately, drive better action).

Legal Design is also well-suited to contemporary life. For example, by focusing on how end users receive information, it enables legal, compliance and business teams to think digitally. While paper-based documentation is still a necessity in some cases, the reality is that most will consume information on a screen—whether they are, for example, a consumer scrolling through terms for a new service, or an employee checking company bribery policy to understand if, when and how they should register a gift from a potential vendor. Legal Design enables us to keep these needs top-of-mind, balancing content with function for better results. Furthermore, Legal Design can draw on scientific evidence to support contemporary aims of inclusivity, and, more broadly, accessibility. For example, colour blindness impacts 1 in 12 men and 1 in 200 women in the world.[10] One of the most common forms of colour blindness is manifested in a confusion of red and green—consider what this means for charts that are innocently color-coded in a stoplight system.[11] In this case, including an icon that conveys the meaning of the original colour—for example, a red 'X' signifying no, or a green '✓' signifying yes—instead of colour coding the content, is a more inclusive solution. At Simmons, we use a 30-point checklist to ensure our outputs are appropriate for the intended audience, including psychology principles and tests for reading level, comprehension, colour contrast and compatibility with assistive technology for the visually impaired (e.g., screen readers). Cultural competency and diversity are also important elements. For example, when a financial institution seeks to overhaul its anti-money laundering guidance videos in the Middle East, Africa, and Asia, the final product must include people who look like the intended audience. Here, Legal Design serves an underappreciated yet significant role as a leader for and driver in deeper, more visible diversity and inclusion.

All of these aspects should not—and cannot—exist in a silo. That is, Legal Design does not happen on the corner of someone's desk. It is not a part-time job. It is also not a stand-alone role that operates separately from traditionally practising colleagues. Each piece requires deliberate, carefully-designed collaboration between experts in various fields: Take, for example, when we redesign an employment handbook. Legal designers often lead the process, coordinating between various stakeholders at the client and colleagues across the firm. After designing the process and building buy-in and engagement, the Legal Designers will lay the foundation by understanding the client's (and, usually their clients') needs, pressures, values and incentives to paint a (figurative) picture of the project's tone and requirements. The Legal Designers will then work hand-in-hand with their Employment Lawyer counterparts to ensure content, order, and structure of the language meets the end user requirements—as well as what is required by law. Sometimes, this results in uncomfortable questions; for example, challenging the status quo. Sometimes, a daringness to be bold may be too bold, or too forward thinking, for regulatory certainty. It is an iterative learning process that requires each side to challenge their comfort zones and abilities (and, of course, grow along the way).

People

Moving from the end users of legally-designed outputs to the doers and champions of Legal Design, we are often asked who should engage in Legal Design. Our answer is simple: Everyone. For example, a General Counsel seeking to modernise and reimagine its customer-facing documentation, a Partner looking to deliver guidance in a more business-ready way, and a law student seeking to enrich their traditional legal career in non-traditional ways are just a few of the many folks who ought to embrace Legal Design.

So it is promising that law schools across the globe—including IE (Spain), Oxford (UK) and Stanford (US)—are starting to embrace Legal Design as an optional part of a student's law school curriculum. From a personal perspective, I now teach this at the undergraduate and master's level at IE University in Madrid, and students' exposure to design thinking goes beyond my innovation in law courses to a number of workshops, events and even intra-university challenges. Thinking back to the broader call for Plain English, we challenge law schools to include Legal Design as a fundamental part of training future lawyers to better service their clients. In practice, Legal Design is now a viable career option, with many lawyers opting to open up successful Legal Design businesses that dot the globe from Colombia to France to Australia. Speaking even closer to home, five years ago, it would have been unimaginable—let alone unprecedented—for a global law firm to fully embrace a Legal Design practice. In the broader legal community, we've seen the rise of Legal Design conferences and events. This enthusiasm and rapid growth is encouraging.

There's a debate that sharply divides the legal tech community: Should lawyers code? Similarly, in Legal Design circles, many ask whether Legal Designers should be capable of graphic design, or, more radically, whether they need to have formal legal training at all. Unlike the binary (i.e., yes or no) question of coding and lawyers, understanding what makes for a good Legal Designer is more complex. By its nature, Legal Design is a collaborative process—more on that later in this chapter. It is not a solo activity; rather, when done right, it is the collective product of a diverse set of mindsets, skillsets, and perspectives. For example, our Legal Design projects include lawyers from various practice groups, stakeholders from across the clients' business units, formally trained designers, accessibility experts, proven innovators and more. What do all of these participants have in common? Characteristics including curiosity, a growth mindset, creativity, strong listening and observational skills and a willingness to iterate. Another key ingredient is an appreciation for the skillsets of others—for example, a data protection lawyer will bring substantive expertise to a Legal Design project that a lawyer with ten years of innovation experience just won't have. Each are equally as valuable and vital to the success of a data protection-focused Legal Design project.

While enthusiasm for Legal Design grows, so too does spend on and the maturity of the Legal Design market. That growth is not without scepticism. Lawyers are famous for their resistance to change, and it's natural that a traditional profession would question new tools, technologies and ways of working.[12] From a commercial perspective, a fundamental and frequent question is: 'Why should I spend money on Legal Design?' Legal departments are under tighter budget and resource constraints than ever before.[13] While many forward-thinking lawyers are already attuned to Legal Design's role in delivering the future of law, convincing clients that Legal Design is a 'must have', not just a 'nice to have', is, more often than not, a complex and uphill battle. Legal Design—especially when backed by proof like increased comprehension, faster reading time, more inclusion, and higher customer satisfaction—often sells itself. Yet, for many established and traditional organisations, trust and confidence in the team delivering Legal Design are key—a true Legal Designer will facilitate the journey for the client, and coach them through the process.

From a law firm perspective, culture is key—and a firm with innovation embedded in its DNA, like Simmons, is ready to embrace Legal Design in full. That said, in true design thinking form, it is the Legal Designers' role to consider their colleagues as end users: What are their needs, pain points, and priorities? How can we best help our colleagues identify opportunities for Legal Design and welcome us to the table? To drive these conversations, we must educate our colleagues and work with them to understand the art of the possible. This means spending the time to chat about problems and potential solutions, showcasing past work and thinking creatively about engagement: emails and webinars alone will not do, but doing it will. The ugly truth? Doing it takes time. Challenging traditions and an institutionalised way of working, be it on the firm or client side, is difficult, but not impossible. At its worst, it's a chance to better understand the end user (be that a Partner or confused client) and try again. At its best, it's witnessing an 'a ha' moment in a pitch or being top-of-mind for a client or colleague when they're facing a novel challenge or wanting to try something new. Two years into our journey, our team, types of work, and network of Legal Design enthusiasts (and even traditional lawyers who put Legal Design to work in their day-to-day tasks, although they might not yet be ready to publicly admit it!) has grown organically. Our Legal Design practice is routinely asked to lead—not just input—into major pitches spanning sectors and offices. Our client work has evolved into market-leading, money-making tools developed by our colleagues in the New Business (product) team. We've also worked closely with other entities within Simmons Solutions (including Adaptive, our flexible resourcing capability) to bring clients an unmatched, multi-faceted way of approaching, understanding, navigating and solving client problems, especially in response to a global pandemic.

Like most innovation, it's the small changes that can yield a big impact, especially over time. At Simmons Wavelength, we launched a firm-wide Weekly Legal Design Challenge in January 2021, where we release a six-minute challenge that reflects some element of Legal Design each week. Some examples include journey mapping, storyboarding, need-finding techniques and even redesigning a complex clause. Everyone at the firm, no matter their role, location or seniority, is invited to participate. To date, we have participants across a handful of countries, ranging in roles from Partners to secretaries, and from Marketing and Business Development to firm leadership. The Challenge has had three primary benefits: generating interest in Legal Design, upskilling colleagues, and creating a community of Legal Design enthusiasts across the business. Together, we tackle communication, cultural and accessibility issues in working through how Legal Design impacts the way we structure and convey information. Sometimes, we focus on something minor, such as reimagining the almost undecipherable, and therefore non-user-friendly icons on an office paper shredder, to creating simple posters that relay a cultural preference or norm that, if others knew, might make our ways of working more productive and collaborative.

Process

Design thinking is a well-documented group of processes, and Legal Design is no different. Traditional legal transactions often go as follows: Client instructs Lawyer; Lawyer performs the work and sends it back to Client; Lawyer and Client exchange a few rounds of emails, phone calls, and amendments are exchanged; Client gets the end product and a bill for the services; and Lawyer gets paid. While this example might be overly simplified, it illustrates the siloed nature of traditional legal work—for the majority of the relationship, Client and Lawyer are working separately. They may have the occasional conversation to troubleshoot, but they are rarely at the same (figurative) table—with the client trusting the lawyer to get their job done, and get in touch should the odd question or concern arise. For many lawyers, the way a deal is structured, or the way due diligence is performed or analysed, doesn't drastically change (although the variables and circumstances might). There is, undoubtedly, comfort in this predictability and stability.

Legal Design is, by its nature, uncomfortable. It is far less certain than a lawyer's traditional ways of working, and is generally full of surprise discoveries, uncovered opinions and a constantly shifting puzzle of reprioritising needs. Lawyers are trained to avoid and avert risk. We are taught to craft careful strategies to gain a certain outcome, with each step methodically planned. We're taught to wield our pens for the power of prose—heaven forbid a diagram or flowchart ever make its way from a brainstorming notebook to the client's desk! This is in direct opposition to the iterative, flexible, and uncertain nature of design thinking processes; naturally, the first steps in a Legal Design process can seem an affront to the many hours of training and years of experience required to take a place in the legal field.

Yet even the most seasoned of lawyers can embrace Legal Design. This shift in mindset may happen overnight, but for most it's a gradual process built on experimentation and experience (in both successes and failures). Every Legal Designer has their own 'secret sauce' that reflects their unique combination of experiences, skills, and techniques, yet there are common elements and features across all teams and projects. Teambuilding is a fundamental part of the Legal Design journey, whether the project is a one-day sprint to solve a quick issue, or a one-year overhaul of a private wealth customer's onboarding experience. Need-finding is critical to understanding the landscape—this includes evaluating who your stakeholders are (hint: there are generally more than initially thought!), and listening to them as closely as possible to identify trends, divergences, motivations, and more. Goal setting is also key: What must be achieved by the end of the process? What would be nice to achieve, but isn't absolutely necessary? In a perfect world, what would be the ideal outcome? Goal setting for the group—and for the individual team members involved in the project—helps to build engagement and buy-in, as well as facilitate continued growth and development. As for the actual design process, it is unsurprisingly iterative. For some projects, the content is created (or updated) simultaneously along with the look and feel. For other projects, these are split into two separate and concurrent streams that periodically intersect. In either case, these two facets inform each other with each iteration. Testing can be one of the most emotional phases of Legal Design—too often an idea seems great, but when tested with actual consumers, it falls flat on its face. For example, one client tried to simplify their language around bereavement policies. The end result? A policy saying 'if you die…'. The customer response was, unsurprisingly, not positive, with some practical consumers arguing that they wouldn't be able to action the policy once deceased. This component of the Legal Design journey requires extreme resilience and humility. Testing can also be joyful—the win of seeing work product meet accessibility tests and result in faster comprehension and a better client experience rightfully feels like a massive job well done. On a related note, knowing when to stop iterating and move on—and when to advise clients to do the same—is a skill developed over time. All along the way, clear communication and feedback help to supercharge the process.

Practicalities

From a practical perspective, there are a few learnings to keep in mind: first, successful Legal Design requires commitment. We've seen even the most well-intentioned projects fail because a key stakeholder promised, but could not follow through on, investing the necessary time. Legal Design is a fully-formed discipline, not a side-of-the-desk activity. Second, good Legal Design requires mental, emotional and creative fortitude. It requires analytical and elastic thinking. It requires observational skills in overdrive. Our brains have a finite cognitive load, so Legal Design requires the support of a great team. Third, a great Legal Designer will embrace failure and feedback. Some may view missteps as setbacks, while the more growth mindset-oriented will appreciate them as informative steps towards an end result. This necessitates a separation of the ego from the project outcome—a more difficult task than often thought. Fourth, Legal Design requires real science: using established methodologies and consumer testing to go from 'well, this looks or sounds or feels right' to showing, for example, an actual reduction in page count, increase in comprehension or growth in consumer empowerment.

Conclusion

When deployed well, Legal Design is interactive, collaborative, user-centric and scientific. Good Legal Design promotes confidence, empowerment, accessibility, understanding and navigability. Good Legal Design drives value by reflecting branding, values, goals, culture and solutions to current and future needs. It is a team effort; it is iterative (small shifts that cumulatively yield big results); and, it is hard, meaningful and rewarding work.

We often say that the best Legal Design is when a client doesn't formally know that they're doing it by name, but they're certain they learn from, value and enjoy the process and end result. As Legal Design grows in profile, this little secret might not be so secret for much longer. This chapter has only scratched the surface of how Legal Design is shaping the future of the legal profession. In addition to the examples above, clients count on us to coach them on how they collaborate and team; to redesign the playbooks that matter most in times of reputational and operational crises so that they are functional and engender confidence; and to clearly communicate some of the most complex cross-border implications in an ever-shifting geopolitical world. Over the past two years, we've worked alongside every single practice group and a handful of our 25+ offices around the world, looking at everything from embedding ESG commitments into the client's business to rethinking the due diligence process on a systematic level. Looking ahead, there's no sign of stopping. It's clear that Legal Design is more than here to stay—it is poised to be a star player in shaping the future of our profession (and the opportunities for new entrants, those seeking a radical change and those looking to continue on their journey, but maybe doing it just a little bit better).

Notes

1 Head of Legal Information and Design, Simmons Wavelength (Simmons & Simmons).
2 Molly St Louis, 'How to Spot Visual, Auditory, and Kinesthetic-Learning Executives' (*Inc.com*, 1 August 2017), https://www.inc.com/molly-reynolds/how-to-spot-visual-auditory-and-kinesthetic-learni.html, accessed 19 July 2021; 30 per cent of the population are auditory learners, and 5 per cent of the population are kinesthetic learners.
3 'Learning Styles as a Myth' (*Yale Poorvu Center for Teaching and Learning*), https://poorvucenter.yale.edu/LearningStylesMyth, accessed 19 July 2021 and 'Exams 2018: The "Myth" of the Visual Learner' (*BBC News*, 3 June 2018), https://www.bbc.com/news/education-44304056, accessed 19 July 2021.
4 Admin-Travis, '30 Key Child Literacy Stats Parents Need to be Aware Of' (*Literacy Project Foundation*, 14 February 2019), https://literacyproj.org/2019/02/14/30-key-child-literacy-stats-parents-need-to-be-aware-of/, accessed 19 July 2021.
5 'Writing for GOV.UK—Content Design: Planning, Writing and Managing Content—Guidance—GOV.UK' (25 February 2016, updated 8 July 2021), https://www.gov.uk/guidance/content-design/writing-for-gov-uk, accessed 19 July 2021.
6 'FCA Fines Barclays £26 Million over Treatment of Customers in Financial Difficulty' (*FCA*, 14 December 2020), https://www.fca.org.uk/news/press-releases/fca-fines-barclays-treatment-customers-financial-difficulty, accessed 19 July 2021.
7 Steve O'Hear, 'Monzo, the UK Challenger Bank, Picks up Additional £60M in Funding' (*TechCrunch*, 2 December 2020), https://social.techcrunch.com/2020/12/02/monzo-the-u-k-challenger-bank-picks-up-additional-60m-in-funding/, accessed 19 July 2021; 'Monzo Help—Monzo Terms and Conditions' (Monzo), https://monzo.com/help, accessed 19 July 2021.
8 See 'Episode 13: Legal Designing Financial Services with Fiona Philipps' (*Legal Design Podcast*, 23 May 2021), http://legaldesignpodcast.com/13-episode-legal-designing-financial-services-with-fiona-phillips/, accessed 19 July 2021.
9 Ronda Muir, ESQ. 'The Unique Psychological World of Lawyers', https://www.lawpeopleblog.com/files/2016/05/LPM-Unique-Psychological-World-of-Lawyers.final_.pdf, accessed 19 July 2021.
10 'Colour Blindness' (*Colour Blind Awareness*), https://www.colourblindawareness.org/colour-blindness/, accessed 19 July 2021.
11 'Colour Vision Deficiency (Colour Blindness)' (*nhs.uk*, 18 October 2017), https://www.nhs.uk/conditions/colour-vision-deficiency/, accessed 19 July 2021.
12 Mark A Cohen, 'Legal Innovation Is the Rage, But There's Plenty of Resistance' (*Forbes*, 30 August 30 2018), https://www.forbes.com/sites/markcohen1/2018/08/30/legal-innovation-is-the-rage-but-theres-plenty-of-resistance/, accessed 19 July 2021.
13 ibid 2.

18 Design in legal publishing

Emily Allbon[1] *and Amanda Perry-Kessaris*[2]

How are designerly ways influencing the culture, processes and outputs of the legal publishing industry; and what impact might this have on legal education? We asked Robin Chesterman, Global Head of Product and Matthew Terrell, Head of Marketing at vLex and Karen Waldron, Director of Product and Matt Wardle, UX Director at LexisNexis.[3] Both publishers have a transnational focus, producing primarily legal materials, including case law series and legislation, and secondary sources, such as commentaries and textbooks, from multiple jurisdictions. While vLex focus exclusively on digital formats, LexisNexis also produce hardcopy products, including managing two hundred years of print legacy. Furthermore, both publishers specialise in innovative interactive online data management and analysis tools with which consumers can make detailed and integrated investigations across a wide range of legal materials.

The rise of the visual in legal publishing

Attractive presentation is always important. Many legal content products now include visual elements, such as diagrams. These can be 'eye-catching', but also, more importantly they can improve 'accessibility' and can sometimes convey information more compactly than text. The ground-breaking vLex Precedent Map is an interactive visualisation of the relationships between cases:

> 'What [the user sees] is a citation network for a family of cases—each case is displayed as a circle node, and citations are displayed as connecting edges. The size of the circle is based on the number of relationships the node has with other nodes within the family, which is a good indicator of similarity, and subsequently a useful way to prioritise further reading. [It offers] an excellent alternative to scanning lists of related cases. With a list, you are only able to sort by a single dimension at once, such as how many times a case has been cited, or in chronological order. With a graph such as the Precedent Map, we can indicate both importance i.e. subsequent citations, and a temporal component i.e. year, simultaneously.'

DOI: 10.4324/9780429021411-21

It was one of the first case law visualisation products in the legal research market when it was launched over a decade ago; and '[i]t continues to surprise new users that discover it. Much of its popularity is because it is a manifestation of something similar to the mental image many of us form when trying to picture how different legal authorities connect to each other'. Partly in response to increased demand from a broad cross-section of users, vLex have recently begun to consider how to incorporate more visual elements, such as visual search results, across their service. For example, the vLex website offers an interactive heat-map for users to explore all countries and regions covered in vLex's databases which 'instantly provides' the user with 'an understanding of the breadth of content' as compared to, for example 'presenting them with a long list of countries' (vLex).

But 'visual representations of the law do not resonate with all users, and being able to read a document is still the killer feature', so carefully considered typography and layout remain crucial (vLex). Perhaps the first rule of visualisation in legal publications is not to visualise just 'for the sake of it', not least because of the costs involved. 'But where it brings value, it can be incredibly powerful.' Where the decision is made to go ahead and visualise, it is essential to ensure that the 'visual metaphor' is appropriate to the content

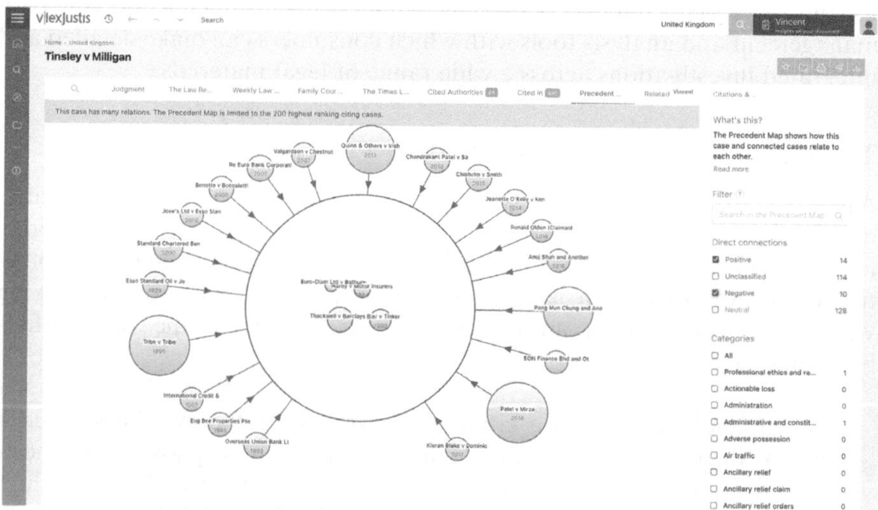

Figure 18.1 Detail of vLex Precedent Map showing the relationships between cases relevant to the case of *Tinsley v Milligan*. The small circles in the centre represent cases mentioned within *Tinsley* and the larger circles outside represent those cases which have cited *Tinsley*. Note that the arrowed lines are in colour which indicates if positive or negative treatment given. The larger the circle, the more the case has in common with the main case. Image: vLex. Reproduced with permission.

and the context. LexisNexis have done extensive research into what makes a visual 'palatable' to lawyers—what brings 'gravitas and utility', as opposed to 'belittling the content or patronising the user'. They found that this is an especially 'delicate balance with a legal customer base' for whom the 'line' between the 'decorative' and the useful is very fine (Matt, LN). What most users 'are actually asking for' is to be able to 'find' and 'understand' legal content. So, what publishers want is to provide a transactional or litigation lawyer 'with more insight, more practical tools to help them do their job' (Karen, LN). They 'spend a lot of time' addressing foundational questions such as 'the layout of a page', 'types of buttons' and data visualisation 'patterns', than on producing superficially 'whizzy flashbang things' (Karen, LN). Legal publishing design choices vary in scale from deciding 'which information to display', to '"pixel-pushing" buttons this way or that. It's all important, and attention to detail pays off in giving users reassurance that they are using a reliable application that can be trusted' (vLex).

Crucially, it is 'fiercely difficult' to develop visual elements, or indeed a complete visual language, in a global context. On the one hand, there is a need to maintain a sense of consistency, both for the brand and for the customer. So LexisNexis are 'moving towards using one standard consolidated design system' across all products including, for example, '[w]hat colour blue a button is, how rounded a corner appears, what a LexisNexis logo looks like, what we name our products' and so on (Matt, LN). Likewise, vLex aim to use a single design system to maintain consistency across user interface elements such as buttons, tabs, cards and icons across all applications (vLex). At the same time, it remains important to maintain a sense of the local. So on the vLex website, pages that communicate product coverage are supported by local photographs and 'showcase local or national content'. Furthermore, all vLex applications 'have internationalisation'—that is, 'the ability to localise languages and dates for a given audience'—built in. For example, each of their roughly 3000 interface elements—'every single button, label, tooltip or fragment of text'—is translated into English, Spanish, French, Italian, Catalan and Brazilian Portuguese.

The team at LexisNexis mitigate some of the complexity of working across, and designing for, multiple jurisdictions by as far as possible adopting a global design structure. This makes for 'incredibly complicated fabrication processes', with people and systems feeding into and interacting with people and systems from across the globe. Members of the design team 'sit within each business that we support', rather than being 'a centralised team that supports the entirety of the global business', so that they 'can be the advocates for the needs of the customers'—pointing out, for example that 'in the UK, that's not a thing' or 'in the UK that needs to be done' or 'needs to be different' (Matt, LN). This structure also affords economies of scale around 'reuse of visual styling, visual elements and [the] design system'; as well as the opportunity to draw on specialist expertise that develops as a consequence of local difference:

> 'For example, some of our colleagues in the United States where case law is far more significant than it is within our transactional workflow in the UK, have done some beautiful design work regarding how to find related cases and case metrics and case analytics. Whereas in the UK we're doing some beautiful work around the presentation of legislation for Halsbury's contents. And what we can do is we can bring both close to the design system, standardise them, then everybody globally can leverage upon that as best in class design system'.
>
> (Matt, LN)

What is especially interesting about these processes in the current context is the extent to which they are influenced—even directed—by designerly ways.

Designerly processes

Designerly ways, especially those referred to as design thinking and human centred design, infuse the production process of both publishers. The vLex team report that '[a]lmost every feature we build involves some degree of design thinking'. Because 'we deal with a lot of data, we design mainly with functional prototypes rather than with wireframes or mock-ups … and we try to use real data wherever possible. It's not possible to account for the unusual edge cases and problems that real world data will give you, so we like to get stuck in right away. All our designers write code—that is just one way of working, but it suits us well' (VLex). Meanwhile, the LexisNexis teams work in a structure that draws on a Silicon Valley Product Group (SVPG) methodology which centres on ensuring that the 'magical trifecta of product, engineering and design' are represented at all times.[4] On the design side there are user interface designers, who are concerned with the look and feel of the product; and experience designers, who are concerned with how users interact with the product. The interface designers set the precise 'specification' or 'blueprint' to which the product is to be built, while the experience designers work in 'lower fidelity' experimenting with the product, and drawing on user research, until they are able to 'define the type of experience that we want' (Matt, LN).

Both publishers find that when producing interactive digital products, the team tends to focus immediately and directly on visual elements (vLex). The 'fidelity' of those visual elements 'increases' over time as the teams progress from 'concept sketches, leveraging existing patterns to producing final blueprints and artefacts for teams to actually deliver' (Matt, LN). And those visuals 'help stimulate discussion and understanding' along the way. 'Not to say how should this look', but rather, for example, 'have we understood the need here, have we completely missed it?' To achieve this 'stimulus' effect 'it's best not to draw something nice and hope people like it', but instead to start off 'really sketchy'. This is because people 'don't want to say that the thing that you've spent ages on is not what they need. But if it's sketchy, they feel much more inclined to scribble on it and rip off pieces and tear it apart' (Karen, LN). At LexisNexis, all feature teams include a designer and, because they are 'able to articulate what people are saying' in visual form, they get disparate team members 'literally on the same page' from the outset. You can 'sketch it out on a whiteboard and say this is what we mean'. Maybe 'everybody goes, oh, heck, no,' but 'that first cycle … very quickly gets people talking the same language.' Crucially, that early sketching 'also changes people's mindset.' The product 'goes from being this ethereal concept to being the tangible reality'; which in turn 'very rapidly focuses the minds of a feature team' on 'working together to deliver that thing, rather than abstract thought[s] around the concept of the thing' (Matt, LN).

The LexisNexis team explain that they used to think of themselves 'as a provider of content to our customers, and that content tended to be books'. Now we understand we are 'a provider of data', and the question of 'what we can do with that data becomes incredibly exciting'. For example, 'how can we leverage that data' by 'rendering it in a way that makes it, by happenstance, more beautiful', but also, 'more consumable' for 'you as a lawyer, doing a task, performing a job' so that you can 'quickly digest this information' (Matt, LN). How can we give the user, who is faced with 'half a million cases' a better chance of answering questions such as 'what is my best argument, which experts should I use, what is their win rate?' This shift to a user centred approach marked a sudden and dramatic turning point for LexisNexis:

> 'I remember the exact moment that we changed mindsets on this … . where we moved from being a business who thought about trying to push something out, who thought primarily about the needs of our content, [to thinking] how do we need to [present it] to them and what segments do they need and want? We had a session with a user group and we had [an interaction designer leading the process] and we sat [users] down and said, what do you do? [W]e never actually asked that directly before. And from [this] discussion about what do you do most, what did you do last [and so on] we very quickly, with the [interaction designer] lead's help, got to [understanding that] there are three main things this [product] needs to do, and therefore we should lay it out like this. So it is not about massive, wonderful visuals [for the sake of it]. It is about displaying and presenting your product to your audience in terms of what *they* need rather than what *you* need. [We know from user feedback] that [i]t had a massive effect. I've never seen anything like it. That simple switch to "how do you guys need this" … was kind of revolutionary because we had spent ages thinking we were publishers. [Now we understood] that we were people with customers with needs that need to be met'.
>
> (Karen, LN)

As we shall see more below, today LexisNexis take a 'research-first' approach, which builds on the Design Council's Double Diamond, which involves first identifying and understanding the 'problem':

> 'We go out and say to a customer, we just want to talk about you for an hour. We don't have any products. We don't have anything to show you. I just want you to tell me what you do. And when we first started doing that, I think people were a bit taken aback'.
>
> (Karen, LN)

Designing for diverse users in a global market

It is an 'enduring challenge' to design for the diverse users of legal communications. The vLex team note that their users range from first term law students, to sole-practitioners to partners at law firms, to judges 'and everything in between'. These users are located in over 80 countries, and 'similar customer segments from different countries have different requirements and subtle differences.' Furthermore, a user's level of legal expertise often does not match their level of technical expertise: 'You always have to remember that any given user could be using the platform for the first time, so you can make no assumptions about their experience'. And '[i]t's always important to gauge user expectations against proposed solutions, to see if we've actually built something useful and desirable'. So vLex perform moderated usability testing with users to see 'which elements of [the] interface frustrate users and which (if any) delight them'. This kind of testing has thrown up some general rules. For example, vLex have established that all of these users place high value on the quality and relevance of search results; but as more content is returned, so it becomes harder to ensure the same accuracy and the relevance diminishes, or the search takes longer. This raises both input and output challenges that must be addressed through design. First, search forms are designed to prompt and facilitate the entry of high precision terms by the user, offering a range of options for query input so that users of all kinds 'can ask for what they need according to their experience and requirements'. Second, effective navigation through search results is ensured through accessible flexibility, to accommodate users who prefer result lists, and those who follow chains of connection between cases and legislation. Overall, 'the answer usually lies in reducing a problem to the simplest possible solution'.

Complexity goes hand-in-hand with legal information and with such a diverse user-base who arrive at the product with varying levels of expertise, one of the toughest challenges is certainly around 'the correct level of detail to show in any given situation' (vLex). So how do LexisNexis manage this?

The team at LexisNexis try to take a 'holistic' view of the user, in particular by leaning on the Jobs-to-be-Done (JTBD) framework.[5] This involves understanding any given product tends to play a small part in the overall 'job' that is 'to-be-done' by the user. So they design with reference to questions such as what 'triggered' the user to move towards thinking about a database, what 'steps' do they take 'before they even start thinking about Lexis Library' and what did they do after? For example, one user may be 'trying to find the piece of legislation that allows them to back up the work that they were about to send a client'; another could be 'double checking something because they've made a mistake last week and they don't want to be in that situation again'; and another may be motivated by 'morbid curiosity to see what the latest legislative change is' (Matt, LN). It is important to start with the question 'do we understand how they're feeling and everything about what they're trying to do? Otherwise you're off on one with assumptions and you haven't really specified what you're trying to do' (Karen, LN). Karen also notes that, rather than thinking of users in terms of their professional standing—as lawyers, information professionals, students—it is more helpful to remember that you have both experts and non-experts reading material in Lexis Library: 'you can be an expert in one practice area and then suddenly be a novice in another' (Karen, LN). The team at LexisNexis are able to learn some of what they need to know about users from anonymised data generated as they engage with the product. They can 'replay sessions', seeing if users were 'successful' in their search, and 'pinpoint which bits are working or not' all of which is 'incredibly useful'. They may see, for example, 'the highly experienced person skipping steps, who just wants the thing that's five steps in'; then 'someone more junior, who's doing it kind of methodically'; and then a beginner 'who would end up in a little loop, who would stay on one step until they understand it and then move to another' (Karen, LN). And they have used core design thinking devices such as creating personas for different users and deploying them in empathy mapping exercises. But they have found that 'it's not necessarily the best way' of understanding how those different users might interact with the product. What they have found to be transformative is regular contact with users. Several years ago LexisNexis ran an 18 month programme during which 150 employees from a diverse range of specialisations were trained to interact with and uncover the needs of over 1000 users (Karen, LN). More generally, 'everybody'—across all specialisations and at every level, from engineers to executives—is 'encouraged to get face time with customers as much as possible … to have conversations with them, hear them talking about the kind of products and services that they are going to be using' (Matt, LN).

This focus on users from outset shifts the mindset of the whole team so that they are:

> 'thinking about producing a system or process or tool for somebody that is actually going to use it. It sounds trite and easy until you see the effects of that not happening within an organisational space. Quite often the designers [and the wider product team come to be] seen as the advocates for the customer within the organisation and the effects of that are manifest in everything that we do, it genuinely can be transformative just to get people thinking about the fact that they're delivering a service for a customer.'
>
> (Matt, LN)

Empathetic research skills can be especially difficult to develop, and especially useful, for those 'who are used to giving advice', such as lawyers. The team at LexisNexis have noticed that empathy training, and the general user-centred approach across the process, has had an impact on how their in-house lawyers interact with the wider team: to be prompted and facilitated 'to collaborate', to work 'collectively', across the whole team, seems to be 'a bit of an eye opener' for them. So it's really important not just for product and not just for UX, but from people across the business to understand customer's point of view' (Karen, LN).

'What we are most proud of is the design work that just quietly heavy lifts the comprehension of quite complicated materials. It's not about putting a picture of a stock photo with somebody pointing at the moon at the top of a practice note to do with conveyancing. That's not useful. But if you can make it so that the type of that page is laid up in a way that allows people to read and comprehend it twice as quick as they would previously, that's the kind of design that we really celebrate here' (Matt, LN).

'We're never going to win a design award' for this kind of work; 'we're never going to get on the cover of Wired' (Matt, LN). But it can be extremely satisfying to produce. For example, when you know, as in the case of Halsbury's Statutes, that the user is likely to be a student: 'You just go, well, yeah, this is actually quite neat because this is all about helping this person understand something that wasn't necessarily written for them, but they're going to need [and we are] providing those little learning loops through it … I get quite excited' (Karen, LN). Similarly, when the team at LexisNexis found that their users were experiencing problems 'around understanding the effects of change of Brexit', they resolved to develop the Brexit Toolkit. It functions as an aggregator of content, which is displayed 'using mixed modality, which means that we change the way that things are displayed so that things have their own identity and plot'. From the users' side it is experienced via a familiar folder structure, which makes it seem simple. That makes it possible to 'display quite a lot of complex aggregated material next to each other' and have it 'make sense' (Matt, LN). Such 'marginal improvements' to the communication of information sets that are 'complex', and that also 'need to be read in context with other things', is more impactful 'than having a particular tool or widget with a flashy thing that does a certain thing for a small percentage of our users.' Conscious of the remarkably high level of uncertainty that users were experiencing around the legal implications of Brexit, the team wanted to ensure that users felt 'guided' and comforted, that 'it's not scary … not overwhelming' (Karen, LN) '[H]undreds and hundreds of hours of contact time' were spent with users to test whether the product was capable of 'support[ing] them through' Brexit –'something the likes of which hopefully we don't have to design around again' (Matt, LN).

'Isn't it amazing what happens when you get design working with product? You can genuinely be transformative' (Matt, LN).

Notes

1 Associate Professor of Law, City Law School, City, University of London.
2 Professor of Law, Kent Law School, University of Kent.
3 All views expressed by Robin Chesterman, Global Head of Product and Matthew Terrell, Head of Marketing at vLex in this chapter are referenced collectively as 'vLex' and were expressed in the form of personal correspondence: Email to authors 30 June 2021. All views expressed by Karen Waldron, Director of Product and Matt Wardle, UX Director, both at LexisNexis, are referenced individually by the speaker's first name followed by 'LN' and were expressed in an interview: Interview, online, 6 July 2021.
4 See Silicon Valley Product Group website https://svpg.com/.
5 See CM Christensen, H Taddy, K Dillon and DS Duncan, *Competing Against Luck: The Story of Innovation and Customer Choice* (Harper Business 2016).

19 Lawyers are still lawyers. Except when they're not.

Rae Morgan[1]

The demands on, and expectations of, the next generation of lawyers will be very different to those faced by lawyers who entered the profession even in recent years. Yes, some things are the same: the traditional 'practice of law' skills are as essential as ever, while building and maintaining relationships with clients is perhaps recognised as an even greater part of a lawyer's job than it has always been. Lawyers are still lawyers.

Except when they're not. There's an interesting shift going on that echoes changes seen in other professional service sectors. The need to consider the holistic needs of the client—something both organisations and individuals now expect—has triggered a change in the role of lawyers that is taking them farther and farther beyond the traditional practice of law. Broader problems need to be solved using more diverse techniques, and, more often than not, demand methods that push lawyers into more creative domains. And this is not just from the more 'progressive' law firms. Today's law students will sense this shift at almost any future employer. Logical, rigorous lawyers will increasingly be expected to be lateral thinking creatives too; and, more specifically, they will increasingly be expected to develop and implement those skills using mindsets, processes and strategies from design.

Many law firms have become comfortable with 'design thinking'—essentially a way for non-designers to think more like designers do—and in those firms, the ability to solve bigger problems more creatively presents a powerful opportunity for potential trainees to differentiate against their more traditionally-skilled peers in the competitive jobs market. Equally, the opportunities for those trained in law to follow a different path to a successful career—even in a traditional law firm—is broader than ever. Whether you follow a traditional path or something different, actively engaging with design has become a basic expectation of the next generation of lawyers and so, arguably, a critical component of a modern legal education. So those receiving a legal education and those providing it are presented with a real opportunity to enhance their arsenal of skills by becoming comfortable with design-centric approaches. How?

To engage with design successfully, needs a different mindset; one that temporarily sets aside the newly acquired legal brain and, in some cases, switches it off altogether. Design is of course a discipline in its own right, and

DOI: 10.4324/9780429021411-22

good design is the product of years of training and experience. Law firms increasingly recognise the importance of employing design professionals to lead these initiatives, but by gaining a good grasp of some basic thinking techniques a student can increase the value they put in (and get out) of relevant projects in practice.

Let's look at six techniques that, when mastered, can unlock even the most complex problems and lead to breakthrough solutions.

First up is one of the core techniques of innovation: *deconstructing truths.*

The aim here is to suspend what is 'known' to be true. Many truths are simply assumptions or long-embedded behaviours: almost anything can be challenged. This can be a difficult position for a lawyer, whose traditional role is usually to be the person in the room most armed with facts. It requires you to deliberately turn your back on your experience for a minute and look at a situation with completely fresh eyes. Simply ask yourself 'why does it need to work like that?' or 'what if that wasn't true?'

Essentially, you need to re-state 'truths' as assumptions and unpick them. It's challenging to identify them (as often they're things that *you've been taught* to be true), but great leaps forward can come from the removal of a single embedded constraint, so it's worth the effort.

Think broadly about where truths lie—it could be a foundational concept of a service, an organisation-wide behaviour, a key strength, an 'industry standard'—if it isn't directly regulated then it should be on the table for deconstruction.

Next, we'll go wide. The ability to recognise and capitalise on behaviours and models from *unrelated* sectors, to apply parallel experiences, is where you'll find some of the biggest historic leaps in innovation.

There's definitely a blind spot in the legal sector here, which often only looks at that which it views as 'relevant' to legal practice and the narrow relationship with clients that that has led to. As a student, learning how to truly partner with a client, means you need to understand their business in a much wider context, to get under the skin of what impacts them and where the behaviours exhibited in an unrelated sector could be applied in their business. The same applies within a law firm: many, many methods and processes involved in the practice of law are not unique. Most have been done elsewhere in a different context, and by drawing on those influences you can almost see into the future. Teaching (or being taught) to look for inspiration more widely before launching a legal career, will add considerable potential value to that candidate.

The influences on a business have never been more diverse, so think about their ecosystem, the competitive landscape they operate in, how they hire, how they make decisions, where their pressures come from and the culture of the organisation itself. All have a tremendous impact on how they function as a business and what their eventual needs will be.

Think about how evolving customer behaviours outside of their sector will affect them—whether that's an increase in remote working or a new app that will set the benchmark for B2C interaction going forward. Uber didn't just reset expectations of how easy it should be to get a cab, it sparked a global shift in the whole value of *ownership.* That shift in customer behaviour is something that another company can exploit for an entirely different purpose.

This translates equally to the experience of an individual accessing the law. More often than not, they will have little knowledge of the law or legal system. Framing their experience in something recognisable, using language and design devices to convey information to someone with no legal education should be a fundamental tenet of real access to justice. Your world in their terms.

Better outcomes and true innovation will come more from influences *outside* your own sector than from within it. As a student you would be well served to learn how to identify, develop and apply different business models, and customer behaviours from unrelated sectors. And if you don't look, you're thinking with mental blinkers on. And if you're peers have embraced this, you'll be on the back foot in the race to your first legal position.

Tackling a problem successfully from a design perspective demands that you *diversify your team.* This is equally true in terms of different life experiences as it is from a cross-disciplinary perspective. To arrive at the *best* solution rather than just *a* solution you always need a breadth of skill sets and viewpoints. If you run a 'design thinking' or 'service design' session that is populated entirely by lawyers then your outcomes will inevitably be constrained. The kicker here is that it will not even be evident to the participants of that session that this has happened. It's a concept to get to grips with in law school, and then effect the change more widely throughout the legal sector with the projects you collaborate on.

To put the problem in context, think of it as an intellectual echo chamber. People with similar life experiences will too frequently agree with each other; a concept called *homogeneity.* Whilst that session can feel very positive, without challenging viewpoints and different perspectives you'll simply think in a very narrow way.

Let's consider it in terms of differentiation. Imagine that three groups of people with similar backgrounds, education and experience are presented with the same body of insight—the evidence if you will—from a range of clients with largely similar needs. Given the same data points and same context, almost all of the time, they will naturally come up with the same solutions. It's why you see law firms frequently launching very similar initiatives. Separating yourself from the pack both from a personal and business perspective requires a broader view, recognising the skill and experience of other roles to bring a different way of thinking to those problem spaces.

There is opportunity within legal education to learn more about specialist resource that is often key to the success of projects. Strategists, product managers, service designers, user experience (UX), visual designers and many more will add cognitive diversity to a team. The experience of these roles is important. You can learn to do some of the things a service designer does, for example, but to be *expert* at it demands those 10,000 hours at the coal face. The more you can bring in people from outside the legal sector, you'll get better, first-hand experience of new concepts and models, often unlocking the breakthrough you need.

Ultimately, breakthroughs are what it's all about. To reiterate an earlier point, given the same data, applying the same logic will lead to the same conclusions. It's one of the reasons that an over-reliance on data spawns the same rational, *logical* types of initiatives again and again. People follow the same data to the same crowded destinations.

There is, however, a beautiful *illogic* to human behaviour that is not only fascinating, but presents perhaps our greatest opportunity to think differently. It's simple: just try adopting a *contrarian position*: do the *opposite* of the accepted norm. It's a different mindset than you'd use in the practice of law, what you've learned at law school up to now, and encourages you to think laterally. The illogical and less obvious avenues are often those that lead to world-changing ideas. Fifteen years ago no-one ever said 'I want to stay in a stranger's bedroom' until AirBnB did the illogical thing and made that easy. Now millions of people every day actively prefer to stay in someone else's bedroom over a room in a hotel.

It's actually very simple: the easiest way to be illogical is to be contrary.

The fifth technique is all about *insight*. Researching your potential 'users' and understanding the context of what they are trying to do is a widely accepted technique these days, although many will still ignore it and jump straight into solutioning. But even when research is conducted, it often focuses on the wrong things: the things that came up most often.

Now I'm sure that makes no sense. Surely the point of doing research is to get closer to the customer and if everyone is doing something or saying something you should run with that, right?

Wrong. Well in this context at least. Always focusing on the most prevalent or most common factors can result in missing critical *sparks of insight*, those golden nuggets, often peripheral to the points of discussion—or simply one aberrant comment from one person—that can unlock big new ideas. Skilled insight specialists will tease out these nuggets and ensure they don't get subsumed by all the common (read 'average') learnings.

The more lively and broad a conversation you have with your potential customer, the less likely it is they'll neglect to tell you that one thing that could prove to be important. A lawyer conducting research on other lawyers is rarely going to lead to a genuine spark of insight. As a student, the trick is to learn how to suspend your own opinion or experience, and conceal your own background, to keep the conversation open. Take that into practice and your research will be infinitely better. And for the record, don't be afraid to go down a few random rabbit holes: you never know what you might find down there.

Even firmly within the legal domain, remember the outputs of a task will often be consumed by someone who is not a lawyer—think about a contract of employment for example. Its most important user is the employee—and probably an HR advisor—lawyers are the beginning of the chain. Researching directly with those users is crucial to understand what the artefact actually needs to do. To truly meet the need and fulfil the purpose. In the design context, how *you* experience your own environment is largely irrelevant—you need to be able to suspend your own outlook and focus on the needs of that user.

Finally, you need to be *loud and lively.* Insular working leads to insular thinking. Get ideas up on the wall and talk about them. Debate, explore and argue about them. Get a version done—just start with *something*—and iterate from there. It won't be right, and that's great, because the lively debate you have with your peers about how wrong it is will help you rethink it for version two. An idea that isn't right yet is not the same as a failure. And in the context of design, everything we try that doesn't work teaches us something. Learning this as part of your legal education will pay you back in spades—it takes some confidence and bravery to get going, but *unlearning* these constraining behaviours later in your career is much harder.

You need to put stuff out there that you are not sure is going to fly so that you can talk about it. Draw it, or write it big, and get it on a wall. Then stand people in front of it and explain the thinking to them. A couple of hours of lively discussion with a bunch of other people is worth a week of insular working every time, because in saying it out loud, often under pressure, your brain engages differently and brilliant new ideas emerge, or you realise that current ideas are terrible. In law school, you aren't trained to present things you're not confident in whereas designers know it's an essential part of getting things right eventually.

Whether you intend to follow a traditional career path, one of the emerging new legal roles or just trying to get your foot in the door, the legal sector has never been more exciting. Getting comfortable with adopting different mindsets to free your creative brain is the key to leveraging these opportunities, and complementing the critical legal skills you've amassed through your legal education. And to top it all off, it's immensely good fun.

Note

1 Principal Consultant, Wilson Fletcher.

Index

access to justice 87, 98, 135, 180, 240; campaigners 151, 152–153; improving/better 11, 84; resources 110; and technology 119; and use of HCD 137; virtual 152, 153
access to law 176, 192–199
accessibility 11, 59, 193; of contracts 206; designing for 63–64; enhancing 5, 39; of information 4, 98, 143(2), 186, 187, 229; of the law 192–199, 218, 222, 225; of legal communications 3, 9–10, 55; of materials 37, 148–149; of physical space 3; of publications 229, 234; of socio-legal studies 18; testing 226
accountability 104
activism 55, 56, 98, 101
actor-network theory 30
actors 34; in peacebuilding 46–47, 48, 49, 50, 51, 55, 56
advice, procedural 135
advice guides 178–179
advocacy 97, 155; graphic 4, 166; tenant 170
advocates 160, 162, 163; customer 231, 235
aesthetics 34, 36, 220; emotional 35; legal 29, 39
affective context 59–60, 64
Affective Context Model of Learning 60
alienation 69, 72
Altera case *127*
ambiguity 88, 92–93, 209
amicus curiae 163
anecdotes 34
anger 135, 156, 187
animation 4, 36
anonymity 162
Anti-Social Behaviour Order, tailor-made 162
anti-subordination 167
anxiety 68, 113, 143, 159; methodological 18–19
argumentation 62, 104
Aristotle 194–195
art 35, 36, 37–38; smart 24; tools and language of 44
artefacts 7, 55, 232, 242
artificial intelligence 98, 99, 100, 196, 211
artists 151–152, 158, 164 *see also* court artists
artists' materials 89, 151–152, 157, 158, 161
assessment 3, 43, 44, 64, 68, 76, 87, 91, 104–105, 111, 122, 124
assignments, written 104–105
attainment 69; gap 67–68, 71
attendance 68, 71
attitudes: changing 136, 137, 148; to design process 144; towards LIPs 135, 136, 137, 142–147
augmented reality (AR) 36
Australia 8, 81–94, 121–129
autonomy 53
avatars 128
awareness 146, 148; raising 110–111

backgrounds 154, 156
bail bond project 168–169, *168*, 175–176, *175*
banana crops 48–50, *49*, 52–53
Bar Council 9, 11
barriers to participation 135, 136; breaking down 142–149
barristers 151, 154–155, 156
behaviour 239–240; controlling 178; driving 121; ethical 198, 199; illogical 241; impact of design on 192; mapping 183; online 154–155; shifting 192; unlearning 242

Bentham, Jeremy 193
biases 171, 198, 205
biodiversity 48, 53
black letter approaches 89, 90
Black Lives Matter 37, 115, **116**
blueprints 232
boundaries 90
boundary objects 73
brain writing 75, 102, 104
brainstorming *20*, 102, 104, 181, 226
bridging tasks 76
Brodie, Howard 158
build phase 112, 137, 141, 167, 194
Bull v Hall 157
Business Law in Practice (BLIP) unit 121, *125*, *127*
business purposes 211
business strategies 69
buttons 231

campaigners 151, 152–153
capitalism 174
care ethics 195
careers 83–84, 105, 223, 238
carelessness 206
caricatures 159
case studies 44, 45–46, 89, 110–119, 126
categorical imperatives 194
causation 36
challenges 8, 102, 103, 179, 186, 234; innovation 89, 91, 122; intra-university 223; normalising 88, 92–93; and Socio-Legal Lab 18, 22–25; visual representations of 46–54; weekly 225
checklists 221, 222
citizenship 98
civil liberties 8, 178, 180
class contact 68
clay models 7, *10 see also* modelling
clients: and contracts 204; experience of 226; focussing on 84, 94; holistic view of 238; internal 111, 119; journeys 224; needs/preferences of 82, 88, 205, 221; vulnerable 113
clipart 89
coca crops 48–50, *49*, 52–53
co-creation 73–75
co-design 3, 167, 170, 175, 192; concepts 171, 197; methods 169, 178, 180; workshops/jams 8, 178–190, 198
co-designers 169, 170, 171, 172
cognitive load 59, 60–63, 64
Cole, Richard 158
collaboration 8, 9, 17, 62, 73, 75, 136–137, 224; with clients 211; and co-design 180, 181–182; with experts/developers 90, 117, 223; interdisciplinary 97; online 185; student 123 *see also* working, collaborative
collectivity 224
Colombia 43–56
colour blindness 222
colour-coding 207, 219, 221
colours 36, 50, 52–53, 174, 222, 231
Coltsfoot Vale 5, *6*, 60
comic book contracts 121–131, *125*, *127*, 207, 221
Comic Contracting Project 121, 122, **123**
comics *173*, 174
commitment 227
communication 18, 221, 225, 236; accessible 55, 63–64; clarity/effectiveness of 90, 122, 227; with clients/customers 64, 219, 220; combining forms of 123; and contracts 204; as core function 36; of ideas/messages 45, 56, 113; lack of 58; by lawyers 192, 211; means/methods of 35, 61; non-textual 37; of relationships 30–31; of results 34; shared 73; visual 1, 3, 5–7, 29, 36, 166, 173–176 *see also* information
communication skills 62, 97, 105
communication strategies 3–9, 20
communicators 60, 211
communities 192; business 203–204; contracting 206; legal design 225; local 46, 48, 49, 50, 51, 53, 54, 55
community, sense of 9
community building 19, 20, 25, 26
community groups 8, 188, 189, 190
community organisers 172
competency, cultural 222
complaints *see* police complaints
comprehension 59, 62, 121, 122, **123**, 124, 126, 222, 224, 226, 227 *see also* understanding
computer modelling 36
confidentiality 25
conflict: armed 43, 48, 49, 50, 51, 52, 53, 54; in contract terms 127; potential 22, 144
conflict resolution 90
connectivity 186, 195
conscience 43
consequence scanning 196
consequentialism 193, 195, 196, 197

consistency 231
consultation 118, 123, 197, 198
consumer credit rules 220
contextualisation 32, 34, 35, 37, 39
contract design 203–211
Contract Pattern Design Library 86
contracting: conscious 125; functional 206; proactive 205–206
contracts 126–127, 241–242; audio 123; camouflaged 206; invisible terms 206; next generation 209, 210–211, **210**; relational 125–126; text-only 122; video 128; visualisation of 121–129, 203–211 *see also* comic book contracts
contrariness 241
co-operatives *173*
counternarratives 166, 173–176 *see also* narratives
courses/modules 8, 68; BLIP unit 121, *125*, *127*; comic book contracting 121, 123–128, *125*; interdisciplinary 43; IT law 98–104; law and technology 110; legal design 81; on legal design thinking 81, 86–94; project management 110; on technologies 83
court artists 155–164
Court of Appeal 157
courtrooms 22, 151–160, 162–164
courts 151, *151*, 152, 153–154
Covid-19-pandemic 25, 171, 178; and the courts 151; lessons from 148–149; and online formats/platforms 25, 123; postponements/restrictions 137, 139, 142 *see also* lockdowns
creativity 70, 77, 104, 119, 128, 224, 238, 242
criminal justice system 175
criminalisation 187
criticality 2, 45, 55, 105, 172
critiques 105
crops 48–50, 54
cross-disciplinarity 240
culture creation 221, 224, 225
curiosity 224
customer journeys 211
customer service 220
customers: behaviour of 239–240; needs of 231–232, 233–234; point of view of 236
cyber-attacks 113
cynicism 92

danger 113, 115
data 72; anonymised 235; on comic contracting 126; Comic Contracting Project **123**, 126; interpretation of 185; messy 92; personal 198; same 240, 241
data analysis 113
data collection 71, 91
data handling 232, 233
data management 229
data protection 99–100, 102, 103, 224
Data Protection Canvas 99–100, *99*
data providers 233
data science 84, 222
data sets 32
data subjects 102
data synthesis 73
databases 117, 230, 234
decolonisation 72, 76, 77
DecoloniseUKC 7
defendants 153, 156
defensiveness 189
define phase 102, 104, 179, *179*, 180
deliver phase 102, 179, *179*
democratisation 169–170
demographics 72, 73, 117, 190
deontology 194, 195, 197
de-personalisation 144
design: community-centred 166; core characteristics of 1, 2; elimination 165–166; ethical 192–199; graphic 1, 36, 90, 223; influence of 4, 77, 193, 196; objectives of 8, 9, 10, 46, 49, 50–51, 55, 136, 146; participatory 166, 167, 169–173; radical 1, 5, 35, 69, 166, 176; universal 3, 63; user-centred 70, 178, 179–180, 181; visual 165, 166, 167 *see also* co-design; human-centred design (HCD); legal design; mindsets; processes; service design; visual, the; visualisations/visuals
design briefs 9, 112, 113
Design Council 70, 102, 233
design jams 68, 198, 207
design labs 1, 101, 103, 198 *see also* learning labs; Socio-Legal Lab; Stanford Legal Design Lab
design principles 24, 112, 187, 197, 198
design processes 2, 11, 102, *179*, 218, 225–227, 238; ethical 196; experimental 3–7; five-stage 112; focussing on 87, 89–90; iterative 75, 85, 87, 91, 92, 105, 136, 137, 179, 223, 226; in legal publishing 232–234; and the legal system 98, 165
design reports 115, **116**
design sprints 1, 8, 11, 112, 118

design strategies 1, 2, 3–9, 11, 25, 98, 104, 166, 170–171, 175, 186, 196, 238
design structures, global 231–232
design systems 231–232
Design the Law Nepal project 181
design thinking 24, 71, 97, 101, 224, 240; devices 235, 240; experimental 23; human-centred 89, 92, 93–94; and legal problems 68; models 70; for non-designers 238; processes 226, 232; for students 223 *see also* Legal Design Thinking course
design turn, the 18
designerly ways 1–2, 3, 5, 18, 19, 35, 88, 203, 205, 207, 211, 229
designers 69, 91, 102; conscious/unconscious 210; curriculum 84; experience 232; importance of 239; information 207, 210; interaction 233; interface 232; legal 223–224, 226, 227; service 240 *see also* co-designers
desk research 71
develop phase 102, 179, *179*, 180
development 53–54, 188, 189, 190; cycles of 136; economic 53; highway project 46–48, 53; models 51
devices 4, 34, 240; electronic 59, 116, 155, 187; learning 23; mnemonic 59; visual 7, 43, 44, 45, 46, 52, 55 *see also* personas
diagrams 29, 30, 31, 39, 122, 185, 192, 207, 210, 219, 226, 229
dialogue 45, 47, 77
dichotomies *20*
digital formats/products 229, 232
digital platforms 37
digital simulations 21
digitalisation 25
Dilemma Game 22
dilemmas: ethical 192, 195, 197, 199; teaching 30–31
disabilities 61, 63–64
disability 24
disability studies 3
discover phase 102, 103, 104, 112, 119, 137, 138, 179, *179*
discrimination 157, 189
dismantling: designing by 165–166, 167, 174; oppressive systems 167–168, 172, 173–174, 176
disputes: elimination of 126; prevention of 207
dissemination 45
dissertations 102
diversification 240–241
diversity 43, 64, 68, 71, 73, 121
dock, the 152, 161, 162–163, *163*
documents/documentation: client/customer-facing 88, 223; complex 219; courts/hearings 22, *151*, 153; designing 220, 221–222; incomprehensible 204; readability 230; reading strategies 61–62
double diamond matrix 70, 102, 179, *179*, 233
drafting 203, 205, 207, 220
drawing 203; illegality of 151, 155, 157; from memory 155, 156, 157, 161, 163; 'quick and dirty' 159; with software 158
drawing materials 158, 159
drawings: of bears 159, *161*; of courtrooms 151–160, *151*, *161*, 162–164

Economic Sociology of Law (ESL) 29, 30–35, *32*, *33*, 36, 39
ecosystems: balancing 48; business 239; education 3; enabling 2, 7–9; inclusive 11; legal 87; for legal design 218; of movements 168
education *see* courses/modules; legal education
embroidery 48–50
emotions 91, 146, 186, 189, 226
empathy 44, 71–73, 136–137, 146, 180, 186, 189, 198; connecting with 88, 91; developing 143, 144; skills 236; theme of 148; training 105; via observation 23
empathy mapping 104, 181, 182–183, **183**, 185
employability 83–84
empowerment 25, 98, 221, 227
engagement 122, **123**, 124, 193, 196, 197–198; active 238; building 226; creative 224; ethical 199; kinaesthetic 37; process 180; statistics 126; student 68, 69, 71; subjective 129; tools for 181; visual 37
environmental issues 46–48, 52
equality 145, 147
ethical lenses 192, 193–195, 199
ethics 180, 192–199
ethnography 22
European IT Law by Design (EITLab) 98–104
evaluation 23; course/module 71, 76, 93, 104–105; of insights *179*, 185–187; product/service 105

eviction resource project 170–171
evictions 170, 171, 172, *172*
evidence-based approach 124, 126, 128
evolution 87, 103, 112, 137, 148, 149
exams 59
exclusion 3, 8, 165; digital 188; of stakeholders 170, 172
exclusivity 11, 83
exemplars 86
expectations 3, 8, 22, 142, 145, 188, 234; shared 29, 32, 35
experimentation 2, 3–7, 18, 19, 20, 23, 35, 55, 87, 112, 136–137, 226; and contracts 205–209, 211; physical 89
expertise, levels of 231, 234
experts 87, 89, 90, 97, 100, 105, 175, 197, 235, 241
explainers 4, 187, 188, 189, 190
exploration 5–7
expressions, facial 155, 156
eyes, believing 152, 164

failure 19, 23, 87, 88, 92–93, 136, 226, 227, 242
fairness 135, 152, 189, 219–220
family courts/proceedings 138, 142, 147, 148
Family Justice Innovation Lab 137
fatigue: digital 25; text 36, 39
fear 135, 146, 148, 160, 186, 189
feasibility 126, 128–129
feedback 115, 169, 170, 175, 206, 227; client 88, 112; collaborative 25; community 168; group 104, 141; neutrality of 174; participant 19, 22, 171; protestor **116**; on prototypes 91, 92; stakeholder 167; student 76; team member 77; TMG 118, 119; user 233; from workshops 198
feelings 5, 60, 71–72, 186, 187, 189
felicific calculus 193, 197
fictitious entities 123–124, 128
fidelity 232
Financial Conduct Authority 220
fintech firms 220
flexibility 3, 111, 118, 185, 205, 234
flipcharts 206, 209
flow charts 190, 207, 226
focus groups 72
food deserts 174
formality 155
Forum for Women, Law and Development (FWLD) 181
foundation subjects 67, 68
friendly classrooms 72
frustration 135, 146
Fuerzas Armadas Revolucionarias de Colombia (FARC) 43, 48
functionality 182, 185, 210

games 21–22, 25
gamification 22
Gantt charts 73
goal setting 226
goals 23, 69, 72, 73, 142, 170; learning 25, 98; political 166, 170
good practice 104
Gough, Stephen 161–164
graffiti 36
grammars 30, 35–36
Graphic Advocacy Project 86, *168*, *172*, *173*, *175*
graphs 101
group work 76, 93, 100, *101*, 110, 123, 128
guidelines, ethical 197

habituation 194
happiness 193–194, 195
HCD Design Group 138, 139, **139**, 141, 143–144, 145, 148, 149
hearings 153–154, 156
'Herod clauses' 124
hierarchies 8, 9, 22; of arguments 101; of ideas 145; page 36
highlighting 207
highway development project 46–48
homogeneity 8, 240
honesty 144
hope 92
housing 170, 171
human flourishing 195
human-centred design (HCD) 1, 98, 101, 136–137, *138*, 147–149, 169, 198, 219, 232; five design principles 137–142; project findings 137–147; stages **140**
humanity 148, 186
humility 226
hydrocarbon extraction 51, 53
hypothetical imperatives 194
hypotheticals 206

icon sets 75, 89
idea clustering 75
ideation 73, 87, 141, 145, 147, 220
ideology 174
IEL Collective 44–45
illiteracy 58, 219

illustrations 36, 122, 186, 189
images 34, 36, 37, 121, 155, 186, 230; banned 157; modification of 157–158 *see also* visualisations/visuals
imagination 2–3, 5, 34, 36, 45, 55
immigration 180, 183, *184*, *185*, 190
impatience 146, 148
imperfection 23
incarceration 169
inclusion 5, 67–68, 72
inclusivity 3, 11, 71, 175, 222
incomprehensibility 204
inequality 56, 171
influences 23, 59, 197, 199, 239, 240
infographics 88
information: clarity of 169; empowered 221–222; gaps/lack of 135, 152; legal 178–179, 196, 233; receiving 61; retention of 59, 60; retrieval of 104; sticky 62; urgent 187 *see also* accessibility; communication
information asymmetries 88
information design 4, 178
information duty 102
information materials 178–190
information technology (IT) law 97–105
information-gathering 21
infrastructure construction 48, 53
innovation 81, 84, 85, 87, 88, 92; challenges 89, 91, 122; contract 121, 122, *125*; core techniques 239–241; embedded 224; legal 82–83; messy 89
insights 8, 148, 169, 170, 240, 241; combining 38; into communities 86; ethical 198; evaluation of *179*; from 113; interdisciplinary 4; for lawyers 231; legal 60; from literature 100; psychological 59, 60, 62; from research 72, 88; from stakeholders 89, 179; into students 71, 76, 122; into teaching/learning 88, 93, 98; into users 71, 77; from workshops 178, 180, 181, 185–187, 189
inspiration 103, 137, 206, 239
insufficiency 167
insularity 242
intangibles 1, 221
integration 77, 83, 85
integrative law movement 125
intelligence 220
intention 112, 118, 171, 174, 176
interactionism, symbolic 32
interactions 18, 30, 35, 37, 55, 76, 99, 206
interactivity 181
interdisciplinarity 17–18, 20, 26, 30, 56, 97, 98, 103, 126
interfaces 38, 102
International Economic Law 44–45
internet access 154
interpretation 24, 32, 34, 37, 38, 55, 126, 152, 174, 209
interviews 71, 75, 82, 87, 104, 170, 172
intimacy 155
intuition 5
InVision 185
irritation 22–23
isolation 68, 73, 189
iteration 8, 23, 224, 226–227, 242; of courses/modules 76–77, 87, 90, 92, 93; of racism reporting tool 112, 114, 115, 116; steps/phases of 102, 179 *see also* design processes, iterative

Jigsaw Seminars 99–101, *101*
Jobs-to-be-done (JTBD) framework 234–235
journey mapping 75–76, 102, 104, 141, *141*, 146, 181, 182, 184–185, *185*, 186, 225
judges 151, 153–154, 155, 162, 163
judgment, ethical 192
Judicial Committee of the Privy Council 161
juries 157
jurisdictions 231
Justice *151*

Kant, Immanuel 194
Kantian ethics 194, 195
Keating, Tom 157
kindness 72
Knight, Laura 157
knowledge 71; co-production 29, 37, 38, 39; sharing 166–167, 169, 172
knowledge construction 17, 20

laboratory turn, the 18
Lancashire Law School 67–80, 197
land law 5, 60
landlords 170, 171, 172
landscapes 62
language 223, 240; barriers 113; common 69; contract 203; creative 44; of instruction 63; legalese 88, 124, 146, 204, 221; mindful 186; negative 189; plain 187, 204, 219, 223; simplification of 226; tested 204; universal 203; visual 231

law: broken 124–125; as communal resource 3, 35; creativity of 23; different standpoints of 17; doctrinal 30; future of 81, 84, 218, 224; humanising 125; mainstream approaches to 30, 31, *31*, 39; neoclassical 30; social context of 32, 35; and social science 52–54; text-centricity of 197; well-being of 3
law curricula 3, 197, 223; core law 105; decolonising 72, 77; redesigning 67–80; traditional law 97, 105; T-shaped 97 *see also* courses/modules
law degrees: human-centred 86; Lancashire Law School 67–80, 197; qualifying 83; redesigning 67–80; vocational emphasis of 83
law in action 18, 19, 211
law in books 211
Law Societies (Australian) 82–83
Law Society 9
Lawbore 4
lawyering 2, 84, 93, 121; collaborative 92; community 166, 170
lawyers 238–242; behaviour of 73, 193; characteristics of 8, 18, 19, 55, 75; community 172; contract 204, 205, 207, 210, 211; designerly 206, 210, 211, 223–224; educating/teaching 61, 81–94, 204, 205; ethical 194, 195, 196; as experts 58; as gatekeepers 166; in-house 205, 236; innovative 94; personality of 92; perspectives of 22; researching 231; thinking like 58–59, 97, 192; training of 23, 89, 223, 225, 226; T-shaped 97, 105
layout 230, 231
learners, visual 219
learning: communities of 26; by doing 18, 98, 148; effects of stress on 63–64; evolutionary 59; experiential 19–20, 81; human-focussed/centred approaches 81; interactive 17; kinaesthetic 36, 88; legal 63; object-based 7(2); psychology of 25, 58; student-centred approach 64, 100; styles 88, 219; textual 22; visual 22, 36, 123, 128 *see also* courses/modules; law curricula
learning environments 37, 69, 71
learning goals 25, 98
learning labs 17–26
learning loops 235, 236
learning materials 24, 75
learning outcomes 23, 68, 73, 75, 76, 98–104
lectures 123–124, 127
legal design 1, 18, 82, 85, 105, 112, 118, 198, 206, 218, 224, 225; in action 101–104, 220; defining 220–223; importance of 218–228; and IT law 97–105; practice 102–103; purpose of 218–220; rationale for 69–71
legal design cycle 101–104, *103*
legal design market 224
Legal Design Thinking course 81, 84–88
legal education 2–3, 22–23, 64, 97; in Australia 8, 81–94, 121–129; courses 67–80; and ethics 195–198; reform of 82–83; traditional 58, 60; use of psychology 58–66 *see also* courses/modules
legal educators 59, 60, 62, 64
legal engineering 218
legal practice 59, 84, 97, 102, 128, 238; changing 82–83, 87; commodification of 84; future of 1–2; importance of legal design in 218–228; innovative 83, 97; preparation for 21, 83 *see also* legal design
legal principles 102
legal profession, future of 82–83, 227, 228
legal publishing 5, 229–236
legal realism 24
legal services 98, 110; access to 119; humanising 121; innovative 101; redesigning 10
Legal Services Board 9–11
legal system, the 18, 58, 86, 98, 135, 137, 148, 162, 172, 240
Legal Treasure Tours 7
legal work, traditional 225–226
legal writing 204, 219
LEGO® 7, 23, 37
lending, predatory 169
life-drawing/modelling 159, 162
life-learning 97
listening/hearing 91, 183, 224
literacy, visual 24–25, 38
Litigants in Person in Northern Ireland (LIPNI) project 135
litigants in person (LIPs) 135, 136, 137, 138, 139, 142, 143–149
litigation 205
lived experiences 187
live-drawing 159
live-streaming 157
locations for drawing 159
lockdowns *151*, 152–156

logos 231
*Lynn Shellfish Limited v Loose*162

MA in peacebuilding 43–56
magic points 184, 185
magistrates' courts 152–153
'magnifying glass' method 31, *32*
mapping 4, 60, 61, 62, 64, 172–173, 219, 229–230, *230see also* empathy mapping; journey mapping
marginalisation 72, 165, 197
markets, global 234–236
masks 52, 54
matrices 172
meaning 29, 35, 37, 39, 55, 204, 207, 222
media coverage 187–188
mediations 153–154
memes 128
memories 59
memory 50, 51, 53, 59, 60–61, 62–63, 155, 156, 157, 161, 163
mental health concerns 180
mentors 111, 119, 137, 148
metacognition 93, 104
metamorphosis 52, 54
metaphors 31, 58, 206, 230
microphones 162–163
milieu, cultural 197
mind maps 21, *21*, 36, *99*, 100, 101, 192
mindsets 224, 238; changing 129, 205, 233, 241, 242; core 198; creative 19, 91; designerly 2, 11, 77; dominant 166; empathic 180; learning by doing 18, 148; new 205, 210; open 126; sending 147–148; shifting 226, 235
Minimum Viable Product (MVP) 111, 113, **114**
misinformation 172
mistrust 50
mnemonics 59, 122
mock trials 21, *151*
modality, mixed 236
modelling 23, 45
modernism 35
modular building 37
modules *see* courses/modules
mono-disciplinarity 17, 22
mood 156
morality 193, 194, 195, 197, 198
movements 54, 165, 166, 167, 169
multi-disciplinarity 90, 97, 205
Museum-House (Casa Museo) 50–52, 53, 54

Naked Rambler, the 152, 161–164, *163*
nakedness/nudity 161–162, 163
narratives 34, 84, 174; visual 36, 173–176, *173see also* counternarratives
National Student Survey 71
navigation aids 207, 210
need-finding 225, 226
negativity 205
negotiation 127, 171, 198
neoliberalism 30, 34
networking/networks 75, 105
neutrality 35, 43, 170, 171, 173, 174
non-designers 238
non-experts 235
non-lawyers 90, 241–242
non-linearity 89, 91
non-textual materials 38
notes 206, 207
notice 206, 207
NuLaw Lab 23
Nuremberg trials 157

objectivity 30, 35, 36, 170
objects 37, 44, 50–52, 53, 55
observations 104
obsolescence 85
online chats 60
online materials 148–149
Onwubiko, Judith *10*
openness 171
oppression 174 *see also* power, oppressive
optimism 92, 148
Organización Femenina Popular (OFP) 50, 51, 53
outcomes 165, 179, 189, 226, 240
outrage 189
overload, cognitive 61, 62, 64
ownership 240

Padlet platform 182–185
page layouts 114, *114*
pain points 71, 136, 141, 184, 186, 187, 224
paintings 36
paper deals 204, 211
participation 18, 22, 54, 55, 87, 166, 169–173, 180, 198
pathfinder tool 142, 146
pattern libraries 209
patterns 62, 86, 209, 231, 232
peace 54, 55
peace agreements 43, 48, 50, 55
peacebuilding 43–54
peacebuilding policies 45, 54, 55

pedagogy 1, 26, 58, 61, 63, 68, 69, 77; 'banking' model 58–59, 60, 64
perceptions 3, 8, 34, 35, 37, 43, 121, 122, **123**, 124, 126, 135
perfectionism 92, 93
permission 152, 159
personas 4, 29, 30, 31–35, *33*, 39, *74*, 75, 103–104, 112, 119, 138, *138*, 139, 141, *141*, 144, 146, 147, 148, 149, 181, 182, 184, *184*, 185, 186, 189, 197, 235; characteristics of 72–73
pessimism 92
photography 36, 155, 157–158, 164
playfulness 5, 23
police 113, 115
police complaints 179, 183, 187, 189–190
policies, compliance and risk 221
pomp and paraphernalia, lack of 161
Pop-Up Museum of Legal Objects 44
portfolios 87, 91, 119, 121–122, 123–128, 129
portraits 157
power 148, 165, 167–168, 169, 171, 172, 174, 198; collective 167, 173, 176; oppressive 166, 171; shifting 166–167, 169, 172, 176
power structures 170
practicality 2, 45, 55, 112
precedents 127, 157
predictability 226
presentations 62, 100, 104, 105, 121, **140**
primal mark 75
print, small/fine 124, 127
problems 86, 89, 220, 233; defining 73–75, 166, 167–169; ideating 73–75; root causes of 167–168; understanding 172, 233; wicked 69–70, 90, 92, 136, 167
problem-solving 23, 85, 90, 91, 97, 98, 101, 102, 119, 148, 165, 170, 220, 225, 238
processes *see* design processes
professionalism 22, 91, 195
project management 110, 111–112, 115, 117, 118
project work 111
props 89
protocols 198
prototypes 2, 23, 90, 92, 110, 111, 141, *142*, 147, 148, 190, 209, 232
prototyping 7, 8, 73, 75–76, 86, 87, 91, 102, 104, 137, 144
psychology 58–66
public gallery, the 152, 161
public speaking 104
publishers 229–236

quality 9, 70, 129, 209, 234
queries 178–179, 180
questions 142, 161, 210; ethical 192, 197; foundational/key 113, 231; 'How might/can we …?' 75, 141; prompt 183; research 104, 143

race-blindness 174
racism 72, 174, 175, 187
racism reporting tool 110–119, *114*, *115*, *117*
rationality 23, 35, 36
readers 61–62
reading 58, 61, 197, 224; contracts 124, *125*; faces 155; levels 219, 222
reading ages 219
real deals 204, 211
real estate developers 172
reasoning 90, 100, 196
refine phase 104
reflection 9, 76, 77, 81, 87, 122, 129, 136, 143, 146, 148, 193
reflective logs 124, 126, 128
reflexivity 32, 38
relationships 30–31, 61, 92, 167, 171, 180, 220; with clients/customers 92, 166, 221, 238, 239; contractual 125, 205; law–design 55; power 135, 174
rent cancellation 171
Research Impact Canvas 25
research methodologies 32, 101, 102, 103, 121; agile 119; design thinking 86–93, 167; ethical 193, 198; pop-up collection 44–45; scientific 227; Scrum 111–112, 116, 118; Silicon Valley Product Group (SVPG) 232; Stanford model 70, *70*, 71, 85; tripartite 198
research methods 17, 19, 87, 98, 137; co-creation 73–75; co-designing 167, 169; core 34; focusing on 89–90; mixed 17–18; qualitative 20, 34, 71, 87, 91, 104, 147, 185; quantitative 20, 71, 104, 147; service design 67, 68–69, 70, 76, 77, 240
research notebooks 104
resilience 92, 226
resistance 52, 53
reskilling 88–89
retrospectives 119
reviews 115, 116, 118
rights: advice guides on 178–179; defendants' 153; disability 24, 63; to

fair trial 135; human 43, 180; intellectual property 112; legal 197; reproductive 181; of victims 52
risk 194, 226
role play 122
rules 22, 24, 153, 157, 159, 188, 194, 198, 206, 220

safeguarding 205
safety, personal 113, 186
saturation 91
saying and doing 183
scenarios 22, 53, 72, 73, 86, 87, 89, 100, 186, 189, 221
scepticism 144, 146, 148, 224
schemas 61
Scott, Matthew 162, 163, *163*
scrapbooks 89
Scrum 111–112, 116, 118
search results 234
seeing 4, 126, 183 *see also* communication, visual
self-awareness 93
self-discipline 105
self-interrogation 124
self-motivation 105
self-perception 8, 32
self-reflection 104, 110
semantic codes 45, 55
sensitivity 43, 166, 198
separation 153
service design 67, 68–69, 70, 76, 77, 240
service safaris 77
shadowing 77
shapes 219
signposting 186, 187–188
silos 8, 9, 31, *31*, 67
simplification 29, 39, 88, 89, 207, 221, 234
simulations 34
sketches 206, 232
sketchiness 232–233
skill sets 121, 224, 240
skills 87, 205, 238; core 110; development of 68; future-oriented 84; innovation 84, 85; key 75; legal 101; methodological 17–18; multi-dimensional 105; observational 227; practical 97; soft 84–85, 98; transferable 84 *see also* communication skills
small talk 60
social change 69
social distancing 153
social institutions 35
social justice 76, 77
social science 52–54
social scientists/sociologists 19, 22
Socio-Legal Lab 9, 17–25, *21*, 26
software 36, 62
solicitors 67
Solicitors' Regulation Authority 67
solidarity 167–169, 171, 173
solitary confinement 162
solutions 87, 104, 105, 141, 144, 146, 186, 221, 234, 240 *see also* problem-solving
spaces: breakout 181, 182; collaborative 37; creation of 54–55; for design 5; emancipatory 45; forms of 37; identities of 51–52; learning 17, 23, 26; negative *162*; pedagogical 19, 20; of resistance 52, 53
spectators 159–160
stability 226
stakeholders 70, 89, 91, 112, 136, 137, 139, 143, 146, 167, 170, 171, 173, 181, 223, 226 *see also* HCD Design Group
standing protocol 163
Stanford Legal Design Lab 103, 198, 209
Stanford model 70, *70*, 71, 85
Starbev case 127
statues 37–38
stereotypes 24, 135, 174, 175
stick figure syndrome 221
sticky notes 75, 181, 182, 185
stop and search 179, 183, 187–188, 190
stories/storytelling 34, 60, 186, 187, 198
storyboarding 225
stress 63–64, 135
students: backgrounds of 67–68, 72, 241; from BAME backgrounds 67–68, 72; characteristics of 68, 88; diversity of 43, 44; experience of 76–77, 86, 93; perspectives of 67, 73; political positions of 43–44; and use of innovation 87
study groups 62
subjectivity 43, 124, 129
subordination 166
summaries, nutshell 60
support groups 187
surveys 60, 122, 172
sustainability 54, 222
symbols 52, 53
sympathy 146
synthesise phase 73, 104, 112, 137, 141, 170
systems, oppressive 167, 168

tableaux 36
Tame (Arauca) 49–50, 52

tangibility 2, 5, 7, 8, 19, 23, 29, 34, 45, 75, 211, 221
teaching *see* courses/modules; law curricula
teams 112, 207, 210
teamwork 90, 105, 110, 118–119, 224, 226, 227, 231, 233
technologies 3, 29, 83, 87, 97, 116, 207; assistive 219, 222; disruptive 82–83, 84, 85, 86–87; impact of 82, 110
teddy bears 161, *162*
teleology 193
templates 86, 119, *138*
tenants 170, 171, 172
tension 144, 156, 167
terms, invisible 206
territory 46, 48, 50, 52, 54
testing phase 111, 112, 118, 119, 137, 146, 198, 226, 227, 234, 236; conclusions/solutions 21, 76, 104
text-based materials 29, 34
texts 21, 24, 29, 36, 61, 62–63, 174, 204; alt 3, 36, 63; combining with pictures 122, 174; legal 59, 61–62, 98
The Monitoring Group (TMG) 110–119
themes 148, 185, 186–187
theology of liberation 51
theories, ethical 192–193
thinking: analytical 227; critical 98, 105; digital 222; graphical 38; iterative 2; lateral 241; legal 23, 86; like a lawyer 58–59, 97; transformation of 146; ways of 23–24
time management 105
timelines 207, 209, *209*
Tinsley v Milligan230
TL;DR 4, *6*, 181
toolboxes/kits: Brexit 236; for contracts 205; design 69, 71, 77, 97, 102, 103–104; ethical 196; methodological 17, 25; visual 99
tools: contracts as 205; creative 44; ethical 198; navigation 210, 234; online 64; project management 112; visual 165; visualisation as 207
topics, sensitive 43
touchpoints 184–185, *185*
tourism 48
transcripts 63
Transform Justice 152
transformation 166
transparency 102, *151*, 152, 157, 189, 190, 221
travel, essential 152
trust 25, 69, 90, 113, 125, 146, 148, 225
truth 54, 157–158, 164, 171, 239
tutorials 123, 128
tutors, interdisciplinary 103
typography 230, 236

UK Supreme Court 152, 157, 159–160, *162*
uncertainty 91, 93, 189, 236
understanding 32, 123, 143, 207 *see also* comprehension
unfairness 189
unlearning 242
unpredictability 23
usability 207, 209, 210, 234
usefulness 207
user centricity 220
User Experience (UX) research 71–72, 75, 77
User Interface (UI) designs 114–115
user researchers 180
user stories 113, **114**
user-friendliness 205, 220, 225
users 4, 11, 92, 119, 136(2), 170, 190, 205, 211, 223, 235, 241–242; centring 70, 236; characteristics of 32; diversity of 234–236; experience of 112, 118, 136, 209, 210; holistic view of 234–235; journeys 104, 138; needs of 4, 71, 85, 87, 91, 111, 179, 198, 219, 224, 242; personas of 72–73, *74*, 75; perspectives of 18, 68–69, 76, 102, 136
utilitarianism 193

validation 189
value 88, 90
value levers 198
value sensitive design 198
values 125
victimisation 189
victims 51, 52, 54, 189
video screens 156
videos 221
viewers 152, 153
viewpoints 240
vignettes 29, 30, 31–35, *33*, 39
violation 189
virtual reality (VR) 36
virtue ethics 194, 197
visibility 2, 5, 7, 8, 19, 45, 211
visual, the 35–38, 87; focussing on 88–89; as illustration 37–38; in legal publishing 229–232; researching 231
visual aids 62–63

visual contract services 121
Visual Law Library 86
visual representations 38, 44, 45, 50; 'Embroidering a future of peace' 48–50, *49*, 52–53, 54; 'Let's make love to fear' 50–52, *51*, 53, 54; 'The marginal road in the jungle' 46–48, *47*, 52
visual strategies 3–9, 25
visualisers 206
visualisation exercises 101
visualisation techniques 196–197
visualisations/visuals 18, 23, 24–25, 29, 31, 61, 75, 98, 126, 192, 204, 207, 231; and contracts 1, 121, 122–123, 127, 203–211, *208*; use in teaching 122–123
vocabularies 30, 35–36
vocalisation 189
voices 49, 53, 54, 55
volunteers 111, 118, 119
voting 75
vulnerability 25, 113, 157, 198

walls 141, 182, 184, 204, 242
websites 142, 146, 178, 231
well-being 93, 195
wireframes 90, 232
witness preparation 64
women 50–52, 53, 58
women's organisations 54
working, collaborative 90, 105, 112, 144, 220, 222, 225, 227
working groups 103
workshop resources 181–185
workshops 19–20, 123, 128, 223; co-designing 178–190, *179*; contract training 204, 206, 207; HCD Design Group 137, 139, **140**, 142–147, 148; kick-off 181, 183, 184; online 181–185
World Commerce & Contracting (WorldCC) 209, 210

Young-jun, Oh 158

Zoom platform 22, 182

For Product Safety Concerns and Information please contact our EU representative GPSR@taylorandfrancis.com Taylor & Francis Verlag GmbH, Kaufingerstraße 24, 80331 München, Germany